THE SHIFTING GROUND
OF GLOBALIZATION

Studies in Critical Social Sciences Book Series

Haymarket Books is proud to be working with Brill Academic Publishers (www.brill.nl) to republish the *Studies in Critical Social Sciences* book series in paperback editions. This peer-reviewed book series offers insights into our current reality by exploring the content and consequences of power relationships under capitalism, and by considering the spaces of opposition and resistance to these changes that have been defining our new age. Our full catalog of *SCSS* volumes can be viewed at https://www.haymarketbooks .org/series_collections/4-studies-in-critical-social-sciences.

New Scholarship in Political Economy Book Series

THE SHIFTING GROUND OF GLOBALIZATION

Labor and Mineral Extraction at Vale S.A.

THIAGO AGUIAR

TRANSLATED BY
EDUARDO CARNIEL

TRANSLATION EDITING BY
SEAN PURDY

Haymarket Books
Chicago, IL

Published in paperback in 2024 by
Haymarket Books
P.O. Box 180165
Chicago, IL 60618
773-583-7884
www.haymarketbooks.org

ISBN: 979-8-88890-224-0

Distributed to the trade in the US through Consortium Book Sales and
Distribution (www.cbsd.com) and internationally through Ingram Publisher
Services International (www.ingramcontent.com).

This book was published with the generous support of Lannan Foundation,
Wallace Action Fund, and the Marguerite Casey Foundation.

Special discounts are available for bulk purchases by organizations and
institutions. Please call 773-583-7884 or email info@haymarketbooks.org for more
information.

Cover design by Jamie Kerry and Ragina Johnson.

Printed in the United States.

Library of Congress Cataloging-in-Publication data is available.

Uma rua começa em Itabira, que vai dar em qualquer ponto da terra.
Nessa rua passam chineses, índios, negros, mexicanos, turcos, uruguaios
Seus passos urgentes ressoam na pedra,
ressoam em mim

• • •

Sou apenas uma rua
na cidadezinha de Minas,
humilde caminho da América

• • •

A street starts in Itabira, that leads anywhere on earth.
On this street Chinese, Indians, Blacks, Mexicans, Turks, Uruguayans pass.
Their urgent footsteps resonate in the stone, resonate in me

• • •

I am just a street
in the little Minas town,
America's humble path
ANDRADE, 2012:121–5

• •
•

Contents

Foreword

Global Capitalism and Social Theory for the Twenty-First Century: What a Brazilian Case Study Tells Us

Shortly after his first inauguration, in 2003, and then again in 2010 during his second presidential term, Brazilian president Luiz Inácio Lula da Silva loaded up a government aircraft with Brazilian corporate executives and headed for Africa. As Thiago Aguiar discusses in the study before us, the presidential-corporate entourage opened up Mozambique and other African countries to investment in the continent's abundant mineral resources by the Brazilian-based transnational mining corporation, Vale, under the rhetoric of "South-South solidarity."

If we interpret the expansion in recent decades of South-South trade, investment and capital flows through the lens of twentieth-century theories of dependency, of the world-system, and of imperialism as core domination over an oppressed periphery, we may reasonably conclude that there is something progressive about the South-South integration agenda so epitomized by Lula's African corporate safaris.

Yet such "solidarity" by transnational capitalists and the capitalist states that promote their interests is patently antagonistic to transnational proletarian solidarity. Social theories frame our understanding of the world in particular ways and are therefore never neutral but politically and ideologically charged. The sweeping transformation of the world capitalist system since the late twentieth century compels us to develop and apply new theoretical lenses in our interpretation of the world and in our political praxis. Left intellectuals and activists may cling on to outdated theories that see in the rise of transnational capitalist classes based in the historic periphery some progressive challenge to world capitalism. But in the end, such views can only end up cheering on the expansion of global circuits of capital accumulation that lead, in Africa and elsewhere, to the violent displacement of local communities, the plunder of resources, the exploitation of workers, and the degradation of the environment.

My colleagues and I have been advancing since the turn of the century a theory of global capitalism as a novel epoch in the ongoing and open-ended evolution of world capitalism characterized above all by the rise of truly transnational capital and the integration of every country into a new globalized system of production, finance, and services. In his 2018 study *Giants: The Global Power Elite*, sociologist Peter Phillips identifies an inner core of 389 individuals

drawn from the upper echelons of what we refer to as the transnational capitalist class (TCC) who stand at the very apex of the global power structure
and who have brought about the transnational inter-penetration of what were
in an earlier era national capital and power networks. We see a cementing
now at the global level of political and economic power in this TCC through
an unprecedented concentration of financial capital and through the political
influence that this economic control wields over states and transnational state
institutions. In short, in 2018 just 17 global financial conglomerates collectively
managed $41.1 trillion dollars – more than half of the entire global gross prod-
uct – "in a self-invested network of interlocking capital that spans the globe."[1]
Moreover, these 17 were cross-invested in each other to such an extent that it
appeared as simply a mass of interlocking global capital, impossible to trace
back to particular national economies.

In the brilliant study before us, Aguiar furthers our understanding of the
TCC through a case study of Vale, one of four global mining conglomerates that
dominate the industry worldwide. He traces the transformation of this corporate behemoth from a Brazilian state company established in the logic of an
earlier era of national developmentalism and the subordination of Brazilian to
core-based multinational capital. Much of the research on the TCC has focused
on the cross-penetration of what were national capitals in the historic core
of world capitalism. As Aguiar's case study shows, Brazilian-based capital in
the form of Vale has transnationalized not only by expanding throughout the
"Global South" but also in the "Global North" through its purchase in 2006 of
Inco, one of Canadian two largest mining companies, as well as in investments
in mining and related industrial operations in the United States, Europe, and
elsewhere. TCC groups around the world are able to take advantage of differ-
ential rates and intensities of exploitation, as well as national borders and cultural sensibilities, to exploit workers and other subordinate classes throughout
the global economy and to force competition on them in a global race to the
bottom.

It is not therefore just that the leading capitalist strata from the historic
periphery have transnationalized across the South and the North, but in doing
so, they have integrated into a global ruling class that exercises its power over
the laboring masses in *both* South *and* North. As Aguiar discusses, Canadian
mine workers organized in the United Steelworkers union faced off against
Brazilian corporate executives in a nearly year-long battle against attempts
by Vale to roll back Canadian workers gains in the mining town of Sudbury.

---

1   Peter Phillips, *Giants: The Global Power Elite* (New York: Seven Stories Press, 2018), pp. 35.

"Southern" capitalists therefore exploit "Northern" workers as much as "Northern" capitalists exploit "Southern" workers. Twentieth century theories of world capitalist development argued that core capital extracts surplus value from workers in the periphery and transfers it to core capitalist coffers, thus draining out of the periphery surplus that could launch processes of endogenous capitalist development. Theories of imperialism saw the world divided into national capitalist classes from the core in rivalry with one another over access to the raw materials, markets, and labor pools of the periphery. These theories are now outdated.

Earlier this century I had the opportunity to give a talk in Manila to a group of Philippine revolutionary activists. One woman in attendance, originally from India, objected to my analysis of the TCC. Visibly disturbed, she told me that in India "we are fighting imperialism" just as Lenin had analyzed. I asked her what she meant by this. Core capitalists were exploiting Indian workers and transferring the surplus back to the core countries, she replied. It was by sheer coincidence that in the very week of my talk, the Indian-based global corporate conglomerate, the Tata Group, which operates in over 100 countries in six continents, had acquired a string of corporate icons of its former British colonial master, among them, Land Rover, Jaguar, Tetley Tea, British Steel, and Tesco supermarkets, making Tata the largest single employer *inside* the United Kingdom. So, India-based capitalists had become the largest single exploiter of British workers! The fundamental contradiction in global capitalism is not between core and periphery but between capital and labor on a world scale. The categories of "external" and "internal," an unproblematized focus on nation-state boundaries and the nation-state/interstate framework of analysis they imply do more to confuse than to clarify the nature of the new global capitalism and its transnational class relations.

Many of us in the global justice movement have insisted for some time now that as capital has transnationalized so too must workers' struggles. Aguiar discusses the Canadian strike, the attempt (ultimately unsuccessful) by Vale workers across borders to set up international worker associations, and Vale's corporate labor relations strategy. As the discussion makes clear, workers around the world continue to face objective material constraints in the endeavor to transnationalize labor struggles, as well as subterfuge by trade union bureaucracies that are often tied informally to the capitalist state, and divisions between formal sector unionized workers and those that are precarious or not unionized.

It is true that labor relations in the historic periphery remain harsher than in the historic core. It is equally true that the historic imperial centers – often operating through transnational state apparatuses – continue to exert undue structural and often direct power over national states and social groups in the historic periphery. It is equally true, however, that in the first instance capital went global starting in the late 1970s in order to break the power of working classes in these imperial centers and to undercut the possibility of an alternative to global capitalist integration in the historic periphery. The study before us underscores that in the end, to reiterate, the transnational class struggle, the global capital-labor contradiction, is at the very core of the global capitalist system and in the larger picture trumps secondary (often derivative) contradictions. As global capitalism descends into an epochal crisis,[2] it behooves us more than ever to understand the nature of this system and the transformations it has undergone in recent decades. For we cannot fight what we do not understand. Aguiar's study makes a critical contribution to our understanding.

William I. Robinson
Distinguished Professor of Sociology, Global Studies, and Latin American Studies at the University of California, Santa Barbara

---

2   On this epochal crisis, see William I. Robinson, *Can Global Capitalism Endure?* (Atlanta: Clarity Press, 2022).

Acknowledgements

This book, like all products of knowledge, is a collective work, with the collaboration of many people. First of all, I would like to thank Leonardo Mello e Silva, my supervisor and friend, and Michael Burawoy, for having hosted me in California during my PhD. internship. Judith Marshall, Paula Marcelino, Ricardo Antunes, Rodrigo Santos, Ruy Braga and William I. Robinson, at different moments, offered their generous reading, suggestions, and comments. I thank Alfredo Saad-Filho and David Fasenfast for the opportunity to publish this book in the *New Scholarship in Political Economy* series. I would like to thank Eduardo Carniel for his careful work in translating the book and Sean Purdy for his translation editing. Without them, this publication would not exist.

I owe a lot to the decisive support of workers and union members who dedicated part of their time to teach me about their activities. I thank the leaders of STEFEM, USW Local 6500, Metabase Carajás, and Guilherme Zagallo for the welcoming, the contacts, and the patience to answer my questions.

Cristina, João and Priscila Aguiar, my mother, father and sister, were a source of unconditional support at all times. Many friends also contributed so that I could complete this book. In particular, Pedro Micussi, Vittorio Poletto and Flavia Brancalion were always close by, even when I was away. Pedro was, moreover, a permanent discussion partner, essential for this book's eventual corrections, without, however, sharing any responsibility for its mistakes.

I thank the Graduate Program in Sociology of the University of São Paulo and the Department of Sociology of the University of California, Berkeley for hosting the research on which this book is based, and Brill for making its publication possible. I am grateful to the National Council for Scientific and Technological Development (CNPq) for the grant which allowed me to carry out my PhD. research; to the Fulbright Commission and the Coordination for the Improvement of Higher Education Personnel (CAPES), for funding my PhD. internship; to the São Paulo Research Foundation (FAPESP), for the resources which made this publication possible (grant #2021/11182–9) and for the post-doctoral scholarship (grant #2019/26020–4) at IFCH-Unicamp, which allowed the updating of the material that gave rise to this book.

Figures and Tables

Figures

Tables

Acronyms

AFL-CIO	American Federation of Labor and Congress of Industrial Organizations
AIAV	*Articulação Internacional dos Atingidos pela Vale* [International Network of People Affected by Vale]
AIP	Annual Incentive Program
AMZA	*Amazônia Mineração S.A.* [Amazon Mining S.A.]
ANM	*Agência Nacional de Mineração* [National Mining Agency]
Aval	*Associação de Sindicatos de Trabalhadores da Vale* [Association of Vale Workers' Unions]
BNDES	*Banco Nacional de Desenvolvimento Econômico e Social* [Brazil's National Bank for Economic and Social Development]
BRBF	Brazilian Blend Fines
BRICS	Brazil, Russia, India and China
BSGR	Benjamin Steinmetz Group Resources
CESP	*Companhia Energética de São Paulo* [São Paulo Energy Company]
CFEM	*Compensação Financeira pela Exploração de Recursos Minerais* [Financial Compensation for the Exploitation of Mineral Resources]
CIPA	*Comissão Interna de Prevenção de Acidentes* [Internal Commission for the Prevention of Accidents]
CLC	Canadian Labour Congress
CME	Coordinated Market Economy
CMM	*Companhia Meridional de Mineração S.A.* [Southern Mining Company S.A.]
CNDTM	*Comitê Nacional em Defesa dos Territórios Frente à Mineração* [National Committee for the Defense of Territories against Mining]
CNQ	*Confederação Nacional dos Químicos* [National Confederation of Chemists]
Contraf-CUT	*Confederação Nacional dos Trabalhadores do Ramo Financeiro da CUT* [CUT's National Confederation of Financial Workers]
CPRM	*Serviço Geológico do Brasil* [Brazilian Geological Survey]
CUT	*Central Única dos Trabalhadores* [Unified Workers' Central]
CVM	*Comissão de Valores Mobiliários* [Securities and Exchange Commission of Brazil]
CVRD	*Companhia Vale do Rio Doce*
DNPM	*Departamento Nacional de Produção Mineral* [National Department of Mineral Production]
EBC	Earnings Based Compensation
ECSC	European Coal and Steel Community

EFC	*Estrada de Ferro Carajás* [Carajás Railroad]
FGV	*Fundação Getúlio Vargas* [Getúlio Vargas Foundation]
FHC	Fernando Henrique Cardoso
FNC	*Floresta Nacional de Carajás* [Carajás National Forest]
Funcef	*Fundação dos Economiários Federais* [Federal Economy Workers Foundation]
Funcesp	*Fundação de Empresas Elétricas de São Paulo* [São Paulo Electric Companies Foundation]
GDP	Gross Domestic Product
GPN	Global production network
GTAMS	*Grupo de Trabalho Articulação Mineração-Siderurgia* [Coalition on Mining and Steelmaking Working Group]
GUF	Global Union Federation
IBGE	*Instituto Brasileiro de Geografia e Estatística* [Brazilian Institute of Geography and Statistics]
IBRD	International Bank for Reconstruction and Development
ICEM	International Federation of Chemical, Energy, Mine and General Workers' Unions
ICMBio	*Instituto Chico Mendes de Conservação da Biodiversidade* [Chico Mendes Institute for Biodiversity Conservation]
IFA	International Framework Agreement
ILO	International Labour Organization
IMF	International Metalworkers' Federation
IMF	International Monetary Fund
INSS	*Instituto Nacional do Seguro Social* [National Institute of Social Security]
INVESTVALE	*Clube de Investimentos dos Empregados da Vale do Rio Doce* [Vale Employees' Investment Club]
KfW	Kreditanstalt für Wiederaufbau
LME	Liberal Market Economy
Metabase	*Sindicato dos Trabalhadores na Indústria de Extração de Ferro e Metais Básicos* [Workers in the Iron and Base Metal Extraction Industry Union]
NGO	Non-governmental organization
OAB	*Ordem dos Advogados do Brasil* [Order of Attorneys of Brazil]
OCC	*Centro de Comando Operacional* [Operational Command Center]
PCdoB	*Partido Comunista do Brasil* [Communist Party of Brazil]
PDT	*Partido Democrático Trabalhista* [Democratic Labour Party]
PFC	*Projeto Ferro Carajás* [Carajás Iron Project]
PRI	Principles for Responsible Investment

PSDB	*Partido da Social Democracia Brasileira* [Brazilian Social Democracy Party]
PSTU	*Partido Socialista dos Trabalhadores Unificado* [United Socialist Workers' Party]
PT	*Partido dos Trabalhadores* [Workers' Party]
PUC-Rio	*Pontifícia Universidade Católica do Rio de Janeiro* [Pontifical Catholic University of Rio de Janeiro]
RBJA	*Rede Brasileira de Justiça Ambiental* [Brazilian Network for Environmental Justice]
SEC	Securities and Exchange Comission
Sindimina-RJ	*Sindicato dos Trabalhadores nas Indústrias de Prospecção, Pesquisa e Extração de Minérios no Estado do Rio de Janeiro* [Union of Workers in the Prospecting, Exploration and Extraction of Ore Industries in the State of Rio de Janeiro]
STEFEM	*Sindicato dos Trabalhadores em Empresas Ferroviárias dos Estados do Maranhão, Pará e Tocantins* [Union of Workers in Railroad Companies in the States of Maranhão, Pará and Tocantins]
STIEAPA	*Sindicato das Indústrias Extrativas dos Estados do Amapá e do Pará* [Extractive Industry Union of the Amapá and Pará States]
TCC	Transnational capitalist class
TJLP	*Taxa de Juros de Longo Prazo* [Long-Term Interest Rate]
TLP	*Taxa de Longo Prazo* [Long-Term Rate]
TNC	Transnational corporation
TNS	Transnational state
UGT	*União Geral dos Trabalhadores* [General Union of Workers]
UN	United Nations
US Steel	United States Steel Co.
USW	United Steelworkers
VBG	Vale BSGR Guinea

Introduction
Walking on Shifting Ground

> True, anatomical knowledge is not usually a precondition for 'correct' walking. But when the ground beneath our feet is always shaking, we need a crutch. As social scientists we are thrown off balance by our presence in the world we study, by absorption in the society we observe, by dwelling alongside those we make 'other'. ... So we desperately need methodology to keep us erect, while we navigate a terrain that moves and shifts even as we attempt to traverse it.[1]

••

The sociologist trying to lean on 'crutches' to walk on shaky ground: this is the comic and suggestive metaphor offered by Michael Burawoy to address the role of methodology in the social sciences. The perception of social change and its relationship to the researcher's condition in a world in motion are perhaps the greatest questions raised by his methodological contribution. Change and movement constitute the very condition of ethnography, conducted in real space and time, while history and its conflicts continue to unfold. The sociologist's dual condition, as observer and participant, in ethnography can become both an obstacle and a tool to help understand the micro-processes in the field and their relationship to social macro-forces.[2]

The perception of the shift and the loss of balance in one's feet, as will be seen, have permanently accompanied the research on which this book is based.[3] Initially, the research aimed to follow the international expansion of Brazilian companies during the first decades of the twenty-first century, its

---

1 Michael Burawoy, *The Extended Case Method: Four Countries, Four Decades, Four Great Transformations, and One Theoretical Tradition* (Berkeley: California University Press, 2009), 40.

2 Ibid, 28.

3 This is a modified version of a doctoral dissertation prepared in the Graduate Program in Sociology at the University of São Paulo (USP) (2015–2019), with a doctoral internship period at the University of California, Berkeley (2016–2017), complemented by new analyses carried out in post-doctoral research at USP (2020–2021) and at the State University of Campinas (Unicamp) (2021).

consequences for labor relations, and the responses proposed by unions and workers' organizations in the face of the global fluidity of capital and the size of transnational corporations (TNCs).

These questions had already been the subject of previous research, a case study on Natura, a national leader in the cosmetics industry with a growing presence abroad, which went public and incorporated assets and factories in other countries.[4] As was then shown, the company is a successful case of the implantation of flexible production concepts and practices, with a concrete impact on the forms of workers' sociability. The principles of Toyotism, namely, quality and flexibility, guide the task performance in production, as well as the relationships in the work units. Parallel to the changes in the organization of production and labor, I emphasized the company's concern in hiring and training a certain type of workforce: younger, educated, with a greater presence of women, consumer and career oriented, and not much inclined to union participation. At the same time, I noted an important vector in this group's constitution: contrary to what happened in the Fordist period,[5] a 'new worker condition' obtained,[6] with the creation of a kind of "company sociability", through strategies such as the "model of skills",[7] "just-in-time production", cells, and goals, which seek to commit the workers to the company's production expectations and to stimulate certain forms of behavior towards their colleagues, their bosses, and even towards the unions.

Such conclusions, concerning a TNC in the cosmetics sector, led to an inquiry about the existence of a possible generalization of cases of domestically originated corporations' restructuring and internationalization. The concern about this theme came on top of the interest in this process's relationship with the Brazilian economy's integration into global capitalism during that period. To find that relationship, a comparative research effort between several companies and economic sectors is necessary. In view of this task's magnitude, I decided to focus on the pursuit of such links through a case study of Vale S.A., a Brazilian mining TNC with a strong presence of domestic capital among its shareholder control.[8]

---

4   Thiago Aguiar, *Maquiando o trabalho: opacidade e transparência numa empresa de cosméticos global* (São Paulo: Annablume, 2017).

5   See Huw Beynon, *Working for Ford* (Harmondsworth: Penguin Books, 1984); Robert Castel, *Les métamorphoses de la question sociale: une chronique du salariat.* (Paris: Galliard, 2016), among others.

6   Stéphane Beaud and Michel Pialoux, *Retour sur la condition ouvrière: enquête aux usines Peugeot de Sochaux-Montbéliard.* (Paris: Fayard, 2010).

7   Claude Dubar, "La sociologie du travail face à la qualification et à la compétence," *Sociologie du travail* 38. no. 2 (April-June 1996): 179–193.

8   Throughout this book, in general, the company will be referred to simply as Vale (the name officially adopted by the company since 2007) or as CVRD (the acronym for *Companhia Vale do Rio Doce*), especially, in the latter case, when referring to its state-owned period.

My choice was not random: in addition to its enormous economic size and relevant international presence – as will be shown in the following chapters -, the researcher's entry into the field could benefit from contact with several domestic and foreign union actors. In particular, the company's presence in Canada – after the acquisition of Inco, one of the world's largest nickel producers, in 2006 – and the subsequent strike of Vale's Canadian workers in 2009–2010,[9] considered the largest private sector strike in Canada in 30 years,[10] were rich empirical sources which illuminated the investigation of the relations between labor, unions and globalization presented in this book.

What is new about this situation? Decades ago, it was common for Northern multinationals to establish themselves in peripheral countries. Fernando Henrique Cardoso and Enzo Faletto called this type of investment 'enclave economies' in dependent countries, in which

> foreign invested capital *originates in the exterior*, is incorporated into local productive processes, and transforms parts of itself into wages and taxes. Its value is increased by the exploitation of local labor forces, which transform nature and produce goods that *realize* again the life of this capital when staples (oil, copper, bananas, etc.) are sold in the *external market*.[11]

Unlike the 'enclave,' in situations of dependency with domestically controlled production, the local bourgeoisie is responsible for the appropriation of natural resources, for the exploitation of labor and for accumulation. For Cardoso and Faletto, dependency and development are not mutually exclusive, since the latter refers to the development of the capitalist productive forces and towards accumulation (whether in the center or the periphery) while dependency relations deal with the need to obtain technology and financing from abroad, even while accumulation occurs nationally, a phenomenon whose origins are in imperialism and in internal and external class alliances. Dependency is at the core of the relationship between center and periphery. The authors clearly referred to the historically developed dependency of Latin American economies on the nations of the global center.

Does the presence of a Brazilian-based TNC in Canada, after buying an important local mining company, exploiting its workforce and exporting

---

9   The Vale workers' strike lasted almost a year at the Sudbury and Port Colborne (Ontario) operations and eighteen months at Voisey's Bay (Newfoundland and Labrador).

10   John Peters, "Down in the Vale: Corporate Globalization, Unions on the Defensive, and the USW Local 6500 Strike in Sudbury, 2009–2010," *Labour/Le Travail* 66 (Fall 2010): 73–105.

11   Fernando Henrique Cardoso and Enzo Faletto, "Preface to the English Edition", in *Dependency and Development in Latin America* (Berkeley: University of California Press, 1979).

natural resources, modify classic dependency relations? Or does it only make them more complex? To what extent does the rugged labor conflict mentioned above shed light on aspects of this problem? This book intends to contribute to this discussion from an ethnographic approach situated within the field of the sociology of labor.

The case presented is, in a way, a novelty for the development of Brazilian TNCs, whose organization of production and labor is in line with the practices of companies from central countries. These have already been widely discussed in the international literature and framed as 'flexible accumulation' or the 'post-Fordist' pattern of work.[12] One can speak of a 'new stage of labor rationalization',[13] in a characterization well known as the 'Japanese model'[14] or the Toyotist model of labor organization. In addition, it is also possible to highlight: the outsourcing of company activities to subcontractors and suppliers in the same country or abroad, which was explored by studies focused on 'commodity chains';[15] the outsourcing or subcontracting of the workforce; and competency-based assessments as a form of mobilizing the workforce.

The effects of such a process are widespread in Brazil and have been extensively analyzed in the national literature.[16] However, the recent period has witnessed the expansion of Brazilian multinationals and TNCs, of which Vale is a significant example.

My research, therefore, is located in a well-established tradition of case studies in the sociology of labor which have followed the changes in the productive base in a globalized economy. I aim to analyze how workers react to structural changes related both to the transition to post-Fordist production, and, now, to the consolidation of domestically originated TNCs, in their operations in Brazil or abroad. To this end, a comparative approach between the practices

---

12   See David Harvey, *The Condition of Postmodernity: An Enquiry into the Origins of Cultural Change* (Cambridge: Blackwell, 2015); Huw Beynon and Theo Nichols, *Patterns of Work in the Post-Fordist Era: Fordism and Post-Fordism* (Cheltenham: Edward Elgar Pub, 2006), among others.

13   Jean Pierre Durand, "A refundação do trabalho no fluxo tensionado," *Tempo Social* 1, no. 15 (April 2003): 139–158.

14   Helena Hirata, *Sobre o modelo japonês: automatização, novas formas de organização e de relações de trabalho* (São Paulo: Edusp, 1993).

15   Gary Gereffi and Miguel Korzeniewicz, ed. *Commodity Chains and Global Capitalism* (Westport: Praeger, 1994).

16   Some examples can be found in Ricardo Antunes, ed. *Riqueza e miséria do trabalho no Brasil* (São Paulo: Boitempo, 2006); Ricardo Antunes, ed. *Riqueza e miséria do trabalho no Brasil II* (São Paulo: Boitempo, 2013); Ricardo Antunes, ed. *Riqueza e miséria do trabalho no Brasil III* (São Paulo: Boitempo, 2014); Leonardo Mello e Silva, ed. *Exercícios de sociologia do trabalho* (Belo Horizonte: Fino Traço, 2016), among others.

promoted by such companies in the different places where they operate, and a sociological perspective focused on the collectivity of workers is inescapable. This is what I present below.

1   A Period of Crisis and the General Direction of Change

The Brazilian corporations understood to have reached the status of 'global challenger' status, with Vale in the lead, project an image of themselves as a "motor of development" both in Brazil and in the countries where they invest, generating employment and economic growth, a symbol of 'global Brazil'.[17]

Brazil is the way it is and Vale is very clever in using the Brazilian flag to project its identity. Vale's 'Brazilianness' was a strong factor.[18]

The creation and expansion of Brazilian-origin TNCs in the first decades of the twenty-first century were sometimes related to the rise of the BRICS and to the Brazilian development model of the period. That picture, however, quickly began to change. The ground was shifting.

When the research that gave rise to this book was designed, a debate about 'global Brazil' was in full swing in the Brazilian social sciences and economics: a heated controversy arose regarding the characterization of the *Partido dos Trabalhadores* [Workers' Party], or PT governments, of the period of economic growth from the second Lula administration onwards (in particular, after the first shock of the 2008–2009 crisis) and its consequences for social classes, of the possibilities for development and of the country's geopolitical location.[19] It was the period of the rise of the BRICS as emerging stars of the

---

17   Judith Marshall, "Behind the Image of South-South Solidarity at Brazil's Vale", in *BRICS: an Anti-Capitalist Critique*, ed. Patrick Bond and Ana Garcia (Chicago: Haymarket Books, 2015), 162–85.

18   Susan, union advisor, interviewed by Thiago Aguiar in Toronto, Canada (October 2016). In this book, the names of the union members and workers interviewed will always be changed. However, Vale's managers, some national union leaders and outstanding agents, for the relevance of their positions and always with their authorization, will have their names presented.

19   It is not the purpose of this work to promote an exhaustive survey on the subject. However, we can briefly mention some works which have dealt with these issues: Cornel Ban, "Brazil's Liberal Developmentalism", *Review of International Political Economy* 20, no. 2 (2013): 298–331; Armando Boito Jr. and Andréia Galvão, *Política e classes sociais no Brasil dos anos 2000* (São Paulo: Alameda, 2012); Ruy Braga. *The Politics of the Precariat: from Populism to Lulista Hegemony* (Leiden: Brill, 2018); Luiz Carlos Bresser-Pereira, "Do

world economy. Several Brazilian companies in this period benefited from government stimulus to create 'national champions' and soon 'global champions', TNCs which expanded their business worldwide.[20] Despite being considered a multinational since the state-owned period, Vale's international expansion during this period can be considered a significant case of the consolidation of a Brazilian transnational as a 'global player' in its sector of activity.

Vale's internationalization coincided with the 'commodity supercycle' (from 2002 to 2012, ore prices increased by an average of 150%) and with the intense Chinese demand for iron ore for its steel industry.[21] The Asian country accounted in 2013 for 64.3% of the transoceanic demand for iron ore, as well as 50% of the global demand for nickel and 43% of the global demand for copper.[22] As we will see in the following chapters, in addition to the external economic scenario, the abundance of capital available for borrowing from Brazil's National Bank for Economic and Social Development, the BNDES, as well as the proximity between Vale's command and the Brazilian federal government are key factors to understand the company's expansion, particularly during Roger Agnelli's term as CEO (2001–2011).[23]

---

antigo ao novo desenvolvimentismo na América Latina", in *Desenvolvimento econômico e crise*, ed. Luiz Carlos Prado (Rio de Janeiro: Contraponto, 2012), 27–66; Luiz Carlos Bresser-Pereira, "O governo Dilma frente ao 'tripé macroeconômico' e à direita liberal e dependente," *Novos Estudos*, no. 95 (March 2013): 5–14; Francisco de Oliveira, Ruy Braga and Cibele Rizek. ed. *Hegemonia às avessas: economia, política e cultura na era da servidão financeira* (São Paulo: Boitempo, 2010); Marcio Pochmann, *Nova classe média? O trabalho na base da pirâmide social brasileira* (São Paulo: Boitempo, 2012); Plínio de Arruda Sampaio Jr., "Desenvolvimentismo e neodesenvolvimentismo: tragédia e farsa," *Serviço Social e Sociedade*, no. 112 (October/December 2012): 672–688; André Singer, *Os sentidos do lulismo: reforma gradual e pacto conservador* (São Paulo: Companhia das Letras, 2012); Jessé Souza, *Os batalhadores brasileiros: nova classe média ou nova classe trabalhadora* (Belo Horizonte: Editora UFMG, 2010); Pedro Paulo Zaluth Bastos, "A economia política do novo-desenvolvimentismo e do social-desenvolvimentismo," *Economia e Sociedade* 21, special issue, (December 2012): 779–810. Good critical analyses of the BRICS can be found in Patrick Bond and Ana Garcia, ed. *BRICS: An Anti-Capitalist Critique* (Chicago: Haymarket Books, 2015); William I. Robinson, "The Transnational State and the BRICS: A Global Capitalism Perspective," *Third World Quarterly* 36, no. 1 (2015): 1–21.

20   Especially through the financing policy of the National Bank for Economic and Social Development (BNDES) and the role of pension funds linked to state-owned companies, as will be seen in Chapter 4.

21   See Marshall, "Behind the Image of South-South Solidarity at Brazil's Vale." 162.

22   See Tádzio Peters Coelho, *Projeto Grande Carajás: trinta anos de desenvolvimento frustrado* (Rio de Janeiro: Ibase, 2014), 22.

23   Aspects highlighted by Marshall, "Behind the Image of South-South Solidarity at Brazil's Vale"; André Guilherme Delgado Vieira, *O mapa da mina* (Curitiba: Kotter Editorial, 2020); among others.

The picture has changed with the end of the commodity boom. In 2016, iron ore reached its lowest value in many years: US$39.60 per tonne. For comparison, in January 2013, the value of iron ore was US$154.64,[24] after reaching a peak of US$187.10 in January 2011.[25] In this period, especially from 2014 onwards, the continuous retraction of commodity prices in the world market, caused by the reduction in Chinese demand, deeply affected the Brazilian economy, by reducing the value of its exports and by the drop in government revenues.[26]

In 2015, Vale suffered harshly from the consequences of this process. The loss of almost R$45 billion that year meant pressure and wage reduction for the company's workers in Brazil, with tougher negotiations on the annual collective bargaining agreement, zero pay adjustments, withdrawal of benefits and non-payment of the profit sharing bonus[27] in 2016, as will be discussed in chapters 1 and 2. In November 2015, the collapse of the Fundão dam, ran by Samarco (a joint venture between Vale and BHP), in Mariana (in the state of Minas Gerais),[28] increased the mining company's losses and setbacks, which retracted investments in the country and abroad.

During the period, Brazil entered a deep recession: in 2015, the Gross Domestic Product (GDP) drop was 3.5%, and in 2016, 3.3%.[29] The economic

---

24 According to information available in http://www.indexmundi.com/pt/pre%E70s-de -mercado/?mercadoria=min%C3%A9rio-de-ferro&meses=60; accessed May 26 2021.

25 Luiz Jardim de Moraes Wanderley, "Do *boom* ao pós-*boom* das *commodities*: o comportamento do setor mineral no Brasil," *Versos – Textos para Discussão PoEMAS* 1, no. 1 (2017): 1–7.

26 Tádzio Peters Coelho, "Noventa por cento de ferro nas calçadas: mineração e (sub)desenvolvimentos em municípios minerados pela Vale S.A," Ph.D. Diss, Rio de Janeiro State University, 2016, 99.

27 Form of variable pay tied to the achievement of annual goals negotiated in an internal commission between management and employees.

28 The Fundão dam collapse left nineteen dead and 262 families homeless. Good analyses of the theme can be found in Marcio Zonta and Charles Trocate, ed. *Antes fosse mais leve a carga: reflexões sobre o desastre da Samarco/Vale/BHP Billiton* (Marabá: iGuana, 2016); and Judith Marshall, *Tailings Dam Spills at Mount Polley and Mariana: Chronicles of Disasters Foretold* (Vancouver: CMP, CCPA–BC Office, PoEMAS, Wilderness Committee, 2018). Years later, in January 2019, Dam I of Vale's Córrego do Feijão Mine in Brumadinho (Minas Gerais) burst, leading to the death of 270 people due to the flooding of about 12 million cubic meters of mining tailings which engulfed the region, covering the Paraopeba River and displacing thousands of families from their homes. Most of the dead and missing were Vale's workers, in-house or outsourced. The events of Mariana and Brumadinho are not the subject of this book, but some of their consequences for Vale's corporate strategy will be analyzed, in particular in Chapter 4.

29 According to data from the *Instituto Brasileiro de Geografia e Estatística* (Brazilian Institute of Geography and Statistics, or IBGE) available in: https://ftp.ibge.gov.br/Contas_Nacion ais/Sistema_de_Contas_Nacionais/2018/tabelas_xls/sinoticas/tab02.xls; accessed May 26 2021.

crisis combined with a political crisis which had been developing since June 2013, when mass demonstrations took place throughout the country, expressing, as is known, opposition to the increase in transportation fares. Soon, they expanded their questioning to the quality of public services, to the billion-dollar expenses with the promotion of international sporting events, to police repression and, finally, to the responses of governments, parties and legislators to the demands presented. Dilma Rousseff's administration – beset by deep recession, rising unemployment, and serial corruption charges which eroded the popularity of the main political parties of the government and the opposition – was overthrown by impeachment in 2016, in a parliamentary coup promoted by an alliance between congressmen hitherto allied as well as opponents, supported by important fractions of the ruling class and sectors of the middle classes mobilized in street demonstrations.[30] Michel Temer's administration deepened the neoliberal orientation of the federal government's economic policy, with visible consequences for mining, such as changes in the sector's legislation[31] and the creation of a favorable environment for changes in Vale's 'corporate governance'.[32]

It is not the purpose of this book to produce a detailed analysis of the Brazilian crisis. However, Vale, since its creation as a state-owned company, has been of decisive importance to Brazil's economy: it can even be said that the company, along with Petrobras, played a fundamental role in structuring industrial capitalism in the country, as will be seen in the next chapter. Therefore, it is necessary to deal with the political and economic transformations which occurred during my research.[33] In what follows, then, I analyze some approaches in the literature to interpret this period. In the next section, in turn, I outline the theoretical framework which will lead my exposition throughout the following chapters.

---

30 Analysis of the crisis and the fall of the Dilma Rousseff administration can be found in André Singer, *O lulismo em crise: um quebra-cabeça do período Dilma (2011–2016)* (São Paulo: Companhia das Letras, 2018); Alfredo Saad Filho and Lecio Morais, *Brazil: Neoliberalism Versus Democracy.* (London: Pluto Press, 2018.); Plínio de Arruda Sampaio Jr., *Crônica de uma crise anunciada: crítica à economia política de Lula e Dilma* (São Paulo: SG-Amarante Editorial, 2017).

31 Bruno Milanez, Tádzio Peters Coelho and Luiz Jardim de Moraes Wanderley, "O projeto mineral no Governo Temer: menos Estado, mais mercado," *Versos – Textos para Discussão PoEMAS* 1, no. 2 (2017): 1–15.

32 Themes which will be analyzed in Chapter 4.

33 Which extended, fundamentally, from 2015 to 2019.

Vale's expansion during the first decades of the twenty-first century is an example of the period of economic growth, investment, and internationalization of Brazilian companies: it is, according to André Singer, the years of Lula's "weak reformism"[34] and the attempt to promote a "developmentalist experiment" in the Dilma Rousseff administration,[35] which was later abandoned, especially after her reelection in 2014 and the neoliberal turn in the government's economic policy. For Singer, the failure of this 'developmentalist experiment' occurred due to a "lack of political base" for the supposed multiple anti-neoliberal battlefronts opened by the government, going against many interests simultaneously and provoking fierce attacks without a base from which to defend itself due to a combination of factors, that involved: 1) the mixing of interests between industrial and finance capital, which reduced the domestic industrial bourgeoisie's interest in supporting the attack on rentierism through the drop in interest rates; 2) the formalization of labor and the real increase in the minimum wage, which reduced the reserve army of labor and increased production costs, displeasing the bourgeoisie; 3) the alteration of the relationship between the domestic bourgeoisie and foreign capital; and 4) the ideological effect of the co-optation of business owners by rentier thinking.[36]

Ruy Braga,[37] in turn, focusing on the June 2013 protests, presented what we may call the hypothesis of spontaneous convergence "between *the political struggle of the urban precariat* demonstrating in the streets in defense of their social rights and *the economic struggle of the working class mobilized in unions* in defense of better wages and working conditions."[38] This is a fundamental aspect of his reasoning because this convergence reveals the "political limits of the Lulist mode of regulation," which combined the *active consent* of the social movements' leadership, in particular that of the "financialized union bureaucracy" (which came to occupy positions in state administration and in pension funds) with the *passive consent* of the subaltern classes, benefited

---

34   Singer, *Os sentidos do lulismo.*
35   André Singer, "A (falta de) base política para o ensaio desenvolvimentista", in *As contradições do lulismo: a que ponto chegamos?* ed. André Singer and Isabel Loureiro (São Paulo: Boitempo, 2016), 21–54.
36   An excellent analysis of the Brazilian industrial entrepreneurs' behavior during the Lula and Dilma Rousseff administrations can be found in Pedro Micussi, "Empresário industrial e governos do PT: o caso do IEDI (2003 – 2016)", Master's Thesis, Faculty of Philosophy, Languages and Human Sciences, University of São Paulo, 2021.
37   Ruy Braga, "Terra em transe: o fim do lulismo e o retorno da luta de classes," in *As contradições do lulismo: a que ponto chegamos?* ed. André Singer and Isabel Loureiro (São Paulo: Boitempo, 2016), 55–92.
38   Ibid, 71.

by public policies, by the raise in minimum wage and by the formalization of labor (although mostly concentrated in jobs which paid up to one and a half times the minimum wage). In the Lulist development model, this mode of regulation was combined with a peripheral post-Fordist accumulation regime, marked by labor precariousness, due to outsourcing, low wages, high turnover and the resilience of informality (in contrast to the trend towards formalization and the rise in minimum wage). During the expansionary cycle, "Lulist hegemony achieved up until 2014 a remarkable success in reproducing both the passive consent of the masses and the active consent of the leadership."[39] With the economic crisis, however, the previous period's accumulated contradictions (expressed in the demonstrations for housing, for the improvement of public services and of the quality of urban life, as well as in the increase in the number of strikes in 2013–2014) led to the "exhaustion of the Lulist development model, supported, above all, by the exploitation of cheap wage labor."[40]

Although hastily developed here, Ruy Braga's argument is useful to frame a fundamental aspect to understand the limits of Vale's union movement. It is the confluence, found in the mining company, between the Lulist administrations' orientations (its economic policy, the arrangement of its foreign relations, the stimulus to investment, etc.); the search for profit maximization by the company's management, its controllers and shareholders; the presence of powerful pension funds in control of the company's capital stock; and the relations between the pension funds' leadership, the labor movement and the PT-led governments. In Chapter 4, these issues will be scrutinized, while also addressing recent changes in Vale's 'corporate governance' aimed at consolidating its transformation into a TNC, following the signing in 2017 of a new shareholders' agreement which terminated the company's controlling shareholders' block established after privatization.

In an assessment of the Brazilian development model, Bruno Milanez and Rodrigo Santos compare the economic discourses of 'neo-developmentalism' and 'neo-extractivism' – present in the first decades of the twenty-first century, respectively, in Brazil and in Spanish-speaking American countries – and contrast them with their results.[41] For the authors, the 'neo-developmentalist'-oriented policies in Brazil did not produce the expected results; on the contrary, they consolidated a path of re-primarization in the country's economy,

---

39   Ibid, 88.
40   Ibid, 91.
41   Bruno Milanez and Rodrigo S. P. Santos, "Topsy-Turvy Neo-Developmentalism: An Analysis of the Current Brazilian Model of Development," *Revista de Estudios Sociales*, no. 53 (July/September 2015): 12–28.

strengthening its extractivist profile and bringing, in the long term, a tendency to low growth. Even though Brazil cannot be defined as a neo-extractivist country, both discourses would be varieties of the same economic route, with socioenvironmental consequences due to the impacts associated with activities such as mining. There would have been in Brazil, then, a kind of "topsy-turvy neo-developmentalism" whose "normative perspective ... ignores the structural limitations imposed by the world's current economic context."[42] The unprecedented Chinese demand for commodities led to a stimulus to the export of primary products and to support for the creation of domestically-originated TNCs, which, however, consolidated a subordinate insertion in the Brazilian economy, given the asymmetry in the exchange relations of mineral and agricultural products exported by these TNCs and the growing import of industrialized products.

A similar diagnosis was proposed by Plínio de Arruda Sampaio Jr., for whom the subordinate insertion of the Brazilian economy within neoliberal globalization was accompanied by the subordination of the country's economic policy to the interests of international capital and by the modernization of consumption patterns, oriented to replicate the central countries' way of life.[43] As a result, patterns of underdevelopment, deindustrialization and reprimarization of the economy were reproduced and transformed into a kind of modern "trading post" with the ongoing "neocolonial regression."

This brief survey of diagnoses serves as a support for a first attempt at locating the changes verified throughout the research on which this book is based. Moving under these conditions is like walking on shifting ground, always in transformation, where it is necessary to find new meanings for the questions initially proposed. While reality and the economic crisis ended up resolving – or, somehow, locating in the past – the theoretical polemics about the Brazilian development model during the first decades of the twenty-first century, the effort to describe and frame labor relations in transnational companies still seems quite valid.

For the case in focus, a TNC of Brazilian origin which has operated, throughout its history, "as an element of transfer and connection between international processes and domestic dynamics,"[44] it becomes fundamental to explore, in the micro-processes in the field, for social macro-forces, as proposed by

---

42 Ibid, 25.
43 Sampaio Jr., *Crônica de uma crise anunciada.*
44 Bruno Milanez et al., "A estratégia corporativa da Vale S.A.: um modelo analítico para redes globais extrativas," *Versos – Textos para Discussão PoEMAS* 2, no. 2 (2018), 2.

Michael Burawoy.[45] Before dealing with the empirical findings, however, it is necessary to advance towards an initial theoretical framework on such social macro-forces: global capitalism and class relations in the first decades of the twenty-first century.

2   Global Capitalism, Transnational Capital and Labor: An Approach

> What I'm feeling, and I think I'll keep feeling it, is that capital … It stops being from one country and starts being international. TAM, for example, is it national? But it has shares in Chile, in LAN. … I think there's an international trend for us to no longer have a Portuguese company, a Spanish company, an Italian company. … The headquarters is not so important anymore. … I think this is going to happen with companies all over the world. And in mining companies, that's what's happening. Mergers and other stuff are happening. Vale was in a situation where it either stayed here and took the risk of being eaten up, or it left Brazil. And we were – and still are – basically a Brazilian iron ore company. Of extraction in Brazil. … So, we were in a situation: we either stayed here running the risk of being eaten up, or we went international. And that's when we started to have operations outside Brazil. And today Vale is the biggest nickel producer in the world. (…) We had to get into the nickel business, get out of others. The Inco opportunity arose and we bought it. … And when you have a company that operates in several countries, it's stronger. … So, that concern about being a 100% Brazilian company doesn't exist. … So, more and more things are going to move towards that. I was in Turin: you got the Fiat CEO's office there, but the rest of the building has become a shopping mall. The Fiat building has become a shopping mall! Now, the headquarters is there, the international headquarters is there. This is more visual. I believe that this is a trend, and Brazilian companies have to get involved in this. So, I don't see a loss of nationality: it's just that we'll be stronger. If we stay in here, we'll be weak.[46]

André Teixeira is the executive manager of labor relations at Vale and occupies a position which, in the company's organizational chart, was previously in the Board of Directors. Having participated for many years in the company's

---

45   Burawoy, *The Extended Case Method.*
46   André Teixeira, Vale's manager, interviewed by Thiago Aguiar in Belo Horizonte, Brazil (July 2018).

strategic discussions and in the formulation of the company's relations with workers and unions, this executive seeks to frame in this way Vale's international expansion movement and the reorganization of its capital stock, after the signing of the new shareholders' agreement, as consequences of an inescapable trend of global capitalism. This involved the denationalization of corporate control – through mergers, acquisitions, and the creation of joint ventures – and the decentralization of production, reaching the paroxysm of iconic factories having become mere symbolic representation of bygone times, as in his description of Fiat's headquarters in Turin, transformed into a shopping mall. At the beginning of the twenty-first century, in a moment of concentration of capital in global mining,[47] Vale, whose history is marked by its state-owned origin and by its dependence on extractive activities in Brazil,[48] would have experienced a disjunctive: run the risk of losing competitiveness and be incorporated or seek new assets and expand globally.

The Vale executive's description illustrates the following attempt at theoretical approximation. After the capitalist crisis of the 1970s and in the following decades, paradigmatic changes in production and labor were part of a series of profound economic, social and political transformations in the world, which we call globalization.

According to William I. Robinson,[49] the introduction of Information and Communication Technology (ICT), the liberalization of financial flows, and the opening of global trade, often imposed by 'structural adjustment' policies of neoliberal orientation, gave capital the mobility which allowed it to disassociate itself from certain constraints of the Fordist compromise, in force during '*Les Trente Glorieuses*'. For Robinson, such transformations are of a qualitative order, a true 'epochal change' in the history of capitalism. Criticizing approaches anchored in national states – and which therefore share an 'international' framework of capitalism – he proposes a Marxist-inspired theory of global capitalism, in dialogue with authors of the 'global capitalism school.'[50]

---

47   Roger Moody, *Rocks and Hard Places: The Globalization of Mining* (London: Zed Books, 2007).

48   Issues which will be examined more closely in Chapters 1 and 2.

49   William I. Robinson, *A Theory of Global Capitalism: Production, Class, and State in a Transnational World* (Baltimore: Johns Hopkins University Press, 2004).

50   See, among others, Leslie Sklair, *Globalization: Capitalism and Its Alternatives* (New York: Oxford University Press, 2002); Peter Dicken, *Global Shift* (7. ed., London and New York: The Guilford Press, 2015); William Carroll, *The Making of a Transnational Capitalist Class* (London: Zed Books, 2010).

For Robinson, "the rise of transnational capital is the basis for economic globalization."[51] Transnational capital, in turn, has its origin in the global fragmentation and functional integration of production which took place in the last decades of the twentieth century and the beginning of the twenty-first century, constituting a globalized circuit of production and accumulation. There is here a clear dialogue with the studies on global value chains[52] and global production networks[53] to show how, for transnational capital, accumulation becomes global, that is, it is no longer circumscribed to a particular region or nation. This is the qualitative nature of the transformation to a global economy, differentiating it from the international capitalism that preceded it.

> What do I mean by *global economy*? I argue that in the new, transnational phase of the capitalist system, we are moving from a *world economy* to a *global economy*. In earlier epochs each country developed a national economy, and the national economies were linked to one another through trade and finances in an integrated international market. I consider this type of world socioeconomic structure a *world* economy. Different national economies and modes of production were 'articulated' within a broader social formation, or a world system. Nation-states mediated the boundaries between a world of different national economies and articulated modes of production. Stated in more theoretical terms, each country developed national circuits of accumulation that were linked externally to other such national circuits through commodity exchanges and capital flows. But what we have seen in the current epoch is the increasing globalization of the production process itself. Global capital mobility has allowed capital to reorganize production worldwide in accordance with a whole range of considerations that allow for maximizing profit-making opportunities. In this process, national production systems have become fragmented and integrated externally into new globalized circuits of accumulation.[54]

Robinson's theoretical approach seeks to point out a trend of global capitalism: the development of global circuits of production and accumulation

51   Robinson, *A Theory of Global Capitalism*, 9.
52   Gary Gereffi et al., "The Governance of Global Value Chains," *Review of International Political Economy* 12, no. 1 (2005): 78–104.
53   Jeffrey Henderson et al., "Global Production Networks and the Analysis of Economic Development," *Review of International Political Economy* 9, no.3 (2002): 436–464.
54   Robinson, *A Theory of Global Capitalism*, 10.

hegemonized by transnational capital. The formation of a transnational capitalist class (TCC), for the author, does not occur in a linear and homogeneous way, since there is a struggle between fractions of the bourgeoisie oriented towards transnational, national and local accumulation – the latter two do not cease to exist, even though they are gradually led by capitalist logic itself to 'globalize or lose.'

The role of transnational corporations is key as they are at the forefront of the fragmentation/integration of global production through mechanisms such as subcontracting and joint ventures.[55] The increase in foreign direct investment (FDI) flows is one of the most important indications of the transnationalization of the global economy. TNCs, in turn, are gradually losing the national identification that once clearly linked certain companies to their home countries. In their shareholder control, investment funds, to which it is often difficult to attribute a national origin, gain importance, with their investors scattered around the world, including in countries of the former 'Third World', whence TCC members emerge with relevant participations or controlling companies with a global presence.[56]

This situation makes the relationships between center and periphery, Global North and South, more complex, challenging the established diagnoses of the sociology of development. For Robinson, analyses centered on the nation-state should therefore give way to a social conception of development, taking into consideration the social classes and fractions within each nation-state, as well as their transnational relations.[57] Globalization has separated the wealth of each social group as well as the nations', widening inequality also within each country. Although inequality between North and South persists, unequal development deepens between classes and fractions within each state, at the center or at the periphery, as an effect of the global division of labor. As we will see, these transformations have brought important challenges for the working class and for the union movement.

---

55   An example of this process can be found in Caroline Knowles' fascinating ethnographic research on the global production, consumption and disposal of a prosaic commodity: the rubber flip-flop. See Caroline Knowles, *Flip-flop: a Journey through Globalisation's Backroads* (London: Pluto Press, 2014).

56   Robinson, *A Theory of Global Capitalism*, mentions, in this regard, the Indian-origin Tata Group, which has become the largest single employer in the UK, interestingly enough India's former metropole.

57   William I. Robinson, "Transnational Processes, Development Studies and Changing Social Hierarchies in the World System: A Central American Case Study," *Third World Quarterly* 22, no 4 (2001): 529–63.

For the theory of global capitalism, transnational financial capital is the hegemonic fraction of the TCC, controlling assets of the major TNCs.[58] As stock markets grow, facilitated by the communications revolution, changes in the shareholding composition of TNCs can occur on a daily basis. It is useful at this point in the exposition to describe the mechanisms by which the transnational capitalist class is formed:

> there is now a considerable and rapidly growing body of empirical evidence that in the latter part of the twentieth century the giant corporate conglomerates that drive the global economy ceased to be corporations of a particular country and increasingly came to represent transnational capital. Some of the mechanisms of TCC formation are: the spread of TNC affiliates; the phenomenal increase in cross-border mergers and acquisitions; the increasing transnational interlocking of boards of directors; increasingly cross- and mutual investment among companies from two or more countries and transnational ownership of capital shares; the spread of cross-border strategic alliances of all sorts; vast global outsourcing and subcontracting networks; and the increasing salience of transnational peak business associations. There are other, less researched mechanisms that spur on TCC formation, such as the existence of stock exchanges in most countries of the world linked to the global financial system. The spread of these stock markets from the principal centers of the world economy to most capital cities around the world, combined with twenty-four-hour trading, facilitates ever-greater global trading and hence transnational ownership of shares. [59]

From the above it is clear that the transnationalization of the economy modifies capital-labor relations not only in terms of the global fragmentation/integration of production. While the TCC has gained global mobility, the working class is more subject to the limits of the nation-state, through the control of migratory flows and the circulation of people, but also through the limitation of its organization on a global scale. If the working class, on the one hand, finds itself increasingly selling its labor power to TNCs and participating in

---

58   Analyses in the French tradition on the financialization of capitalist economy in the context of globalization can be found in François Chesnais, *La mondialisation du capital* (Paris: Syros, 1998); and Thomas Coutrot, *L'entreprise néo-libérale, nouvelle utopie capitaliste?* (Paris: La Découverte, 1998).

59   William I. Robinson, *Global Capitalism and the Crisis of Humanity* (New York: Cambridge University Press, 2014), 21–2.

geographically dispersed production processes, on the other hand, it faces the TCC as a national or even local working class, with few instruments for extranational organization. The working class has an objective transnational existence from the standpoint of its location in global production.[60] Yet this emerging 'global proletariat', subjected to post-Fordist restructuring and to new capital-labor relations, is fragmented: it is neither self-conscious as a transnational class nor organized as such. This is the root of the working class' difficulties in dealing with the challenges of globalization.[61] It is necessary to face legal, political, ideological, cultural, economic and communication barriers, among many others, that the transnational bourgeoisie finds it easier to transcend.

This does not mean that TCC's do not have differences and disputes. While these tend to manifest themselves less and less as national rivalry, as in the epoch of world capitalism, there is a fierce global competition between TNCs and fractions of the TCC. The fundamental issue is the ability of the TCC to recognize its common interests – such as increasing trade openness, liberalization of financial flows, advocacy of structural adjustment policies, etc. – and organize itself supranationally, for example, in spaces such as the World Economic Forum.[62] At the same time, the TCC can make itself represented by an army of managers, economists, journalists, academics, high-level technicians, bureaucrats and political operators at the service of its interests, who are materially rewarded and ideologically committed to the interests of the TCC. Without being strictly speaking members of the TCC, they make up a 'transnational elite', often trained in the same top universities and schools, who occupy management positions in companies and states.

Such an elite is fundamental to what Robinson defines as the creation of 'transnational state (TNS) apparatuses'.[63] In short, the concept does not express the existence of a state with global regulatory capacity, but in fact the gradual capture and interrelationship between supranational and international agencies and institutions – such as the United Nations (UN), the World Trade Organization (WTO), the International Monetary Fund (IMF), the World Bank, the European Union, the G7, the G20, the North Atlantic Treaty Organization (NATO), etc. –, nation-states and their institutions in a network

---

60   Robinson, *A Theory of Global Capitalism*, 43.

61   This issue will be analyzed in Chapter 3, when I will focus on Vale's presence in Canada.

62   Robinson named the member of the transnational capitalist class who is class-conscious and politically organized in the spaces of the global bourgeoisie the 'Davos Man,' in reference to the Swiss city where the annual meetings of the World Economic Forum traditionally takes place.

63   Robinson, *Global Capitalism and the Crisis of Humanity*.

which operates in order to guarantee the conditions for global accumulation.[64] Indeed, because of their origin in the old international system, hegemonized by countries of the Global North, the most important TNS apparatuses have a strong presence of institutions and states from the central countries. Thus, it can be said that the Federal Reserve, for example, is one of the main TNS apparatuses. The discussion about the validity of the concept of TNS apparatuses will not be the object of further attention in this book, but in chapters 3 and 4 it will be possible to return to some related questions.

What interests us here, above all, is to point out the chief tendency in the theory of global capitalism: the tendency towards transnationalization of the economy and of social classes as synonymous with globalization or global capitalism. This is an ongoing process, whose outcome will be determined by the class struggle on a global scale, among comings and goings, but in which the TCC has become the hegemonic fraction of the bourgeoisie on a global scale.

> The TCC therefore can be located in the global class structure by its ownership and/or control of transnational capital. What distinguishes the TCC from national or local capitalists is that it is involved in globalized production and manages globalized circuits of accumulation, which gives it, spatially and politically, an objective class existence and identity in the global system above any local territories and polities. Transnational capital constitutes the 'commanding heights' of the global economy ... [and] *has become the hegemonic fraction of capital on a world scale.* ... At the level of agency, the TCC, as represented by its inner circle, leading representatives, and politicized elements, is class conscious. It has become conscious of its transnationality. ... The TCC is increasingly a class-in-itself and a class-for-itself.[65]

For the TCC's, the global crisis of 2008 was a landmark event, which revealed the growing difficulties of articulating and imposing its agenda. The historic and structural character of the crisis – a true "crisis of humanity"[66] – revealed

---

64   On the other hand, for Robinson, the TCC has found it difficult to strengthen such TNS apparatuses and ensure greater power of global coordination, a key element in understanding the crisis of global capitalism. At the same time, the internal legitimacy of nation-states has been eroded, bringing serious difficulties for the domination of the transnational bourgeoisie and its political agents. This instability has increased the dispute between fractions of the TCC.

65   Robinson, *A Theory of Global Capitalism*, 47–8.

66   Robinson, *Global Capitalism and the Crisis of Humanity.*

the TCC's inability to build a hegemonized historical bloc capable of providing a global direction. As a result, the more clearly repressive and authoritarian features of globalization are becoming apparent, and capitalism seeks to find valorization for the over-accumulation of capital by intensifying mechanisms of primitive accumulation,[67] deepening speculation, and developing forms of militarized accumulation which make spatial repression and segmentation profitable by controlling surplus populations.[68] It is not our aim to deepen the analysis of the 2008 crisis, but only to highlight elements which will be taken up again in the conclusion of this book.

If a more detailed presentation of the theory of global capitalism has been chosen here, it is because of the need to indicate the contours of capitalist globalization as a process of transnationalization of the economy and of social classes. This is a fundamental definition, even if it is criticized and part of a long and ancient controversy about the very notion of globalization and its definition.[69]

---

67   This is a fundamental aspect for the framing of mining TNC activities. Starting from different theoretical premises, the notion of "accumulation by dispossession" points in the same direction. See David Harvey, *The New Imperialism* (Oxford: Oxford University Press, 2003).

68   See William I. Robinson, *The Global Police State* (London: Pluto Press, 2020).

69   Paul Hirst and Grahame Thompson, *Globalization in Question: the International Economy and the Possibilities of Governance*. (Cambridge: Polity Press, 1997), for example, question the qualitative character of the change represented by globalization and consider that international companies would be predominantly multinational rather than transnational. In Robinson, *A Theory of Global Capitalism*, this diagnosis is criticized, linking it to these authors' methodological nationalism, that organized the empirical data nationally, instead of verifying, for example, the enormous intra-firm trade flows. In Sebastián Madrid, "Elites in Their Real Lives: A Chilean Comment on Robinson," *Critical Sociology* 38, no. 3 (2012): 389–393, empirical elements are sought to evaluate the pertinence of aspects from the thesis about global capitalism: for the author in question, analyzing the Chilean case, there is a temporal anticipation to the conflict between 'modernizing' technical cadres who adopted the neoliberal ideology and the national dominant class; furthermore, there would be a contemporary confluence between the transnationally-oriented capitalist class and the more traditional dominant class in Chile. However, would this not be precisely a sign that transnationalization has been successful? William Carroll, "Global, Transnational, Regional, National: The Need for Nuance in Theorizing Global Capitalism," *Critical Sociology* 38, no. 3 (2012): 365–371; Andrew Schrank, "Conquering, Comprador, or Competitive: The National Bourgeoisie in the Developing World," *New Directions in the Sociology of Global Development* 11 (2005): 91–120; Michael Hartmann, "Internationalisation et spécificités nationales des élites économiques," *Actes de la Recherche en Sciences Sociales* 190, no. 5 (2011): 10–23; and Anne-Catherine Wagner, "La bourgeoisie face à la mondialisation," *Mouvements*, no. 26 (2003): 33–9, like most critics of the global capitalism thesis, emphasize, from different theoretical premises, the still current relevance of the national character of the capitalist class. There is

Finally, to illuminate an additional theoretical aspect, it is useful to present more precisely the contours of the notion of transnationalization (of production, of corporations, of classes) and its differences with internationalization. In dialogue with Dicken[70] and Sklair,[71] Robinson associates transnationalization with the "globalization of the production process itself," as distinct from internationalization, a mere "extension of trade and financial flows across national borders." The former, therefore, is qualitatively different from the latter.

> Internationalization involves the simple extension of economic activities across national borders and is essentially a *quantitative* process that leads to a more extensive geographical pattern of economic activity, whereas transnationalization differs *qualitatively* from internationalization processes, involving not merely the geographical extension of economic activity across national borders but also the *functional integration* of such internationally dispersed activities.[72]

Thus, it is possible to associate internationalization with multinationals, as a phenomenon typical of the era of international capitalism, with nationally-based companies which expand their activities to other national economies. The internationalization processes of companies, which become multinationals, continue to exist, since, within the capitalist class, there are regionally and nationally oriented fractions, which can seek international expansion of their business. A nationally-based company can extend its activities beyond its national borders without becoming a TNC. Although the criteria for defining the borders between national and transnational bourgeoisies are subject to debate, from which more consensual empirical verification criteria may be established, it is possible to define the process of transnationalization as the fusion and interpenetration of national capitals – for example, through foreign direct investment, cross-border mergers and acquisitions, interpenetration of boards of directors, and subcontracting – giving rise to global processes of production and accumulation.

---

an extensive survey of other authors critical of the thesis of transnational class formation and an attempt to answer them in William I. Robinson, "Debate on the New Global Capitalism: Transnational Capitalist Class, Transnational State Apparatuses and Global Crises," *International Critical Thought* 7, no. 2 (2017): 171–89.

70   Dicken, *Global Shift*.
71   Sklair, *Globalization*.
72   Robinson, *A Theory of Global Capitalism*, 14.

Are capitalists transnational only in the sense that they span the globe with their economic power, or are they transnational as they are beginning to merge as a global bourgeoisie through corporate mergers, banking interests, and so on? I suggest that the former situation is an indicator of an international bourgeoisie, while the latter situation is an indicator of a transnational bourgeoisie. Internationalization occurs when national capitals expand their reach beyond their own national borders. Transnationalization occurs when national capitals fuse with other internationalizing national capitals in a process of cross-border interpenetration that disembeds them from their nations and locates them in new supranational space opening up under the global economy.[73]

It would then be possible to combine both processes in a broad understanding of transnationalization. If the latter can be understood as the merger and interpenetration of national capitals, whose accumulation is based globally, internationalization is not contradictory to it. On the contrary, we can identify internationalization as a moment of globalization/transnationalization. It is through processes of internationalization that national capitals expand internationally and can then merge into a transnational network which makes them less dependent on their national origins and less identifiable with them.

The incorporation of conceptual categories from the global capitalism school allows us to frame Vale's transnationalization process described in this book by means of ethnographically inspired research conducted in two countries. It is a privileged case for understanding aspects of globalization and its relations with Brazilian internal dynamics. Thus, the objective of this study is to analyze Vale's transnationalization process and its effects on labor relations. In doing so, I hope to glimpse the forms of the Brazilian economy's incorporation into global capitalism, in the first decades of the twenty-first century, and its consequences.

Our effort will be dedicated, therefore, to the description of this long movement of the company's transnationalization: the preparation for privatization while still under state control;[74] the privatization, in 1997, with a majority of domestic shareholder control by pension funds of state-owned companies; the increasing stimulus to the company's internationalization during Roger Agnelli's management and the 'commodity supercycle', with the acquisition of Inco in Canada and the opening of new operations, for example, in

---

73   Ibid, 54.

74   Maria Cecília Minayo, *De ferro e flexíveis: marcas do Estado empresário e da privatização na subjetividade operária* (Rio de Janeiro: Garamond, 2004).

Mozambique;[75] the recent changes in its corporate arrangement with the signing of the new shareholders' agreement; the consolidation of the company's transformation into a TNC and its consequences for Vale's future.[76] The focus will be on the company's labor and union relations in recent years, during the commodity post-boom, in Brazil and Canada, through an ethnographic approach.

Between the 'clouds' of theory and the 'marshlands of empiricism',[77] however, a way must be found to analyze complex issues such as those already outlined. How to operationalize notions like 'transnationalization' and 'globalization' without remaining in the 'clouds'? How to value field data and the ethnographic approach without sinking into the 'marshlands'? Theoretical 'crutches' are needed that allow one to walk on such slippery ground: this is what is presented below.

3   Framing Multi-situated Social Phenomena: Global Production Networks (GPNs), Corporate Strategies, and International Trade Union Networks

Understanding globalization as a process of the transnationalization of the international economy does not mean ignoring that different national realities condition the way the process of the global economy's integration takes place. The 'varieties of capitalism' approach can illuminate some interesting aspects of this question: focused on the analysis of central countries, it suggests that national differences in terms of innovation policies, sources of corporate financing, worker's training policies, and relations with unions, among others, are due to the role of specific institutions constituted over time.[78] History, culture, and the informal rules developed by economic agents and their representative organizations create certain 'institutional infrastructures' which condition the economic specialization of regions and countries.

---

75   Marshall, "Behind the Image of South-South Solidarity at Brazil's Vale."

76   Rodrigo S. P. Santos, "A construção social de uma corporação transnacional: notas sobre a 'nova privatização' da Vale S.A.," *Revista de Estudos e Pesquisas sobre as Américas* 13, no. 2 (2019): 230–270.

77   Burawoy, *The Extended Case Method.*

78   Peter Hall and David Soskice, "An Introduction to Varieties of Capitalism," in *Varieties of Capitalism: The Institutional Foundations of Comparative Advantage* (Oxford: Oxford University Press, 2001), 1–68.

This institutionalist approach aims to show that specific economic activities – developed in regions such as California's 'Silicon Valley' or Germany's Ruhr River Valley – benefit from such 'institutional infrastructures' which allow companies to gain 'institutional comparative advantages' and to design corporate strategies consistent with the variety of national capitalisms in which they are embedded. In general, these are the frameworks with which this literature divides central country economies into Liberal Market Economies (LMES) – of which the United States is a typical example – and Coordinated Market Economies (CMES) – of which Germany is a typical example – whose characteristics will not be detailed here.[79] Peter Hall and David Soskice, however, state that the typical 'institutional infrastructures' of each of these groups of economies have undergone transformations due to globalization.[80] One can mention, for example, the change in financing sources in CMES, whose companies are increasingly dependent on capital markets – and subject to short-term pressures – with the proximity shrinkage to banks from their own countries; or even the changes in unionization rates, which drop more rapidly in LMES, starting from historical levels already low compared to those of CMES.

The point in dealing with 'varieties of capitalism' is that even if these produce only "varieties of integration into global capitalism,"[81] *varieties still exist and matter*. Therefore, not only the tendencies towards homogenization stimulated by globalization should be underlined, but also the way in which differences are articulated for the benefit of global capitalist accumulation. This observation will have consequences for the analysis, carried out in Chapter 3, of Vale's labor and union relations strategy in Brazil and Canada, in tracing what the company intends to make common and how it deals with local differences in its operations. At the same time, such observations appear as a background, in Chapter 4, for the treatment of the relations between pension funds of state-owned companies, the union movement, Vale's management, and the PT administrations (2003–2016). By analyzing the interview conducted

---

79   There are attempts to use the notions of 'varieties of capitalism' for the analysis of Latin American countries. This is what was done by Ben Ross Schneider, "Hierarchical Market Economies and Varieties of Capitalism in Latin America," *Journal of Latin American Studies* 41, no. 3 (August 2009): 553–75, by proposing to classify them as Hierarchical Market Economies (HMES), a description of which is beyond the scope of our concerns at this time. In Chapter 3, we will point out some features of LMES, especially in regard to the relationship between companies and unions, which facilitated the restructuring promoted by Vale in its Canadian operations, leading to the 2009–2010 strike.

80   Hall and Soskice, "An Introduction to Varieties of Capitalism."

81   Robinson, "The Transnational State and the BRICS," 16.

with Sérgio Rosa, former president of Previ[82] and of Vale's Board of Directors (2003–2010), for example, it was possible to shed light on the orientation of an important group of political and union leaders favorable to the international-ization/transnationalization of Brazilian companies, making it possible, at the same time, to gather elements for an assessment of this period.

In dealing with the process of transnationalization, I do not intend to ignore the theoretical heritage of the Brazilian sociology of development – which continues to address issues such as those proposed above, relating them to the class dynamics in the country – even though its more detailed appropri-ation is not the objective of this book. Rodrigo Santos, for example, has res-cued the 'forgotten' tradition of the sociology of development by historically locating mining projects in the Eastern Amazon to propose a framework for Vale's metamorphosis from an old state-owned company, whose roots go back to the period of national developmentalism, to a TNC, in a process conditioned by "privileged access to the largest iron ore reserve in the world, the Carajás Mineral Province."[83]

This type of framework demonstrates the importance of articulating multi-ple scales and levels of analysis when dealing with Vale's mineral production. In particular, investment projects such as Carajás Iron and S11D[84] should be analyzed as 'nodes' of mining and steel global production networks (GPNs). Global production networks allow "the suppression of privileged scales in the discussion of development in favor of multi-scale approaches."[85]

It is necessary to avoid, on the one hand, methodological nationalism and, on the other, a hasty global-national dichotomy in the analysis of multi-situated social phenomena. It is clear, therefore, that an analytical approach that seeks the "social macro-forces" in the "micro-processes in the field,"[86] as proposed here, can benefit from a multi-agent and multi-scale understanding, such as that proposed by the GPN literature presented below.

> Globalization ... has undercut the validity of traditional, state-centred, forms of social science, and with that the agendas that hith-erto have guided the vast majority of research on economic and social

---

82   Provident Fund of *Banco do Brasil* workers, the largest pension fund in Brazil and Latin America.

83   Rodrigo S. P. Santos, "Desenvolvimento econômico e mudança social: a Vale e a mineração na Amazônia Oriental," *Caderno CRH* 29, no. 77 (May/August 2016): 302.

84   Analyzed in Chapters 1 and 2.

85   Santos, "Desenvolvimento econômico e mudança social," 306.

86   Burawoy, *The Extended Case Method.*

development. Investigations adequate to the study of globalization and its consequences demand of social scientists the elaboration of analytic frameworks and research programmes that simultaneously foreground the dynamics of uneven development transnationally, nationally and sub-nationally. Such investigations require us to focus on the flows *and* the places *and* their dialectical connections as these arise and are realized in the developed and developing worlds alike. Additionally, ... *we need to study what firms do, where they do it, why they do it, why they are allowed to do it, and how they organize the doing of it across different geographic scales.* ... The framework we propose is that of the 'global production network' (GPN).[87]

Approaches such as those presented so far allow us to affirm that methodological nationalism in the social sciences hinders, or even prevents, the perception of new processes arising from capitalist globalization. In a short summary, it can be said that the GPN framework starts from the notions of commodity/value chains,[88] but takes a critical view of some of its aspects – such as a 'linear and vertical' conception of production and distribution processes – to propose an understanding of production systems as networked structures, emphasizing the "*social processes* involved in producing goods and services and reproducing knowledge, capital and labour power."[89] These allow for the transcendence of the 'chain' metaphor's fixity and the centering of the analysis on the structure of the 'firm', facilitating the perception of the relationship between economic and social agents, and of multi-scale phenomena more in tune with the complexity of global production. In the following paragraphs, three conceptual categories of the GPN model (*value, power,* and *embeddedness*), which were mobilized in the research on which this work was based, are presented as a way to guide readers throughout the exposition:

1) *value* – a) its *creation* through the labor process and the generation of rents (technological, organizational, relational and 'brand'); b) its *enhancement,* e.g., through transfers and technology sophistication, rent creation and institutional influences; and c) its *capture,* which involves

---

87   Henderson et al., "Global Production Networks and the Analysis of Economic Development", 145–6, emphasis added.

88   Gereffi and Korzeniewicz, ed. *Commodity Chains and Global Capitalism*; Gereffi et al., "The Governance of Global Value Chains."

89   Henderson et al., "Global Production Networks and the Analysis of Economic Development," 152.

government policies, issues of firm ownership, nature of 'corporate governance' and of ownership rights and profit sharing, etc.;

2)   *power* – the sources of power in the GPN and the forms of its exercise,
      divided into a) *corporate power*, related to "the extent to which the lead
      firm in the GPN has the capacity to influence decisions and resource
      allocations – *vis-à-vis* other firms in the network – decisively and con-
      sistently in its own interests.";[90] b) *institutional power*, relating to the
      exercise of power by national and local states, international agencies,
      supranational institutions and rating agencies (the latter as a form of pri-
      vate institutional power); and c) *collective power*, exercised by collective
      actors, such as unions and NGOs, which seek to influence firms, govern-
      ments and agencies by organizing locally, nationally or internationally;

3)   *embeddedness* – firms are embedded, connecting social and spatial
      arrangements, carrying a past history, an origin,[91] which influences their
      strategies and relationship with workers, communities, the state, institu-
      tional agents, etc. It is divided into a) *territorial embeddedness*, by which
      GPNs can absorb or be constrained by economic activities and social
      dynamics existing in the places where they are installed; and b) *network
      embeddedness*, which deals with the connections of GPN members, the
      durability and stability of their relationships.[92]

Examples of the potential of the GPN approach can be found in the research
of Rodrigo Santos and Bruno Milanez,[93] who describe Vale's global iron ore
production network in Brazil and demonstrate how this model allows for shedding light not only on iron ore extraction as a productive activity, but also on
the 'network of contestation' that is organized at Vale, involving several agents,
such as trade unions, environmental social movements, movements in defense
of indigenous lands, non-governmental organizations (NGOs), as well as local

---

90   Ibid, 157.
91   Ibid, 159, draw attention to the fact that "some lead firms when investing overseas may
      carry the institutional 'baggage' of their home bases with them." This aspect is fundamen-
      tal to the analysis of 1) the restructuring of the Canadian operations promoted by Vale in
      2009; and 2) the company's labor and union relations strategy, which provoked a strong
      reaction from unions in that country.
92   Milanez et al., "A estratégia corporativa da Vale S.A.," 6, propose two other dimensions
      of embeddedness: *social embeddedness*, "which relates to the firms' plane of origin, and
      can even be associated with the notion of varieties of capitalism"; and *material embed-
      dedness*, "based on physical-material aspects of the territories, relevant for the study of
      natural resource-intensive sectors".
93   Rodrigo S. P. Santos and Bruno Milanez, "The Global Production Network for Iron
      Ore: Materiality, Corporate Strategies, and Social Contestation in Brazil," *The Extractive
      Industries and Society*, no 2 (2015), 756–65.

and national political and legislative institutions. Throughout chapters 1 and 2, analyses on Vale's iron ore GPN will be mobilized to support the observations registered in the field.

It may be possible to associate the emergence of international union networks with the development of GPNs, as an effort of the labor movement to transcend its local and national boundaries, and to seek forms of articulation with unions and workers which participate in other GPN nodes. As Leonardo Mello e Silva shows, union networks seem to be a response of the labor movement to counteract, or at least to mark its position, against the initiatives of globalized capital.[94] Trade union networks consist of regional, national or international articulation between unions and union centers as a way to coordinate the interests and positions of workers in companies which now operate on a global scale.

In Chapter 3, I will discuss the attempt to organize an international trade union network at Vale, based on the initiative of the *Central Única dos Trabalhadores* [Unified Workers' Central], or CUT, Brazil's main national trade union center, and the international union United Steelworkers (USW). As we will see, the trade union network, which even organized some meetings and activities in solidarity with the strike in Canada, was closed before it was consolidated. Interestingly, the Brazilian Vale union movement's response to the company's internationalization was insufficient, and there seem to be deeper reasons for this, related to the way the company's shareholder control is organized and to the interaction, developed during the PT administrations, between the controllers, the federal government and the union movement's leadership, as we will see in Chapter 4.

Finally, in this discussion, it is necessary to make explicit the definition of 'corporate strategies' in light of the appropriation of the GPN conceptual categories outlined above. Rodrigo Santos and José Ricardo Ramalho, in a comparative study of four multinational groups operating in Brazil, described corporate strategies as the process of rational definition and continuous execution of specific objectives aimed at obtaining value by companies. The authors analyzed corporate strategies in the following dimensions:

1. Financial, involving the ways of obtaining resources on a global scale;
2. Investment, defined by the ways of 'entering' and expanding within the Brazilian market;

---

94 Leonardo Mello e Silva, "Inovações do sindicalismo brasileiro em tempos de globalização e o trabalho sob tensão," in *As contradições do lulismo: a que ponto chegamos?* ed. André Singer and Isabel Loureiro (São Paulo: Boitempo, 2016), 93–122.

3. Market, sales and services, by means of the main goods and/or services offered, and positions occupied in key markets;

4. Technological, relating to the technical and organizational integration of the [GPNs]; and

5. Labor and union relations, addressing the forms of management and impacts over the workforce.[95]

A collective study on Vale proposed a model for the specific analysis of the company's corporate strategy, taking into account five strategies: 1) market; 2) financial; 3) institutional; 4) labor relations; and 5) social.[96] The last strategy takes into consideration the importance of agents such as NGOs, social movements, and local communities which suffer the impacts of mining and relate to the company. The description of these five dimensions of Vale's corporate strategy will be the object of attention throughout this book. What can be stated at this point is that an ethnographic approach has much to contribute to understanding the strategies mobilized by TNCs to exercise their corporate power, enhance value capture, and embed themselves.

The exposition of these concepts is only intended to allow a more precise definition of our objectives in the field. This book aims to describe, through a case study, mainly Vale's labor and union relations strategies in Brazil and Canada. Certainly, in doing so, fundamental aspects of other dimensions of Vale's corporate strategy (financial, market and institutional) will also be revealed, through the information obtained in interviews with local, national and international union members, and with members and former members of Vale's management and of Previ.

The study investigated the following hypotheses: 1) the transnationalization of Vale is underway, with consequences for labor and union relations in the company, on the one hand, and revealing aspects of the dynamics of insertion of the Brazilian economy into global capitalism, on the other; 2) the company's labor and union relations strategy seeks the weakening and dispersion of workers' representative organizations, as a way to mitigate threats to the exercise of corporate power in production and lower labor costs; and 3) in Canada, Vale sought to restructure the operations of the former Inco plant and frame the relations with the union USW Local 6500 and its local workforce within

---

95   Rodrigo S. P. Santos and José Ricardo Ramalho, "Estratégias corporativas e de relações de trabalho no Brasil: uma análise preliminar de 4 grupos multinacionais," *Anais do XIV Encontro Nacional da ABET* (2015): 3.

96   Conducted by the multidisciplinary and inter-institutional research and extension group "Politics, Economics, Mining, Environment and Society" (PoEMAS). See Milanez et al., "A estratégia corporativa da Vale S.A."

the framework of the labor relations strategy developed historically, since the state-owned period, in Brazil, which would be, in our view, the underlying reason for the 2009–2010 strike in that country.

The investigation of such hypotheses was carried out within the limits of the ethnographic record of a specific period. This book presents a kind of photograph of a moment of transition and crisis. In the following pages and chapters, one finds a set of records: 1) of the reaction of workers to the degradation of their working conditions and pay; 2) of the weakening and often the inability of unions to offer a counterpoint to the effects of the company's transnationalization, as is the case with workers' organizations around the world in the face of the dilemmas of globalization; 3) of the organization of production, outsourcing and of the successful (in spite of conflicts) strategy of labor and union relations; 4) of a political project, which has reached a crisis point, through the voice of some of its protagonists less exposed to the spotlight; 5) of the contradiction between the union leadership's diagnoses and its practical responses; and, finally, 6) of the corporate discourse which covers and intends to justify Vale's corporate strategy.

In effect, this book is an attempt to offer meaning to chaos and intense change: a search for 'crutches' and for a compass, through the resources of ethnography, to the shifting ground of globalization. To close this Introduction, I describe some additional aspects of the 'extended case method' adopted.[97] Finally, I briefly describe the four chapters which make up this book.

4 Some Methodological Notes: Ethnographic Inspiration and the 'Extended Case Method'

The study privileged information obtained in interviews and field observations, in addition to the collection of secondary materials, such as documents and corporate reports of Vale directed to the public and its shareholders, union publications, and the Brazilian and Canadian press. Interviews were conducted with workers, local, national and international union leaders of Vale's unions in Brazil – Metabase Carajás,[98] *Sindicato dos Trabalhadores em*

---

97   Burawoy, *The Extended Case Method.*

98   *Sindicato dos Trabalhadores na Indústria da Extração do Ferro, Metais Básicos, do Ouro, Metais Preciosos e de Minerais Não Metálicos de Marabá, Parauapebas, Curionópolis e Eldorado dos Carajás* [Union of Workers in the Industry of Iron Extraction, Base Metals, Gold, Precious Metals and Nonmetallic Minerals of Marabá, Parauapebas, Curionópolis and Eldorado dos Carajás] (Pará).

Empresas Ferroviárias dos Estados do Maranhão, Pará e Tocantins [Union of Workers in Railroad Companies in the States of Maranhão, Pará and Tocantins], or STEFEM,[99] *Confederação Nacional dos Químicos* [National Confederation of Chemists], or CNQ, and CUT – and in Canada – USW, Canadian Labour Congress (CLC) and USW Local 6500 (the local union representing workers in Sudbury, Canada). Also interviewed were André Teixeira, executive manager of labor relations at Vale, and Sérgio Rosa, former president of Previ and of Vale's Board of Directors.

Additionally, production sites were visited, that involved access restrictions imposed by the company. In Brazil, Vale facilities were visited in São Luís (in Maranhão) in May 2016 and in Parauapebas (in Pará) in July 2016. In Canada, in November 2016, I visited Vale's facilities and conducted interviews with workers and union leaders in Sudbury (Ontario). In addition to the locations already mentioned, several interviews were conducted in Brazil, in Belo Horizonte (in Minas Gerais), Rio de Janeiro, São Bernardo do Campo (in the state of São Paulo) and São Paulo, and in Canada, in Toronto (Ontario).

This book is the result of a case study of ethnographic inspiration, which sought to be guided by the methodology of the 'extended case method' proposed by Michael Burawoy, which means treating the 'context effects' present in any ethnography as a fundamental part of knowledge production.[100] The interaction established with the others and the appreciation of the interview guided the contacts that were made. The objective was to extend the case study beyond the limits of the visited locations and of time, in order to establish comparisons between national realities which are diverse and geographically distant, but that are linked by capitalist valorization and by the organization of production by the transnational company. Such power relations have presented themselves in many situations described throughout the work. To deal with them, some methodological assumptions were adopted that are presented below.

The 'hard core' of Burawoy's methodology is the 'extended case method', which takes into account the limits and issues related to 'power effects' in sociological research and mobilizes, as a virtue, the very difficulties created by the method.[101] For Burawoy, the social sciences emerged under the shadow

---

99   Whose headquarters is located in São Luís (Maranhão).
100   Burawoy, *The Extended Case Method*.
101   In addition to the work already mentioned, methodological reflections by this author can be found in Michael Burawoy et al., *Ethnography Unbound* (Berkeley: University of California Press, 1991); Michael Burawoy et al., *Global Ethnography* (Berkeley: University of California Press, 2000).

of the old positivism. The postulates of positive science affirm the observer's isolation, their separation and distancing from the object. The observer is an 'outsider' who must perform the most accurate mapping of the world through procedural objectivity. Quantitative research, then, is the method *par excellence* of the social sciences conceived as a positive science.

The 'extended case method' rejects such assumptions, since positive science has many obstacles in realizing its own dogmas, such as: 1) non-reactivity (impossible to achieve insofar as the interviewer always affects the interviewee in some way); 2) regularity of data selection (affected by the multiple ways in which a respondent may interpret the same question); 3) research replicability (affected by the effects of economic, political, and social context in which the interview takes place); and 4) representativeness (open to question when reflecting on whether the product of an interview is a sample of a population of individuals or, in fact, a sample of a social situation).

Therefore, the 'extended case method' intentionally disregards the precepts of positive science in favor of accepting the 'ethnographic condition,' its virtues and challenges. The social sciences should deal with 'methodological dualism', since it is possible to do science also by means of a reflexive model, which uses "not detachment but engagement as the road to knowledge" through "multiple dialogues": between observer and participants, between local processes and extra-local forces, and of theory with itself. In this way, objectivity is guaranteed not by "an accurate mapping of the world but by the growth of knowledge, that is, the imaginative and parsimonious reconstruction of theory to accommodate anomalies."[102] The two models of science, positive and reflexive, are therefore coexistent.

Quantitative researchers recognize 'context effects' and systematically seek to minimize them. Burawoy, however, suggests that social scientists assume that context is the very reality in which they live. Reflexive science, as an alternative model, then has the role of taking "context as a point of departure but not a point of conclusion." The coexistence between positive and reflexive science would be possible because "it is not the problem that determines the method but the method that shapes the problem," that is, reflexive science deals with problems for which positive science has no answer.[103] The principles of reflexive science are thus drawn from the 'context effects' themselves, by using dialogue and intersubjectivity as tools, uniting participant and observer, knowledge and context, situation, popular and academic theory. This scientific

---

102   Burawoy, *The Extended Case Method*, 21.
103   Ibid, 71.

duality thus corresponds a methodological duality, in which the 'extended case method' can take its place.

The vicissitudes in the field lead social scientists to thematize the ever-present 'context effects' in the field and, subsequently, the 'power effects' which can jeopardize the 'extended case method'. Context brings to the researcher elements such as: 1) the 'intervention', which should be considered a virtue to be exploited, since the ethnographer acts in an environment which is not their own and where there are participants with whom they will relate and who will react to them all the time; 2) the 'process' by which one follows the participants in time and space, allowing one to know the 3) 'structuration', since the every-day world is structured by relations outside the field and is, at the same time, a structurer of these relations; and, finally, the possibility of 4) 'reconstruction' of the theory, to assess whether its postulates hold, whether it accounts for the anomalies brought about by the field, and whether it broadens or narrows. Here are the four principles of Burawoy's 'extended case method,' unified by the 'dialogue' present in and between each of them.

These principles are realized through four 'extensions': 1) extending the observer to the participant, since 'interventions' bring valuable lessons to the ethnographer and it is not possible to behave as a pure 'foreigner,' evading the questions and dangers related to entering and leaving the field, as well as an eventual return to bring back the findings to the participants; 2) extending observations in space and time, taking into account the processes which produce and reproduce social relations; 3) extending from process towards social forces, from the differences in the field to external forces, whose questions can only be answered through theory; and 4) extending theory, taking it as a starting and ending point, evaluating its possibility of absorbing 'anomalies' or having its central postulates challenged.[104]

Ethnography is in constant dialogue with history and theory, since the present "constitutes the lens through which we can see the past .... It supplies the vocabulary, the concepts, and the theories through which we translate the past

---

104   It is possible to identify many convergences with this type of methodological approach in the work of Stéphane Beaud and Michel Pialoux, French sociologists of labor with a long trajectory of ethnographic research inspired by Bourdieusian reflexive sociology. Beaud and Pialoux reject the mechanical transposition of theoretical categories but show how theory is an inescapable presupposition. From it, in the field, it is possible to bring out categories from the collected data to better develop it. In addition, they address the impossibility of 'replicating' an ethnography, given the researcher's unique relationships with the environment and individuals. See Stéphane Beaud and Michel Pialoux, "Partir para o trabalho de campo em Sochaux com 'Bourdieu na cabeça'," *Cadernos CERU/Centro de Estudos Rurais e Urbanos* 24, no. 2 (December 2013): 31–51.

into history."[105] Therefore, the 'extended case method' values the 'revisit' as an ethnographic practice which allows for the identification of changes and permanence through the comparison of a participant observation in a research field with another study in the same field, conducted at some point in the past, by the same or another ethnographer.[106]

Burawoy understands fieldwork itself, in a 'historicized world,' as 'ethnography-as-revisit': a succession of observation periods which accumulate in time and in which there are 'constructivist' moments, when the researcher confronts the changes of the field location itself, and 'realist' moments, which allow for glimpses of changes brought about by internal and external forces. In the field, therefore, a 'rolling revisit' is in progress, which allows for the extension of the case study in question.

Theory, in this way, is a condensation of the knowledge that unites a scientific community, moving more by its mistakes than by its successes. Therefore, it needs to be revised, expanded and reconstructed as a way to reveal its capacity to absorb anomalies, progressing, or not, when it degenerates. The 'extended case method' methodology thus allows the treatment of issues which go beyond the limits of the case, the field, and national boundaries towards global social macro-processes, as a 'multicase ethnography'. In this book, the approach to data collected through observation and interviews in the two countries was inspired by this methodological tradition.[107]

The following chapters present information gathered in the field, interviews, documents and theoretical analysis of this material. Chapter 1 deals with Vale's economic and productive dimension, as well as the reconstruction of its history as a state-owned company, the privatization period, the subsequent restructuring of its Brazilian operations and the consequences of this process for its workers and unions.

Chapter 2 follows the tracks of the company's labor and union relations strategy in Brazil, focusing on the field description, workers' accounts and interviews conducted in São Luís (in Maranhão) and Parauapebas (in Pará). The focus was on the leaders of two important Vale unions: STEFEM and Metabase Carajás. I analyzed and contrasted the positions of two people who, for decades, have led the organizations and have held the seat of workers' representation on Vale's Board of Directors. I also describe in this chapter how the

---

105   Burawoy, *The Extended Case Method*, 169.

106   Ibid., 100.

107   To state that the research was *inspired* by the 'extended case method' method means to recognize the limitations of time, budget, and time in the field in the context of doctoral research such as that which gave rise to this study.

company bargains with its unions and how the division of the latter weakens the workers' organization in the face of corporate power.

In Chapter 3, I present the field observations in Canada, the interviews conducted in Sudbury, the description of Vale's entrance in the country after the purchase of Inco in 2006, the strike of 2009–2010 and its unfoldings. This chapter also reflects on Vale's attempts to organize an international trade union network and the reasons for its failure, promoting a review of the literature on union internationalism and its possibilities.

Chapter 4, as a conclusion, promotes the analysis of Vale's ownership structure after privatization, in which pension funds of state-owned companies had a central role. In addition, I explore the changes promoted by the new shareholders' agreement, signed in 2017, after years of changes in the global mineral commodity market and political changes in the company's management and in Brazil. The analysis of the interview with Sergio Rosa sheds light on the choices of a generation of union members, who placed their bets on the participation in pension funds of state-owned companies in the control of large companies of Brazilian origin, and on their role in an obscure future. The epilogue, finally, brings the final considerations of the book.

The following pages present the observations made in different locations where the global mining giant of Brazilian origin operates. I sought to find meaning for the transformations in the field and in the world. If change is the very condition of ethnography, one could say that it is also the common condition experienced – under the Amazon heat of Carajás or the freezing cold of Ontario – by the workers who move the ground and the underground, creating the wealth and the power of a company once seen as a symbol of Brazil's development and today a fundamental part of transnational mining.

From *Companhia Vale do Rio Doce* to Vale S.A.

The company named *Companhia Vale do Rio Doce* (CVRD) was created in 1942 in the region of Itabira, in the state of Minas Gerais. Its enormous iron ore reserves had been known since the beginning of the twentieth century, when they were bought, along with control of the Vitória-Minas Railroad (which links the Minas Gerais region to the port of Tubarão, in the state of Espírito Santo), by the British Itabira Limited group, creating the Itabira Iron Ore Company in 1911.[1]

The company controlled by British capital, however, was unable to effectively exploit the purchased reserves. Many reasons for that can be numbered, among which are certain restrictions, at the time, on the activity of foreign capital by the local government of Minas Gerais, the difficulties in raising capital due to the context of the First World War and even perhaps a strategy of the British group not to exploit the reserves and only to ensure the monopoly of resources against competition.[2]

Decades later, especially after the 1929 crisis, import substitution industrialization began in Brazil, stimulated by the new international situation and the drop in coffee prices in the world market (which was then the main Brazilian export product). During the nationalist administration of Getúlio Vargas, the country maintained for some time an ambiguous posture, conversing with both the Axis countries and the United States in search of the best conditions for locating Brazil in the pre-war situation of tension between powers. US pressure, as well as offers of loans and economic partnerships, made Vargas decide to cede the Natal Air Force Base to the Americans, as well as to enter the war against the Axis.[3]

In exchange for Brazilian participation in the conflict, the 'Washington Agreements'[4] were signed between Brazil, the US and England in March 1942. The latter countries were interested in obtaining a supply of raw materials

---

1 Maria Cecília Minayo, *De ferro e flexíveis: marcas do Estado empresário e da privatização na subjetividade operária* (Rio de Janeiro: Garamond, 2004). Minayo's work, as will be seen, was an important reference for the research that gave rise to this book.

2 Ibid, 49–50.

3 See Lira Neto, *Getúlio (1930–1945): do governo provisório à ditadura do Estado Novo* (São Paulo: Companhia das Letras, 2013).

4 Brazil-United States Political-Military Agreement.

from Brazil for the war industry.[5] The agreement established the return, by England, of the British Itabira Company's iron ore deposits and also financing from the U.S. government through the Eximbank, so that the Brazilian government could create a company to exploit the iron mines and reform the Vitória-Minas Railroad. This company would be the state-owned *Companhia Vale do Rio Doce*, which pledged to sell, in its first three years, 1.5 million tonnes of iron ore to the USA and England. The 'Washington Agreements' also made it possible to obtain financing for the construction of the state-owned steel production company – *Companhia Siderúrgica Nacional* [National Steel Company], or CSN – to which CVRD began to sell part of its iron production. CVRD was created to supply iron ore to the international market. Between 1942 and 1961, the company exported 98% of all the iron ore it extracted; while between 1967 and 1997, "on average, at least 80% of the iron ore extracted by CVRD was destined to international markets."[6]

The creation of CVRD (and CSN) can be described as a successful example of the 'seizing the chance' strategy described by Immanuel Wallerstein,[7] who criticized bipolar models for development – such as the center-periphery view proposed by structuralists – as insufficient to analyze the world economy as a single system: center and periphery would not be two distinct types of economies, but parts of the same world-system for centuries. Wallerstein argued for mobility in the world-system: a tri-modal system of center – semi-periphery – periphery, based on unequal exchanges due to differences in technology, wage patterns and profit margins. The semi-peripheral countries would then have developed, in the mid-twentieth century, three strategies to conquer parts of the world market for their products or even to guarantee their own domestic market for their national products: 1) seizing the chance; 2) promotion by invitation; and 3) self-reliance.

The creation of CVRD and CSN were fundamental for the development in the following years of a relatively diversified industrial park in Brazil, also with a large presence of multinationals (combining the 'seizing the chance' with the 'invitation' strategy). If, on the one hand, a new type of dependency was created, since the new companies required the import of machinery and technology from the center, on the other, the combination of strategies ('seizing the

---

5   Minayo, *De ferro e flexíveis*, 57–58.

6   Bruno Milanez et al., "A estratégia corporativa da Vale S.A.: um modelo analítico para redes globais extrativas," *Versos – Textos para Discussão PoEMAS* 2, no. 2 (2018): 3.

7   Immanuel Wallerstein, "Dependence in an Interdependent World: the Limited Possibilities of Transformation within the Capitalist World Economy," *African Studies Review* 17, no. 1 (April 1974): 1–26.

chance' and 'invitation') allowed for the presence of 'heavier industries' of an 'intermediate level' in Brazil.[8]

CVRD, since its creation, was an export-oriented company. After the war, in the 1960s, West Germany and Japan were the main buyers of Brazilian iron ore. During the military dictatorship, CVRD accelerated iron ore exports, stimulating its workers to increase production through an ideology that associated the miners' work with a patriotic mission to produce foreign exchange in order to pay the country's foreign debt.[9]

With this goal in mind, the *Projeto Ferro Carajás* [Carajás Iron Project], or PFC, was created in the Amazon Forest, where the largest open-pit iron mine in the world is located. The resources of the Carajás Mineral Province, which were fundamental for Vale to become a TNC, were "discovered in 1967 by *Companhia Meridional de Mineração S.A.* [Southern Mining Company S.A.] or CMM, a subsidiary of the international market leader of steel at the time, United States Steel Co. (US Steel)."[10] The concession to explore the reserves would occur two years later, when "a joint venture between CMM (49%) and CVRD (51%), named *Amazônia Mineração S.A.* [Amazon Mining S.A.], or AMZA, was created in 1970."[11] Later, in 1977, CVRD would buy CMM's share, constituting the PFC into a 'megaproject' of mineral exploitation, primary processing and exportation. As a milestone of its construction, the first detonation took place in 1981 for the opening of mine N4E – a mine from the 'northern system', one of CVRD's iron ore extraction systems in Brazil. To transport this production, the Carajás Railroad (EFC) began operating in 1985 with 900 kilometers of tracks that connected the producing region, in the heart of the Amazon, to the port of Ponta da Madeira in São Luís, in the state of Maranhão. The EFC crosses 23 municipalities (19 in Maranhão and four in the state of Pará) and has shipping stations in Parauapebas and Marabá in Pará, and in Açailândia, Santa Inês and São Luís in Maranhão.

The opening of the Carajás Iron Project consolidated CVRD's position in the 1980s as already the world's largest iron ore producer. In this period, the Asian market became the main destination of CVRD's iron ore, accounting for almost 48% of its exports. Japan was then the main buying country.[12] Asia continues

---

8   Ibid, 14.

9   Minayo, *De ferro e flexíveis.*

10   Rodrigo Santos, "Desenvolvimento econômico e mudança social: a Vale e a mineração na Amazônia Oriental," *Caderno CRH* 29, no. 77 (May/August 2016): 302.

11   Ibid, 302.

12   Tádzio Peters Coelho, *Projeto Grande Carajás: trinta anos de desenvolvimento frustrado* (Rio de Janeiro: Ibase, 2014).

to be Vale's largest market, with the difference that China became, especially since the 2000s, the largest consumer of iron ore produced by the company.

The PFC was made possible "based on the establishment of a coalition of state interests and multinational steel capital ... densifying CVRD's global production network" as "a node of mining and steel [GPNs]."[13] The project's financing underscored that feature, since, of the project's total capital of US$3.642 billion, 51.4%, or US$1.872 billion came from domestic sources, especially resources from CVRD itself (US$852 million) and BNDES (US$1.02 billion), while the remaining 48.6% came from external sources, such as financing from the European Coal and Steel Community (ECSC) (US$600 million), Nippon Carajás Iron Ore Co. Ltda (US$ 500 million), the IBRD (US$ 304.5 million) and the German bank KfW (US$ 122.5 million).[14]

These figures help to illustrate a fundamental aspect we intend to highlight in this brief history of the company: CVRD, since its foundation, united state and multinational interests and capital to build the extraction, processing and transportation infrastructure needed to export iron ore to the international market. In the 1980s, with the inauguration of the PFC operations, "a strategy of growth via natural resources came into play, coupling the Eastern Amazon to the Southeast-centered economic internationalization process, and reconstituting it as a regional extractive economy."[15]

1   The CVRD's Privatization and the Internationalization Leap

The relationship in some Latin American countries between industrialization, economic transformations, presence of state-owned enterprises and strengthening of the state during the 1970s was analyzed by Fernando Henrique Cardoso and Enzo Faletto,[16] who back then considered CVRD and Petrobras the only Brazilian multinational companies. The strengthening of state-owned enterprises in the country during the authoritarian regime was explained as follows:

> A basic problem exists, posed by the present moment and by Latin American situations of dependency: the very penetration of

---

13   Santos, "Desenvolvimento econômico e mudança social", 302–03.
14   Ibid, 303.
15   Ibid.
16   Fernando Henrique Cardoso and Enzo Faletto, *Dependency and Development in Latin America* (Berkeley: University of California Press, 1979).

multinationals requires a state that is capable of furnishing the multinationals with the resources for accumulation. So national wealth is
necessary for foreign private accumulation. But this process is contradictory: for this to work, the state must fortify itself and expand its functions at both the administrative and economic levels .... Faced with the
political challenges of dominated classes to radically reorder society, this
entrepreneurial-regulative state militarizes itself, becoming even stronger and more autocratic.[17]

The relationship between multinational companies, their allies in the national
ruling class, and the state bureaucracy sustained the autocratic regime. Because
of its authoritarian nature, however, such relationship often lacked institution-
alized channels and depended on 'bureaucratic rings' which would link busi-
nessmen and multinationals to figures from the regime. 'Developmentalism'
was the basic state ideology.[18]

The successful creation of CVRD, the expansion of its production and its
profitability during the state period illustrate the importance of state action
in the economic transformation and industrialization of Brazil. State intervention requires the development of a cohesive yet decentralized, bureaucratic
state apparatus. State-owned enterprises, therefore, fulfilled the role of ensuring coherent state intervention.[19]

Peter Evans[20] analyzed the relations between states, industrial transformations and development in the then-'Third World' countries through a typology
of state apparatuses. 'Predatory states' would be those in which patrimonial-
ist and traditionalist practices, instead of creating a professional bureaucracy,
would have led to the creation of a personalistic circle around power, interested in extracting 'predatory' rents from the state. In the opposite case, the
'developmental states' – such as the late industrialized countries in East Asia
(following the pattern previously followed by Japan) – would have established
a professional and meritocratic bureaucracy, with stability and long-term
careers.

---

17   Ibid, 212.
18   Ibid.
19   See Dietrich Rueschemeyer and Peter Evans, "The State and Economic Transforma-
      tion: Toward an Analysis of the Conditions Underlying Effective Intervention," in
      Bringing the State Back In, ed. Peter Evans, Dietrich Rueschemeyer and Theda Skocpol
      (Cambridge: Cambridge University Press, 1985), 44–77.
20   Peter Evans, "Predatory, Developmental and Other Apparatuses: a Comparative Political
      Economy Perspective on the Third World State," *Sociological Forum* 4, no. 4, (Dec.
      1989): 561–589.

In this classification, Brazil would be an 'intermediate case' between the 'predatory' and the 'developmental' pattern, since, despite the existence of a certain meritocratic professional bureaucracy, there would still be much dependence on Executive Branch appointments and clientelistic relations in the professional government apparatus, whose origins go back to the historical presence of traditional rural elites with political power. This situation would make it difficult to create stable relations with the private sector, stimulating the emergence of 'individualized channels', the 'bureaucratic rings' of Cardoso and Faletto.[21] However, in Brazil certain 'pockets of efficiency' have developed within the state, in agencies and institutions such as the BNDES, with its stable and qualified professional staff, whose mission is to finance investment. State-owned enterprises also fulfilled such a role, creating a certain autonomy from the pressures and 'individualized' channels traditionally developed within the Brazilian bureaucratic apparatus.[22]

Maria Cecília Minayo[23] points in the same direction when she shows how CVRD maintained a posture of distancing itself from the demands of the local Itabira government (the city where it began its operations) and, at times, even from sectors of the federal government. In essence, however, the company's administration was totally focused on the need for increasing exports and profit as a way of obtaining foreign exchange for the country. The 'national-developmentalist ideology' integrated the entrepreneurial state, the managers and the workers during the CVRD's state ownership period. Labor relations in the company responded to this principle through paternalistic and authoritarian practices, especially in regard to untrained workers. Workers' resistance and conflict were considered serious faults and insubordination, to which the company responded with economic punishments or even intimidation and dismissals, especially in the case of union activists.

The company's relationship with trade unions is an example of such practices. Vale workers are represented by a myriad of local unions. Historically, many of these unions were created by the company's own management,[24] placing managers and men of trust in leadership positions. As will be argued later, the dispersion of worker representation allows Vale to 'divide and conquer', almost always imposing its own determinations in annual collective bargaining. For now, we can affirm, based on Minayo's indications about the

---

21   Cardoso and Faletto, *Dependency and Development*.
22   Evans, "Predatory, Developmental and Other Apparatuses".
23   Minayo, *De ferro e flexíveis*.
24   This is the case of the two Brazilian Vale unions surveyed: Metabase Carajás and STEFEM.

CVRD's relations with the union in Itabira during the state-owned period,[25] that the company preserved certain practices of the authoritarian period in its strategy of labor and union relations under the new private management. Field observations and interviews conducted in São Luís and Parauapebas, in Brazil, as well as reports from workers and union members on strike in Sudbury (Canada) corroborate this finding. Rodrigo Santos and Bruno Milanez point in this direction by associating authoritarian practices with previously state-owned TNCs:

> The *social* form of embeddedness concerns the origin of its agents and their constitutive processes. Regarding companies in particular, social and cultural contexts (largely national ones) tend to shape specific behavioral patterns ... , although sectoral trajectories and historical patterns of interaction with the state, workers and consumers are also relevant. In exemplary fashion, previously monopolistic and state-owned TNCs tend to preserve organizational aspects that are inappropriate to competitive conditions, such as the maintenance of disused real estate assets, authoritarian practices in managing labor and union relations, reactive denial behaviors in the face of social contestation, etc.[26]

It is useful to highlight such authoritarian remnants of the state-owned period in the shaping of Vale's strategy of labor and union relations. It will be possible to resume this discussion when analyzing the tense negotiations of the collective agreement in 2015 and the profit-sharing bonus agreement in 2016 with Brazilian unions and, above all, in the 2009–2010 strike in Canada.

André Teixeira, currently the executive manager of labor relations at Vale, started working at CVRD in 1984, at the end of the military dictatorship, in a technical area. Without having dealt directly with the area of labor relations during that period, Teixeira describes the negotiations between CVRD and trade unions during the state-owned period and, in particular, during the military dictatorship based on his experience with managers and directors who preceded him in that area:

> Look, in the state-owned period I didn't work with this issue. ... Our negotiations were very limited. ... The decision that would be presented about

---

25 Minayo, *De ferro e flexíveis*.

26 Rodrigo Santos and Bruno Milanez, "Redes globais de produção (RGPs) e conflito socio-ambiental: a Vale S.A. e o complexo minerário de Itabira," in *Anais do VII SINGA* (*PPGEO, LABOTER, IESA, UFG*) (Goiânia: 2015), 2098.

our proposal was discussed with the Ministry of Mines and Energy, the secretariat of this, the secretariat of that. So, external interference was much greater. Our autonomy to resolve things was much weaker.

... The relationship with the union was about the summer camp, the club, the drugstore, all the welfare unionism that is very present until today. ... The people didn't become members of the union on a matter of believing that it represented what they were doing. It was all with government incentive. In the dictatorship, the government encouraged the unions to be directed towards welfare.

ANDRÉ TEIXEIRA, Aguiar Interview

It will be possible, in later pages and chapters, to analyze the way Vale negotiates with its unions and its labor relations strategy, in whose formulation Teixeira currently plays a decisive role.

It is also possible to consider the difficulties of self-organization among the company's workers as a legacy of the authoritarian period. In all of Vale's history, only two strikes have been recorded: in 1945, still in its first years of operation, and in 1989.[27] In the latter case, the strike meant the 'guardianship release' of the workers against the state-owned company, often pointed out in the workers' discourse as a 'mother.'[28] Interestingly, as will be shown in Chapter 3, the Canadian miners also called Inco, a company bought by Vale, 'mother Inco.' Conversely, in Brazil, "the remaining workers from the state-owned era ... today call the company 'stepmother Vale' as opposed to the previous expression 'mother Vale.'"[29]

The fact that the workers call the state-owned CVRD and the former Inco 'mother' is significant and makes it necessary to open a parenthesis in this reconstruction to relate this feeling of belonging and closeness (which even reaches affectivity) to the 'company town morphology,' by which there is "a set of structural limitations ... typical of mono-industrial cities where the power of the large company predominates over local politics and union action." In

---

27   In Carajás, according to information from the Metabase Carajás union, following the events in Minas Gerais in 1989, there was a local strike in 1990. Vale, in its 2017 annual report, highlights the absence of strikes in Brazil since 1989 as a sign of the "stability of operations." See Vale, *Relatório de sustentabilidade Vale 2017*, 40, note 6. Available in http://www.vale.com/PT/aboutvale/relatorio-de-sustentabilidade-2017/Documents/v _VALE_RelatorioSustentabilidade_2017_v.pdf. accessed May 26, 2021.

28   Minayo, *De ferro e flexíveis*.

29   Laura Nazaré de Carvalho, "Análise da ação dos sindicatos dos trabalhadores da mineradora Vale S.A. na região Sudeste brasileira," *Textos & Debates* no. 23 (January/July 2013): 92, note 1.

company town circumstances, the company has an "extremely hierarchical and authoritarian view of its role ... exercising a combination of repression and paternalism over ... the local union."[30]

Such features – described from research into the relationship between the National Steel Company and the municipality of Volta Redonda, in the state of Rio de Janeiro – have similarities with what happens in Itabira, Parauapebas and Sudbury, among other locations where Vale has extractive operations. It is true that there are also specificities and differences. One can point out contrasts between CSN's practices in Volta Redonda and CVRD's in Itabira, showing that the latter company was established in an already established city, in whose territory CVRD

> induced a disruptive action ... , formulating a social structure more in tune with its specificities as a state-owned mining company; [saw] a process of "rupture of domination" in the 1980s,[31] when an active civil society opposed to the predatory action of mining was formed; and witnessed the emergence of an alliance between public authorities and the business community, who were dissatisfied with the company's historical domination and with the low productive diversity of the city.[32]

The very existence of the municipality of Parauapebas, in turn, is largely due to the Carajás Iron Project. The municipality started in the nucleus built by the company – which will be described in Chapter 2 – and subsequently experienced a large population and urban growth. The permanent proximity between worker and company, the access to services and the paternalistic element of its concession are fundamental to understand the treatment of the company as a 'mother.' Guilherme Zagallo illustrated the relationship between the 'company town morphology' and the difficulties for union action:

> Carajás, specifically, is a difficult place to have a union movement. It's not that I am condescending. It's just that it is very difficult to control, to mobilize in one place ... Even though, today, most of them live in Parauapebas, originally, most of them lived in the projects, up there, a place where the club,the school, the hospital are controlled by the company, I mean, you don't leave your work environment at any time. At

---

30 Raphael Lima, "CSN e Volta Redonda: uma relação histórica de dependência e controle," *Política & Sociedade* 12, no. 25 (2013): 48.

31 Minayo, *De ferro e flexíveis.*

32 Lima, "CSN e Volta Redonda," 58.

every moment, at soccer ... You're there somehow, at the Friday beer ... So, generally speaking, union activity in this kind of occupation, in an enclave-city, it's usually more difficult. ... In Parauapebas, most of the people went there for the mining, for Vale and for the activity it generates. It is not an easy place to build a more autonomous union movement. [33]

Sudbury, in turn, is a centennial city deeply marked by the creation of Inco,[34] although, in recent decades, technological and organizational changes in extraction activities, as will be seen in Chapter 3, have led to an increase in labor productivity and a significant decrease in local nickel mining jobs. Be that as it may, the features of a 'mono-industrial city' can be used to describe the three localities mentioned.

The strike at CVRD in 1989 took place in a troubled period of economic crisis and high inflation rates in Brazil. The workers' main demand was for wage adjustment. The flourishing of the union movement in the company in the following years was, however, aborted by the productive restructuring plans that CVRD was already developing and whose realization was also stimulated by the strike, in a kind of turning point.[35]

The early 1990s marked the 'preparation for privatization'.[36] Fernando Collor's victory in the first direct presidential election after the military dictatorship accelerated these plans. CVRD organized an extensive voluntary redundancy programme which put the unions back on the defensive.[37] Under the argument of the need to reduce costs, reduce hierarchies and increase productivity, changes also occurred in the production process with the introduction of group labor and principles of multi-skilling.

During the Fernando Henrique Cardoso administrations (1995–2002), privatizations were boosted. In 1997, CVRD was privatized through a process in

---

33   Lawyer and union advisor, whose trajectory will be presented in the following paragraphs, Zagallo authorized the reproduction of his name and statements given in meetings and assemblies attended by the researcher, as well as in interviews conducted by Thiago Aguiar in São Luís, Brazil (May 2016) and in São Paulo, Brazil (July 2018).

34   Jamie Swift, *The Big Nickel: Inco at Home and Abroad* (Kitchener: Between the Lines, 1977).

35   Chapter 3 will show that the 2009–2010 strike in Canada was also a kind of turning point, during and from which Vale introduced its labor and union relations strategy – developed mainly from the company's experience in its Brazilian operations -, differing from the strategy previously adopted by Inco.

36   Minayo, *De ferro e flexíveis*.

37   The dismissals at CVRD were part of a plan to lay off 108,000 federal civil servants during the Collor administration. See Ibid, 283.

which victory came to a group of companies led by Benjamin Steinbruch (who shortly before had bought the state-owned steel company CSN), banks and pension funds. The arguments for privatization presented by the government at the time followed the ideological pattern – very much in evidence at the time all around the world and in Latin America in particular – of the 'Washington Consensus'. According to its formulator, the main reason for privatizations

> is the belief that private industry is managed more efficiently than state enterprises, because of the more direct incentives faced by a manager who either has a direct personal stake in the profits of an enterprise or else is accountable to those who do.[38]

CVRD, however, was historically a very profitable company. In the three years prior to privatization, CVRD's profits were US\$304 million (1994), US\$721 million (1995) and US\$558 million (1996).[39] However, structural adjustment policies, such as privatizations, price stabilization, market liberalization, deregulation and fiscal austerity, were an agenda formulated and implemented undemocratically, designed in Washington and imposed without debate through the tutelage of institutions such as the IMF and the World Bank, whose goal was to ensure the payment capacity of debtor countries.[40]

Robinson,[41] in turn, associates the neoliberal policies of structural adjustment and the abandonment of developmentalism in peripheral and semi-peripheral countries with the victory of fractions of the national bourgeoisies whose accumulation became transnationally oriented (especially, but not limited to, banks and new investment funds), and which gradually began to compose the ranks of the transnational capitalist class (TCC). These factions were aided by cadres of the transnational elite (in most cases, graduates of internationally prestigious universities attended by their foreign counterparts), installed in key institutions of the nation-states, such as the central banks and ministries responsible for economic policy, and also holding important

---

38   John Williamson, "What Washington Means by Policy Reform," in *Latin American Adjustment: How Much Has Happened,* ed. John Williamson (Washington, D.C.: Institute for International Economics, 1990), 16.

39   Coelho, *Projeto Grande Carajás*, 17.

40   Henry Veltmeyer, James Petras and Steve Vieux, *Neoliberalism and class conflict in Latin America: A Comparative Perspective on the Political Economy of Structural Adjustment* (New York: St. Martin's Press, 1979).

41   William I. Robinson, *A Theory of Global Capitalism: Production, Class, and State in a Transnational World* (Baltimore: Johns Hopkins University Press, 2004).

positions in academia and the local press, contributing to the ideological dispute in favor of open trade, financial liberalization and privatization. The dismantling of the strategy of import substitution industrialization and of national-developmentalism – both fundamental for the creation of CVRD – in a context of economic crisis in the 1980s and 1990s increased the presence of transnational capital and accelerated the integration of semi-peripheral and peripheral economies into global capitalism. Also, for this reason, Robinson[42] considers theories such as those of the world-system and of dependency to have been superseded in the epoch of global capitalism, since these took the nation-state as the unit of analysis and produced valid explanations for that epoch of international economy.

Shortly after CVRD's privatization, Benjamin Steinbruch clashed with other controlling shareholders and left the company.[43] In his place, in 2001, Roger Agnelli took over as CEO of Vale, appointed by the Bradesco bank. He was a former economist of the bank and, at the time, president of Bradespar,[44] who had previously acted in the controversial process of CVRD's evaluation for privatization. Bradesco's presence in the company's controlling block was questioned since this would be prohibited by the Brazilian Bidding Law regarding CVRD's sale,[45] precisely because of the bank's participation in the evaluation process. According to Judith Marshall:

> The sale of Vale is considered to be the most scandalous privatising episode in Brazilian history. The company was sold for only R$3.4 billion in a period of parity between the real and the US dollar. A submission to the Federal Regional Tribunal (TRF) in Brasilia in 2004 made explicit a series of irregularities that proved that Vale was undervalued. Some mines were ignored in the calculations, others undervalued. The forestry sector was also undervalued. Intangible assets of enormous value (technologies, patents and technical knowledge related to geology and mining engineering) were not considered. Vale's stock holdings in Açominas, CSN, Usiminas and CST were ignored. The list of irregularities is enormous.

---

42   Ibid.

43   With the support of the Fernando Henrique Cardoso administration, which feared the concentration of power in Steinbruch's hands, according to André Vieira, *O mapa da mina* (Curitiba: Kotter Editorial, 2020).

44   The equity arm of the bank.

45   Nazareno Godeiro, ed., *Vale do Rio Doce. Nem tudo que reluz é ouro. Da privatização à luta pela reestatização* (São Paulo: Sundermann, 2007), 95.

Bradesco, the bank responsible for the evaluation, took over control of Vale one year later.[46]

In the same direction, Nazareno Godeiro argues:

> CVRD's sale price, US$3.338 billion, was deliberately underestimated (...). This value did not include all the companies of the group and the shareholdings in dozens of companies, nor the value of CVRD's mineral reserves .... A conglomerate of some 60 companies was left out of the minimum price ..., including a 9,000 km railway infrastructure ... and several port terminals.[47]
>
> In order to determine the minimum prices in the privatization, it was reported that CVRD had 2.8 billion tonnes of iron ore. However, the company had already informed the New York Stock Exchange that CVRD's total ore reserves in Brazil were 7,981 billion tonnes. It was reported in 1997 that CVRD had reserves of 197 million tonnes of bauxite, when the correct figure was 392 million tonnes. Of manganese, a total of 30.4 million tonnes ... was reported ..., when the total number was 63 million ... . Of potash, 4.4 million ... while the correct figure was 19.2 million tonnes.[48]

Guilherme Zagallo is a lawyer who worked for 10 years at CVRD in São Luís as an electronics technician. He studied law while working at the company and subsequently, since leaving the company, has been advising Vale workers' union STEFEM for over 20 years. Currently, in addition to his work as a prestigious lawyer in the Maranhão state capital,[49] he is one of the organizers of the *Justiça nos Trilhos* (Justice on the Rails) network.[50] This initiative can be associated with other movements contesting mining activities in Brazil.[51]

---

46   Judith Marshall, "Behind the Image of South-South Solidarity at Brazil's Vale," in *BRICS: an Anti-Capitalist Critique,* ed. Patrick Bond and Ana Garcia (Chicago: Haymarket Books, 2015), 170.

47   Godeiro, *Vale do Rio Doce,* 86–7.

48   Ibid, 94.

49   Zagallo was president of the state section of the Order of Attorneys of Brazil, the country's National Bar Association, and national counselor of the Order.

50   It is an articulation of social movements, associations and individuals, organized in 2007, with the objective of "demanding from Vale do Rio Doce fair compensation for the damage caused to the environment and to the population living in the areas crossed by its railway", according to the description available in http://justicanostrilhos.org/quem-somos/. accessed May 26 2021.

51   "By adopting the GPN framework, ... it is assumed that the structure of economic actors influences the organization of social actors, whose contestation strategies, in turn,

Because of his profound knowledge of Vale, accumulated over decades of working at the company and participating in union negotiations, Zagallo was invited by the United Steelworkers Local 6500 (Sudbury, Canada) to advise them during the strike and the tense negotiations of the 2009–10 collective agreement. Regarding the privatization process and the possible undervaluation of CVRD's reserves, he states that

> Bradesco was one of the companies hired to evaluate Vale's sale. It has lawsuits to this day. There is already ample proof that Vale was undervalued. ... Carajás, just to give an objective example, was discovered in 1967 with a capacity of 19 billion tonnes. When you talk about geology, you talk about proven, probable, estimated and inferred reserves, each with a level of certainty. What was done when privatization came? Vale had these 19 billion distributed [among all types of reserves]. They revalued them downwards in the accounting documents, in the SEC documents, in the CVM[52] documents, for what? To lower that asset's value. If you only have two billion tonnes of proven reserves, it's different than having three billion or four billion tonnes. There is a value, they will have to be removed, it will cost money to remove them, but it is an estimable value. And, post-privatization, these values returned to what everyone knew since 1967, to the actual size, to the actual cubage of that province's mineral reserves. ... I don't know how the Judiciary will face this. There is a strong lobby, with the participation of Supreme Court justices, who

affect economic actors' decision-making." See Rodrigo Santos and Bruno Milanez, "The Global Production Network for Iron Ore: Materiality, Corporate Strategies, and Social Contestation in Brazil," *The Extractive Industries and Society* 2 (2015): 763. One can point to an interdependence between global production networks and the emergence of contestation networks, such as *Justiça nos Trilhos*. Santos and Milanez mention the Brazilian Network for Environmental Justice (RBJA), the Coalition on Mining and Steelmaking Working Group (GTAMS), the International Network of People Affected by Vale (AIAV), and the National Committee for the Defense of Territories against Mining (CNDTM) as examples of (national or international) contestation networks which respond to the effects of mining companies' actions in their territories, and stress that "Vale is the only company with an exclusive contestation network that is also the target of global campaigns." (Ibid.) Such campaigns may focus on exposing the company through statements at shareholder meetings, stock exchanges or rating agencies. These actors can also seek institutional power (through court actions and pressure on local and national governments) to confront the company's corporate power or even take direct action, such as disrupting operations and transport activities.

52   SEC (Securities and Exchange Commission) and CVM (*Comissão de Valores Mobiliários*) are, respectively, the U.S. federal agency and the Brazilian federal agency responsible for regulating the stock and securities markets in their respective countries.

have granted decisions, delayed the processes' judgment for years. I don't know what will be the legal system's final position about this. There is a considerable risk that the shareholders will be called to complement the amounts paid, but an interesting thing is that Bradesco, which was the appraiser, appears in the controlling block three or four years after the sale, it buys a participation of a North American bank which had participated in the block which won the bidding. And it not only buys it, it starts leading the trust, appointing one of its executives. It was the period when Benjamin Steinbruch left, who until then was leading the trust in a very unstable relationship – the Board did not trust his leadership, the management levels, the decision levels of the Board of Directors were very low, which means that the board's limit of authority was very low, the company's management had a certain level of immobility due to this absence of a higher level of trust, of delegation. And then Bradesco appeared as a leader, appointing one of its executives. But, even in the Roger Agnelli/Bradesco period, when the Lula administration came, you had a very close relationship between the government and Vale.

GUILHERME ZAGALLO, Aguiar Interview

Benjamin Steinbruch's departure from Valepar[53] is also pointed out by Sérgio Rosa[54] as a decisive moment in shaping the corporate strategy that guided Vale's internationalization after privatization, during a period of rapid growth in the company's profits and market value during the commodity boom. Sérgio Rosa was an important figure in the PT administrations. As a member of the São Paulo Bank Workers Union, Rosa was one of the enthusiasts for disputing positions in the pension funds of state-owned companies in the 1990s. Elected Equity Director at Previ in 2000, Rosa became CEO of the pension fund upon Lula's electoral victory in 2003, holding the position until 2010, which led him, during the same period, to take up the presidency of Vale's Board of Directors.[55]

---

53   Vale's controlling group after privatization, with the presence of pension funds from state-owned companies (Previ, Petros, Funcef, Funcesp), Bradesco, BNDES and Mitsui, established by a shareholders' agreement that was in effect until 2017, when Valepar was dissolved. The description of the 1997 shareholders' agreement and the new agreement signed in 2017, as well as the 'corporate governance' of Vale, will be addressed in Chapter 4.

54   Rosa authorized the use of his name and statements in an interview with Thiago Aguiar in Rio de Janeiro, Brazil (January 2018). His background and relationship with the PT administrations, as well as the role of pension funds in Vale, will be the focus of Chapter 4.

55   Under the shareholders' agreement then in effect at Vale, the chairmanship of the company's Board of Directors fell to Previ because it had the largest shareholding in Valepar.

It is useful to follow Rosa's long exposition on Steinbruch's departure, Roger Agnelli's inauguration as CEO and the strategic formulation for the years to come, debated at that moment by Vale:

> When I arrived at Previ, the privatization of Vale do Rio Doce had already taken place, Previ was already a shareholder and a process that was called 'unwinding of Vale's shares' was practically concluded, because, in the privatization, the main shareholder was Benjamin Steinbruch of CSN and there was a conflict, [which] was understood, at that period – I mean, Vale and CSN were more competitors than complements. So Benjamin's presence at Vale ended up, let's say, making it difficult to plan with greater independence. ... Then, in 2000, there was a general agreement to buy and sell shares, and exchange shares, which we called 'unwinding'. Benjamin left Vale do Rio Doce and the remaining shareholders were the pension funds – Previ with most of the shares – Bradesco, BNDES and Mistui: the four major shareholders. Previ, along with Petros and FUNCEF, but [the latter two] with a much smaller proportion of shares. ... A shareholders' agreement was made at that time between the shareholders of Valepar, which was Vale's parent company, and this shareholders' agreement governed Vale do Rio Doce.
>
> ... So, in this process, a new CEO was chosen. At the time, Roger Agnelli was appointed, and a cycle of strategic planning began at Vale. With Benjamin's departure, it was understood that Vale was free to think about what it wanted to be in the world. ... And, among the elements of Vale's planning, there was also the idea of growing outside Brazil. What for? ... First, because indeed it was already seen that, in the 2000 cycle, a process of economic concentration was beginning – we could say in one sector, but unfortunately in almost all of them – because the larger mining companies (BHP Billiton, Anglo American, Rio Tinto) were always looking for relevant assets and a mining company with good mines, good assets, that came up would become an immediate acquisition target. So, in order to maintain a relevant share of the iron ore market, competition was permanent, it was a way to continually acquire either ore with a higher content or closer to consumers – at that time, China was already appearing as a major iron ore consumer market for the period. ... And, for that, you also need to be sizable, otherwise you have no financing capacity, no capacity to exchange shares .... A second reason, which became even stronger over time, was the idea of Vale not having only iron ore as its main source of revenue, which amounted to 80% or more of it at the time.

... As it was already estimated in that period that the price of iron ore and the demand for it is historically very cyclical, ... we imagined that there would be a consumption growth cycle, which in fact occurred, but we also imagined that this would be short-lived, so Vale was interested in seeking some kind of diversification, entering into mining sectors in which it had no stake up until that moment. ... The wager was not that restricted, but it was the coal sector which Vale found attractive, interesting – coal is an input for steel production itself, and also ... coal was still being used for energy on a reasonable scale. ... First, they bought it in Australia, as Australia had a great coal tradition, there were smaller mines, not as expensive ... The idea was to buy a mine in Australia and, with this mine, try to learn how to deal with coal, to incorporate people who could bring experience in coal management, and later betting on taking larger steps. So, coal was one area, nickel ... It was understood that nickel is also a metal, again, used in steel production, but on a larger scale in the production of electronics ... , which is linked to an even more dynamic sector of the economy today than was iron ore and coal. ... The third sector was potash, for which Brazil is a major power in agricultural production, has no potash, and imported it, so the idea was that Vale could be associated with the cycle of Brazilian agribusiness, the growth of Brazilian agriculture, as a major supplier of potash. So, this desire to grow and diversify were the two great motivators for Vale's planning.

... When the unwinding took place, I remember Vale had a market value of less than 10 billion dollars. By the end of 2010, Vale was worth $180 billion. The plan was for us to multiply Vale's market value by five in 10 years. It was much higher than that. So, the planners' idea was already bold. Taking a company and multiplying its market value by five is not something you can put on paper and easily do. So, it was an ambition of the shareholders and it was achieved to an even greater extent. For Previ properly, it was an extraordinary gain.

SÉRGIO ROSA, Aguiar Interview

Sérgio Rosa's description is very rich for relating several aspects involved in the privatization of Vale. Steinbruch's departure freed the company from conflicts of interest with CSN, allowing it to launch a market strategy distinct from the one that had characterized CVRD until then. Market strategy is related to "(i) geographical and/or sectoral patterns of resource allocation; (ii) technological patterns; and (iii) the portfolio of assets and commercialization structure of goods and services, seen as relational." Based on these, the company "structures its options for entering, remaining in, and exiting markets and their specific segments."[56]

Rosa was a key figure in the development of Vale's corporate strategy at the beginning of the twenty-first century. According to him, the investment expansion in Brazil and the internationalization of Vale, both of which gained momentum after privatization and the 'unwinding' of shares, took into account the need to: 1) deal with the competition with mining TNCS, such as BHP Billiton, Anglo American and Rio Tinto, among others, which at that moment were seeking to acquire new operations; 2) create conditions to meet the growing demand for iron ore by the Chinese market; and 3) diversify revenue sources, seeking new operations, such as, for example, Inco, a leader in nickel extraction, which was bought in 2006. This last aspect also influences Vale's financial strategy – which is related to the means of "mobilization, ... internal management, and mainly ... external raising of economic resources."[57] Even if, during this period, the company had been fundamentally supported by national sources of financing (such as, for example, BNDES and even its own profits), the purchase of operations in Canada expanded and cheapened international financing sources, since Vale also became a 'Canadian company' with the purchase of Inco. This movement of diversifying the ores explored by the company retreated after the fall of mineral commodity prices in 2015–2016. Vale then changed its market and financial strategies, seeking to make divestments, such as in the fertilizer area, and to focus again on its core business, iron ore extraction, as will be discussed in more detail in Chapter 4. André Teixeira thus summarizes the relationship between corporate strategy and Vale's internationalization:

> What was the vision at that time? ... I need to diversify. Now, today, the vision is this: I have to do good business. We did terrible business: coal in Colombia ... , copper in Chile ... , a coal mine in Australia that was not a good business ... We did bad business. Now, all mining companies have made bad deals. The volume of bad deals that mining companies had was very large, and today all of them have this same vision: you have to do good business. It's not about diversifying for diversifying's sake: I have to do good business. So, in this world, ... I think companies will be stronger to the extent that ... When you are a Canadian company, we have access to a lot of financing that a Brazilian company does not have. That's where

---

56   Milanez et al., "A estratégia corporativa da Vale S.A.," 10.
57   Ibid, 15.

it starts. Since we have operations in Canada, we can get some loans that, as a Brazilian company, we wouldn't be able to get. ... I believe in this kind of internationalization, I believe that business ... It's not that the company is Brazilian or not. Is Ambev Brazilian? So, companies will have to follow this vision.

ANDRÉ TEIXEIRA, Aguiar Interview

Privatization was a decisive moment for the still ongoing transnationalization of Vale and the Brazilian economy. The analysis of CVRD's privatization shows some features of this process: led by transnationally oriented elites in the FHC administration, privatization led CVRD to orient its accumulation towards the global stage, seeking not only international export markets – as it already did successfully during the state-owned period – but also acquiring or opening up new extraction operations outside Brazilian borders (internationalization), as well as diversifying its sources of financing and seeking valorization in international capital markets, as described by Sérgio Rosa. This last aspect, as will be seen, became a decisive guideline for corporate strategy. If, at some point, Vale's internationalization had the appearance of expanding a 'national champion,' the changes in the post-2015 corporate strategy have made it clear that Vale's controllers, in search of capital appreciation, intend to make it more dispersed, more 'global,' if not in the origin of most of its revenues – still very dependent on the extraction of iron ore in Brazil -, certainly in the control and guidance of its strategic decisions. The origins of this process, still under the 1997 shareholders' agreement, and its consequences will be analyzed in Chapter 4.

For now, it is useful to trace the contours of the commodity boom and post-boom, mentioned above, as a backdrop to the transformations which led the former CVRD to become Vale S.A. Following that, it will still be necessary to address some additional aspects of privatization related to unions and labor relations in the company.

2   The Mineral Commodity Boom and Post-boom

The conclusion of the 'unwinding' of Vale's shares and the formulation of its internationalization strategy, carried out during Roger Agnelli's term as CEO (2001–2011), coincide with the period of the commodity boom at the beginning of the twenty-first century, particularly from 2002 onwards, "as a reflection of the increased demand from emerging countries, particularly China, to fuel the growth of their domestic economies and the productive impetus of growing industries."[58] Global iron ore imports in the period expanded from 500 million tonnes in 2001 to 1.394 billion tonnes in 2014, an increase of 178%. A significant part of the increase in consumption came from China, which accounted for 67% of global iron ore imports in 2014, up from 18% in 2001. Global iron ore supply more than doubled between 2001 (1.06 billion tonnes/year) and 2014 (3.4 billion in 2014) and remained higher than global demand.[59] This reveals that the rise in commodity prices had "a strong speculative component, which caused prices to rise well above the growth in demand or ... departure from the supply-demand relationship."[60]

The boom period extended until 2011, in a first part of the cycle which

> corresponds to the period of constant and sharp price appreciation of mineral commodities in the international market. Iron ore with 62% content, which in May 2002 cost US$ 12.60 a ton, reached US$ 187.10 in January 2011, an appreciation almost 15 times greater in 10 years. This phenomenon also affected the price of other ores, increasing: the nickel tonne by 1072%; the tin tonne by 897%; the South African coal tonne by 789%; the gold troy ounce by 665%; and the aluminum tonne by 239%.[61]

The growth of Vale's market value, celebrated by Sérgio Rosa, is closely related to the figures presented above, especially the increase in value of iron ore. The impressive 1072% appreciation of the nickel tonne in the period of 2001–2011 explains Vale's interest in buying Inco in 2006 for almost US$19 billion. The effects in Brazil were sensible. Iron ore exports accounted for 6.8% of Brazil's total exports in 2000, rising to 17.6% in 2011. Between 2001 and 2011, the mineral extraction industry's participation in the national economy increased from 0.63% of the GDP to 1.77%, also increasing the collection of the CFEM[62] tax from R$160 million to R$2.38 billion between 2001 and 2013.[63] In this context,

> we had expansion through extensification of production in already consolidated areas, with the opening of new projects in new locations (greenfields) and the incorporation and return of areas with deposits

---

58   Luiz Jardim Wanderley, "Do *boom* ao *pós-boom* das *commodities*: o comportamento do setor mineral no Brasil," *Versos – Textos para Discussão PoEMAS* 1, no. 1 (2017): 1–2.
59   Ibid.
60   Ibid, 2.
61   Ibid, 1.
62   Financial Compensation for the Exploitation of Mineral Resources.
63   Wanderley, "Do *boom* ao *pós-boom* das *commodities*."

that were previously considered economically unviable .... With the high price, it became profitable to invest in technological innovation and infrastructure to explore new deposits and expand production scales. ... As a reflection on the territories, there is an increase in the pressure of mining capital and, with it, the installation and expansion of new productive, logistical and disposal infrastructures .... Social conflicts spread, and rural and urban socio-environmental impacts worsen .... [64]

This situation began to change with the global economic crisis that emerged in 2008, and intensified from 2012 onwards, when its effects started to be felt more deeply in Europe and in the retraction of Chinese economic growth. The commodity post-boom began with the "steady decline of mineral commodities ... until a new average price was found" to which contributed the "speculative component arising from the financial market and expressed in negotiations in the futures market", contributing to a "rapid and sharp price depression."[65] Iron ore had a 79% retraction in its price by 2016, with the tonne retreating to a low of US$39.60; nickel, another important ore exploited by Vale, had an 84% retreat in its market price by 2016.[66] Mining TNCs had to adjust to the new prices and rework their corporate strategies.

In the post-boom period, mining companies lost market value in their shares, suffering, above all, from the high indebtedness acquired during the expansion period and with declining and sometimes negative operating and financial results. In other words, low profits and even losses put pressure for the transfer of dividends to their shareholders, which has kept investors away. Between 2011 and 2016, the shares of Brazilian Vale S/A devalued 87.2% and the shares of BHP Billiton, the world's largest mining company, fell 68.4% ....

... More companies have changed their corporate strategies: retracting and reviewing investments; promoting divestments with the sale of non-strategic assets; seeking to reduce operating costs and increase productivity; and concentrating activities in strategic businesses and priority regions. [67]

---

64   Ibid, 2.
65   Ibid, 3.
66   Ibid.
67   Ibid.

This framework assists the analysis of the information collected in the field. The variation in ore prices, such as iron and nickel, helps to understand the company's relationship with its workers and unions. The search for reducing operating costs led to the harsh imposition, in 2015 and 2016, of not granting annual wage adjustments or profit-sharing bonus agreements to its workers in order to reduce labor costs, as we will see in the next chapter. In addition, the sharp reduction in nickel prices, still under the impact of the first shock of the global economic crisis in 2008 and 2009, is the backdrop, as will be shown in Chapter 3, to Vale's decision to restructure its Canadian operations and accept a long conflict with its workers, since the depressed prices of ore did not compensate its extraction in view of the possibility of expanding the productivity of operations in the subsequent period.

Divestments were also part of the changes in Vale's corporate strategy in the post-commodity boom period: the company sold its fertilizer segment; a coal mine in Australia; exited its partnership with ThyssenKrupp in *Companhia Siderúrgica do Atlântico* (Atlantic Steel Company); reduced its stake in less profitable companies and projects;[68] sold part of its naval fleet; as well as a 15% stake in the Moatize mine and 50% of the Nacala Logistics Corridor, both in Mozambique, to Japan's Mitsui.[69]

We will return to the issue of Vale's focus on its core business, iron ore extraction, in the post-boom period in Chapter 4. For now, it is useful to address some of the consequences of this process. In response to the fall in prices, the large mining companies expanded their extracted volume, seeking to gain more market share against competitors weakened by the new market situation. For Vale, this represented a priority investment in the conclusion of the S11D Project in Carajás.[70] As a consequence of the post-boom,

> In the medium term, what is expected is a new round of capital concentration in mining, with the strengthening of large groups which will control the market of each ore in an oligopolized manner. In the case of iron ore, it is estimated that more than 80% of production will come from the four large mining companies: Rio Tinto, BHP Billiton, Vale and Fortescue from 2018 onwards.[71]

---

68   Ibid, 4.
69   Milanez et al., "A estratégia corporativa da Vale S.A.," 18.
70   About which Chapters 2 and particularly 4 will deal.
71   Wanderley, "Do *boom* ao pós-*boom* das *commodities*," 4.

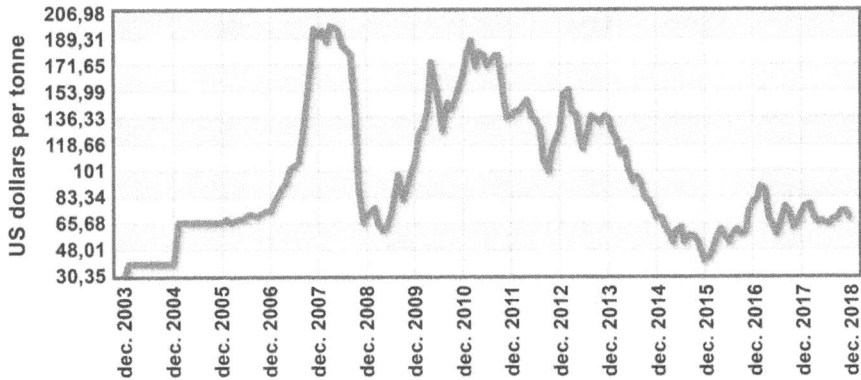

FIGURE 1   Monthly prices (US dollars) of 62% grade iron ore (Dec. 2003/Dec. 2018), based
on iron ore tonne import prices at the port of Tianjin (China)
SOURCE: INDEXMUNDI, WITH INFORMATION FROM THOMSON REUTERS
DATASTREAM AND WORLD BANK. AVAILABLE IN HTTPS://WWW.INDEXMU
NDI.COM/PT/PRE%C3%A7OS-DE-MERCADO/?MERCADORIA
=MIN%C3%A9RIO-DE-FERRO&MESES=180. ACCESSED MAY 26, 2021

Figures 1 and 2 illustrate the trajectory of iron ore and nickel prices in the international market over 15 years: from December 2003 to December 2018. Since
they cover a relatively long, time span, the interest in reproducing the figures is,
above all, to allow us to follow the often-sudden periods of growth and retraction in the prices of these ores, as detailed in the exposition above.[72]

Figure 1 shows the evolution of monthly prices of 62% grade iron ore. The
price went from around US$ 32.00 in December 2003 to US$ 65.00 in February
2005, from which point on there was an intense and constant price growth until
it surpassed the barrier of US$ 190.00 in April 2008. Subsequently, throughout
this year, with the global unfolding of the crisis that began in the US real estate
market, prices fell rapidly to around US$60.00 in April 2009, from which point
they started to rise again. In 2008, Vale dismissed about 2,000 direct workers
and 12,000 outsourced workers (the company had, at that time, 120,000 workers worldwide), under the justification of the global crisis and the intense drop
in iron ore prices,[73] starting the friction between Roger Agnelli and the federal

---

72   In Chapter 4, the increase in mineral commodity prices in 2020–2021 in the wake of the
Covid-19 pandemic crisis will be analyzed.

73   Carvalho, "Análise da ação dos sindicatos dos trabalhadores," 93, note 2.

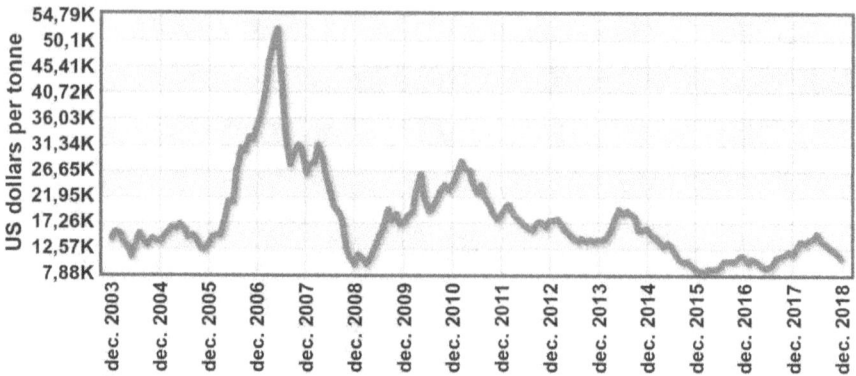

FIGURE 2   Monthly prices (US dollars) of nickel tonne (Dec. 2003/Dec. 2018)
             SOURCE: INDEXMUNDI WITH INFORMATION FROM PLATTS METALS WEEK,
             THOMSON REUTERS DATASTREAM AND WORLD BANK. AVAILABLE IN
             HTTPS://WWW.INDEXMUNDI.COM/PT/PRE%C3%A7OS-DE-MERCADO/?MER
             CADORIA=N%C3%ADQUEL&MESES=180. ACCESSED MAY 26, 2021

government, which was contrary to the dismissals, leading, among other reasons, to his departure from the company's CEO chair in 2011.[74]

The price of a tonne of iron ore reached a new peak, close to US$ 190.00, in January 2011, as mentioned above. Thereafter, marking the beginning of the post-boom period, prices fell back to below US$ 100.00 in May 2014 and to below US$ 40.00 from December 2015. Over the following three years, considering variations, the price remained between US$60.00 (from November 2016) and US$80.00, having reached close to US$90.00 in February 2017, but without sustaining itself at this level. In December 2018, the price was close to US$70.00.

It is possible to associate such variations in iron ore prices, Vale's main source of revenue, with the company's search for lower operating and labor costs and increased productivity, as will be seen in the description of the collective bargaining agreement negotiations in 2015 and the profit-sharing bonus agreement negotiations in 2016. Likewise, the new iron ore price levels in the post-commodity boom period conditioned the formulation of Vale's divestment strategy and formed the backdrop for discussions on the company's new shareholders' agreement in 2017.

---

74   Vieira, *O mapa da mina*, also points to the crisis with the Guinean government over the operating licenses for the Simandou mine (a joint venture between Vale and BSG) as a source of friction between Agnelli and the Dilma Rousseff administration, which would have contributed to his departure as the company's CEO.

Figure 2 shows the evolution of nickel prices also over 15 years. There are similarities with the evolution of iron ore prices analyzed above. The data help to frame the period of hard confrontation and strike in the company's Canadian operations between 2009 and 2010 and also, as will be shown in Chapter 3, shed light on Vale's choice to extend the conflict, ensuring the restructuring of those operations rather than seeking an immediate return to nickel extraction in a context of depressed prices.

As with iron ore prices, Figure 2 shows the growth of the nickel tonne prices from just over US$ 14,000 in December 2003 to a peak of over US$ 52,000 in May 2007. Vale's interest in Inco and the purchase's realization occurred exactly during this moment of intense rise. Over the year 2006, when the acquisition was made, nickel prices jumped from around US$15,000 in January to almost US$35,000 in December.

However, throughout 2007 and 2008, as also occurred with iron ore, nickel prices fell sharply as an effect of the global crisis. The price per tonne was below US$ 10,000 in December 2008. Thereafter, there was a recovery in prices – which, however, unlike what happened with iron ore, did not return in the following years to the previous peak of 2007. In July 2009, when the Vale workers strike in Sudbury (Canada) began, nickel's price per tonne was US$ 16,000, and a year later, in July 2010, when the strike ended, the price was US$ 19,500.

We highlight these two ores in the exposition because the extractive activities in the locations surveyed (Carajás and Sudbury) are concentrated on them. Vale is the global leader in the production of iron ore, pellets and nickel.[75] In 2020, the company produced 300,4 million tonnes of iron ore[76] and 214,700 tonnes of nickel,[77] had record net revenues of US$ 40 billion, EBITDA of

---

75   In 2019 and 2020, Vale temporarily lost its position as the largest global iron ore producer, which it held for years, to Rio Tinto due to restrictions in its production caused by the collapse of the Feijão Dam in Brumadinho (in Minas Gerais) in 2019, and due to the temporary closure of some mines as a result of the Covid-19 pandemic and for climate reasons in 2020. News indicated a tendency to recover the former position of largest global producer with the recovery of iron ore production at the end of 2020 and in 2021. See Marta Nogueira, "Vale perde posto de maior produtora global de minério de ferro para Rio Tinto." Available in: https://economia.uol.com.br/noticias/reuters/2020/02/11 /vale-perde-posto-de-maior-produtora-global-de-minerio-de-ferro-para-rio-tinto.htm. accessed May 26, 2021.

76   Vale S.A., *Formulário 20-F. Relatório Anual 2020*, 50. Available in http://www.vale.com /PT/investors/information-market/annual-reports/20f/20FDocs/Vale%2020-F%20FY2 020%20-%20Final%20Version_pt.pdf. accessed May 26, 2021.

77   Vale S.A., 64.

US\$ 16.6 billion and a net income of US\$ 4.5 billion.[78] Of Vale's revenues, most came from iron ore (68.2%), iron ore pellets (10.6%) and nickel (12.5%).[79]

3   Changes and Continuity in the Strategy for Labor and Union Relations after Privatization

As stated above, from the point of view of the production process and of labor relations, many transformations consolidated in the private period were introduced during the state-owned period, at the stage of 'preparation' for CVRD's sale.[80] For example, outsourcing, productivity bonuses (profit sharing) and the individualisation of earnings were deepened.

> The 90s came, a terrible crisis ... . And then Collor, with the political philosophy that he had to open up to the neoliberal project, so he had to dry up the state-owned companies and sell them. And then we in PT did everything so he wouldn't win. He won. But outsourcing was accelerated, automation was also accelerated and dismissal was the same, right? The company also left its administrative system, which was Fordism, and we had to adapt to Toyotism. That is, I had studied electrical engineering, I had to go back and take other courses, right? ... So that we started the 90's with 2700 men, with this process of downsizing so as to privatize, automation, outsourcing being accelerated ... We reached the year 2000 with 900 men on top of the mine. And production increased: we reached 35 million tonnes [of iron ore, the initial goal of the Carajás Iron Project], we went to 40 million, 40-something million tonnes, production ran wild. The country with very complicated hardships, you remember Collor's time. It is a crisis that we are practically repeating in this cycle right now, because, at that time, ore prices reached 40 dollars a tonne, ... we lost our colleagues who were fired, many of whom returned through

---

78   Vale S.A., *Relatório Integrado 2020*, 40. Available in http://www.vale.com/PT/investors/information-market/annual-reports/sustainability-reports/Sustentabilidade/Vale_Relato_Integrado_2020.pdf. accessed May 26, 2021.

79   The rest of the revenues comes from copper (5,4%), coal (1,2%), manganese and ferroalloys (0,6%) and others (1,5%). According to data from Vale S.A., *Formulário 20-F*, 2.

80   Minayo, *De ferro e flexíveis*.

outsourcing and there was a request for Collor's impeachment, when he later resigned. So, today we're practically repeating those days, right?[81]

With these words, Tonhão, leader of the Metabase union, described the changes in Carajás during the period of preparation for privatization. At that time a member of the PT, Tonhão stated that he was critical of the company's sale. During the interview, in fact, in the few moments when the union leader presented a discourse opposing Vale or the government, he recalled the period when he fought the 'neoliberal project,' of which, however, he became an enthusiastic supporter today, as we will see in the next chapter.

Tonhão and Ronaldo Silva are two union leaders that hold top positions at Metabase Carajás and STEFEM, respectively. Ronaldo, in a union election in 2012, left the top position he had occupied for many years and moved to a lower position,[82] although he was still very well positioned in his union's board. In addition to having been on their entities' boards for many years, both also have in common the fact that they have held seats on Vale's Board of Directors, representing workers. Ronaldo was a full member of the Board for six years, for three terms, while Tonhão was an alternate member for two terms. The leaders, however, have contrasting views, not only on the company's privatization process, but also on the relations between Vale and its unions. Despite their differences, the unions they represent are affiliated to CUT.

After a stressful internal conflict, Ronaldo took over STEFEM's leadership precisely during the period of CVRD's privatization. In his opinion, the unions were very weakened after the 1989 strike, in the context of the preparation for privatization organized by the Collor administration and the state-owned company's management. The defensiveness was caused by the withdrawal of benefits in exchange for bonuses: Ronaldo mentioned the end of the five-year benefit, the fourteenth salary and the education allowance for workers' children.[83] But, above all, the defensiveness was related to the huge number of dismissals in a company that adopted, during the state-owned period, despotic management practices and an anti-union stance characteristic of the dictatorial period. This legacy, even after the 1989 strike, would have been decisive for the lack of worker mobilization against privatization.

---

81   Tonhão, union leader, interviewed by Thiago Aguiar in Parauapebas, Brazil (July 2016). As indicated in the Introduction, the names of local workers and trade unionists interviewed will be changed throughout this book.

82   Possibly because of his actions in solidarity with the strike at Vale Canada in 2009–2010, as will be argued in the following Chapters.

83   Details about this process, again, can be found in Minayo.

This I can assure you: no worker participated in the plenary meetings. If they did, we couldn't recognize them. ... It was perfectly understandable, because the pressure was so great. Vale was, in a way, militarized. That regime ... I entered a sector where I had to walk with my beard removed, my hair cut, my shirt tucked in, my shoes shined, my pants buckled. I was from this sector. That was how it worked. Mainly because they alleged that our transportation sector was the image of the company and had to be like that. What could you do? Command those who can, obey those who are sensible. ... There was a very strong process of dismissals, very strong even at the time of this transition and we lost hundreds of comrades .... It was during Collor's time. The company became very lean and the target workers were the most diverse possible. There was an incentive programme, but it reached those who were on the eve of retirement, those who were in poor health and those who had salaries that were, always according to the mapping that they did, above market. So, these people were easy targets ... to be disconnected from the company. It was not optional, it was compulsory. You were chosen and had that incentive to leave, contrary to what is propagated. It wasn't voluntary, it was compulsory.[84]

The union's leadership, wrapped up in an internal dispute,[85] was split into two groups in a provisional commission created by the Labor Court until new elections solved the conflict. Ronaldo says that his group organized in STEFEM the campaign *O Brasil Vale Muito* 'Brazil is Worth a Lot', against privatization, bringing to Maranhão national union leaders, intellectuals and political leaders. The meetings and gatherings were full, but only with an external public: "We did not have the participation of any Vale worker, but we mobilized society."[86] To the unions, in face of the emptiness of worker mobilization, only the discourse in defense of national sovereignty would have remained, which was not convincing or, at least, it was not enough reason to put the workers in motion – ahead of the offensive of dismissals and, perhaps, by the attempts to convince workers to buy shares in the firm organized by CVRD through the INVESTVALE program. According to Godeiro,

> On the eve of privatization, CVRD executives created INVEST-
> VALE – *Clube de Investimento dos Empregados da Vale* [Vale Employees'

---

84   Ronaldo Silva, union leader, interviewed by Thiago Aguiar in São Luís, Brazil (May 2016).
85   Which will be the object of attention in the next Chapter.
86   Ronaldo Silva, Aguiar Interview.

Investment Club]. The Club's goal was to enable the workers to acquire CVRD shares, subsidized by BNDES through a loan of R$ 180 million to INVESTVALE. Each worker who joined ... received 626 shares which in principle would be blocked within the Club ....[87]

The company adopted a kind of carrot and stick tactic, which made the path to privatization easier: a combination of pressure, due to the layoffs in the previous period, added to the stimulus of INVESTVALE – with the perspective of some future gain on account of the shares – and the discourse of partnership of the new privatized company with the 'shareholding' workers.

[The workers] didn't get involved, they were cowed, they were already under pressure from the incentive plan, from dismissals. Nobody got involved. ... All over Brazil. What we saw in Brazil were some leaders, not all from the unions, making viable, by their own initiative, campaigns involving society. When they didn't do that, they were towed by society, by society's organized movement, which dragged the union leaders to make this campaign viable. Not here, over here it was our initiative, coordinated by this party, by this group. ... Vale used another economic trick which was the creation of an investment club called INVESTVALE, where each worker, up to the time of privatization, had the right to ... It was compulsory, 1 real would be deducted from his paycheck for him to join the club and receive a participation of 626 shares, something like that, for him to be a shareholder of the company. This generated a huge expectation of money for the worker. ... The workers, in fact, due to their economic situation, many of them left almost immediately. The club had only started opening the possibility of getting rid of the shares and they were already selling. There were people who offered cars, economy cars, in order to have access to the shares of Vale's workers.

RONALDO SILVA, Aguiar Interview

---

[87]   Godeiro, *Vale do Rio Doce*, 82. Following that, Godeiro describes a series of suspected irregularities in the purchase and sale of shares, in addition to the fluctuation of share value, which to this day motivate legal disputes. Ronaldo Silva raised similar suspicions, whereby workers without proper information or even victims of bad faith would have sold their shares to other shareholders for lower prices: "The guy having a hard time would sell his shares for 4,000 reais and sometimes they were worth an economy car" (Aguiar Interview).

Tonhão presented an opposite assessment of the privatization process, based on the company's performance after 1997 and on the increase in hiring over the following decade, which would have been results of the new private administration. For him, not only was privatization positive: INVESTVALE was a good opportunity for gains for the workers, who would depend only on their individual capacity to manage the shares, becoming themselves responsible for gains and losses in an eventual sale.

> In that crossing, we were lucky when the year 2000 came. ... Then came Fernando Henrique, who sold Vale. We were against Vale's sale in 1997. In the 90s, we were against it. As a PT activist, we did a lot of movement here, a union affiliated to CUT. We were radically against it, but Fernando Henrique sold Vale. ... Today we realize it was a great deal. Because it had around 12,000 something to 13,000 men and, after it was sold, after the private sector took over the company, the number of workers increased. We saw that insourcing was prioritized, reducing outsourcing. And the result is that the company went from 12,000 men to 60,000 men. In Brazil and all over the world. We reached five continents, 34 countries[88] and 12 Brazilian states. It has expanded so much in the private sector management. It didn't use to yield one billion of profit per year. We started in the next year to yield two, three, we reached 24 billion per year. So, from the company's point of view, it was excellent, right? And the result of this was that in 2014 we helped contribute to the balance of trade with over 47 billion. ... So, the difference Vale made from then to now, and has been making, was very big for this country. The privatization was excellent, it was a great deal for Vale, for those who stayed with Vale. We, the workers, were left with 3% of the shares, with a total of 626 shares for each worker. These shares, we got them for 30-something reais. They came to be worth as much as 900 reais. So, people made money. I myself held on to mine and put my family's house in order with this money. When it reached 800 and some, 900 reais, I sold a part of it. Now, many colleagues went and handed over these shares for a car, a used car, a new car, they gave it away. So it was an excellent deal. If, at the time, Fernando Henrique had ... Today we know he did everything right. And we see that the one who really socialized capital for the worker was Fernando Henrique, it was the

---

88   Vale managed to reach a presence in 33 countries at the peak of its expansion, according to Marshall, "Behind the Image of South-South Solidarity at Brazil's Vale."

PSDB.[89] Me, as a former PT activist, today I realize it because he authorized us to buy shares of Vale and Petrobras. At the time, I invested half of my FGTS[90] in Petrobras and it yielded a thousand percent. If I managed to collect it today, that's another problem, right? That's no longer in his hands. And our PT administration, which we really thought would defend workers' capital, it didn't let us invest in Petrobras and Vale shares, but it opened the coffers for the so-called PAC,[91] doing construction work abroad, which I was steaming mad about. He was doing construction work in Ecuador, Odebrecht dams there and their guy saying he wasn't going to pay and we didn't understand why, right? That was a serious mistake of PT, it sinned with the workers in that part, that it didn't give us conditions to invest with our little shares, with our FGTS money, to buy company shares and make money. No! I think he left each one to their own place: businessman over there, worker over there.

TONHÃO, Aguiar Interview

As we will see in the next chapter, Tonhão openly defends the privatization not only of Vale, but of all state-owned companies. He even says that they should be 'given', without payment, to private capital, since only the latter would be capable of generating jobs and preventing corruption. It will be necessary to scrutinize the reasons why a neoliberal union activist runs the main Vale workers' union in Brazil (it should also be said, still affiliated to CUT).

The transformations in CVRD were not, however, restricted to the period of preparation for privatization. Soon after the company's sale in 1999, the workers' pension plan underwent drastic changes. Up to that moment, CVRD offered to the workers, through its pension fund Valia,[92] defined benefit plans, by which the retirees received from the company a complement to the values of the state pension (from the INSS, the National Institute of Social Security) so that they could maintain the salaries of their active period. This plan gave way to Vale Mais, an individually-defined contribution plan, whereby the retired

---

89   *Partido da Social Democracia Brasileira* [Brazilian Social Democracy Party], Fernando Henrique Cardoso's political party.

90   *Fundo de Garantia do Tempo de Serviço* [Time of Service Guarantee Fund], a worker protection fund.

91   *Programa de Aceleração do Crescimento* [Growth Acceleration Program], a government infrastructure program.

92   This is the *Fundo Vale do Rio Doce de Seguridade Social* – Valia, Vale's pension fund. Founded in 1973, with "10,934 participants, it currently has over 120,000 participants", according to information available in https://www.valia.com.br/sobre-a-valia/nossa-histo ria/. accessed May 26, 2021.

worker receives a complement according to the amount he has invested over time, without the high counterpart paid until then by the company, which guaranteed the maintenance of his active period wages.

> The first battle we had [after the privatization] was that struggle to remove the pension plan model, which went from a defined benefit to a defined contribution. ... Because the defined benefit gave you a safe situation: you contributed with a given percentage – a very small one at that – and the company offered you a benefit that guaranteed, in the case of retirement, your full salary in the future. You would have stability in the future, at the end of your working life. Today, with this defined contribution model, which is the same as the ones in the market, you have a maximum contribution parity of 9%. Vale contributes 9% and you can also reach 9%. But it is difficult for workers to reach 9%, because they cannot. From the reference salary, from his nominal salary. You can hardly get there. And then, if you contribute to this model, you are subject to market rules. If the market breaks down, everything you have contributed there is gone.
>
> RONALDO SILVA in a meeting with STEFEM's board of directors

Ronaldo experienced such a transition in Vale's pension plans already holding a very important position on STEFEM's board of directors. According to him, managers exerted enormous pressure on workers, since it was necessary to individually accept the replacement of the old Valia plan (the defined benefit plan) by Vale Mais (the defined contribution plan), by signing documents. Very few – in particular union leaders who, by law, cannot be dismissed – refused to do so.

> **Ronaldo Silva:**   Soon after it was privatized, ... [there was an] attack by the company on our pension fund, which was Valia, and they implemented Vale Mais like a steamroller. Valia was a defined benefit model and Vale Mais a defined contribution model, the same model that they took to Canada. ... In the defined benefit, you paid a monthly contribution, deducted from your paycheck, to a pension fund that would guarantee you a certain comfort in the future on your retirement. If I get paid a certain amount at Vale, I will receive, according to the criteria stipulated in the manual, this same amount [in retirement]. I won't have a loss. ... I would keep my salary, all good, the same salary. That is, you would not have this loss that those who

are retired by the INSS have. ... The fund complements it. In the defined contribution [Vale Mais], you contribute to this fund, subject to the rules of the market, which can suddenly yield an exorbitant profit as well as suddenly break down so you lose everything. ... They drove the steamroller and the union group did not have the mobilization capacity, for several reasons, we won't go into specifics, to oppose the company. Because we could have gone on strike, we could have done a lot of things. Nobody did. Our union was again one of the references at a national level. I am the example because I was not, even as I was 'pressured', in quotes, because they didn't have the courage or the audacity to come to me and say that I had to adhere to their new model. I was an example, until the end, and until today I remain as a defined benefit. I didn't sign it.

Thiago Aguiar: *And did they force people to sign?*
Everybody. From manager to drudge, everybody signed. Here, in the union, Geraldo [another board member] stayed with me and also another one who has already left. In all of Brazil, we are only eleven: me, Geraldo and nine other active members [who didn't sign the adhesion to the new plan]. We held several meetings, several assemblies, we brought lawyers who had full technical knowledge of the coup that was behind it, we alerted the workers, we made banners, campaigns ... But there was no way. Because the workers were forced to sign. They either signed or they were canned. There were several examples of people there. Coercion. They would come here and say: "Oh, I was threatened." But how do you prove it? It's just like moral harassment. It's hard to prove it.
Aguiar Interview

The emphasis on the privatization period lies in the fact that it was there when fundamental measures were taken to shape what would be the strategy of labor relations adopted by the company in the following period in Brazil and abroad. We can see, in the Canadian case, for example, the implementation, after Inco's purchase, of measures similar to those which were taken in Brazil in the period of preparation for privatization – especially, the plan of encouraged dismissal to downsize the workforce and the changes in the organization of production – as well as changes in the pension plan, made, in Brazil, shortly after private capital took control of Vale.

According to Ronaldo, few benefits from the state-owned period have been kept, such as health insurance and food stamps, whose value today is close to R$ 500.00 per month. The downsizing of personnel, technical modernization and benefit reduction reduced Vale's production costs, increasing workers' productivity at the same time that their earnings were reduced.

> If in the state-owned period, productivity was encouraged by the appeal to the civic sentiment of generating foreign currency for the country, today it has several other ways of being required: by collective, group or individualized economic reward (through profit sharing bonuses); by goals established and controlled daily, and, not least important, the veiled threat of an excessively inflated labor market, in the face of an increasingly reduced demand from the company. Today, hiring is meager and does not occur in the necessary proportion at times of increased demand, and to cover eventual needs, the company uses the outsourcing mechanism.[93]

With the increase in production and profits and with external demand heated up from the first decade of the 2000s, the hiring of new workers occurred upon new frameworks, thus enabling the replacement of a significant part of the state-owned period's workforce by another with greatly reduced wages and benefits, in addition to the increased use of outsourcing.[94] For Ronaldo, there was an intensification of labor as well as risks to workers' health as a counterpart to the increase in productivity:

> The level of production reached by these Vale workers because of this new private model is something that deserves to be studied, especially considering their health. Because what I'm going to tell you here is what they said to us at the negotiation table: the workers at Vale, their working life is 10 years. It's 10 years because their productivity level is so high.

---

93   Carvalho, "Análise da ação dos sindicatos," 93.
94   Carvalho. The increase in outsourcing in Sudbury following the incorporation of Inco by Vale is also described by Reuben Roth, Mercedes Steedman and Shelley Condratto, "The Casualization of Work and the Rise of Precariousness in Sudbury's Nickel Mining Industry", in *33th International Labour Process Conference* (*ILPC*) (Athens, 2015).

> Their stress level is so high. So they have back problems, or RSI, or mental problems.
>
> RONALDO SILVA, Aguiar Interview

As shown in the previous sections, the legacy of the authoritarian period and the changes brought about in the 'preparation' period and after privatization were fundamental in shaping Vale's labor relations and union strategies, which will be described in the next two chapters, with the analysis of field observations and interviews conducted in Brazil and Canada.

Judith Marshall, through a survey applied to company workers in three different countries – Brazil, Canada and Mozambique – synthesizes some tactics employed by the company:

(1) Vale is noted for being very anti-union; (2) A Vale worker tends to earn less than workers in similar workplaces; (3) Vale managers engage in constant bullying of workers; (4) Vale imposes unrealistically high production goals, thus creating the atmosphere of permanent stress which Vale promised to eliminate; (5) Vale workers live with the constant threat of being fired without due cause; (6) Vale supervisors impose arbitrary disciplinary measures with great frequency; (7) To work at Vale means to work in dangerous conditions because Vale puts production above all else and often covers up health and safety incidents; (8) Vale regularly tries to buy union and government leaders by offering them vehicles, travel, credit cards, etc.[95]

Ten years after privatization, in 2007, the former *Companhia Vale do Rio Doce* (CVRD), whose name honors the region where it was created by the Vargas administration in 1942, was renamed Vale S.A. The company adopted the green and yellow of the Brazilian flag in its modernized global brand.[96] The workers, who previously wore beige uniforms, better suited to the iron ore dust that fills all the company's facilities, now wear the light green that can signify both the concern with 'sustainability'[97] as well as the Brazil 'brand' which the TNC uses in its expansion around the world.

---

95   Marshall, "Behind the Image of South-South Solidarity at Brazil's Vale," 172.
96   Marshall, 180.
97   In the words of Guilherme Zagallo: "now, in the past few years, ten years, they haven't used this expression, but they have already tried to be a 'green mining company' in their advertising discourse, which is a contradiction in terms. There is no sustainable mining."

The green in the uniforms. There is a factor: the previous color was khaki, it was khaki, beige, which is more appropriate for those who deal with ore, it gets less dirty, it is more appropriate from a functional point of view. But they make an option for the green in their brand, when they change their brand they adopt the green and yellow. It has a lot to do with that [attempt to identify itself with the colors of Brazil]. Over time, they saw that this 'green company' discourse would not prosper, they end up abandoning this strategy, although they continue with a strong discourse for, supposedly, sustainability, but then, finally, the facts show that this is an unsustainable discourse.

GUILHERME ZAGALLO, Aguiar Interview

Besides being the world's largest iron ore producer for decades, Vale became the largest nickel producer after the purchase of the Canadian company Inco in 2006. At the time, Vale came second among the largest global mining companies in market value, and currently occupies the third position.[98]

During Roger Agnelli's term (2001–2011), the company's shares appreciated 834%, stimulated by the enormous growth in the value of iron ore during the commodity boom.[99] During this period, there was a great concentration of capital in global mining.[100] Even though Vale continues, from the point of view of its revenues, to be highly dependent on the extraction of iron ore in Brazil and that, abroad, it has only commercial offices in many countries, with no production activities, it is undeniable to recognize the adoption by the company, after the privatization, of an aggressive expansion posture, through which it began to operate in 25 countries in five continents.[101] André Teixeira and Sérgio Rosa spoke about this expansion:

Thiago Aguiar: *In how many countries does Vale now operate?*
André Teixeira: We have functioning operations in Brazil, Canada, in England we have a small refinery, but we have the railway issue in the UK, in Mozambique, in Malawi. We have it in New Caledonia, which is in Oceania, part of France, in Indonesia, in China there is also a nickel refinery.

98   PwC, "Mine 2020: Resilient and Resourceful" (2020): 26. Available in https://www.pwc .com/gx/en/energy-utilities-mining/publications/pdf/pwc-mine-2020.pdf. accessed May 26, 2021.

99   Coelho, *Projeto Grande Carajás*.

100   Roger Moody, *Rocks and Hard Places: The Globalization of Mining* (Londres, Zed Books, 2007).

101   Vale S.A., *Relatório Integrado 2020*, 35.

We have a stalled project in Argentina, which is the Rio Colorado project, which we bought and, because of Cristina Kirchner, ... we suspended it, it was a confusing government. ... And we have exploration in some other countries, we have exploration in Chile, we have exploration in Peru. ... Oh, and we have it in the United States, which is California Steel.

Are all these places Vale's operations?
Operations, you got production. Now, we have commercial offices in Singapore, for example. In Sanit-Prex, near Geneva, we have an office ...
Aguiar Interview

We invested up to 20 billion a year! We reduced dividend payments to be able to invest. I don't know if it was 20 [billion], but large investments to be able to guarantee that. This is a strategic board decision. So, there was an investment decision by the company. So, if the company grew, it is because the company decided to invest and invested money, especially its own, which no longer became dividends, but investments. (...) Inco had important assets which represented a diversification in Vale's mining portfolio. So, there was nickel, there was some coal stuff ... There was some very complicated stuff in Indonesia, very complicated ... But it was a package, a package, right? It was a company from a country, ... from a developed market. That is, this business combination sometimes helps you to improve brand perception, the business combination. You have assets from a country with a more unstable economy, you have a relevant asset in a more stable economy, you have a little improvement in the rating of the business as a whole. So, you have some gains that come just from the composition of the business, but, above all, the focus was on nickel. ... If we could have bought only Inco nickel, we would have bought only Inco nickel. During the negotiations, there were attempts to select, to fraction Inco and buy only what interested us, but then the guys didn't want to sell only the nickel, they wanted to sell the whole package.

> ... It was the biggest acquisition that Vale made in the
> period, a high acquisition by Vale's standards up to that
> point. That was the wager: we had size, we had the capac-
> ity to swallow it and it brought about a change in Vale's
> status because we were incorporating a company with
> diversified assets with a new and important metal for us.
>
> SÉRGIO ROSA, Aguiar interview

Most of Vale's workers are concentrated in Brazil, but there are significant contingents in other operations. Of Vale's 186.200 workers worldwide (74,300 in-house workers and 111,900 outsourced ones), 80% are in Brazil; 6.6% in Asia; 6.2% in Africa; 5.7% in North America (but 8.2% among in-house workers); and the rest among Europe, Oceania and other South American countries.[102] In turn, of Vale's revenues in 2020, 57.8% came from China; 13.7% from other Asian countries; 13.3% from European countries; 7.3% from Brazil; 4.1% from other countries in North, Central and South America; and 3.8% from the rest of the world.[103]

4 Some Characteristics of Vale's Iron Ore GPN in Brazil

Vale, as already stated, is the largest iron ore production company in the world. Brazil had the world's second largest estimated reserves and third largest production of iron ore in 2011.[104] Mineral deposits belong to the federal government, which regulates mining activity. Companies need operating and environmental licenses. Chapter 4 describes some recent changes in the Mineral Code, such as the creation of a regulatory agency, the National Mining Agency (ANM), replacing the former National Department of Mineral Production (DNPM), which was until then responsible for granting operating licenses and inspecting the activity.[105]

As a way of framing the field observations presented in the next chapter, it is useful to describe some elements of the economic dimension of the Brazilian node of the iron ore GPN. Mining is a major economic activity in

---

102   Vale S.A., 124.

103   According to data from Vale S.A., *Formulário 20-F*, 106–107.

104   Santos and Milanez, "The Global Production Network for Iron Ore," 759.

105   In the legislative debates on changes in the mineral legislation, there was prominent participation of deputies whose campaigns were financed by mining companies. (Santos and Milanez, 760). There will be opportunities throughout the book to return to this aspect, analyzing, in Vale's institutional strategy, lobbying practices and campaign financing by the company in Brazil and abroad.

Brazil, underpinning most industrial sectors and involving intense consumption of natural resources with environmental impacts. The following paragraphs highlight five aspects of the iron ore production network: 1) exploration; 2) extraction; 3) processing; 4) logistics; and 5) consumption, following the description of Rodrigo Santos and Bruno Milanez.[106]

Exploration is marked by uncertainty. It is an activity that requires geological research and mapping work to identify and characterize mineral deposits, which involves high costs. In Brazil, the Brazilian Geological Survey (under the Mineral Resource Research Company, or CPRM) is the public agent responsible for mineral research, although, given its underfunding, smaller private research companies are increasingly taking on geological research activities in association with large mining companies.[107]

Extraction, in turn, takes place mostly in open pit mines and includes drilling, blasting, loading and transportation activities. Vale concentrates 80% of its iron ore production in Brazil, a consequence of its rooting in the country and its state-owned origin. Extraction occurs mainly in mega-mines due to the need to reduce fixed costs.

> As a result, mining companies are usually the main employers in mining towns, particularly in rural areas in the Amazon region. This condition is a key element to understanding the high level of corporate power of mining companies at the local level.[108]

Iron ore processing involves grinding, separation, concentration and pelletizing activities, generating multiple ore grades. With the exception of the latter, at Vale, these activities are generally carried out in areas close to the mines. Only 17% of the ore extracted by the company undergoes pelletizing in Brazil. The rest occurs mainly through Vale "in partnerships with international steel mills from Australia, Italy, Japan, South Korea, and Spain in a process of network embeddedness."[109]

---

106   Santos and Milanez, 760–1.
107   Bruno Milanez, Tádzio Peters Coelho and Luiz Jardim Wanderley, "O projeto mineral no Governo Temer: menos Estado, mais mercado," *Versos – Textos para Discussão PoEMAS* 1, no. 2 (2017): 3, when addressing the changes in the Brazilian mineral policy during the Michel Temer administration, showed the latter's willingness to reduce state participation, through CPRM in mineral research, making room for junior companies, "small mining companies, primarily of research or with few operations, listed on stock exchanges and that have intrinsic relationship with the financial market and high degree of investment risk".
108   Santos and Milanez, "The Global Production Network for Iron Ore," 760.
109   Ibid.

Logistics involves the transportation infrastructure necessary to ship iron ore to consumers or to pellet plants from which it is shipped to consumers. Consumption by domestic steel mills is mainly supplied by railroads – such as the Carajás Railroad and the Vitória-Minas Railroad – and pipelines. Global consumption is met by sea. Transportation costs represent a major part of the iron ore price, which shows the importance of economies of scale and explains the use of private terminals and the fact that ore export ports are operated by mining companies, such as the port of Ponta da Madeira in Maranhão. Vale projected it to become the largest port in the world in shipping capacity at the end of the investments in the S11D project:

> Brazil's leading cargo-handling hub, Ponta da Madeira is undergoing capacity expansion works to meet the increased production resulting from S11D, which will make it the largest port in the world. Its current shipping capacity is 150 million tonnes/year, but by 2018, it will reach 230 million tonnes/year – a level of handling that will be reached in stages that will include matching the capacities of the mine, railroad and port.[110]

Finally, regarding consumption: the steel industry is the primary consumer and, of all iron ore produced in Brazil, only 30% was consumed in the domestic market, concentrated in five main groups: ArcelorMittal, Gerdau, Usiminas/Nippon Steel Corporation, Companhia Siderúrgica Nacional and ThyssenKrupp. International consumers, therefore, are key in the iron ore global production network.[111]

Vale's iron ore extraction is concentrated in Brazil, regionalised by the company into four systems (northern, southeastern, southern and central-western). The empirical research in Brazil focused on two strategic areas of the 'northern system' – the mines of Carajás (in Pará) and the port of Ponta da Madeira (in Maranhão), through which its production is shipped.

> [The northern system] (North, East and South mountain ranges) is located in Pará, and is integrated to the Ponta da Madeira Port Terminal (in Maranhão) by the Carajás Railroad, and is aimed at the Asian and

---

110   Vale S.A., *Relatório de Sustentabilidade Vale 2015b*, 39. Available in http://www.vale.com /PT/investors/information-market/annual-reports/sustainability-reports/Sustentabilid ade/relatorio-de-sustentabilidade-2015.pdf. accessed May 26, 2021.

111   According to data by Santos and Milanez, "The Global Production Network for Iron Ore," 761.

European markets. The importance of this system in the corporate strategy has been progressively increasing, particularly since the start of the operations of S11D, the world's largest iron ore mine, which accounted for 46.2% (169.2 Mt.) of the company's supply in 2017.[112]

The southeastern (Itabira, Minas Centrais and Mariana complexes) and southern (Itabirito, Vargem Grande and Paraopeba complexes) systems cover the Iron Quadrangle (in Minas Gerais), accounting for 29.6% (108.5 Mt.) and 23.6% (86.4 Mt.) of extracted ore, respectively. The southeastern system is also integrated by the Vitória-Minas Railroad (EFVM) to the port of Tubarão (in Espírito Santo), which also serves some mines of the southern system. The others are served by the operator MRS up to the private port terminals of Guaíba Island and Itaguaí (in Rio de Janeiro). The fourth system, the central-western, is located in the state of Mato Grosso do Sul, allowing for the flow of ore on a smaller scale – 0.7% (2.4 Mt.) of supply – through the Paraguay River and Argentine ports .... [113]

The next chapter presents the field observations and interviews conducted in São Luís (in Maranhão) and Parauapebas (in Pará), which will enable a deeper theoretical and, above all, empirical analysis of the company's labor and union relations strategy.

---

112 Of the total production of 366.5 million tonnes of iron ore by Vale in 2017, the percentage mentioned refers to the production of the northern system as a whole (169.2 million tonnes of iron ore), of which 22 million tonnes came from S11D. In it, Vale expects to produce, in 2018, "50 to 55 million tonnes and, in 2019, 70 to 80 million, reaching a capacity of 90 million tonnes in 2020," according to Vale S.A., *Relatório de Sustentabilidade Vale 2017*, 112. Available in http://www.vale.com/PT/aboutvale/relatorio-de-sustentabilidade-2017 /Documents/v_VALE_RelatorioSustentabilidade_2017_v.pdf. accessed May 26, 2021.

113 Milanez et al., "A estratégia corporativa da Vale S.A," 12.

Corporate Power and Union Fragmentation
Vale's Labor and Union Relations Strategy in Brazil

The first contact with the unions STEFEM and Metabase Carajás took place at a time of tense negotiations with Vale. Iron ore prices in the world market, in freefall after peaking at almost US$ 190 in 2011, declined intensely throughout 2014 and 2015, reaching, by the end of that year, a price below US$ 40, the lowest in more than a decade.

As a result, in 2015, Vale's net revenues, heavily dependent on iron ore extraction and exports, declined 31.8% in one year.[1] The mineral commodity price drop and the onset of the Brazilian recession, in turn, led to foreign exchange losses and the revaluation of the company's assets, which generated a loss of US$12.129 billion[2] that year.[3] Although the huge loss was caused mainly by exchange rate and accounting factors, the company announced that its operating expenses were "reduced, by US$ 1.6 billion, as a result of efforts to maintain competitiveness in the mining industry, efficiency and austerity."[4]

As analyzed in the previous chapter, the commodity post-boom led to changes in the corporate strategy of mining TNCs, which began to divest and prioritize profitable, large-scale investments. Vale made the same move over the following years, reorienting its corporate strategy, which led to changes in its shareholder arrangement and in its investment, financing, and market tactics, among others.[5] With these measures, coupled with the relative recovery in mineral commodity prices in the following years, the company returned to profit. In 2016, Vale would highlight a new round of operating cost cuts of

---

1   Vale S.A., *Formulário 20-F. Relatório Anual 2020*, 91. Available in http://www.vale.com/PT /investors/information-market/annual-reports/20f/20FDocs/Vale%2020-F%20FY2020%20 -%20Final%20Version_pt.pdf. accessed May 26, 2021.
2   Vale S.A., 86.
3   Vale's R$44.2 billion loss in 2015 was the largest among publicly traded Brazilian companies since 1986, according to information available in https://www.valor.com.br/empresas/4454 094/prejuizo-da-vale-em-2015-e-o-maior-entre-companhias-abertas-em-29-anos;   accessed May 26, 2021.
4   Vale S.A., *Relatório de Sustentabilidade Vale 2015*, 36; Available in http://www.vale.com/PT /investors/information-market/annual-reports/sustainability-reports/Sustentabilidade /relatorio-de-sustentabilidade-2015.pdf; accessed May 26, 2021.
5   As will be seen in more detail in Chapter 4.

US$1.841 billion, in addition to a reduction in investments. Net profit was recovered, reaching US$ 4 billion;[6] in the following year, it increased 38%, reaching US$ 5.5 billion.[7]

The first to feel the effects of the changes in Vale's corporate strategy, however, were the company's workers and their unions. Even before the disclosure of the 2015 annual results, during the annual collective agreement's negotiations held at the end of that year, the company brought to the table its willingness to extract harsh concessions, such as not granting any wage adjustment, in a year of high inflation, and withdrawing benefits: the payment of the '14 th and 15th [monthly] salaries,'[8] for example, to which the workers in Carajás were entitled by regional agreement, was terminated. In 2016, the company announced that there would be no profit-sharing bonus payment related to the previous year, generating great dissatisfaction among its workers, for whom variable earnings are fundamental.

This chapter will present field observations in São Luís (in the state of Maranhão) and Parauapebas (in Pará), in addition to interviews with workers, union members and members of Vale's management. The focus will be on the company's labor and union relations strategies, and the forms of worker organization and resistance in the face of corporate power. Vale has historically been able to circumvent labor conflicts, imposing on its workforce the flexibility – in terms of working conditions and payment, for example – it needs to reduce operating costs and recover profit margins and remuneration for its shareholders.

The labor and union relations strategy is decisive for the creation, expansion and capture of value. Within the GPN framework, multiple actors (companies, the state, workers and unions) relate to each other, seeking to influence the decision-making processes along the networks or to formulate resistance. Strategies can be divided into different tactics,[9] such as: 1) professional qualification and training; 2) working conditions; 3) labor relations (hiring, payment, working hours and dismissals); and 4) union relations.

---

6 Vale S.A., *Relatório de sustentabilidade 2016*, 34; Available in http://www.vale.com/PT/invest ors/information-market/annual-reports/sustainability-reports/Sustentabilidade/relatorio -de-sustentabilidade-2016.pdf; accessed May 26, 2021.

7 Vale S.A., *Relatório de Sustentabilidade Vale 2017*, 109. Available in http://www.vale.com/PT /aboutvale/relatorio-de-sustentabilidade-2017/Documents/v_VALE_RelatorioSustentabili dade_2017_v.pdf. accessed May 26, 2021.

8 Named as such because the Christmas bonus is traditionally called the '13th salary' in Brazil.

9 Following the arguments of Bruno Milanez et al., "A estratégia corporativa da Vale S.A.: um modelo analítico para redes globais extrativas," *Versos – Textos para Discussão PoEMAS* 2, no 2 (2018): 1–43.

Regarding the first tactic, there is a "coexistence between distinct forms of qualification/training of the workers who act in its facilities" in "three distinct training proposals", by which: (a) in management positions, the qualification aims at preparing to deal with the increasing automation and mechanization of production; (b) the workers in the operation itself, in turn, receive training, through lectures and courses, whose indirect objective, however, is the "ideological control of workers, keeping them away from union organization", to "manage the conditions of company embeddedness in contexts of labor conflict" and collaborate to the "co-optation of unions"; c) finally, outsourced workers, "mainly in maintenance, construction and cleaning, do not receive training or are precariously qualified."[10] In the following pages, it will be possible to empirically verify how the tactic of co-opting unions and establishing forms of direct control of the workforce operates to avoid conflicts. This is a constant concern of the company's labor relations management and is seen, perhaps, as the main obstacle for union organization by the interviewed leaders.

The second tactic, related to the "standard of working conditions at Vale", "specifically with regard to health and safety, focuses on reducing costs, particularly in the maintenance and cleaning sectors,"[11] in addition to records of salary delays, poor housing, healthcare and food conditions for Filipino and South African subcontracted workers in the Mozambique operations, as well as unhealthy conditions and health risks in Brazilian operations.[12] Corroborating this diagnosis, field research in Sudbury revealed changes in safety and health policies after the purchase of Inco, which led, according to workers interviewed and the union USW Local 6500, to an increase in the number of accidents, including fatalities. The changes also included the implementation of a new alcohol and drug policy, which established the possibility of management subjecting workers to frequent urine tests, as will be seen in Chapter 3. According to the interviewees, these measures are aimed at persecuting and demoralizing stewards,[13] union activists and workers who are critical of management's role.

In terms of labor relations tactics, Vale exercises its corporate power seeking to influence – through its 'institutional strategy,' lobbying the National Congress and establishing relations with the various spheres of state power – aspects of the legal and judicial labor framework.[14] Chapter 4, for example, will show how Vale sought mediation in the Superior Labor Court with STEFEM, in the first

---

10   Ibid, 23–4.
11   Ibid, 24.
12   Ibid.
13   Union rank and file representatives at mines and production facilities.
14   Ibid.

national case of recognition by the courts of a negotiation fee, established in a workers' assembly, as a way to compensate for the extinction of union dues by the 2017 labor reform. Thus, if, on the one hand, the company seeks to co-opt the unions, on the other hand, it recognizes the importance of these entities to establish stable relationships with its workforce, in a predictable relationship arrangement with its unions, in which it can exercise its corporate power with less friction. At the same time, its labor relations management is largely supportive of labor reform and has sought to adopt elements of the new legislation in recent negotiations with unions, despite resistance from the latter.

The widespread use of outsourcing is the main aspect of Vale's labor relations tactics:[15]

> Although it is not exclusive to Vale, outsourcing at the company covers a large part of labor relations and is central to the expansion of value creation. In 2015, of the total 166,300 workers, 92,200 were outsourced, or 55.4% of the total. In 2017, the number fell to 57,000 outsourced out of a total of 130,600, or 43.6% of the total ... This drop is explained by the demobilization generated by the completion of projects, especially the S11D, in Carajás, since the use of outsourced workers is more intense in construction, expansion and infrastructure renovation works.
>
> Outsourcing tends to be accompanied by increased flexibility and deterioration of working conditions. In this sense, Vale does not seem to effectively monitor working conditions and compliance with labor standards by service providers. Thus, the worker is subjected to an intense routine with strenuous demands for productivity.[16]

In recent years, the investment increase in capital goods and in automation of ore extraction and transportation – the most important of which is the S11D Project – has allowed Vale to reduce the number of workers and hire workers through outsourcing and short-term contracts.[17]

---

15 As was also pointed out by Laura Nazaré de Carvalho, "Análise da ação dos sindicatos dos trabalhadores da mineradora Vale S.A. na região Sudeste brasileira," *Textos & Debates*, no. 23 (January/July 2013): 91–114.

16 Milanez et al, "A estratégia corporativa da Vale S.A."

17 Ibid. Just as an illustration, the turnover rate indicated by Vale in 2017 (the information does not appear in more recent reports), considering only its own employees, was 9% in general (in 2016, the general rate was 7.2%) and also 9% if only the Brazilian operations are considered. In Brazil and Canada, countries with the largest contingent of Vale workers in the world, there was an increase in turnover from 2016 to 2017: in Brazil, the

Most of the company's tactics aim to 'fragment and weaken workers' agency.'[18] To achieve this, Vale: a) seeks to bring the union leaders closer to its interests, subordinating them; b) offers support to certain slates and promotes the dismissal of opponents, making them unviable (a situation of which Metabase Carajás would be the main example); and c) upon finding obstacles in the attempts to co-opt the union leaderships, seeks to reduce the resistance and negotiation capacity of the unions, expanding outsourcing, which occurred in Canada in its confrontation with the USW.[19] For now, the presentation of this framework is sufficient for an approach to the problem.

André Teixeira, executive manager of labor relations at Vale, began working in the company in the 1980s. A mechanical engineer, Teixeira initially worked in CVRD's maintenance and information technology areas, before starting to work in the human resources area in 1994 and assuming management positions in the area from 2000 onwards.[20] He said in an interview that in the beginning he kept restrictions on union action, but with time he realized the interdependence between the company and the unions and the importance of this relationship to 'alleviate tensions' in production.

Therefore, as head of the labor relations area, his focus would be to establish close relationships with the entities, almost like the relationship of "a couple," preventing negotiations and conflicts from exceeding the limits of this proximity. This approach, according to the manager, would be responsible for the absence of strikes at Vale, a reason for "pride" to him:

> **André Teixeira:** Today I believe that unions are extremely necessary to our society. If you take the history of world trade unionism, you see that trade unionism appeared in the *Belle Époque*, in fact, that was when Karl Marx created the Socialist International. It was the period of greatest growth in Europe. ... But in the beginning I had a relationship ... I thought that unionism was a problem for companies. But now, where unionism has grown, capitalism

---

rate went from 6.8% to 9%; in Canada, from 4.3% to 6.9%. See Vale S.A., *Relatório de Sustentabilidade Vale 2017*, 39.

18   Milanez et al., "A estratégia corporativa da Vale S.A."

19   Ibid, 25–6.

20   Teixeira also teaches at Fundação Dom Cabral, a world-class Brazilian business school, in order, he says, to prepare for a new activity when he retires. His work at the institution, as he stated in an interview, is unpaid: "I have never earned a penny from Fundação Dom Cabral. ... I negotiate with them, in exchange for the courses I give there, scholarships for Vale employees."

has grown. The union works, our relationship with the union works by relieving tensions. Where tensions are not relieved, like in Russia, for example, you had a revolution. ... So, as I was saying, I believed that the union had one goal and the company had another goal, and that one wanted to destroy the other. ... And my great discovery was – it was little by little, right? – that they need each other. And that, incredible as it may seem, in most situations, our goals are not different. Sometimes, we have different ways of reaching the same goal, right? And I'm proud of the fact that I've experienced strikes, but they weren't generated by us. Companies that we took over and that came with the strike, here in Brazil and outside Brazil. ... In Vale Mining, you may not have known, we have had strikes, but you may not know of any strikes.

Thiago Aguiar: *The last one was in '89, wasn't it?*
'89. No, but within the group, we had another one at Vale Fertilizers, here in Brazil, two strike days and, since I didn't give them a cent for the day off, it's something that I find absurd, but after the strike, my relationship, our relationship, with the union only improved. Even moving towards a relationship of friendship. Why? Because we left the strike without trying to destroy the union, we didn't pay a cent for the day off, but we negotiated. ... I think that the joint construction between capital and labor is extremely important. In the same way I also think that the negotiation has to be directly with us, not showing up in the press. ... If you look in the press, you'll find it very difficult to find reports of our negotiations. ... And, well, for our union members, going to *Folha de São Paulo, Globo,* even on television to give interviews, for them it would be very good, but we managed to show them that this is not good for the workers. This was great learning.

But was that because you thought it would expose Vale before its shareholders or before society? For what reason?
There's nothing to expose Vale in that respect, the content can come out later, because the negotiation

is ... Let's say, a couple. A couple is not going to discuss through the press, people, we have problems, right? The discussion is much more effective when these parties are discussing directly, right? ... When the party, when the union goes to the press, at least what I see with other companies, at least the impression that I get, is that they are also trying to promote themselves. Their goal is not to promote themselves; the goal is to get stuff for the employee. And, when we have a more direct negotiation, we are clearer, more assertive in what we say. Many times you can even see the result of the negotiation in the press. ... There are threats in the negotiation, right? Oh, I'll go on strike, and so on ... The more exposure you have, the more threats arise. ... When you don't have as much exposure, the language is much more direct, you get more assertive, more frank, more transparent.

Aguiar Interview

In this and in the next chapter, some examples of this "direct"[21] way of conducting relations with unions will be assessed, as well as its effects on the exercise of collective power by unions and their workers.

1   Entering the Field in a Period of Crisis

The company is proposing a profit-sharing model for 2016 with a one-paycheck advance: half a paycheck 10 days after signing the agreement and another half-paycheck conditioned to a trigger, again, of R$2.75 billion in EBITDA minus current investments. Why are we here? Because the company introduced – it wasn't a union proposal – risk clauses in the previous agreement. The company introduced operational cash flow. At the time, no one thought it wouldn't be achieved, so much so that in 2014 a profit sharing bonus agreement was paid above five salaries. But in 2015,

---

21   In Chapter 3, for example, it will become clear how uncomfortable the company was during the strike in Canada with protests and actions which exposed shareholders and the Board of Directors, and with attempts to make public abroad the events in the Canadian operations.

with the drop in ore prices – ore prices were around 40 to 50 dollars – that indicator was not reached and, since there was this risk clause, what was provided for in the contract, in the collective agreement signed and approved by the workers, was that there was no payment. The 2015 agreement, from a judicial standpoint, is legal. It's perfectly valid, although the union had recommended not signing the agreement in exchange for the possibility of raising the cap to seven salaries. The workers decided to take the risk. Well then. The workers took the risk and paid the price for it. The price was that almost everyone here is in debt, almost everyone here is in economic hardships. After 15 years of the workers receiving profit sharing bonuses ranging between four and five average salaries, we had zero profit sharing bonus in 2015 with this proposal that the company is presenting now.

> GUILHERME ZAGALLO, at an assembly of Vale workers held
> in the port of Ponta da Madeira, on May 4, 2016

It was seven o'clock in the morning at a bus terminal that provides internal transport for workers to Vale's facilities in the port of Ponta da Madeira, in São Luís. STEFEM was organizing an assembly of workers who were arriving for the morning shift, along with those who had just finished their shift after a long night's work. Around 350 people listened to Guilherme Zagallo, the union's lawyer, struggling to explain to the workers, among the intricacies of the profit-sharing bonus agreement previously in force, the reasons why nobody had received the long-awaited annual amount. Accompanied by Geraldo Andrade and Ronaldo Silva, Zagallo showed how the deep drop in iron ore prices the previous year, the historic loss that had just been disclosed by the company and the cash generation below expectations meant, by the agreement previously voted by the workers, zero profit sharing bonus.[22] Months earlier, in a collective bargaining agreement frustrated at the end of 2015, Vale workers also suffered zero wage increases in a year in which inflation, according to INPC/

---

22   The crisis faced by the company was aggravated, as the union members also highlighted in their speeches at the assembly, by the impact caused by the collapse of the Fundão dam, ran by Samarco (a joint venture between BHP Billiton and Vale), located in the municipality of Mariana (in Minas Gerais), in November 2015. Guilherme Zagallo explicitly dealt with the Samarco case when addressing the unpredictability of mining activities and the need to reject the imposition of cash generation targets for the payment of profit-sharing bonuses.

IBGE data,[23] was 11.28%. The tension in the environment could be identified by the expression on the workers' faces.

The arrival in São Luís for interviews with members of STEFEM, the *Justiça nos Trilhos* network and Vale workers could not have occurred at a more elucidative moment of Vale's unions' articulation troubles. Pressured by the discontent of its rank-and-file members and by the company's decision to compress costs in a context of reduced prices in the global iron ore market, the union needed to react. Two weeks before my arrival, STEFEM had taken the initiative to close the company's main gate in protest at the announcement of the profit-sharing bonus non-payment. The union members' expectation was to pressure Vale into presenting a proposal for a profit-sharing bonus agreement for the next two years, without making the payment conditional on cash flow, so as to avoid a repetition of the situation experienced.

The day before the assembly, at STEFEM's new headquarters located in a modern business complex in São Luís' new downtown, Ronaldo Silva talked about the union's reaction to the protest:

> Recently, we mobilized differently than everyone else at the national level. And this was a motivating element that made Vale back down and present a proposal. We had to go to the company's door, it's been fifteen days more or less. We had to set fire to the company's door, tires, everything, we stopped the company for four hours. We didn't count on any workers, just us. The ones who stayed there, around 300, 400, listening to us. But most of them were in the surrounding area. No one came in.
>
> RONALDO SILVA, in an interview with STEFEM's board of directors

Despite the successful stoppage for a few hours, the union members regretted that the adhesion to the protest was very low. The workers, they described, had followed the union members' speeches in front of the burning pile of tires with a certain amount of suspicion. If this was, in STEFEM's opinion, the most radical protest made by Vale's unions against the company's hardening negotiations, the consequence was equally harsh: the company quickly obtained in court a prohibitory interdict which prevented another similar mobilization at the company's gates, establishing a heavy fine in case of non-compliance.

---

23   National Index of Consumer Prices, the average life cost in the eleven most important metropolitan areas. The index is measured by the IBGE. Information taken from a spreadsheet with the indicator's historical series available in https://www.ibge.gov.br/estat isticas/economicas/precos-e-custos/9258-indice-nacional-de-precos-ao-consumidor .html?=&t=series-historicas; accessed May 26, 2021.

The company also obtained the same type of decision from the courts in Pará, after a demonstration by the Metabase Carajás union, at the same time, in protest against the profit-sharing bonus non-payment and the cuts in benefits received only by local workers.[24]

Moving through the assembly, it was possible to talk to several workers. Most, at first, seemed afraid of the researcher's approach. Others, after a while, became convinced that the strange character in the landscape was not seeking information for supervisors or for the union, and decided to express some opinions about the lack of profit-sharing bonus that year and about their relationship with the union.

Nei, a maintenance mechanic at Vale for over twenty years, is one of them. His answers are more evasive while the recorder is on. For him, the gate shutdown promoted by STEFEM was not really unanimous among the workers, most of whom – although they would not be against the initiative because of the indignation caused by the lack of profit-sharing bonus – would consider any union mobilization ineffective. On the other hand, managers and supervisors showed their annoyance with the protest: "Oh, it did. They don't let it show, but they're bothered, that's for sure ... I even talked to a manager and he said he knew that the stoppage was going to happen."[25] With the tape recorder turned off, when the conversation seemed to be over, Nei resumes the subject and shows more disagreement with the events. He says that workers would certainly vote against the new proposal for Vale's profit-sharing bonus agreement for the next two years, out of indignation at the lack of payment for 2015, despite the fear that many would be feeling, since supervisors would daily emphasize to workers the bad situation of the labor market in the region. Alumar, another large company installed in the city, had been making many layoffs, which brought concern and insecurity about the future for Vale workers as well. Nei valued the union's role in showing the limits of the company's proposal. He, however, did not believe that his colleagues were willing to

---

24 In dealing with the social aspect of Vale's corporate strategy, that is, the influence of the corporation over civil society from emotional, cognitive and agency perspectives, Milanez et al., "A estratégia corporativa da Vale S.A.", 26–8, mention actions of 1) corporate social responsibility; 2) culture; 3) science/education; 4) justice; and 5) police. If the first three are related to the company's social and territorial embeddedness projects and the search for legitimacy for its actions, the last two refer to the coercion of social agents (such as unions or social and environmental movements), for which, above all, the use of the prohibitory interdict instrument is recurrent, in addition to lawsuits against social leaders and recourse to police action and to the company's private security bodies.

25 Nei, Vale's worker, interviewed by Thiago Aguiar during the assembly in São Luís, Brazil (May 2016).

mobilize, much less strike. The majority would vote in favor of the 'state of strike' proposed by the union in the assembly only for the desire to pressure the company in search of some improvement in the new agreement. This, by the way, was the same disposition of the union's board of directors. Another worker with over twenty years in the company, Anastácio, summed up his feelings and those of his colleagues:

> The company had accounting losses and decided not to pay us the profit sharing bonus. ... All the employees are outraged, everyone's in debt, unable to pay the debts. So, the employees kind of want to go on a state of strike. I think Vale should be sensitive and give some amount, even if it's a bonus for the work done in 2015, to the people who did a good job, a bonus to improve workers' lives.[26]

In his speech, Guilherme Zagallo says that the union had warned workers, when voting on the profit-sharing bonus agreement in 2014, that the proposal offered by Vale was risky because of the conditions present, including a 'trigger' that linked the profit sharing bonus payment to the company's cash generation. Ronaldo and Geraldo also emphasized and repeated the argument, trying to keep the union away from any responsibility for the situation experienced by the workers. Probably, the union members intended to avoid that, among the workers, visions like that of Vanderlei, a mechanic technician for six years at Vale, spread. For him, there is a strange relationship, "doubtful" in his words, between the union and the workers' collective. The profit-sharing bonus agreement proposal presented by the company, again conditioned by cash generation criteria, in his opinion, took into account "the market conditions." On the other hand, he opines that the non-payment for 2015 was due to unrealistic or poorly conducted negotiations by the union:

> The feeling today is against the union because ... the union should be firmer or bring a more real proposal, because sometimes we see the union's proposal, they ask for an adjustment that, in our opinion, we know Vale won't accept. Then, the union presents this proposal to Vale, it decreases a little and gets close to what they really wanted and what Vale was willing to accept. But then, when we see a proposal like this, people know that this is out of the question ... We know that Vale won't accept.

---

26   Anastácio, Vale's worker, interviewed by Thiago Aguiar during the assembly in São Luís, Brazil (May 2016).

So a lot of people think that this union ... that, in the end, it won't do any good, it seems that everything has already been arranged.[27]

Gustavo, 28 years old, who had been working at the company for a few months, followed the assembly with an apathetic expression. When asked about the discussions, he said he found the situation "boring," that he didn't understand what was going on and what the dispute between the union and the company was about. For him, what was important was the fact that he got a job with a signed contract after two years of unemployment.

After around 45 minutes of speeches by the lawyer and the two union members, the voting took place and Vale's proposal for a profit-sharing bonus agreement was rejected. According to STEFEM, the main problem with the proposal was the continuity of cash flow conditionality for profit sharing bonus payments, even though the company had signaled a higher cap of seven salaries, if all targets were met. For union members, this was a hoax, since it would never be possible to achieve what was established and the risk of not receiving profit sharing bonus again would be real in a context of instability in ore prices. The company signaled – in an attempt to convince workers who were under material pressure because they had not received the profit sharing bonus for 2015 – that if they accepted the new profit sharing bonus agreement, they would receive an advance of the eventual payment for 2016, in the amount of one salary, half of which would be paid ten days after signing the agreement and the other half about two months later. This was the proposal, the harms of which Guilherme Zagallo was trying to explain to the workers. In new rounds of negotiations, the new agreement was reached, still including conditions, which were lower than those initially proposed by Vale, since the cash generation trigger for the minimum profit-sharing bonus payment was removed from the agreement.

As a result of the agreement signed in February 2017, workers received profit sharing bonuses capped at 3.9 salaries relating to the 2016 results, an amount lower than that received before the drop in iron ore prices, but celebrated by the unions after the zero profit-sharing for 2015.[28] After the zero adjustment in salaries in 2015, with some recovery in iron ore prices throughout 2016, a new collective agreement was signed at the end of that year: there was an

---

27   Vanderlei, Vale's worker, interviewed by Thiago Aguiar during the assembly in São Luís, Brazil (May 2016).

28   As can also be seen in the virtual STEFEM and Metabase Carajás newsletters available in http://www.stefem.org.br/noticias/noticia.php?id=22 and http://metabasecarajas.com .br/noticias/noticia.php?id=133; accessed May 26, 2021.

8.5% adjustment in salaries, 13.6% in the food stamps and a R$ 1.000 bonus. Although the wage adjustment was slightly higher than the inflation rate for 2016 (6.58% according to INPC/IBGE data[29]), the small increase was far from recovering the accumulated losses from the previous year.

With the crisis and the deterioration of ore prices in the world market, Vale's workers in Brazil saw their wages flattened. The unions, however, celebrated the agreement reached,[30] given the conditions in the labor market and the challenges in negotiations with the company in the previous period. According to Guilherme Zagallo, the collective bargaining and profit-sharing bonus agreements in 2016 and 2017, in general, recovered the inflation rate of the period, but did not allow the recovery of the intense losses of 2015, even though the profit-sharing bonuses for 2017 was higher, with a seven base salaries cap:

> This generated a lot of wear and tear and led to the negotiations in 2016 and 2017, of Vale trying to, let's say, recompose its relationship with the workers and the unions, especially with the workers, who had been left with this double ... in the same year, zero profit sharing bonus and adjustment. In '16 and '17, these were years in which inflation was conceded, in which there was practically no ... We can't say that rights were taken away. There were some changes in the collective agreement that reduced rights: form of acquisition, period of enjoyment ... But we can't say that it was a pure and simple suppression, as had been happening in previous years. ... [In 2017,] it was a collective agreement of inflation concession, of renewal. The profit sharing bonus agreement was the highest in history, by the way. ... It was, on average, seven base salaries for each worker. ... A little above average. But this, let's say, is a form of recomposition of the company with its staff after what happened in 2015. ... Low inflation also facilitates wage replacement.
>
> GUILHERME ZAGALLO, Aguiar Interview

Profit sharing bonuses play a fundamental role in Vale workers' pay. With average salaries quite low, profit-sharing bonuses have become, along with some benefits such as healthcare plans and food stamps, the differentiating factor

---

29   Information taken from a spreadsheet with the indicator's historical series available in https://www.ibge.gov.br/estatisticas/economicas/precos-e-custos/9258-indice-nacional -de-precos-ao-consumidor.html?=&t=series-historicas; accessed May 26, 2021.

30   As can be seen in the virtual STEFEM and Metabase Carajás newsletters available in http://www.stefem.org.br/noticias/noticia.php?id=19 and http://metabasecarajas.com .br/noticias/noticia.php?id=130; accessed May 26, 2021.

between working at Vale or at any of its outsourced companies, since their salaries are often the same, as we will see through the workers' reports. When dealing with its payment policy, the company states only that it "respects the local minimum wage as defined by legislation."[31]

André Teixeira explains that Vale holds three different negotiations with its unions every year (a collective bargaining agreement with all unions in Brazil, regional agreements with local unions and a profit-sharing bonus agreement) and emphasizes the importance of variable pay for the company and for the workers:

> And another thing too that I believe very much is that I cannot bind because collective bargaining is a haggled relationship, right? Now, I can't bargain targets and other kinds of things. So, the Profit Sharing Program is a separate negotiation and today it's more important than the general negotiation for the unions and for the employees. It represents much more. The profit sharing bonus agreement, for instance, we paid an average of seven salaries last year. What other company in Brazil paid that last year? None.
>
> ANDRÉ TEIXEIRA, Aguiar Interview

Based on a survey of Vale's unions in the states of Minas Gerais and Rio de Janeiro,[32] Laura Nazaré de Carvalho concluded that variable pay at Vale is very important to the workers, whose gains, however, are tied to "their individual performance, that of their team, their department and the company, including issues of sustainability."[33] The fear of unemployment and the weakness of the unions make profit sharing bonuses "the only option in a false zero-sum game," which leads to "increased worker productivity and, consequently, stress-related illnesses."[34]

---

31 Vale S.A., *Relatório de Sustentabilidade Vale 2017*, 41.

32 Metabase Inconfidentes (Minas Gerais), Metabase Itabira (Minas Gerais) and Sindimina (Rio de Janeiro).

33 Carvalho, "Análise da ação dos sindicatos," 99.

34 Ibid, 110–1. The identification of the effects of profit-sharing bonuses in the increase of productivity, in the individualization of pay, in the weakening of collective organization and, eventually, in the dissemination of occupational diseases is not exactly new. It is a widespread situation mapped by the sociology of work literature. Similar effects were pointed out in the cosmetics sector in Thiago Aguiar, *Maquiando o trabalho: opacidade e transparência numa empresa de cosméticos global* (São Paulo: Annablume, 2017).

Because many people are deluded by the Vale worker. Roger did this very well, he publicized this very well to society. Internally he worked a lot on these issues, he put the Vale workers [as] the reference of 'backpackers' in Brazil. The guys with laptops, first generation computers, this and that, but if you look at the essence of their salary, they didn't have ... The portfolio of benefits that we had, that we built when we had the state-owned model, today, [in the] private model, [is] totally different. We're working, in the benefits portfolio, at the threshold of the law, nothing much above the law. It's no longer a company from the point of view of benefits, of salary, inter-esting to wager that it's worth working in Vale .... Vale workers have always been very threatened, mainly by the economic issue. Vale workers don't have a salary. They've always been bullied. Their wages, their average, ... either because of the profit sharing bonus agreement or because of those inherent professions, which involve overtime, involve night shifts, daily rates, risk premiums. That is, they earn a little more. ... [The base salary] is always low. ... If there's no profit sharing bonus, if it continues with this policy, nobody will stay in the company. Those good professionals don't stay because most of them are good. They don't stay, they go looking for another market. With the market heated up, there was a lot of movement at this time of the good peak, without the crisis starting to descend, a lot of movement mainly within Vale. Vale was very concerned about this. They even made an agreement, here in our region, they had an agreement so that Alumar wouldn't take workers from Vale, Vale wouldn't take workers from Alumar and from the other large companies here.

RONALDO SILVA, in a meeting with STEFEM's board of directors

Therefore, after not having received a profit-sharing bonus payment for 2015, great attention was paid to the targets proposed by Vale in the 2016 profit shar-ing bonus agreement, which generated a gate shutdown in the company's doors at São Luís and a similar action in Carajás, whose union is known even by peers as not very confrontational. There, however, in addition to the profit-sharing bonus non-payment, as will be seen below, Vale cut the payment of the '14th and 15th salaries,' established by previous regional collective agreements (only for that production unit).

João, who works in a maintenance cell (specializing in lubricating vehicles at one of the mines in Carajás), serves as a rank-and-file director at Metabase Carajás. According to his account, the loss of the '14th and 15th salaries' and the absence of wage and profit sharing bonus increases in 2015 have made jobs in service providers for Vale more interesting and better paid. For him, the fact that there are outsourced workers performing the same functions as Vale workers in mining activities in Carajás, eventually receiving higher wages, is a cause of great discontent among workers. João also said that, in his area, while tractor, mining truck and lubrication train drivers at Vale received no wage adjustment in 2015, outsourced workers from a company that provides transport services to the mining company received a 10% adjustment that year.[35] João spoke about his dissatisfaction with the wage gap between company and outsourced workers, mentioning an episode experienced in his team:

João:
Our company is a very good company. What kills our company today, as far as we can see, is bad management. Because, like, we see our friends, ourselves, complaining because, let's say ... You see the truck. If you see it up close, it's almost as tall as this building here. So what happens? You'll be amazed. The other day I was there and there were these trucks that haul diesel oil, there are these large trucks, aren't there? There are some that bring diesel from Belém to there, Marabá, and take it there. In this heavy station where we work, there are some barrels, a very large reservoir where the trucks come and distribute it. The guy fills the drums there, this reservoir, which is to supply the trucks, the machinery. ... And there are trains which fill up there [at the mine]. Then one of these days a group of people arrived from Belém. They were taking diesel oil there. Then there's contact, everyone stays in a room there. And when there's nothing to do, we stay there talking, chatting. Then he saw one of these trucks [refers to the huge trucks transporting ore] and took some photos. ... Then he asked me: 'João, a truck like that, this guy must make good money ... 450 tonnes?' I said: 'Yes, 450 tonnes.' Then he asked me what his paycheck was. I think, we think that's what the company leaves to be desired, there are many failures. ... The actual paycheck doesn't help. A truck like this has an operator who gets only R$1.400. A responsibility for someone who's just entering! Now to find someone who earns R$ 2.000 it is hard work. Only those who are very old. ... That was the

---

35   Especially the transportation of workers from certain points of Parauapebas to the mines.

answer I gave him: no, it's not as much as you think. 'You mean he makes less than me?' And he makes R$3.000 there. He makes R$3.000. I said, 'You make enough for two of those operators.' So, those on the outside think it's one thing, but the reality is something else.

Thiago Aguiar: *In what ways do you think the outside impression is different from reality?*

Paycheck, for example, right? Paycheck, like I told you. For example, it says: 'Valuing those who make our company.' 'Life first' ... You know what I mean? So, when you preach something and you don't do it, it's as if you were cheating, as if you were selling a fake advertisement. And today we feel, the worker in general, we feel harmed. Because, like, what is it that you value? 'Growing and evolving together', which is what it preaches, right? This is what you think: growing and evolving together, whatever good I achieve for myself, I wish the same for you. But now it's different. For example, now, with this S11D project, many people got a position to work there. They asked for a transfer and everything, but the supervisor, by order of the company, won't let them go, you know? So it's preventing the person from growing and being happy, from evolving. They preach one thing and do another. There are many little details that get in the way. There are many people leaving the union and blaming them, who think that the union is to blame.[36]

Located in the municipality of Canaã dos Carajás, S11D is a huge complex of iron mines, inaugurated in December 2016, from which Vale expects to extract 90 million tonnes of iron ore per year.[37] The creation of the S11D project in Carajás, mentioned by João, also revealed another discontent that, according to him, is very present within the workers' collective: opaque criteria that are very dependent on affinities with supervisors to obtain mobility in the internal

---

36   João, Vale's worker, interviewed by Thiago Aguiar in Parauapebas, Brazil (July 2016).
37   In Chapter 4 it will be possible to approach the project's implementation in more detail, which was the company's biggest investment in recent years, and to deal with its centrality in Vale's current corporate strategy.

labor market. Several workers who would like to leave their cells in the Carajás mines and occupy open positions in the new S11D mines were prevented by the restrictions imposed by supervisors and managers, while the company recruited its workforce from outside the company for the new open positions.

Using the opportunity offered by the company (which pays 75% of a technical or higher education course to workers who study), João graduated as a technician and wants to leave his job as a mechanic to work, with better pay, as a technician in S11D. However, the encouragement for workforce schooling generates frustration due to the impermeability of internal mobility and the inaccessibility of supervisors and managers. "But it's like this: you graduate and it doesn't give you an opportunity. ... Today, if you talk to workers in the company, in any area, everyone's unhappy,"[38] summarizes João.

This aspect is consistent with the indications of Maria Cecília Minayo[39] on the frustration of Itabira workers with the internal labor market, highly dependent on personal favoritism in the then state-owned company still in the period of military dictatorship.

> The workers of this period metamorphosed into true iron men, as if they were equal to the steel strength of the equipment, allowing themselves to be exploited to the utmost, compensating for the alienation from the product by the mastery of that part of the labor process for which they were needed. In turn, this willingness to serve CVRD at all times and in all circumstances, reminiscent of the barracks readiness regime, will also be capitalized by the workers. Their attitude of total dedication will allow them to claim promotions, personal favors, placing themselves closer to the echelons of decision-making or as possible candidates for positions of responsibility.[40]

> I think it's bad management, bad administration, you know? It formed a kind of monopoly, ... because you have a position up there, you think it has to be done the way you want. ... It's from the top down. That's why it hurts us. Because, like, we see something like this that's wrong. Then you take it to your superior and complain: look, this is happening, this and this, I think it's wrong, take action. And the person does nothing, doesn't take action, becomes complacent, that is, agrees with what's happening,

---

38   Aguiar Interview.

39   Maria Cecília Minayo, *De ferro e flexíveis: marcas do Estado empresário e da privatização na subjetividade operária* (Rio de Janeiro: Garamond, 2004).

40   Ibid, 143.

do you understand? So it becomes something unviable. Nowadays, you
see something wrong, you can't even say anything, because you know
that the person won't solve it. So, I mean, the person who's there doesn't
give a damn.

JOÃO, Aguiar Interview

Minayo's records on the arbitrariness of the criteria for registering workers[41] at
CVRD in Itabira are repeated in João's statement about the situation in Carajás
more than four decades later. Among the consequences, one can point to
worker fragmentation, competition and conflict in a "real dispute among partners."[42] According to João, only trainees, with a base salary of R$1.350, enter
the company with a defined salary. The other positions are paid according to
an agreement made individually with the recruiter. In João's cell, for example, there are workers registered as 'Mechanic I' and others as 'Mechanic II',
although they perform the same function and earn different salaries.

| João: | What people think is bad is, for example, I have the same time as you ... We both enter together. And you enter with [R$] 2,000 and me with [R$] 1,500. There are a lot of people like that. ... They say the guy has to 'know how to register,' right? The guy who will give you the job, the manager who will put you in the company, will evaluate you and will register you, it depends on him. It's his word. If he wants to give you a salary of [R$] 2,000 he'll give you; if he wants to give you a smaller one, he will. That's what it is. The company doesn't have a rule that can ... Not from the company. The manager is the one who says the word, when he calls you in the cold room to register you. 'I can pay you R$2,000 in your wallet: can you do it?' Then you say: 'no, give me [R$] 2,500, then I'll stay with you.' 'Well, that's good. I'll file you at [R$] 2,500.' Or if by some chance he says, 'You're going to enter with [R$] 1,500, do you accept?' Then you say, 'I'll do it.' 'Then you'll get [R$] 1,500, the other one who came and spoke first will get [R$] 2,500.' |

---

41   The process by which a new hire is assigned a position and given a salary.
42   Ibid, 201.

> *Thiago Aguiar:*   *And does that create conflict among workers?*
> Absolutely! ... Because you feel devalued, discouraged. I
> even have several friends who have left for this reason.
> ... Arguments. I know it's not your fault. I know it's bad
> management. A certain annoyance with the people up
> there. These guys leave a lot to be desired, you know?
> Aguiar Interview

Despite experiencing common problems and having the challenge of conducting local, scattered discussions with Vale based on proposals submitted nationally by the company (annual collective agreement or profit-sharing bonus agreement), Vale's workers' unions have many challenges in coordinating unified actions. The company obviously benefits from this situation, and we will show later how it stimulates division among its unions. Such problems are openly mentioned by the union members during the interviews. At the assembly in the port of São Luís, Ronaldo Silva addressed this issue in his speech to the workers:

> We can't passively accept this imposition and then what we're used to
> hearing comes along: 'The union in Pará has already approved, why is
> Maranhão resisting? Unions in Minas Gerais will already receive one
> month paycheck, why is Maranhão resisting? The union somewhere has
> already approved, why is Maranhão resisting?' Unity is fundamental in
> any association. Unity is fundamental in any party, in family, with friends.
> Now, we can't accept a unity which puts the workers in a humiliating con-
> dition. We have to reject it. It's a problem for those who accepted it.
> RONALDO SILVA, during the assembly

2   Collective Power Weakened

As discussed in the Introduction, collective power refers to "the actions of collective agents who seek to influence companies at particular locations in GPNs, their respective governments and sometimes international agencies." Examples of collective power agents include "trade unions, employers associations, and organizations that advance particular economic interests ..., NGOs concerned with human rights, environmental issues, etc."[43]

---

43   Jeffrey Henderson et al., "Global Production Networks and the Analysis of Economic Development," *Review of International Political Economy* 8, no. 3 (2002): 451.

In this book, the focus of our attention has been directed to the collective power exercised by Vale's unions. The imposition of a collective agreement which froze wages and the absence of variable pay, essential for the reproduction of workers and their families in a context of high inflation, showed the unions' constraints in offering opposition to corporate attacks. Vale, therefore, has favorable conditions to deal with market fluctuations through flexibility (in hiring and payment) of its workforce, making it absorb part of the operational adjustments to the benefit of the company's profits and the distribution of dividends to its shareholders.

In a comparative study of corporate power in three mining contexts in Minas Gerais,[44] Rodrigo Santos and Bruno Milanez[45] describe three dimensions of power: 1) the first "focuses on the influence of one actor over another (or others), as 'power over' ... specific actors", a conception that "emphasizes the exercise of power to the detriment of the ownership of power and its related resources;" 2) the second is related to "the actor's capacity to create obstacles to the emergence of grievances as public issues," treating "not only the influence of one actor over another (or others), but also the obstruction of his/her capacity for action;" finally, 3) the third refers to "'latent conflict' situations [which] are based on the possibility of an actor granting legitimacy to another's action despite his/her own objective interests," bringing out the "possibility of false or manipulated consensus."[46]

Based on this three-dimensional power dimension, Santos and Milanez state that there is an "absence of contestation to the corporation"[47] in Itabira, in which Vale can exercise its power in all three dimensions, "fram[ing] the (non-) emergence of public issues [and mobilizing] adherence of individual and collective actors, a process which illustrates the third dimension of power [through a] contradictory combination between granting legitimacy to powerful agents and opposition to the objective interests of a collectivity."[48] This would be due to Itabira's company town context and the end of the mineral cycle, given the economic dependence on mining activity, which reduced the

44   Anglo American in Conceição do Mato Dentro, CSN in Congonhas and Vale in Itabira.

45   Rodrigo S. P. Santos and Bruno Milanez, "Corporate Power and Economic Action: Considerations Based on Iron Ore Mining." in *'Civilizing' Resource Investments and Extractivism: Societal Negotiations and the Role of Law*, ed. Wolfram Laube and Aline R.B. Pereira (Zurich: LIT VERLAG, 2020), 259–260.

46   Steven Lukes, *Power: A Radical View* (Basingstoke: Palgrave Macmillan, 2005), 28 quoted in Santos and Milanez, "Corporate Power and Economic Action," 260.

47   Santos and Milanez, "Corporate Power and Economic Action," 271.

48   Ibid.

propensity to contestation by Itabira's political and social actors. Therefore, Vale was successful in sustaining a "manipulated consensus regime" in Itabira.[49]

The analysis of Vale's corporate power in Itabira presents similarities and differences with what was found in field observations. In Parauapebas, for example, Vale is also the major local employer, even though, unlike Itabira, Carajás is in full expansion of mineral extraction. As seen, in 2015, workers and union members, from STEFEM and Metabase Carajás, said that unemployment exerted great pressure on workers, who feared mobilization initiatives even though they experienced great dissatisfaction with the company's impositions.[50] In spite of that, in the end, the collective agreement with zero adjustment and the proposal for a new profit sharing bonus agreement were accepted, despite clauses similar to the ones which caused the absence of payment in the previous agreement. In other words, forms of 'manipulated consensus' were organized there as well – whereby legitimacy is conferred to the action of another, even if it goes against one's own objective interests. The dispersion of Vale's local unions all over Brazil and the company's union strategy, which seeks to keep them fragmented and submit them to its corporate power, seem to be at the root of the company's success in frustrating the emergence of latent conflict.

Field observations in São Luís and Parauapebas shed light on the various tactics employed by Vale to weaken the unions' collective power. It is useful, in this regard, to reproduce André Teixeira's lengthy reconstruction of the 2015 collective agreement negotiations and the acceptance, by unions and workers, of the absence of an adjustment and of profit-sharing bonus payment. The labor relations manager showed how he obtained a kind of tacit acceptance of his justifications and proposals, to which the proximity with the union leadership and the direct action of the company's managers in convincing the workers contributed, who mostly voted in favor of the agreement in assemblies.

This last aspect – the managers' action in convincing workers – is always mentioned by union members as a source of problems for worker mobilization. In São Luís, workers interviewed with no relation to STEFEM confirmed to the researcher the massive presence of managers in the workers' assembly. The aforementioned segmentation of the company's worker qualifications,

---

49   Ibid.

50   For Guilherme Zagallo, this aspect was determinant. With little mobilization history, in a period of recession and with high unemployment, the unions simply could not resist: "In fact, it's not that there was support. In fact, there was a weak confrontation capacity for that moment, proportional, let's say, to the intensity of the measures that were adopted by the company."

whereby operational workers receive courses and lectures with the indirect objective of keeping them away from union organization, seems to play an important role in the mobilization challenges at Vale.

André Teixeira: In 2015, late 2015, 2016, the price of iron ore, which today is around [US$] 65 – it had already reached almost [US$] 200 -, was [US$] 36. Our share value reached R$11. Our debt was unpayable. That year, we ... offered zero adjustment, in the general agreement, zero, okay? And, in the bonus, in a difficult year – and that other companies in Brazil were giving – because we were hit directly by the issue of the Asian market, of Asia. We had an approval, with a secret voting, secret voting! Some were with open voting, others with secret voting, but, on the ones that were with secret voting, our proposal had 85% of approval. Higher than in previous years, [in which] we had real gains. So, that helped me a lot to show this to the company internally: the workers understood and accepted it. Now, in the following year, when we were just too bad, that was the craziest – this was the craziest! – profit sharing bonus was zero. Because of an agreement we had made since 2015, profit sharing bonus was zero, okay? ... In 2017, we did a mood survey, the survey is confidential, it's not identified, no one has ever been identified there. ... Engagement, engagement was measured, they even took external people, it was one of the highest. People realized that we could have had higher unemployment and today, even the people themselves when we talk – I mean supervisors – [say:] thank God we got through that phase and the staff reduction was very small.

Thiago Aguiar: *But, when these proposals appeared, zero adjustment in 2015 and, in the following year, zero profit sharing bonus, were there no objections? Were there no issues in the relationship with the unions?*
It's not easy, no, this business that it's easy, there's no such thing, okay? It was very difficult. It was a period in which we had a very extensive negotiation. ... So, our negotiation is long. We started to show to the unions what we were going through. He said: 'But, André, I'm not going

to defend zero. How could I go there and defend zero? So I won't go, I'll never go'. So, I had meetings with the supervisors, with the managers, so that they could show the company to them. And, at this point, Vale has something that goes back a long time. People know the company. If you go around Vale today, if you ask a mechanic, he'll tell you with great precision how much the price of iron ore is. So, the openness of information at Vale was very great, and this is one of the things that helps us a lot in the relationship between capital and labor. So, people knew about the difficult moment we were going through. Now, it was very difficult. We had contestation. Internal movements arose contesting, wanting it ... Some movements arose wanting to strike and other stuff, but they were very localized. We had many problems, yes.

So you managed to get around this situation by having a direct relationship with the workers, informing, discussing ...
Directly and indirectly as well, I mean, directly, informing about the negotiation and the company's situation. And also through the union. Because the union ... It has several ways, it doesn't need to be defended. It can even hit, but it doesn't have to hit very hard. The language of the unions – and I had a hard time understanding this, and my language also has to be like this – the union ... it's emotional and zero rational. Emotional to the extreme, right? Very emotional. And I always had very rational communication. My communication with the union was extremely ... with the employees, it was extremely rational. Today, I try to counterbalance a little. Why? Some people like this emotional communication. But, the union doesn't get there and say: 'Oh, people, this year it has to be zero.' Now, it goes like this: 'This is the situation of the company and we have this option, this option, this option. It's up to you.' That's one thing. Now, 'This company is making millions and millions in profit' – which wasn't true – 'It's this, that and the other thing.' They could have built a discourse that would have greatly complicated our action. They didn't.

Do you believe that this is due to an effort to talk to the unions? Why haven't they done that if they could have?

I told you that in the beginning I thought that the positions were antagonistic, right? And I built my vision about the union very much in function of the bulletins that I saw from the union, and the bulletins attacked the company. Man, if he's attacking my company I'm going to attack him too, ok? That was how I saw it. Until, in a certain moment, when I started to realize – and I was also helped – ... that we can have different opinions. And, when the union member realizes that the company doesn't want to destroy him, he also starts not wanting to destroy the company. ... So, the big change that took place in this relationship, and that I tell people, is this: I'm not a partner, because a partner also isn't true, but we're not enemies. Now, how does the company see the union and how does the union see the company? You can see it as a partner, as an opponent, or as collaboration or as a partner, as understanding. It's not a partner, do you understand? But we're not enemies, we're not opponents: we're in divergent positions, in many cases, but many times we reach an understanding. So, this discovery ... is that today we achieved this good relationship.

Aguiar Interview

The "collaboration" of unions described by Teixeira is certainly related to the way union negotiations are organized at Vale. The dispersion of workers' representation and the obstacles for unions to act in unity are key features of the company's union strategy. According to union members, in negotiations for annual collective bargaining agreements and for the profit-sharing bonus agreement, the company presents a single proposal to all unions. However, negotiations are carried out separately by the company in three groups, bringing together fourteen mining and railway unions:[51]

---

51   There is some disagreement about the composition of the three groups, as it is common for unions to change groups for negotiation, for example after changes in the board of directors. The fourteen unions from the production sectors which negotiate in three groups are not the only ones in the company. Mentioning data from the *Instituto Observatório Social* (Social Observatory Institute), Carvalho counts 52 unions, "which represented the

1)   Railroad workers of Belo Horizonte (Minas Gerais), Metabase Belo Horizonte (Minas Gerais), Metabase Brumadinho (Minas Gerais), Metabase Carajás (Pará), Metabase Mariana (Minas Gerais), Extractive Union of Corumbá and Ladário (Mato Grosso do Sul), *Sindicato das Indústrias Extrativas dos Estados do Amapá e do Pará* [Extractive Industry Union of the Amapá and Pará States], or STIEAPA;

2)   Metabase Itabira (Minas Gerais), Metabase Rio de Janeiro, Sindifer (Espírito Santo), STEFEM (Maranhão, Pará and Tocantins);

3)   Metabase Inconfidentes (Minas Gerais).[52]

Although the negotiations involve groups, the results are the same for all fourteen unions in Brazil, with the exception of any specific collective agreements signed between the company and any of the local unions. Some benefits (such as the '14th and 15th salaries' withdrawn by the company in Carajás in 2015) were the result of agreements of this type. In a meeting with STEFEM's board of directors, Ronaldo Silva said that negotiating in groups would have the practical effect of consolidating a kind of 'divide and conquer' game, which we could infer from the various statements of union members on the subject:

> This is one more tactic, one more pressure instrument that it uses, that all the unions get together, which are distributed in three groups. But these groups, in reality, are just the name. In the end, the proposal is the same for all. And these groups play the company's game, because, as soon as it finds more fragility in a group, that's where it starts to put its proposal to vote. And this reflects all over Brazil. Especially when there's money involved, because, generally, there's either a bonus, a premium, but in exchange for some benefit that it will take away. And then those who are more fragile, already from a very fragile group between the three, these more fragile already serve as a reference for the debate. ... It negotiates with the three groups, but at the time of the agreement's discussion, it starts to extract results through those who start making assemblies.
>
> RONALDO SILVA, in a meeting with STEFEM's board of directors

---

diversity of professional categories verified in the company: miners, railroad workers, engineers, administrative, technicians, among others." See Carvalho, "Análise da ação dos sindicatos," 93.

52   The Metabase Mariana (Minas Gerais) union also belonged to this group when the union's former leadership was linked to CSP-Conlutas. There are still two other entities – Químicos da Baixada Santista (São Paulo) and SIMA (from Fertilizantes Araxá in Minas Gerais) – which the interviewed union members could not indicate to which of the negotiation groups they belonged.

The company, despite the negotiation in groups, would then carry out a two-pronged pressure: on the one hand, involving closer unions, which would quickly approve the proposal presented, thus pressuring unions who were willing to hold more assemblies or to resist the company. This was because, as some unions begin to approve Vale's proposal, in which some kind of bonus or premium was usually included, supervisors and managers of the eventually 'rebellious' areas took the stage to convince workers to pressure their union to approve the agreement and guarantee the receiving of bonuses which, in other parts of the country, were already being paid.

> **Ronaldo Silva:** We've already had several cases of this nature. In the last one, what happened? Only us and the people from Mariana rejected it. Everybody had already approved. It's that pressure. ... It starts over there with the less politicized, weaker, less interested ones, then this political pressure comes over to those who are resisting. 'Look, everybody already got it, you didn't get it'. Then the worker, on the other hand, comes against the union. We reject it ... The most we have ever done here, not in profit sharing bonuses, but in collective agreements, with this kind of posture, rejecting, contradicting other unions nationwide, is to take it to the Superior Labor Court to try to make a bargaining agreement viable. But, even so, the workers don't have the patience needed, they don't have the understanding, maybe, so you end up giving up halfway through.

> ***Thiago Aguiar:*** *If, then, you are the only ones not to accept it, this becomes a legal dispute ...*
> It becomes a legal war. Now, for that to be sustained, the workers would need to support us. Then, there's the story of the petition, Vale throws in a petition, it pressures ...
> Aguiar Interview

André Teixeira is explicit when affirming that the union division favors the company, but he is evasive as to the reasons for the fragmentation of the entities. For him, the division does not occur because of different affiliations to union centers or different political orientations, but simply because of 'fights' and 'divisions' among the unions. The creation of three-group negotiations was, according to Teixeira, a request from the unions to make the negotiations more 'evolved'.

André Teixeira: I will refer to Vale S.A. only – I am not referring to the Vale Group – just companies that are 100% Vale. We have fourteen unions. These unions, for historical reasons, have already negotiated together and had fights among them. We had a negotiation, for example, it was scheduled – I didn't go near this area, I just tell the story – ... to start at 2pm. At 7 o'clock in the morning there were already people in the room to get the central place at the table, they fought a lot among themselves. Then, at a certain moment, in order for the negotiation to be more evolved, at their request ... At their request! Many people say the company was setting them up. At their request. Of course the company benefits from that. They divided themselves into groups. Today, we have three negotiation groups, we already had four, today we have three groups.

Thiago Aguiar: *Do groups organize for ideological or political reasons?*
No, no. At Vale, it's for historical reasons. The division by union centers is just a figure of speech. We have CUT unions that don't sit down together. It's very much in function of the union's leadership line. So, if, for example, the leadership changes, their organization changes, it doesn't bother them. The influence of the union centers in our negotiations is zero. It's zero! It's not zero because Conlutas[53] has some influence, but apart from Conlutas, it's zero. The Conlutas union sits apart from the others. ... One of the groups is Conlutas, but this one is separated. What leads to this division are the political fights between them. ... So, these compositions often lead to division. There's a bigger concentration of a group that is CUT's, but there are unions from CUT that are not [of the same group]. And there's another group that has predominance, which used to be *Força Sindical* [Union Force],

---

53   *Coordenação Nacional de Lutas* [National Coordination of Struggles].

today there are many people from UGT,[54] but today
there are also people from *Nova Central*. But, I mean,
it's not the centers which determine it. It's the disputes
between the unions that are there. And there are also
some cases of disputes between the unions at the rank
and file level. So these are the disputes between them.
Now, in conducting this process, I try to have a lot of
respect ... Actually I don't just try, we do have an absurd
respect for all the unions. ... Some have the posture of
being more quarrelsome with us, others favor more the
search for dialogue. It doesn't mean that one gets more
and the other gets less. And we make the tables, we make
separate and simultaneous tables. And it's even funny
that, when we're going to present the proposals, which
are the same, we set a time: 'at 11 o'clock we are going to
present proposals.' ... And sometimes they keep sending
me messages, for us to make the compositions. Then we
interrupt, we talk ... We interrupt and talk a lot, but when
we formulate our proposal, we present it simultaneously
at all the tables so that there is no ... that one feels more
privileged than the other.

Aguiar Interview

When dealing with the divisions, the labor relations manager affirms his
"respect" for the unions, but the tone he uses sometimes borders on infantiliz-
ing the union leaders – as when he brings up the anxiety about the meetings'
schedule and the existence of some more "quarrelsome" unions -, which helps
to reveal the subordinate position of the union organizations in negotiations
in which they are weakened by dispersion.

Sérgio Rosa, former president of Vale's Board of Directors, when asked about
the fragmentation of unions, also implicitly recognizes that it benefits the
company's labor relations strategy:

You can't say, in a game ... If we understand that capital and labor are two
things in opposition, you can't blame the other team for my team's flaws.
... You can't place the blame. I'm not the one to say that your defender is

---

54   *União Geral dos Trabalhadores* [General Union of Workers].

too short and my striker is tall: look, do something ... So the game is the game. If they can't get it together ...

SÉRGIO ROSA, Aguiar Interview

Trade union members lament the retreat of unity since the end of the state-owned period, when a national coordination of unions was created in the period of resistance to privatization. It was called *Associação de Sindicatos de Trabalhadores da Vale* [Association of Vale Workers' Unions], or Aval, based in Rio de Janeiro and maintained by contributions from Vale's unions. After privatization, dispersion was imposed until, from 2002 to 2009, CUT (with support from Conlutas and the participation of other centers) tried at times to organize a national (and later international) trade union network for Vale. For reasons which will be presented in Chapter 3, the network failed.

For Artur Henrique,[55] former president of CUT (2006–2012), the links to different centers explain the division: "In Vale's case, there are a lot of unions and a lot of unions from different centers, with different conceptions. ... This unity is very difficult." However, Carlos Andrade,[56] a CUT leader who participated in the unsuccessful initiatives to organize the Vale union network, points to the company's action to stimulate conflicts between unions:

These unions, when the unit that existed at Vale was dissolved, it was due to Vale's interference, which made this division, giving stuff to some people and not giving to the others. Like, for example, the people from Pará had a '14th salary' that nobody else had. Why did it give a '14th salary' to all the workers in Tonhão's local after Tonhão took over the union? Because he was already old there, ... he took over the union two or three years after the union had been formed. I mean, there was the first board and then he joined the second one. He must be there until today. ... So, Vale had this posture and this caused fights, like, for example, the guy from Espírito Santo ... and the other railroad, with the miners who throw ore inside the wagon, which was [represented by] the Minas union. They had an ugly fight between the two, which ended up in court, and there was a lawsuit between the two. Then the union from Pará joined the fight too and the one from Espírito Santo sued Pará's union president.[57]

---

55   Who authorized the use of his name and statements in an interview with Thiago Aguiar in São Paulo, Brazil (August 2018).

56   Fictitious name.

57   Carlos Andrade, CUT organizer, interviewed by Thiago Aguiar in São Bernardo do Campo, Brazil (April 2016).

Tonhão, leader of Metabase Carajás, agrees that the division of Vale's workers' unions makes negotiations difficult, but points out the "radicalism" of certain union currents as responsible for the fragmentation, making union action inefficient and unable to promote improvements for workers in production.

> ***Thiago Aguiar:*** *Does this dispersion make negotiation time difficult?*
> **Tonão:** It does, it does ... Oh ... One doesn't want to see the other's face, says the other one is a coward, I don't know what else, blah, blah, blah. The other is a neoliberal, the other wants to be a socialist and then all hell breaks loose. A rotten radicalism. ... The more it's divided, the better to manage. The more divided, the better. Which company wouldn't like it? We're the ones who are selfish and irresponsible, who can't organize ourselves and have unity. We fight for a piece of the cake, for a burnt matchstick, because one looked at the other wrong ... We fight for nothing. Then we get divided and that's great for the company. It's really our fault, isn't it?
>
> *And have there been attempts to unify the unions? Is there any effect on production?*
> Oh, many. CUT intervened trying to help, *Nova Central,* several heads in action and they can't unify it. The guys are crazy. ... In production? It doesn't affect anything. They fight like cats and dogs all the same. The union yells here, yells there and production continues the same way, it doesn't interfere at all.
> Aguiar Interview

In turn, Geraldo Andrade[58] – who, in the port assembly, showed his discontent with Vale's profit-sharing bonus agreement proposal and tried to convince workers to vote for its rejection – did not hide his resignation with the situation in an interview. Due to the usual dispersion and logic imposed by Vale in negotiations, as in many other times, STEFEM would not be able to resist for long:

---

58   Geraldo Andrade, union leader, interviewed by Thiago Aguiar in São Luís, Brazil (May 2016).

Geraldo Andrade: The right thing at this moment would be if we had everybody together. The great demotivation of some of our comrades, and of yours truly, is because of that. Because you can't do it. You can't do anything alone. It's no use thinking that a single union, like this one, or any union at all … Alone … 'Oh, it has political autonomy, it has legal autonomy, the legislation'… But it alone won't be worth anything because the pressure from others, the behavior of others … Can we say we'll never sign this agreement? We can't. Are we a strong union? Yes, we are. But can we guarantee that we won't sign this agreement? At the end of the day nobody knows, because we can be dragged by the workers …. So, in other words, we're living a moment in which, let's say, it's a globe of death. Any failure … Why? There's no point in setting up any instrument of resistance and guaranteeing that we'll succeed. Because the external set is not favorable, economically speaking, the country's political condition, everything is conspiring against us … The emerging needs of the workers, especially at the base of the pyramid. Because telling them that in ten days after signing they'll receive a month's paycheck is better than nothing. … And because of this process of not having a union collective action, and not having a set of actions, … together, all the unions in the same line: then whatever's good for João is good for Manoel too, right? But, no. Tomorrow we'll probably have a local already approving it, and it's no small local. Do you know which one is it? The largest one, Carajás! … And from Carajás the others come too.

Thiago Aguiar: *Is the negotiation with Carajás always smoother?*
[After a brief silence] I don't know.
Aguiar Interview

3   The First Driver of the Carajás Railroad

STEFEM occupies two floors of a modern business complex in the new and wealthy downtown of São Luís. The ground floor is where members are attended to: there is a spacious reception area, with new and comfortable furniture, and reception rooms. On one of the upper floors, the board of directors is installed. The environment is very reminiscent of a well-equipped corporate office. The board meeting room is large, with a huge table, where we had our first conversation. On one of the side walls, there is a panel with a gray world map, showing Brazil in orange and all the other countries where Vale operates in a darker silver color. Facing the room, a work area organizes the union secretariats' workshops and the president's office. A hallway leads to the large and well-equipped room where Ronaldo Silva works.

The union member was very receptive to the researcher and his questions. With the tape recorder on, in formal interview situations, he did not evade answering any of the questions, even though, in informal situations[59] he was more explicit, especially on some issues where there are divergences within Vale's union movement and his own union's board of directors: among such controversial issues is the support to the strike in Canada. Regarding Vale – especially concerning labor relations in the company – Ronaldo kept a clearly oppositional speech, even though he recognizes and honors the company's history and its economic success.[60]

STEFEM's new and modern headquarters replaced the big house in São Luís' historic center, where the union operated from for decades. Ronaldo said he was proud of both, since, according to him, by his own initiative, the entity was able to organize itself and accumulate such an estate. The union leader took me to see the old headquarters on a rainy day in the capital of Maranhão. He almost always drove around the city in a big pickup truck, one of the union's vehicles – according to him, the truck is necessary to travel to its countryside branches, traveling along the railroad's path over bad roads. When we arrived at the big house, he showed me the details of a renovation he intended to complete on the site. According to his plans, it would be used to host a course provided by the union in partnership with government institutions through Pronatec (the National Program for Access to Technical Education, a federal

---

59   It was possible to live with the union member for practically a week, accompanying him in meetings, in the assembly held in the port that week and in social occasions, such as meals shared with him and other union members.

60   This information is highlighted here because of the very different attitude of Tonhão, leader of Metabase Carajás, as will be shown in the following.

government scholarship program). The economic and political crises – the interviews in São Luís occurred days after the Chamber of Deputies accepted the request for impeachment of President Dilma Rousseff – cast doubt on the viability of the plans, but the renovation of the historic mansion continued.

After the visit to the old headquarters, Ronaldo took the researcher to one of the city's main postcards, the *Palácio dos Leões* [Lions Palace], which houses the state government, and made a point of calling a friend of his who was the governor's aide. We were asked to come inside. Inside the palace, surprised by the impromptu 'schedule' the union member had organized that afternoon, I watched Ronaldo's conversation with government advisors about the crisis in the country and the future's uncertainties. Prudence kept me quiet during most of the time I spent seeking to listen and getting to know the concerns of some members of the local governor's team,[61] who, little more than a year ago, had removed José Sarney's political group from the state government. One of the advisors – the aide who took the phone call and invited the visitors in – showed us on his cell phone a video of PT's local party's political broadcast, the party of which he is state leader. This advisor also joked about Ronaldo's popularity in their state, which, in his opinion, should make him run for federal deputy: "I always insist." Ronaldo, who liked the compliment, smiled. The visit wouldn't end before we were escorted, both Ronaldo and the researcher, in a walk through the halls of the huge palace, an old colonial fort. Currently a PT member, the trade unionist was a supporter of the *Partido Comunista do Brasil* [Communist Party of Brazil], the PCdoB, in the early 1990s, soon after starting his union activism forged in the 1989 Vale strike.

In his room at the union's new headquarters, Ronaldo told me how he became a company worker. Born in the countryside of Maranhão, he moved to São Luís to take a technical course in the late 1970s. In 1982, shortly after graduating, he was recruited by one of the companies that worked in the construction of the Carajás Railroad and, in 1983, he joined CVRD. The mining company would then hire young graduates from technical schools and Senai courses (National Service for Industrial Training, a network of professional schools) in Maranhão and in neighboring states, such as Pará, Piauí, Ceará and Paraíba. Of his 180-student class, 100 were recruited for the Carajás Iron Project, most of whom were hired as brakemen, who work on the railroad helping to maneuver the trains. Like his colleagues, however, Ronaldo had no previous experience with trains: "It was an impact", he says.

---

61   Flávio Dino (at the time, a member of the PCdoB).

We were all technicians and we were suddenly recruited for a railway activity, specifically, for the train. Because there are many railroad workers who are administrators, mechanics and so on. But this job was to pull trains. ... I came from the countryside, I had no idea of Vale's size, but I already knew it was a big company, a state-owned company, in a region like ours. So, it was a great opportunity, mainly, it provided me, in my specific case, with a trip to another state. I went to Vitória, in the state of Espírito Santo, to do some recruitment there. ... I had a fast career inside the company. The group who trained us were from Minas Gerais and Espírito Santo, who came here to run the project because of the knowhow they had down in the Southeast region. And our career was fast, especially mine, because we were a group of six who became the first train drivers of the Carajás Railroad in Maranhão. So, we were Vale's first train drivers.

RONALDO SILVA, Aguiar Interview

Ronaldo worked in the Carajás Railroad since its construction period, in the countryside of Maranhão and Pará. After three months as a brakeman, a position young technicians were initially recruited for, he worked for six months as a train driver's assistant, and finally, a year later, he became a driver himself. Because of his experience in the company, Ronaldo usually presents his trajectory as that of a pioneer, both in Vale and in the union: he describes himself as one of the "first of Vale's drivers in the Carajás Railroad" or "the first train driver", as when he told me the episode of the bridge inauguration over the Tocantins River:

I was at the inauguration of the Tocantins bridge, which is the princess of the company, of Vale, because if that bridge collapses, brother, it will take a year to recover it. It will be an incalculable loss. ... And, at the inauguration, I had the privilege of driving the first passenger train, accompanied by an inspector, because I saw it up close and there were two ministers with me, at the time, from the military government: César Cals [1926–1991, Minister of Mines and Energy] and Jarbas Passarinho [1920–2016, Minister of Social Security], as well as the company's director who was also here. It was a very upscale train, full of managers, full of politicians. It was something else, plenty of parties. I had this privilege: besides being the first train driver, being the driver of the first passenger train to inaugurate the bridge of the Tocantins River.

RONALDO SILVA, Aguiar Interview

A member of the first generation of Carajás Railroad workers, Ronaldo approached the union movement because of the 1989 strike, of which, according to him, the train drivers were an active part. However, he would only join the union's board of directors later on, after being invited by the former union's president, from whom he would drift apart some time later.

STEFEM, whose creation is very similar to other Vale's unions, such as Metabase Itabira[62] and Metabase Carajás, was created from an association organized by the company itself, originally headed by company managers. After the association was transformed into a union, a leadership group was organized among activists, who later participated in the 1989 strike, and in which there were members from parties such as the PT and the PCdoB.

> This union here, its construction – and that's not different from all the others – started with an association. But get this: the association was formed by Vale's directors. The managers themselves, Vale's directors, were the ones who built the association at the time and handed it over – which we only discovered over time – to a worker who became a reference for the union movement from '89 until '97, when he lost the election to us, you see?
>
> RONALDO SILVA, in a meeting with STEFEM's board of directors

> And then a colleague of ours here, my predecessor, from Maranhão, he became the first union president. ... And we supported all of his movements. My first party membership, as a matter of fact, in the heat of my excitement, was in the Communist Party, in PCdoB, in '90, '91. [The president] was not from PCdoB, but we had many people in the area where I worked who were influential, who later became union directors, much earlier than me. And they were from PCdoB. So, we formed this group and we were supporting the union's actions.
>
> RONALDO SILVA, Aguiar Interview

According to Ronaldo, CVRD's reaction right after the strike, dismissing workers who were active during the conflict, generated discontent among the worker collective and suspicions about the behavior of the then union president with regard to the company's management.

---

62   Minayo, *De ferro e flexíveis*.

But [the president], there, we realized his true intention. We realized that he had other interests, besides defending our interests as workers, and an opposition was formed there. Vale fired many people from the opposition. ... And he became somehow very weakened because the opposition, that mass of people who were fired, all of the responsibility was attributed to him. And he, very intelligently, sought to recompose that area with other new names, in order to be able to fill that political need of his. ... And I don't know who it was that told him that I could be an option, a reference to replace his colleagues there, those who were his colleagues up to then, the ones who were persecuted and fired. My first gesture was, I volunteered ... We joined the strike, the sector with the biggest support for the strike was my own. The train drivers' sector did not want to leave the strike under any circumstances. ... Then I saw that, since there was no way to revert our colleagues' dismissal cases, I went and volunteered for the company to throw me out because I didn't want to work at Vale anymore.

RONALDO SILVA, Aguiar Interview

He had his role, his important moment. He founded the union, helped build the workers' history. But, over time, he became a coward. ... That was the factor which made him lose the union to us. And, at the time, he already had a ... We started to feel it in our skin, the older workers, when all the collective agreements ... We felt there was a major benefit coming and Vale always bet on it, making the worker extremely needy economically and they would come from behind us with extra money and take another one of our benefits with them. And that's how it was: every year it came with extra money, but taking a benefit in return. And, practically, when it came time for privatization, we were rid of that '14th,' '15th,' no more pharmacy assistance ... All of what I told you about went away. Most of it was gone [before privatization].

RONALDO SILVA, in a meeting with STEFEM's board of directors

Due to pressure from managers, who offered him a more advantageous position from a salary point of view that even reached his older sister,[63] Ronaldo backed out of the decision of leaving CVRD. He was then around 25 years old.

---

63   Pressure from managers on the relatives of workers – who were involved in union activities or who, for some reason, created discontent with their supervisors – was a common procedure also at CVRD in Itabira, according to Minayo. The next Chapter will show how

Because he was young and inexperienced, he said he couldn't deal with the situation back then. Not having adapted to the position offered to him by management, he resumed his work as a train driver and was sought after by the union president, who nominated him, in an assembly, to be part of STEFEM's board of directors. The former president sought to reorganize the board with younger activists who had participated in the strike, to counteract the discontent caused by his handling of the strike.

> Vale, you got to take your hat off to the company, because it's very efficient in this respect: it supervises all its people's activities, it has all this internal and external control, of their personal life. So, I don't know why in hell, but there was a manager who liked me, he liked me a lot because I had a responsible attitude, I had no problems with attendance or punctuality, I was committed to my activity in the company, I was a reference. I was the first company's first train driver, so I had trained several people. [He] thought I was being hasty, that I was being supportive of a movement that had nothing to do with me. ... Then they did a job within my family. In one of the trips I made – I traveled a lot because of my routine activity as a train driver -, when I came back, my sister, who was the bulwark of my life, she was my second mother, the one who supported us, a poor family, all that, she came and said to me this: 'What is this madness? Why are you handing in your notice? Go back to your job, forget about unions! That gesture, the guys are asking you to stay.' Then I said: 'Well, I've already handed in my notice, I went to his office, am I going to have to go back?' 'Work it out!' They had set me up so I wouldn't be fired. Then he told me: 'I just want to ask you something. I know you're an activist, but don't get involved with unions. Forget about unions. We are giving you an opportunity at the CCO'. That was the Operational Command Center, it was really an elite group, they had a better paycheck, they had a better social life, different from train drivers. I was there on probation with them for a year: I was approved, they wanted me to stay, but I had no identity with the business. I didn't. Then I said: no, it's okay, I don't want to get involved with the union. Really, I didn't have any will, except to be there ... I was young, fearless, but I didn't have it ... And then [the president] of the Railway Workers Union, with the internal fight in there which sponsored everybody's dismissal, he went and started to choose

---

Vale in Canada used pressure, threats and lawsuits against family members to weaken the Sudbury strike in 2009–2010.

those leaders along the railroad. And he got to my sector, someone told him that I would be a good name. ... And he started to harass me: he came to my house, started to offer me trips to visit the union, which up to then I knew nothing about. And I went on like that, with a lot of resistance, because I didn't trust him.

RONALDO SILVA, Aguiar Interview

So, in 1993, Ronaldo became part of STEFEM's board of directors. Since then, he has left his activities at the railroad and has been hired to fulfill union duties. According to him, union activism changed his life: he had the opportunity to travel around the country, in the 1990s, during the campaign against privatizations, he met CUT and PT national leaders,[64] graduated from Law School and, for six years, he was a board member of Vale, representing workers.

At first, Ronaldo occupied a less important position in a leadership hegemonized by the former president, who managed to reestablish his control after the questioning which took place during the strike. Years later, however, a new opposition group emerged in STEFEM, this time internally. The former president, motivated by political ambitions, had, according to Ronaldo, managed the union's finances for his own benefit, raising resources for his political allies' electoral campaigns in the city. This situation even caught the eye of the local press and community, bringing disagreements among the workers and within the union's leadership, which split up. Ronaldo started to lead the opposition group, taking over STEFEM's leadership alongside it in 1997.

I was faithful to [the president], within the activities that we exercised here, until the point where it was no longer possible, when we had a falling out, in '95 to '96. Because he had a personal project. He wanted to be a councillor, a deputy, the mayor of São Luís, the governor. He had an ambitious project. ... But he didn't get any of it. And, since he was very influential at Vale, he had very easy access. In Rio, he could easily get into the office of Vale's CEO, he was very well-known, very articulate. ... He was the one who made the union a CUT affiliate. ... He took a bigger risk when he raised some money from the union to make a party campaign and that was the rupture, because we didn't know it until then, and I told him that we couldn't share that responsibility. ... It was public.

---

64 According to Ronaldo, this was a period of great political debate within Vale's union movement, stimulated by CUT and the PT: "There was this political debate, which today we don't have anymore. And I lived through all of this. This was a good phase, which I consider, because it gave me a lot of political knowledge" (Aguiar Interview).

I was the only one against him. Me, the president of the audit committee and another older union director. ... But from the executive board I was the only one against them, all the others stayed with him. What was my advantage before him? He, because of all his responsibilities, didn't travel the railway corridor anymore and he was losing his representativeness. ... It was difficult to build an opposition group because he had a lot of political strength with Vale, with the municipality. Actually, the mayor for whom he had raised money was elected.[65] His name was already in line to be secretary, and he was this mayor's secretary. We started a fight with him, without any money, just with our reference among the rank and file workers and with this hook, with this possibility of exploring that he had been dishonest, that he had deviated from the union's interests.

RONALDO SILVA, Aguiar Interview

The longevity of union leaders in Vale's workers' unions is an aspect that, despite clear differences in political orientation, brings the two unions studied closer together: in both unions, leaders established for decades control the union and have been away from the daily life of production and the workers for many years. In the boards, there are younger members and several rank-and-file directors who are still in production. However, the most important positions in the entities are occupied by veteran leaders, which indicates a clear bureaucratization process.

When questioned about the subject, union members almost always state that Vale recurrently dismisses members who lose elections and, therefore, their job stability, which encourages leaders to seek to perpetuate themselves in the entities' command. Intervention in union election processes, as already mentioned, is an important part of Vale's union strategy.[66]

Sérgio Rosa, former president of Vale's Board of Directors, stated that on some occasions he had acted on the Board to reverse cases of union leaders' dismissals when these were denounced by unions or board members representing workers:

---

65   The former president, according to STEFEM members, had been a member of the Democratic Labour Party (*Partido Democrático Trabalhista*, or PDT) and supported the campaign of Jackson Lago, elected mayor of São Luís in 1996. It is not known – nor is it the object of our attention in this book – to what extent the interests of the union's leading group and those of the company would converge or diverge in relation to local politics. In the following Chapter, however, the election of a former manager of Vale, with no previous political experience, as mayor of the Canadian city of Sudbury, will be addressed.

66   Milanez et al., "A estratégia corporativa da Vale S.A.".

Sérgio Rosa: We never supported firing union leaders. We intervened. Playing dirty, in the sense of going beyond the limits of a tough negotiation, using practices that we could clearly say: these are illegal, these are dirty. We always tried to block this kind of thing, so much that we never accepted it.

Thiago Aguiar: *Were there cases like that?*
There were at least attempts in this direction and we always tried to correct them. Now, to say that a company negotiator can't be tough in a negotiation ... I've faced that my whole life. ... Whenever we had complaints about these cases, we took them to the Board and curbed this kind of thing. ... There were reports of it once or twice, and we always intervened to make it clear that we wouldn't accept this kind of thing.
Aguiar Interview

Thus, here we have another example of a relatively common topic in the characterization of the corporate structure of Brazilian unions:[67] the way union resources and the unicity of representation, among other aspects, stimulates the bureaucratization and control of the labor movement. Such a tendency is reinforced, in Vale's case, by the company's pressure on oppositional groups and by its anti-union stance. The consequence is the crystallization of positions on the entity boards which may, over time, facilitate the creation of less conflictive relations between unions and the company. For union members, in this scenario, maintaining their positions on the entities' boards becomes a pressing need for survival, to maintain their jobs or even to conserve material resources (besides benefits and pensions[68]) as well as symbolic ones (the importance of the position and the social and political relations arising from it) which are unavailable to rank and file workers.

---

67   On that topic, see Armando Boito Jr., *O sindicalismo de Estado no Brasil* (São Paulo: Hucitec/ Editora da Unicamp, 1991).

68   Ronaldo, as seen in Chapter 1, was able to lean on union stability to maintain the old Valia pension plan.

4   Employee Representation in Vale's Board of Directors

The fact, moreover, that some of the union members interviewed have sat on Vale's Board of Directors – Ronaldo and Geraldo (from STEFEM, in different periods), and Tonhão (from Metabase Carajás, as Ronaldo's alternate) – brings upon them additional pressures of the material and ideological kind. Ronaldo, as a board member, has remained active in the union movement to the point of creating conflicts with the company's management. However, the union member, in an informal conversation, stated that the extraordinary income brought by his board position raised his living standards. Tonhão, on the other hand, as we will see, when talking about his period in the Board, openly undertakes the goals of Vale's shareholders such as the defense of the company and its projects' profits, even when these affect the company's workers, since his main objective as a union and board member, as he said, was the defense of job creation.

The contact with Ronaldo was established after suggestions from the Solidarity Center's[69] office in São Paulo and from CUT's national leaders. They all made explicit reference to Ronaldo as one of the most engaged Brazilian union members in the actions of solidarity with the strike of Vale workers in Canada. This information was confirmed by the Canadian union members and activists from the 2009–2010 strike interviewed in Sudbury. Ronaldo proudly showed pictures of his participation in the Canadian strike, wearing the USW Local 6500 union jacket. At the time of the conflict, he held a seat at Vale's Board of Directors, in addition to his senior position at STEFEM.

Ronaldo described the contradictions of his position during the period, since while he was a union leader, responsible for defending the interests of the rank-and-file workers, he was also a company board member, responsible for the company's administration and its profitability, even though he held a seat reserved for the workers.

Because he had access to confidential information – undertaking to preserve it as a requirement of his position – and because he signed documents as a board member, Ronaldo had to opt, at times, not to expose himself, asking other STEFEM members to hold public confrontations with the company in assemblies and demonstrations. Meanwhile, he said he had used his position in the board to bring worker demands not only from São Luís, but from all over the company.

---

69   Center for solidarity and organization of international relations maintained by the American Federation of Labor and Congress of Industrial Organizations (AFL-CIO, the US union federation described in Chapter 3).

It was very difficult for me, because I was the first experience. At the beginning, I saw that in fact I had that role in that instance, not as a manager, but I was there not around managers, but company directors, shareholders and so on, the company's owner. It wasn't even as directors, it was as company owners. ... Then the workers, without understanding very well, started to label me as the company's manager. What did I do? I didn't lose touch, but even because of the level of responsibility that I had – because I had a lot of information, privileged information that I can't disclose, I sign the commitments, terms of civil responsibility, these kinds of things, under the penalty of liability -, I attributed many times the union's political responsibilities to other colleagues inside here. It came to Geraldo especifically to play my role of direct confrontation along with the workers. But always together, as much as possible, always together, but with a lot of concern to always police myself about what I said.

RONALDO SILVA, Aguiar Interview

Before Ronaldo's election, the Vale workers' seat was appointed by the company's management itself and represented the workers who were shareholders of INVESTVALE. After union pressure, the seat became subject to an election (organized by the company) during Sérgio Rosa's term as Chairman of Vale's Board of Directors:[70]

When we created the conditions for them to elect a member to the Board ... I felt able to do that: I was on the Board, it was a matter of changing the charter, we ... Now, the capacity to organize themselves, to have a platform to be inside the Board, to know what they are doing with that function, is theirs. I'm not the one to tell them, even though we may have a historical identity, each one plays a different role. At the moment, it's not me who's going to teach someone: do this or do that.

SÉRGIO ROSA, Aguiar Interview

Ronaldo said that the first time he was elected, Vale had supported another candidate, but when there was a dispute between the slate he represented, from CUT, against another slate from Conlutas, the company would have preferred that the 'CUTists' won.

---

70   However, Carvalho, "Análise da ação dos sindicatos," 99, mentioning the statements of a leader of the Metabase Inconfidentes (in Minas Gerais) union, linked the election of the workers' representative on the Board of Directors to the company's initiatives to co-opt the union movement, bringing it closer to its interests.

We had, in my first election, a clash with the company and we won the election. But Vale also had an interest in my election because it was very clear that it was a dispute between CUT and PSTU's[71] union center. That was very clear. ... Vale, in a way, had a greater interest that the CUT slate won, even though I was someone who offered them resistance. But there was another kind of resistance here. Maybe a more ideological resistance, which wanted to mess with its international interests.

RONALDO SILVA, Aguiar Interview

After a somewhat calm beginning, Ronaldo reported having experienced more intense clashes exactly for having taken to the Board, at the request of the Canadian union members, the demands of the Vale strike in Canada, which bothered Roger Agnelli, then CEO of the company, and brought upon reprisals against Ronaldo and other union members involved in strike solidarity activities.[72]

I also had the opportunity to set myself against Roger because of the Canada strike. ... [The relationship had been] good until the Canada strike. Then came my confrontation with Roger. Then, Roger realized that I wasn't at his service. If he got that mixed up, that's his problem. I wasn't at his service. And I don't even think that our union has been at his service at any time. ... And here he started a campaign aimed, let's say, at causing some wear and tear to the union's image internally, along with some rank and file fellows, to see if he could destabilize it. But he didn't succeed either.

RONALDO SILVA, Aguiar Interview

The discomfort that the performance of Brazilian union members in support of the Canadian strike brought to the company can be noted through André Teixeira's statements in which he disqualified an up-and-coming union activist, whom he did not identify, that was prominent in the discussions for the organization of an international network of Vale's unions:

There was a Brazilian union member – I won't name him. ... Steelworkers said: 'You're going to be president of the international network of Vale's unions!' Then he said: 'Man, I started from the bottom, now I'm going to

---

71   *Partido Socialista dos Trabalhadores Unificado* [United Socialist Workers' Party], the Trotskyist political party tied to Conlutas.

72   As will be discussed in more detail in Chapter 3.

be president.' He got all interested! He went to Canada, held a demonstration in front of Vale's building ... That was one, but the rest wasn't like
that. The rest weren't captivated.

ANDRÉ TEIXEIRA, Aguiar Interview

It may well be that the company really didn't manage to break STEFEM after
the union had become notable for its solidarity with the strike in Canada,
for Ronaldo vocalizing the Canadian demands in the company's Board of
Directors, for his presence in Sudbury during strike activities, and for sending
lawyer Guilherme Zagallo to Canada to advise USW Local 6500 in negotiations
with Vale. However, the company's pressure had consequences. Shortly after
the end of the strike, the union withdrew from the *Justiça nos Trilhos* network,
which, according to Ronaldo Silva, particularly bothered Roger Agnelli: "He
also criticized the organized social movement, *Justiça nos Trilhos*, which ... he
considered a 'ridiculous' movement. He used to say that. He came to me and
said in a Board meeting: 'Right, Ronaldo? It's a ridiculous movement!'. But he
was already hating me then because I had embraced the Canada strike and he
was trying to get to me. He said I was a signatory, confirming it, that I was a
Justiça nos Trilhos signatory."[73]

All of this shows that representation on the Board has a contradictory
role: if, on the one hand, it allows Vale to approach certain union leaders, and
eventually to make them compromise with the company's goals, on the other
hand, the position may, in exceptional mobilization circumstances, be used to
hinder the company's management.

Before STEFEM's 2012 board election, the first one held after the Canadian
conflict, there were differences in the leadership group which almost led to
its split. Unity was maintained by moving Ronaldo to a different board position. He does not confirm that this was due to Vale's demands, although he has
hinted at this many times.

> This Canada strike, the only unions actually involved were ours, STEFEM,
> led by me, and the one in Mariana, which was the PSTU people, from
> Conlutas. But STEFEM was the one who really stood up to the challenge.
> And I was in a very uncomfortable situation, because I was there three
> times. My last term ended in 2013, as a Vale board member. I was also the
> first Vale board member elected by the workers. It was the first experi-
> ence at it. And, in my second term, the second time I was elected board

---

73   Aguiar Interview.

member, the strike in Canada exploded. So, imagine me wearing both hats: as president of the union and as Vale's board member. And creating a middle ground ... I mean a middle ground, because, knowing the company's reality, I was looking for this middle ground, in the sense of opening a negotiation at the company's core, so as they wouldn't apply that type of policy they were taking to Canada, which was ours here, and which we fought against. And, on the other hand, I also had to put myself as the legitimate representative of the workers, and behave as such. So I had to be at the front of the picket line, I had to strike, make speeches. And without incurring the civil responsibilities that I had, that were inherent to the position, because of the information I had, privileged information. It was a ... crazy business, I couldn't understand it. Even here, internally, we had some trouble. We had some trouble here internally. But I don't regret anything, on the contrary. I think we played our role, maybe not rising to what someone else thought or would like it to be. But as far as possible, I did what I thought was possible to do and I don't regret it. I had to do it and I did it.

RONALDO SILVA, in a meeting with STEFEM's board of directors

Other interviewees – among them an AFL-CIO member who worked at the Solidarity Center's office in São Paulo during the Canadian strike,[74] a retired CUT national leader, and Canadian union members who made close contact with Ronaldo, besides Guilherme Zagallo – confirm that Ronaldo's change of position within the union's board of directors was due to the pressure the company put on the entity's leadership and on the workers themselves, wearing him down.[75] For Guilherme Zagallo, STEFEM's lawyer who advised the Canadians,

there was an internal pressure within the union itself. There was a split within the board of directors itself. Some directors didn't like it, and

---

74 This interviewee talked about Ronaldo's role on the Board and Vale's retaliation against his home union in an interview with Thiago Aguiar in São Paulo in February 2016: "The leader stayed in that position [on the Board of Directors] and kept helping. But I think he was then punished a little bit by the company and lost his position [in his union]."

75 In addition to Ronaldo, interviewees in Brazil and Canada also mentioned the removal of a leader of the Union of Workers in the Prospecting, Exploration and Extraction of Ore Industries in the State of Rio de Janeiro (*Sindicato dos Trabalhadores nas Indústrias de Prospecção, Pesquisa e Extração de Minérios no Estado do Rio de Janeiro*, or Sindimina-RJ) as retaliation by the company for his participation in activities in solidarity with the strike in Vale Canada.

ended up incorporating the business discourse contrary to these solidarity actions. So, I didn't suffer, but there was tension. There was an underlying indirect threat that, in an eventual leadership change, in a union split, this could lead to consequences.

GUILHERME ZAGALLO, Aguiar Interview

The divisions in the Brazilian union movement at Vale regarding the Canadian conflict, the way the company instrumentalized them and the unsuccessful attempts to build an international union network will be discussed in Chapter 4. For now, we can close this section with a brief assessment made by Ronaldo about these challenges:

Ronaldo Silva: You can't get anything alone. But, together with people who don't want anything, you can't achieve anything either. So, I have a clear conscience here that I gave the contribution that I had to give. And I think it was important because our union built a reference, even with all the problems, at an international level, a certain respectability. We have a lot of ease and integration with some social movements that still support us, that believe in our politics.

Thiago Aguiar: *Why was there not greater unity in support of the Canadians?*
Diffuse interests, unknown interests, other people there that we didn't ... didn't allow that ... because people didn't want to commit. They didn't want to commit to that for other reasons. ... Because ... I don't know if I've ever explained this clearly to you, because I don't want to get into these nuances. Interests that we don't know about.

Aguiar Interview

A former CUT national leader[76] makes a harsh assessment of the absence of another important Vale workers' union, Metabase Carajás, in the actions of solidarity with the Canadian strike which were sought to be organized at that time:

---

76   Interviewed by Thiago Aguiar in São Bernardo do Campo, Brazil (April 2016).

In Pará, we have the worst problem. Because it's a union that's in the hands of a guy who has been in the union since its foundation and who eats in the company's hand. The company built the union building, it was the company that did it. The union belonged to the company. When the union was founded, it wasn't like that. It was people from CUT who founded the union and [Vale] did everything they could to fire these people for just cause. ... It was founded by the CUT in Pará, which supported a slate, they set up the union .... They didn't even have time to do it, and Vale already started winning over the union. What was the guy's name? Tonhão! I don't even know if he's still the president ... 'If it's Tonhão, I'll give the union its headquarters. If it's Tonhão, I'll sign the fifth shift. If it's Tonhão, I'll give you a 15th salary'. That's how it was. It really gave it, by the way, Vale made a deal, sent the guys out, put Tonhão there. He's a thug, a gangster. He kept the union a CUT affiliate so as to not to change the name, but he's a guy who eats in the company's hand ... For example, he refused to offer solidarity to Canada. He wouldn't go there even if we paid for the ticket. It was the greatest challenge to bring him to a meeting. And it's Vale's main union, the main mine.

> Former CUT leader, Aguiar Interview

Marcelo Sousa,[77] former leader of the CNQ, supervised Vale's unions through that entity and now works on CUT's national leadership. His position is equally harsh on the relationship between the Metabase Carajás union and Vale:

In Pará, there is very strong co-optation, man! Very strong! ... There is a co-optation process .... They work a lot with worker misinformation. ... They [the company] contest the [union] elections so that the group supported by CUT doesn't win. They don't win. It's bankrolled! Bankrolled! Of course, I can't prove it. But I know, when I'm racing against you, that you have a lot of money, that you have the availability to [campaign for] eight hours. ... Why all this fear? Why is that? Because Vale understands that Pará is so far away from the thinking center of the union movement that it makes it as difficult as possible for this information to get through.[78]

---

77   Fictitious name.
78   Marcelo Sousa, former CNQ leader, interviewed by Thiago Aguiar in São Paulo, Brazil (May 2018).

5   The Challenges of Entering Carajás

Under the Amazon sun, I was walking along the avenue and looking for the exit to Parauapebas (in Pará). Towards the PA-275 highway, which leads to Vale's iron mines in the Carajás Complex, it is not possible to follow without first finding a huge gate, visible from a long distance. The sign informs: "Carajás National Forest," in large letters, between the green and yellow brand of Vale and the identification of the *Instituto Chico Mendes de Conservação da Biodiversidade* [Chico Mendes Institute for Biodiversity Conservation], or ICMBio.[79]

It was the second time I found the gate. In the first one, by taxi, I entered the city after landing at the Carajás/Parauapebas airport,[80] whose area is within the perimeter under ICMBio's jurisdiction, responsible for the Conservation Unit for *Floresta Nacional de Carajás* [Carajás National Forest], or FNC's[81] sustainable use, as informed to me some time later by Larissa, BA in Environmental Resource Management, former outsourced worker of Vale and today a member of a local ecotourism cooperative. It can be said, based on the attempt to reach the area of the Carajás mines, that there is, however, a dual jurisdiction, since Vale, in practice, controls the accesses to the FNC.

At the airport exit, there were vans picking up workers, many of whom boarded in Confins (in Minas Gerais) already wearing their green mining company uniforms. Not having anyone with a car waiting at the local airport, the only possible way out is the taxi. After about half an hour going down the Carajás mountain range, one reaches the gate controlled by the company at the entrance to the União neighborhood. João, a taxi driver from Piauí who has lived in Parauapebas for around thirty years, asked me if I had arrived with the Aerovale which had landed just after my commercial flight. I answered negatively and found out that Vale, in addition to its partnership with aviation

---

79   Autarchy linked to the Ministry of the Environment, responsible for managing the country's Conservation Units.

80   Built by CVRD in 1981 and handed over to Infraero (Brazilian Company of Airport Infrastructure) since 1985, "to meet the activity demand of the largest iron ore deposit in the world, in exploration. The main gateway for investors from the world financial market visiting the Carajás complex, the airport receives an ever-increasing number of passengers, which may double with the new investments of the mining company in the region," as stated in the history prepared by the state-owned airport company, available in https://www4.infraero.gov.br/aeroportos/aeroporto-de-parauapebas/sobre-o-aeroporto /historico/; accessed December 2, 2021.

81   An area of 391,263.04 hectares according to ICMBio data, available in https://www.gov.br /icmbio/pt-br/assuntos/biodiversidade/unidade-de-conservacao/unidades-de-biomas /amazonia/lista-de-ucs/flona-de-carajas; accessed December 2, 2021.

companies,[82] maintains an Embraer-190 to transport workers, technicians and engineers from Minas Gerais to Carajás.

I was surprised when we stopped in a line of vehicles which were identified to the armed security guards who control the roadblocks on the three lanes. João told me that the situation on the city accesses' "got a lot better" after pressure from the city government, years ago, for greater freedom of movement. Quickly recognized, the taxi driver was allowed to pass, and I entered the city for the first time. The curiosity to access the mines, however, increased even more with the feeling that it would not be easy to do so.

I confirmed this impression when I personally insisted on asking some leaders of the Metabase Carajás union, having previously done so by phone, to provide indications or some assistance to visit the mine area. Everyone always changed their expressions and said it was 'almost impossible,' besides not knowing what the procedures were and to whom such a request should be directed. "The company won't let us. It has to be done well in advance and even then it's difficult for them to let us through the gate."[83] This is what Carlinhos, a union director for almost fifteen years, said, adding that he himself didn't remember entering the mines during the whole period away from production as a union board member. I understood that there were indeed restrictions on the part of the company, but at the same time I began to suspect that it couldn't just be that. There is a distance between the union and its workers, an issue we will return to later, and, perhaps, little willingness on the part of union members for the researcher to go into the mines to talk to workers or to visit the nucleus, a neighborhood where technicians, engineers and administrative staff live, but also a place of daily passage for hundreds of workers at lunchtime in search of restaurants, banks and shops.

As recommended by the union, I sought a permit and some information on how to access the mine area at a Vale service office located at the checkpoint. Earlier, when simply trying to cross it on foot as a test, I was stopped by a security guard with a curious expression. He affirmed that it was not possible to pass without formal authorization from the company. I identified as a visitor and said I wanted to see the area in front of the gate. I was informed that, besides the distance of over forty kilometers to the mines, I would necessarily need authorization from the company or from ICMBio, and that I should go to the identification office next door, under the same structure, where Vale and the Institute maintain spaces for this purpose. The company's office is bigger,

82   Information and flight details available in http://www.vale.com/brasil/PT/aboutvale /news/Paginas/parceria-vale-gol-traz-novo-voo-carajas.aspx; accessed May 26, 2021.

83   Carlinhos, union leader, interviewed by Thiago Aguiar in Parauapebas, Brazil (July 2016).

but I find a lineup of people searching for assistance. There, I discovered residents of Parauapebas who did not work for the company (and, therefore, did not have identification to pass through) seeking authorization to access the nucleus or the airport. According to them, to get it, you have to justify it (presenting the airline ticket in case of going to the airport, for example).

The clerk at the counter informed me that, in order to access the area without a link to Vale, it would be necessary to bring the matter to ICMBio, in whose office a few meters ahead at the same checkpoint, however, the attendants said there was no one who could handle the matter. There, they suggested I go to the central headquarters of the institute in the city, less than two kilometers away from the gate, which only seemed many more because they had to be walked under the strong Amazon heat that afternoon. A short time later, when I arrived at the indicated address, I found an extensive and high wall protecting what seemed to be a large house, with a one-piece gate that made it impossible to see what was inside. As I knocked on the gate, I saw through a crack a security guard approaching with his hand pressed against the revolver held in his waistband. Without opening, he asked from behind the gate what I wanted there. Quickly, so that there was no doubt, I explained that the office at the gate had recommended I go to the ICMBio headquarters to obtain a permit to visit the FNC and the area of the mines. "No, no, you won't get that here. The tourism cooperative does that. They have a room lent by ICMBio here, but now there's no one here." Through the same gap, I kindly received from the guard, who never took his hand off his revolver, a member of the cooperative's phone number, with whom I then talked about how to access the area beyond the gate.

Cooperture, the Carajás Ecotourism Cooperative, is conducted by local guides with ICMBio authorization to circulate through FNC areas and offer ecotourism services. With the cooperative, visitors obtain authorization from the institute to access the area, including the mines, since the road passes through them and, being an open-air activity, it is possible to see several mining facilities. The next day I met up with Larissa, the guide, who took me by car again through the FNC gate. The plan was to drive around the area of the mines and make a few stops so I could see the facilities up close and talk to workers. We also decided to drive through the nucleus, the neighborhood where she lived during the time she was married to a Vale worker living there. Again, I was stopped at the gate, now accompanied by Larissa, who was surprised to have to argue with the security guard about the authorization she carried. He didn't want to accept the tourism cooperative identification badge given by ICMBio, since my name didn't appear on the document. Larissa was surprised and said it was the first time that had happened, since the cooperative crosses the gates several times a week, sometimes even in vans with dozens of people, none of whom had individual authorization documents. After speaking to another security guard, possibly a supervisor who soon approached us, we were finally released. According to her,

> this is the function of this gate: to limit people, because there have been robberies: people come down, bring some kind of material, equipment, right? It can be stolen. So, they restrict it to make this inspection of people ... We know where we are, we have authorization, so they can come and say whatever they want. We are within our rights. So, I mean, once someone came and said: 'Oh, do you have clearance?' Generally they're people without the knowledge, they don't know. 'How did you get in here? How come this and that?' No, we have ICMBio authorization. So, we explain that. Sometimes, there are some newcomers, they don't know. Because the gate staff go through a training to know what kind of card we use, what kind of clearance we give, how many people the authorization is for ... Because, in my case, one authorization, one guide, is good for 15 people.
>
> LARISSA, during the trip to the mines in Carajás, July 2016

Finally, after passing through the (first) gate, we continue on the highway, climbing the mountain range, in the midst of dense and intensely green forest, towards the mines. Before finally reaching the area where Vale's installations are located, we stop in front of a gate, smaller than the previous one, also interrupting the flow of all lanes of the highway in both directions. "Welcome to the Carajás industrial complex," it reads. Passing through there is quicker. We went on and heard a shout from the security guard. This time it was just a warning for Larissa to turn on her headlights, following the new traffic directions.

It can be said that the control of the FNC space and the restrictions to its access are part of Vale's "territorial strategy," "to control surfaces, lines and points through the management and control of space ... , in the sense of giving fluidity or creating restrictions to the flow of people and goods in the corporate territory," promoting "spatial reconfigurations", such as the installation of surveillance cameras, construction of gates and walls in access roads "to delimit areas under the control of the mining company, restrain the circulation of people and create control mechanisms for the residents who live around the developments."[84] Guilherme Zagallo said that Vale's controls were even greater

---

84 Milanez et al., "A estratégia corporativa da Vale S.A.," 30–1.

years earlier and that pressure from social movements was fundamental to expand access to the FNC:

> Until eight or nine years ago, ... it was a national forest, but it functioned as a protection area for the company's activities because it wasn't a national forest that could be visited. That's when the social movements started: 'If it's a national forest, it belongs to the entire Brazilian population. It has the right to be visited! You don't have the right to prevent us from visiting! This is not your land! Your land is one thing, the national forest is something else.' So, access to the Carajás National Forest itself is relatively recent, more than two decades after its creation.
> GUILHERME ZAGALLO, Aguiar Interview

The piles of waste rock take over the passage after the gate. They are small hills made of soil taken from the mines and covered with grass to prevent landslides. Taller vegetation doesn't grow there. Soon we saw the Waste Materials Management Center, the sorting facility for waste produced throughout the mine, where Larissa had previously worked. Then the road became redder, from the mixture of earth and iron ore dust, suspended in the air and omnipresent wherever you see or touch. The landscape, then, became red: jagged soil, conveyors transporting ore, trucks in a frenzied rhythm, metallic structures crossing the road over our heads, buildings where ore is milled, distribution structures ... Piles of red dirt pile up from bank to bank. The road also narrows as we enter Vale's facilities. Next, we also saw a red water reservoir, where the cyclonic separation process takes place, by which the ore is washed, and the resulting water is carried through pipes to the dams located more than fifty kilometers from the urban centers. Along the way, I stopped from time to time to try to identify some opportunity to talk to the workers who were sometimes outside of trucks or machines. Talking to them, I began to understand the way the Carajás installations work.

We soon reached a kind of terminal where the tangle of conveyor belts and metal structures converged. In three lines, a multitude of wagons, whose length was out of sight, was loaded with ore, practically ready for the journey towards the port of Ponta da Madeira, in São Luís (in Maranhão). There, the ore is shipped in huge ships to Vale's international buyers. At the port where the trains are headed to, and where I had been a month earlier, there are also huge metal structures and similar conveyors responsible for loading the ships. At the other end of the Carajás Railroad, in Maranhão, I had watched the bitter union assembly of Vale workers at the port facilities.

It is impossible not to mention the gigantic dimension of the facilities observed at Carajás, the likes of which totally absorbed my attention – which may also have been because it was my first contact with that landscape or because my interest in mining had been built from other themes and concerns. At first, I was less interested in the ore and its production process, and more interested, in fact, in globalization and its consequences for development, workers and unions. Later I understood that all these issues are found in mining. What I had not seen before came to life and gained color.

The biggest surprise, in fact, occurred when I reached the viewpoint from where the N4 iron mine can be seen. Before I even went to the tip to contemplate the mine in all its vastness, I saw a worker running towards me speaking on a radio. Before getting into the car and speeding off, I heard a quick part of his conversation: "The railway is closed by the Indians today. So all the wagons stopped down there. I'm running down at 120 km per hour!"[85]

The crater in the middle of the forest is so huge that it is not really possible to clearly identify the beginning and the end. Amidst the many steps, it was possible with some effort to see tractors, conveyors and trucks. Those huge machines, whose tires – I could see up close – were twice my height, seemed from a distance, given the size of the mine, like children's toys. I had enough time, as I followed the activities, to reflect on the grandiosity of what I saw and on the contradictions of Brazilian development exposed in the landscape. During the military dictatorship, national engineering reached the heart of the Amazon, where it built hundreds of kilometers of railroads and the largest complex of open-pit iron mines in the world. From these, in 2020, 192.3 million tonnes of ore were extracted.[86] Since the beginning, the foreign market has been the destination of most of what is produced there: iron ore in an almost raw state, with little processing. Before our eyes, the wonder and tragedy, the greatness and poverty of Brazil were revealed.

On the way back down the mountain range, we arrived at the nucleus, a neighborhood originally built by Vale to provide housing for workers recruited to the PFC. Currently, as Larissa said, the residences in the nucleus are occupied only by managers and their families, since the operation workers live mostly in Parauapebas. The nucleus, however, is quite busy. In the early afternoon, hundreds of workers circulate through its streets, restaurants, banks and

---

85   As the railroad crosses indigenous territories, these populations frequently protest against Vale's actions by interrupting the circulation of trains.

86   Vale S.A., *Formulário 20-F. Relatório Anual 2020*, 50. Available in http://www.vale.com /PT/investors/information-market/annual-reports/20f/20FDocs/Vale%2020-F%20FY2 020%20-%20Final%20Version_pt.pdf. accessed May 26, 2021.

shops. There, it was possible to conduct some interviews with workers who finished lunch and went to the bank branches. There are a number of other public facilities, such as a health center, schools, gymnasiums and churches. A zoo,
maintained by Vale, operates very close to the neighborhood. The Vale nucleus
in Carajás is the closest to the company town features analyzed in Chapter 1.

6   "It's Always Good to Know Who You're Talking To"

After arriving in Parauapebas, I settled in a simple hotel in the União neighborhood, near the access gate to the FNC. The place is often used by Vale workers
passing through the city. I could see this as soon as I arrived, because in the
corridor leading to the rooms there were pairs of boots with the red clay of iron
ore in front of each of the doors. It was easy, by exclusion, to know which room
was reserved for me. Apart from that first impression, I did not intend to linger
there, even though I had just arrived.

The trip to Carajás was organized based on contacts provided by STEFEM.
Since the first conversations by phone, the director of Metabase Carajás with
whom I kept in touch was somewhat evasive, although he never explicitly
opposed the request to interview union leaders. As if to make the job a little more difficult, this leader, with whom I had arranged the interviews in
Parauapebas, informed me, days before the trip, that he would not find me in
the city due to engagements in Minas Gerais on the same date. "But you can
rest assured that the people already know. Tonhão will greet you, but there's no
schedule because he's been busy. Stop by the union's headquarters when you
arrive and the staff will see what they can do," he concluded.

The chosen hotel allowed me to walk to the union, always accompanied by
the city's intense sun. When I arrived at Metabase Carajás' headquarters, I sat
while I waited to talk to a receptionist who was listening to a worker complaining about the delay in making his resignation request from the union. Two
other workers, behind him in line, encouraged their colleague and said they
were there for the same reason. As I learned through the interviews conducted,
the cut in benefits and the lack of salary increases in the 2015 collective agreement, in addition to the non-payment of the profit-sharing bonus at the beginning of 2016, had motivated a wave of resignations from the union. This was
one of the most visible effects, for the entity, of the crisis Vale went through.

Authorized to go upstairs after a phone call, I entered a room with three
people. Sitting behind a table, Tonhão looked at me with a distrustful expression and asked me who I was. I explained to him that I was the university
researcher, who had arranged, with the other union director, for an interview

with members of Metabase Carajás. "That I already know, but I want a document from you, if it has your face in it, even better," he replied coldly. I gave him a university ID card with my picture on it and the information that I was a graduate student. Tonhão put the document on the table, took out his cell phone and asked: "Can I take a picture of this? "It's always good to know who you're talking to."

After a conversation which did not seem very promising, Tonhão soon seemed to be more at ease and less suspicious of the researcher's intentions. So comfortable that he was practically the only one who answered the questions posed. One of the other two union directors present soon left the room. The second, João, followed the entire conversation and in a few moments agreed, in short sentences, with some of the ideas presented by Tonhão. The conversation flowed at length for much of the afternoon.

Tonhão was born in Maranhão but moved to southeast Pará when he was still young to work in the construction of the Tucuruí power plant, like thousands of other northeasterners who migrated to the region to build what would be, at the time, the largest Brazilian hydroelectric plant (since Itaipu is bi-national), responsible for providing electricity to the PFC, then under implementation. In 1982, Tonhão went to Parauapebas, where he took a technical course at Senai, and, in 1985, he was hired by CVRD as an electrician. Before that, in much the same way as Ronaldo did in São Luís, he worked for a contractor which provided services to CVRD. It was at the beginning of the Carajás mines operation.

The Metabase Carajás union, like STEFEM and other Vale workers' unions, arose as an association organized by the company, with managers in its command. In 1987, the entity became a union and received the union certificate from the Ministry of Labor, ensuring the right to represent CVRD's workers in the PFC area, until then under control of STIEAPA, an old miners' union from Amapá and Pará.

> At the time, we had an interstate union here. You know that industrial mining in the Amazon starts in Macapá, right? Macapá was Pará territory. So, sixty years ago, when industrial mining starts in the Amazon, it starts up there in Macapá, in Serra da Mesa, a manganese mine. ... So, at that time, they founded a union which covered all of Pará and Amapá. So, when we started over here, these comrades were already almost bankrupt because the manganese mine closed, it was exhausted. So, this union was almost finished there, it was just in a little mine over there. And then, when it started here, in the region of Marabá, this was all a municipality of Marabá, so we started to found a little association ... In

'84, I was at Vale, but it was because of the contractor, but I already operated the mine, I had taken Senai. So, in '84, in November, we had a meeting and started an association. Then they [the Amapá union] started
harassing us, we fought, we fought, we went to court, and so on and so
on ... When it was September 15, '87, we received the union certificate in
the municipality of Marabá. The municipality of Marabá, with the mines
in the region, started to fragment. They had big mines, the biggest gold
mine in the world, Serra Pelada, with more than 50,000 men in it, so they
opened up and founded the city of Eldorado. Then comes Curionópolis,
which is in Serra Pelada. Then comes the municipality of Parauapebas,
then Canaã. So, as these cities were created, we extended, the rank and
file worker base extended, we held it here. But up to a certain moment it
was in conflict with the people from Macapá.

TONHÃO, Aguiar Interview

The Metabase Carajás union's area of activity includes five municipalities
in southeastern Pará: Canaã dos Carajás, Curionópolis, Eldorado do Carajás,
Marabá and Parauapebas. There are 13,000 Vale workers registered in the
union. By far, it is the main company in which the union works. According to
Tonhão, five other smaller companies are also in the Metabase Carajás area.[87]
The interviewee, despite knowing the union's history deeply, was not a member of its board of directors at the time of its foundation, in 1987. Tonhão mentioned several times his participation in the CVRD workers' strike in Carajás in
1990: "We claimed 84% of the loss from the Collor Plan, the Summer Plan, all
kinds of plans. We went on strike for ten days."[88] He joined the union a little
later, in the early 1990s, when the union also joined CUT. Since then, Tonhão
has been a director of Metabase Carajás and, from the end of that decade,
for about twenty years, he has occupied a prominent position in the entity's
hierarchy.

On the walls of the upper floor of the union headquarters, there are references to CUT and photos of a visit made by Lula to Metabase in 1996, as part
of the 'Citizenship Caravans.' In one of them, Tonhão pointed out his location
close to the PT leader. During that period, the union leader was a PT member and fought against "Fernando Henrique's neoliberal project", to which he

---

87   One of which, Colosso, ended its attempt to reopen gold mining in Serra Pelada, after
      conflicts involving foreign investors in the project. During the interview, Tonhão showed
      the stack of dismissal approvals and blamed 'the politicians' for a supposed intervention
      in the issue, which would have 'scared off' foreign capital.

88   Aguiar Interview.

later attributed Vale's success, considering it an example to be adopted in all state-owned companies. It is perhaps an inaccuracy to say that Tonhão simply defends the privatization of state-owned companies following what was done in the FHC administration, since the union leader went even further: he openly stated that such companies should be handed over, "given" to the private sector without compensation:

> Market, high quality ore and, thirdly, private management. We were lucky. The Chinese market buying a lot of our ore; us with good logistics; high grade ore here in this region; and this other [factor] that I told you about: private management. ... So, Roger made Vale grow a lot. It was these three conditions that allowed us to keep going. Because, also, if it had been left in the government's hands, it would be like Petrobras, helping to bankroll political campaigns, right? Then it would have died, it would be finished. It only survived thanks to privatization too. So, as an activist, as a representative of the workers, I realize today that privatization was Vale's salvation. I think that Petrobras ... I don't just think so, I'm sure that if Petrobras had done that too, or even if it had been given away. Petrobras should have been given away for free to several groups. Not just to one. ... Like he did with the telephone companies. Where is the telephony scandal, right? Fernando Henrique sold it. We stayed here in the bush to call our cities, at that time, only on Sundays. We would face a line, a kilometer-long line. ... Today, with telephony's sale, you can buy a little 10-dollar chip, call wherever you want. Kids walk around with cell phones in their pockets and everything. If Petrobras had been given along with it at the time – I don't even mean sold: I mean given to various groups for operation – the country wouldn't be in the poverty it is today. ... So, we, as workers, deep in the productive sector, and participating in this union and party politics, we're opening, we're broadening people's vision of how the country should be managed.
>
> TONHÃO, Aguiar Interview

This is a highly relevant conversion of an activist who still acknowledges the strike in which he participated over 25 years ago and who keeps old photos of Lula on the walls of the union he commands. His departure from the PT, he said, was due to internal party disputes and alleged conflicts with members who wanted to remove him from the entity's command.

> I left, I left PT. ... Here, there were some factions. You know that there are in PT three lines at the national level, political factions, religious ones,

just like the Jewish people. The Jewish people were all divided in Jesus's time, right? ... I was even there at that time because I am a Spiritist, right? According to my 'collectors,' I was there. So, we're also similar at the national level. They have political currents, three at the national level, up to 57 regional ones, and we were part of the *Articulação* [Articulation] current here and we were kind of suffocated by the other socialist current, which is that of Ana Júlia,[89] [who] was elected here by PT and everything. I saw that I was spending too much energy in this internal dispute and I left. We kept the union a CUT affiliate, but we left. Also because we saw the kind of administration that it was, the kind of involvement within the party. I preferred to stay out. ... So, we started to see that the way things were headed was a little bit crooked and I left. And we started to be persecuted for being in a union this size here. This other group attacked us many times. PT won here[90] and they set up a machine to take control of the entity. They kicked me out at that time. They kept us away for 45 days, right? They made an intervention here. Even though it was the state's role, even though they were persecuting us, we took them to court in Belém, removed them and came back again, right? Because PT has this habit of also wanting to control the social movement and ends up not being able to learn how to manage. PT had a management problem that we could already see was going to get in the way. Because there was no manager, there were agitators to break into farms, occupy factories, occupy railroads, but there were problems when it came to managing. So, I left PT. Though we are in CUT here.

> TONHÃO, Aguiar Interview

When asked about the maintenance of the CUT affiliation, however, Tonhão gave evasive answers, saying that it was due to the possibility of greater articulation with other entities in the union center. Likewise, when asked about the presence of Metabase Carajás in CUT, the answers of the union center leaders were also usually evasive and often the questioning made the interviewees uncomfortable. To Marcelo Sousa, former leader of CNQ and currently in CUT's national leadership, Metabase Carajás remains in CUT because its

---

89   Ana Júlia Carepa, governor of Pará from 2006 to 2010.

90   He refers to the administration of Darci José Lermen, PT mayor of Parauapebas from 2004 to 2012. In March 2016, in the midst of the political crisis which gripped the Dilma administration, he resigned from the party and returned to the mayor's office, as a member of the Brazilian Democratic Movement Party (*Partido do Movimento Democrático Brasileiro*, or PMDB), after winning the municipal election that year.

charter makes it difficult to set up an opposing slate, also from CUT, to dispute the leadership of an affiliate union. Staying in CUT, then, Tonhão could block more open oppositional initiatives. This explanation makes sense, but it doesn't seem to solve the question, since Marcelo Sousa himself talked about his attempts to organize opposition groups in Carajás. In the same direction, Artur Henrique, former CUT president, argued:

> There are many union leaders who say they are CUT members so they are not challenged by an opposing slate also from CUT. ... To run with a CUT slate, you have to discuss with the state CUT or with the branch. You have a whole process. It's different from other union centers.
>
> ARTUR HENRIQUE, Aguiar Interview

Tonhão seemed, at many moments, to simply reproduce corporate discourse. He spoke all the while as if he were still a member of Vale's Board of Directors and represented it in the interview. He was not speaking as a representative of the workers, but as an administrator of the company. With aplomb, he dealt with the obstacles that Vale should overcome to supply ore to regions in conflict, the challenges brought about by the slowdown in the Chinese economy's growth, the disputes with competitors for the market and the decrease in iron ore prices. In these moments, he almost always spoke in the first person about the company and its goals:

> In 2007, we came to be number one in iron ore. We lost out to Anglo and Rio Tinto, which joined and moved over part of our market share, and got ahead of us .... We're surviving, behind Rio Tinto and Anglo, we're struggling to keep the mines open, operating, but it's not so easy, you know? We're in a crisis of consumption retraction ....
>
> The experience [as a board member] was good. It was two terms despite having been the alternate. We were also lucky because it was a period when the market was consuming a lot of ore at Vale, right? It was the time when the S11D project was planned. I was there, I was part of it, I helped, it's there in the minutes. And it was a great moment, a very good one, because the market was consuming ore.
>
> TONHÃO, Aguiar Interview

The union member also mentioned, in passing, the achievements obtained during the period of the company's profit growth and international expansion, in particular the '14th and 15th salaries,' established in a regional agreement for the Carajás mines, and removed during the 2015 crisis.

> Well, the salaries, they came to improve our little earnings through profit sharing bonuses. Some of the workers were promoted, those closest to them. We were, too, in the collective struggle. I remember there was an agreement in which we had real gains, above 3% in the agreement, right? In 2010, for example, we had a real gain. The market was booming, selling a lot of ore, ore at 140 dollars a tonne. So, we had profit sharing bonuses ... And, in the 1990s, despite the crisis and everything else, we started to get the first profit sharing bonus payment. And, when we got to 2000, with a higher demand, sales increased, so we started to increase profit sharing bonuses too. There was a time when workers received six salaries with profit sharing bonuses!
>
> TONHÃO, Aguiar Interview

Most of the time, however, his attention was dedicated to assessing the advantages and disadvantages of the business deals made by the company from the standpoint of the profitability of the capital invested. For him, the purchase of Bunge and the Rio Colorado project, in Argentina, would have been a great opportunity ("a good deal for us"), since it would have positioned Vale as a supplier for agriculture, with a growing demand for fertilizers. Tonhão regretted, therefore, the discontinuation of the project in Argentina, a responsibility of that country's "politicians", who would not have allowed the business to move forward. When asked if there would be any effects or consequences for the workers of the company's international expansion in recent years, Tonhão answered negatively and assessed the issue from the angle of the company's profitability, since international expansion would reduce Vale's dependence on iron ore exports:

> There's no consequence for us, no. There isn't. I don't see any consequences ... The consequence is this: in Argentina, for example, the project that didn't work out. If you dig deeper, the loss could be much greater, right? There are things in the project that can go wrong, right? It can be inside the country, it can be outside the country, it can go wrong, right? That project there, with the mines in Africa.[91] I thought at first it would be a problem, because it's a different legislation, you know? The

---

91   He refers to Vale's coal extraction operations in Mozambique.

shift schedules are all different from ours. But we see that the company
started working with ore, coal, for example, producing. Now, I honestly
don't know the details of these other mines, I don't. But I understand
that it was essential, it didn't hinder Vale's growth. Especially because we
export iron ore, right? If we reduce our operations abroad, it complicates
things, right?

TONHÃO, Aguiar Interview

The positions sympathetic to Vale's management expressed by the union
leader did not prevent the Carajás area to be also affected by the company's
hardening in negotiations with the unions after the billion-dollar loss in 2015.
Although Tonhão says that the union tried to hold a demonstration and distribute print material about it, his assessment of the problem is particularly
focused on one aspect of the issue: Metabase Carajás' finances would have
been shaken by the growing resignations from the union, caused by workers
who can no longer pay membership fees due to their material vulnerability.
Solving this problem – and not mobilizing to pressure the company because
of the workers' salary losses with no raise and no profit-sharing bonus – was
the challenge, in Tonhão's view, brought on by the economic crisis and the
fall of iron ore prices in the world market. In fact, the responsibility for the
losses brought to the union would not be the company's – which decided to lay
off, reduce wages and reduce the gains of its workers as a way to mitigate the
losses with the drop of its main export product. The problem would be, in fact,
caused by opponents who would stimulate the resignations.

Tonhão:	So, the workers started to increase their earnings, and then, the regulator for this was the profit-sharing bonus part, which was variable pay, right? Last year, as it was a loss, we didn't get anything, right?
Thiago Aguiar:	*I read the union material. Are you critical of this situation?* Very critical. So, it's one thing when you have a high paycheck, which is a danger because, when there is a crisis, you're the first one the company discards, as it's now discarding the ones with the highest paychecks. The low ones, they survive. When they have profit shar- ing bonuses, they also get a bigger share. But, at the time of the crisis, they get hurt, because the company had a loss and they're also paying for the crisis. Now, they're the ones who escape the most in times of crisis.

When the crunch comes, who's being discarded? They don't even want to know: the highest paychecks.

Has the company been dismissing during this period?
It keeps streamlining. ... This is a very difficult moment for us. These are the reports we've just closed. We lost many partners out in those crossings. ... From January 2015 to now, we've already lost 1,400 members: 500 and some were fired and the rest are resigning because they can't even pay the union. The fellow's salary is so fucked up that he can't even pay the union. And others who borrow money, retire with a state pension, who stopped paying the union. ... We've been taking losses, as has the company, as have the workers. We have 288 defaulters who were forcibly dismissed by the INSS, owing almost R$ 400,000 to the union. And the total loss, due to dismissal and resignation, from 2015 to now, is 1,349. Today it must be reaching 1,400. The grand total of member loss.

And what strategy is the union adopting in face of this situation?
This situation now. Good question. Praying that the market reacts. Many people think that they should do as Getúlio Vargas determined: open a hairdresser's salon or a cheap restaurant. There's no other way out. In the 90s, we were like that too. We started the mine with 2,700 workers. We had almost 2,000 members. When we arrived in 2000, with 587 members, we were almost finished too. There were directors who considered the union finished. They left. So, the union was almost finished. So, now, it's also dropping, the company took a loss like always, the worker took a loss too and the union is also taking a loss with layoffs, with resignations and it will come to a point where we'll really be squeezed and we'll depend on the union dues. We talk about that every day here. We're seeing a campaign inside Congress to end the union dues. We're seeing a big tractor, a steamroller, being prepared to hit us, to hit the Brazilian union organization. In the company, the guys started a perverse anti-union campaign

within the union movement, from the end of last year to now, right?

The company?
There, inside the company, the guys up there are dressed in uniforms, but they are angry with the union, they launch an anti-union campaign for people to resign, they say with R$ 40 you can buy I don't know how many kilos of beans, this and that. And then those who are also weak join in, right?

But is that done by workers or by the company?
It's the people who are running, irresponsibly too, and they do this. So, the damage is there, right? It happens every time there's a crisis, right? Because then the fellow says: "Oh, but we're not getting any more profit-sharing bonuses, I don't know what else." So they're going to resign from the union, they're going to end the union. They think that the union is to blame. Exactly: they hunt someone down to crucify. So, it's a heavy campaign to wipe out the union. ... So, you have to lower your guards, turn off the engine and manage only the rowing in order to save up costs. We're even making CUT a report, to send it to them, showing the loss and the amount we're contributing to it, we'll have to reduce it. There's no way we can contribute as we were contributing. We're making adjustments here, right? Reducing the bulletins, exploring more electronic means. So, it's a difficult time. We're going through a very difficult time.
Aguiar Interview

In the last election of Metabase Carajás, held in 2014, before our interview, the emergence of an opposing slate led to a conflict with the current leaders. Soon after being organized, the opposition group had some members dismissed without motivation by Vale and was prevented by the union board from registering. The opposing group, however, was not able to reverse its removal from the dispute in the courts.

Marcelo Sousa, former leader of CNQ, says he has followed other cases of dismissals of opposing slates' members in Carajás:

The opposition can't do it. It just can't do it. ... I know two workers there who were disconnected because they were in the slate that I myself was leading there. ... And there have been releases [from work]. The other slate managed to get 24 [members] together and I knew – because I had information there, from my snitch [laughs] – that the 24 were meeting at 3pm on a Wednesday and I couldn't get mine together on a Saturday! What can I do? I know, but I can't prove it. Unless I filmed it! So, there's an indirect persecution.

MARCELO SOUSA, Aguiar Interview

When dealing with Vale's union relations strategy, Bruno Milanez et al.[92] state that the company intervenes in union elections, supporting the formation of slates that are close to it and creating obstacles to opponents, through the dismissal of members of groups opposed to the unions which are more submitted to its interests. Metabase Carajás is an example of the use of such tactics by Vale. The union would also systematically seek recourse to the Superior Labor Court, alleging irregularities in the participation of opposition groups.

In Brazil, one of the main tactics has been to support the formation of slates which compete for the leadership of the unions, in addition to dismissing employees who are willing to form slates to oppose Vale, thereby making them unviable. The Workers in the Iron and Base Metal Extraction Industry Union (Metabase) Carajás is an example of this tactic. In this case, since the privatization of the company, the leadership has remained the same.[93]

In the interview, Tonhão stated that his goal as a union leader was to defend the creation and maintenance of jobs.[94] Therefore, in his opinion, the great virtue of Vale in recent years would be a process of "primarization," through which hiring was expanded to replace the work of service providers. However, as already seen, in the process of preparation for privatization and afterwards, Vale cut benefits and the wages of its workers, which, without profit sharing bonuses, have become close to or even lower than those paid by the companies

---

92   Milanez et al., "A estratégia corporativa da Vale S.A."

93   Ibid, 25.

94   Tonhão talked at length about the case of an agreement made on the East Mountain Range mine, whereby the workers' salaries were halved, and they remained on leave for three months. According to the union leader, Vale had presented a disjunctive: either they accepted the leave, or the workers would be fired.

providing services to the mining company. Be that as it may, the data and inter-view statements presented seem sufficient to show that outsourcing is at the heart of Vale's labor relations strategy.

Tonhão's statements suggest that, for him, the company has no major responsibility to preserve the jobs of its workers in the face of the risks and vicissitudes of its own business. However, the workers should make conces-sions to share risks and keep their jobs, under the seal of the union, whose role is not to threaten the profitability of the company with "philosophy," especially in a region notorious for tough conflicts, often solved with violence.

Tonhão:	Ore is only valuable when there is an investor and a machine producing it, otherwise ... There's no point in philosophy. Philosophy doesn't always bring food to our mouths, to our tables. If it was like that, Greece would be employing a lot of people, the cradle of philosophy, you know that. ... Within our country, there are many intellectuals like that. It's what I tell the boys: if I came from Maranhão today like I did, I wouldn't pick up a toolbox anymore. I would get a sound box and a micro-phone and go to the middle of the street to rail against [Michel] Temer and Vale. That's what gets the most hits here: railing against the investor and the President of the Republic. You can put up a fight, and soon there will be a crazy person listening to you, two, three, four. Then your campaign investor will show up. Now, you have a price to pay him later. That's what we see in our movement. We started our movement here. We used to pool for the Workers' Party. It was R$ 5 to make lunch. And a bunch of people leaning close to the fool to make fun of him and we clapped our hands. I always say that I don't clap for fools to dance anymore. I grew tired of it. I've clapped too much for fools to dance. And then, in a little while, you go into the fool's house, there are already three or four cowboys holding guns, and they won't let you in. They've already got their hands on the guy. He wins the election and that's it. ... So, that's what we're afraid of. I lost a son because of these conflicts. We went through a harsh elec-tion in 2010 and I had a couple of children. My son, at twenty years old, was ambushed. The guys came with hoods: 'Who is Tonhão's son?' 'It's me.' 'Lay down there!'

Bang, bang, bang, bang. And it came to nothing. They killed my pretty boy. I got his picture right here.

Thiago Aguiar: *Because of an electoral dispute?*
The dispute, the harsh movement, everything. So, I don't back down. If I have to die in the struggle, I'll die, but I'll fight for the workers. We've had times when the mines closed, like in the East mountain range: there were times when business got tough. ... So, in the movement here, that's how it is. We're those men who face wasps, snakes, the enemy. I've been shot at, they kill your son: it's for you to run, to take control. And they threaten us and we face the snake. The important thing is to bring food to those who depend on you.

And who is the enemy to face then?
The political and ideological currents within the move-ment. There are a lot of thugs in the region, knee-deep in politics and in social movements. Criminals, all kinds of things to take advantage of. A lot of thugs. It's not the boss, no. There are thug bosses, but there are a lot of thugs among the workers. A lot of them in party pol-itics, in the social movement, a lot. And we have to pray every day, ask God they won't catch you. And warn the kids: don't fool around. If you don't, they'll take our kids and run. And that's how it is. That's how the region here is like. There have already been several colleagues who have been buried, union presidents. ...
Aguiar Interview

For Tonhão, it's necessary to face the "enemy" to defend the workers. An "enemy" who's not on the other side of the labor exploitation relationship, but in the dispute over the directions of the union movement itself. Maybe this is the reason why the union leader refused to participate in activities in solidarity with the strike in Canada, and presented an almost disdainful position towards a year-long production stoppage when comparing it to the ten-day strike in Carajás in 1990:

I never went to Canada to participate. I didn't know the mine there. Vale bought a mine with a product that was even at a good price in the market at the time. Then, that product dropped. ... It was expanding very fast. And that business over there, I honestly didn't see a good deal for Vale, not because the price dropped. The way they interact with each other: they have their legislation which is totally different from ours in terms of union organization. ... We also lag far behind Canada. Canada is way ahead. Vale there had a lot of courage. The guys over there, the comrades who were ahead of us, bought it there, they thought it was a good deal. At the time it was, then we saw that it wasn't, it was hard to operate. The country legislation there, they took advantage of it and stood up to Vale. I didn't follow it word-for-word. I wasn't on the Board, I didn't go on any visits. I have little information about it. We only see people talking about a strike, that they went on a strike ... But we also went on strike here in '90! And we started, it was practically 99% [who] were joining the strike. We went on strike for ten days and Vale held a group inside and kept up production.[95] When we ended the strike, only 20% of the workforce was present. And we went for a bargaining agreement and lost in the Labor Court by one vote. Five votes for Vale and four for us. Vale submitted a production chart, showed that there was no interruption in production, so we also didn't get what we were claiming. I don't know if they got what they were claiming, if production even came to zero there. I don't know. I don't have this information neither from them nor from Vale regarding the production, regarding what the courts determined, given what they claimed. And I don't have this information, so I can't ... All I hear is that they went on strike, they went on strike ... And what did they achieve? Was their goal reached? Because it's easy to start a strike, but how is it going to end?

TONHÃO, Aguiar Interview

Judging by the stances of one of the leaders of the union that represents workers from Vale's largest mines, the company has managed over time, through its corporate power, to impose stability and predictability in the relationship with its unions in Brazil, preventing the eruption of conflicts and strikes. The field visits, the assembly debates at São Luís and the interviews with union members provided a picture of weakened union entities, with little capacity to oppose the company's initiatives due to its imposed negotiation logic. Collective (and profit-sharing bonus) agreements are concluded through a polarization between national proposals and localized negotiations, which

---

95   This is an interesting similarity between the 1990 strike in Carajás and the 2009–2010 strike in Sudbury (Canada), as we will see in the following Chapter: in both cases, the company sought ways to weaken and demoralize the strike by keeping workers in production.

encourages union fragmentation and largely favors the company to succeed in its strategy.

Understanding how Vale relates to its unions in Brazil helps shed light on how it operated in Canada, three years after buying the mining company Inco, when it went to the negotiating table for the first time with the union USW Local 6500. The result is well known: the largest Canadian private sector strike in thirty years.

CHAPTER 3

Vale Buys a Canadian Treasure

Restructuring, Strike, and International Trade Union Network

We heard stories ... We heard stories of Agnelli coming in to town and renting a helicopter and flying all over to see some of the Inco. And he would say: 'Holy Jeez! Whose vehicles are in the parking lot?' And they'd say: 'Well, that's the workers'. That's where they park.' 'Well, they shouldn't be making enough money to afford a car like that.' You know? We heard rumors of that, wheter or not it's true, but they certainly tried to take lots away from us.

MICHAEL, miner and Steelworkers advisor[1]

It's talked about quite a bit. Some people came from Brazil, some of the owners came from Brazil ... They went into a room for a meeting and they were talking. They were looking out the window at the parking lot and asking who owned all the trucks, all the nice trucks over the parking lot. And they said: 'Those are the guys' trucks, those are the workers' trucks.' 'How can your workers afford to spend that much on a vehicle?' They were quite surprised.

SAM, miner and Steelworkers advisor[2]

I don't know if it was Murilo Ferreira or someone else, but someone took the Brazilian guy to see the community. And he saw many big houses, with room for two big cars, very solid houses. He asked: 'But who lives in all these houses anyway?' 'Oh, your workers live in these houses.' Some even claimed that the strike happened because Vale was angry with some people, because when they got there they said: 'We don't want a Third World company coming here and creating a situation where we become Third World-type workers.'

SUSAN, Aguiar Interview

One of the statements back when Vale first came in 2006 ... [The former USW Local 6500 president] and a bunch of other union people took a

---

1   Interviewed by Thiago Aguiar in Sudbury, Canada (November 2016). All names of workers and union members interviewed in this Chapter, as indicated earlier, will always be replaced by fictitious names. The interviews were conducted in English.
2   Interviewed by Thiago Aguiar in Sudbury, Canada (November 2016).

tour with the operational [staff] of Vale. And, when they went to one of the mines, they couldn't believe: 'Who owns all these vehicles?' And they said: 'Well, the workers do. That's how they get to work because there are no buses.' They were kind of insulted that there's no way workers should have that much money to buy all those trucks ... [For them,] workers should just show up and be very happy that we just give you a job that basically makes a buy that you can feed yourself, not to have other things.

JOHN, from a fifth-generation mining family of Inco/Vale[3]

As soon as they walked in the parking lot when they took over the company, they looked at all the people's vehicles and they said: 'There's not many staff here.' And then they told them that [those] were the workers' vehicles and they said: 'No, no, that's gonna change.'

GREGORY, miner fired from Vale[4]

We hear stories, and I never heard by myself, you know? Higher-ups would come from Brazil and look at the stuff: 'Oh, whose cars are those? Those are the workers' cars? Workers don't have cars.' Here they do have cars! That's the way it is, right? We hear stories like that so it makes you wonder what the hell we're getting into here. But in the beginning I didn't notice much of a change for myself ... Higher-up managers and stuff, they knew what was coming, right? They probably had experienced dealing with the way Brazil, the way they manage, the way they run their companies.

LEONARD, Inco's miner since 1991[5]

·· ·

These testimonies were repeated by virtually all the workers and union members interviewed in Canada. In several versions, the story tells of Brazilian executives arriving in the city, flying over, walking around or looking at their new workers' cars in a parking lot, or at their large houses. A mining TNC from the Global South had just bought a century-old Canadian company, with operations in other countries such as Indonesia.[6] Three years later, as the previous collective contract expired, negotiations for a new contract reached an impasse and led to the largest Canadian private sector strike in thirty years,

---

3 Interviewed by Thiago Aguiar in Sudbury, Canada (November 2016).
4 Interviewed by Thiago Aguiar in Sudbury, Canada (November 2016).
5 Interviewed by Thiago Aguiar in Sudbury, Canada (November 2016).
6 Jamie Swift, *The Big Nickel: Inco at Home and Abroad* (Kitchener: Between the Lines, 1977).

involving 3,300 workers, with the equivalent of 845,000 work days lost.[7] The strike in Sudbury, Canada's historic mining town, lasted one year: from July 13, 2009 to July 7, 2010.

In the testimonies, the supposed clash with the community's standard of living was one of the reasons why the company decided to lower bonuses and pensions, weaken the union and impose greater discipline in the workplace, in search of increased productivity. What became a rumor, or a kind of local legend, illustrates a series of conflicts related to Vale's transformation into a TNC, which at that moment was becoming the second largest global mining company, expanding its activities to dozens of countries. When faced with a workers' collective that was very attached to their union and to the company, the new managers faced great resistance in adopting, in these new operations, their labor relations and union strategies, which were mainly based on the company's experience in its mines and activities in Brazil.

Differently from what is usually seen, therefore, such a conflict reverses the well-known relationship between multinational companies from the Global North, or originating from developed countries, and their workers in under-developed countries,[8] with often scarce union experience, high turnover, low wages and benefits. The case in point, therefore, sheds light on the effects of Vale's transnationalization process on its workers and unions.

1   "The Great Canadian Mining Non-disaster"

This was the cover headline of the dense economic section of the weekend edition of *The Globe and Mail*, one of Canada's most widely read newspapers, published in Toronto, and distributed across the country. I came across the report by chance on a very cold and rainy autumn morning while taking refuge, reading the paper, in a Montreal café, after days of research in Toronto and especially in Sudbury. On the inside, the report[9] took up two of the newspaper's

---

7   John Peters, "Down in the Vale: Corporate Globalization, Unions on the Defensive, and the USW Local 6500 Strike in Sudbury, 2009–2010," *Labour* 66 (Fall 2010): 73–105.

8   An example of this type of approach, dealing with the presence of Canadian mining companies in Latin America, can be found in Todd Gordon and Jeffery Webber, *Blood of Extraction – Canadian Imperialism in Latin America* (Halifax and Winnipeg: Fernwood Publishing, 2016).

9   Ian McGugan, "The Great Canadian Mining Non-Disaster," *The Globe and Mail* (November 5, 2016). Available in https://www.theglobeandmail.com/report-on-business/industry -news/energy-and-resources/sudbury-mining-foreign-acquisition/article32675450/; accessed May 26, 2021.

pages and proposed to take a detailed look at the denationalization of the mining sector in the country, which had occurred some ten years before with the purchase of Falconbridge by Xstrata (now Glencore) and, above all, of Inco by Vale. Both companies have a strong presence and identification with the mining town of Sudbury, located in the north of the province of Ontario.

In the economic journalist's view, the "disaster" expected at the time the companies were bought would be the loss of control of the mining revenues, which would no longer remain in the country, apart from the "emotional" reasons, which would bring opposition to control of these companies by foreign firms, since they were a kind of Canadian treasure. However, a decade later, what we could see was a profitable and modernized sector, a part of currently powerful transnational companies. Instead of revenue loss, the local mining companies' sale would have reportedly brought gains in productivity and technology, introduced by the foreign controllers, submitted to national legislation and taxpayers. Vale, in addition, transferred, as a commitment after the purchase of Inco, its global Base Metals (non-ferrous) business division to Toronto, an office with 300 employees headed by a Canadian director.[10] The report also mentioned the reversal of expectations with nickel prices in the world market, which in 2006 were around US$ 20,000 a tonne.[11] However, contrary to the continuous price increase that was expected during the commodity boom, there was a strong price reduction, especially after the 2008–2009 crisis burst. According to the report, had Inco and Falconbridge not been sold, they would have suffered heavily from their high dependence on nickel exports. Vale would have reportedly "got off to a rocky start", with the 2009–2010 strike, but nowadays would have built a "decent relationship with the United Steelworkers," an assessment with which the president of the powerful international union,

---

10   At the time, Jennifer Maki, a Canadian who began her career at Inco in 2003, was Vale's executive director of Base Metals (where she remained from November 2014 to December 2017). On January 1, 2018, Brazilian executive Eduardo Bartolomeo took over as director, the position in which he remained until March 2019, when he became the company's chief executive officer (CEO), following the departure of Fabio Schvartsman in the wake of the crisis caused by the collapse of the Córrego do Feijão mine dam in Brumadinho (MG). Currently, Canadian Mark Travers holds the executive vice-presidency of Base Metals at Vale, based in Toronto. According to information available in http://www.vale .com/pt/aboutvale/leadership/documents/perfilcompleto/jan-15/cv_%20jennifer_po rt_jan_2015.pdf, http://www.vale.com/brasil/PT/aboutvale/leadership/Documents/cv /pt/Eduardo_Bartolomeo_diretor_presidente_Vale.pdf and http://www.vale.com/brasil /PT/aboutvale/leadership/Documents/cv/pt/Mark_travers_diretor_executivo_vale.pdf; accessed December 3, 2021.

11   And in 2007, they peaked at over US$52,000 a tonne, as described in Chapter 1.

Leo Gerard, interviewed at the time, disagreed. For him, with Vale's arrival, a "mature relationship" with the union was replaced by a "confrontational" one, the result of an attempt to impose "authoritarian, Brazilian-style labour relations."

The celebratory tone which covered Vale's presence in the report also contrasts starkly with what I had heard during the previous days spent in Sudbury. I arrived in the mining town by bus, leaving from Toronto. Before entering the city, from afar, it was already possible to identify one of the mining landmarks which distinguishes the place. In the sky, I could see the Superstack, a famous smelter chimney, the second largest in the world at 381 meters high, erected by Inco in the 1970s to mitigate the then serious local pollution problem. The tall height is explained by the need to disperse the sulfuric gasses away from the city.[12] Hans Brasch, a German immigrant who worked at the Inco mines in Sudbury from 1952 to 1992,[13] said that the construction of the Superstack transformed life in the town and profoundly changed the air quality. Despite local affection for the record-breaking smokestack, Vale announced[14] in January 2017 the decision to decommission the Superstack by the first quarter of 2020 and demolish it over the following years. In its place, two smaller smokestacks have been built,[15] which will certainly change the local skyline, but will not cause Sudbury to lose its characteristic sights, which I saw as I approached the small bus terminal late on a freezing afternoon: the train line that takes mined nickel to Port Colborne, where the metal is refined and shipped across the Great Lakes to consumer markets in the United States and around the world; the gray water tower downtown, bearing Sudbury's name; and the peaceful look of its residents walking along the unpaved streets.

---

12   Informations available in http://www.vale.com/canada/EN/aboutvale/communities /sudbury/Pages/Superstack%20History%20Fact%20Sheet_FINAL.pdf; accessed May 26, 2021.

13   And author of several books on photography, mining history in Sudbury and the USW Local 6500 union. It was a privilege to be able to interview Brasch in Sudbury, Canada (November 2016), when the retired miner was 86 years old. His statements and records about union activism at Inco were an important source of information for the research on which this book was based, for which I am very grateful. His name has been mentioned with his consent.

14   Information available in http://www.vale.com/canada/EN/aboutvale/communities/sudb ury/Pages/Superstack%20Announcement_FAQ.pdf; accessed May 26, 2021.

15   With which the company aims to reduce particulate emissions by 40% and sulfur dioxide emissions by 85%, according to CBC News available in http://www.cbc.ca/news/canada /sudbury/vale-announces-superstack-done-1.3949500; accessed May 26, 2021.

2   A Brazilian Mother-in-Law for the Orphans of "Mother Inco"

> We still call it Inco. It's hard to say Vale and it's not because it's a bad
> word. It's because it's a great name in our community. Personally myself,
> I'm from the third generation in the mines ... There's a lot of history in
> mining in the community here ... In that transition time, I felt deceived
> by my own government for allowing foreing companies to come in and
> buy Inco, which was an iconic Canadian company ... We always referred
> to Inco as 'mother Inco', we thought that this was a huge company. And
> then when you hear about this Vale, Inco was just a ... small, little mining
> company. But our perception, in our real ignorance of the mining world,
> we were just nothing. Vale bought us in cash ... I tell a lot of people we
> had mother Inco, and then now we have the ugly mother-in-law [laughs]
> ... Not to say that Inco was all roses and nice fluffy clouds, but certainly a
> different management style that we are still trying to adapt to.[16]

Inco was the largest nickel producer in Canada and the second largest in the
world, a position which Vale inherited after buying the company in 2006,
then to become the largest global producer in 2014.[17] Its largest facilities
are in the Greater Sudbury region (Ontario), in addition to units in Kronau
(Saskatchewan), Port Colborne (Ontario), Thompson (Manitoba), Long
Harbour, Saint John and Voisey's Bay (Newfoundland and Labrador), and the
aforementioned Base Metals business division offices in Toronto. Nickel mining in Sudbury dates back to the late 19th century, with the establishment of
the Canadian Copper Company. In 1901, the Creighton Mine, still in operation
today, began operations, and in 1902 the International Nickel Company was
created (after the incorporation of the mining company by United States capital), whose acronym Inco came into use in 1919.[18] Years later, because of US
antitrust measures, the company's Board of Directors exchanged shares and
Inco "came to be considered Canadian, escaping US legislation against market
monopolies."[19]

---

16   George, miner, interviewed by Thiago Aguiar in Sudbury, Canada (November 2016).
17   Tádzio Peters Coelho, *Noventa por cento de ferro nas calçadas: mineração e (sub)desen-
      volvimentos em municípios minerados pela Vale S.A.* Doctoral dissertation (Rio de Janeiro
      State University, 2016), 241.
18   See Swift, *The Big Nickel*; Coelho, *Noventa por cento de ferro nas calçadas*, and Vale Canada
      history available in http://www.vale.com/canada/EN/aboutvale/history/Pages/default
      .aspx; accessed May 26, 2021.
19   Coelho, *Noventa por cento de ferro nas calçadas*, 233.

Sudbury was also home to another traditional local mining company, Falconbridge. Indeed, the town is historically dependent on nickel mining and is home to a number of mining families who have been established in the area for five generations. During the period of capital concentration in the sector, Inco and Falconbridge, the two largest Canadian mining companies, attempted a merger that did not advance due to legal restrictions pointed out by government competition agencies – the operation would practically create a nickel production monopoly in the country. Even though it is not dependent on a single company, Sudbury has the characteristics of a mono-industrial city, similar to the description of company towns presented in Chapter 1.

Up to the 1970s, the town was defined by its connection to mining, as most of Sudbury's population at that time worked at either Inco or Falconbridge.[20] The community has thus forged a common collective sense in its years as a company town, even though in recent decades the restructuring of the nickel industry in the city – an effect of globalization, technological change, and pressure to expand profits – has led to a reduction in the number of workers (mostly unionized) in the mines and an increase in outsourced workers. The number of workers who are members of USW Local 6500 has dropped from 20,000 at its peak in 1971 to less than 3,000 today. In Sudbury, two-thirds of the workforce was employed in mining in 1971, and by 2006, two-thirds of the city's workforce was employed in the service sector.[21] Sudbury's great mineral wealth, however, would not, apparently, be reflected in city life today:

> In northeastern Ontario, the Sudbury Basin, formed by meteorite impact, contains one of the world's top ten concentrations of minerals. More than 1.7 trillion tons of ore have been mined over a hundred years, and reserves of nickel, copper, iron, gold, silver and platinum remain large. Yet, the city of 160,000 reflects little of that wealth. Household income levels were 10 percent lower than the provincial norm in 2005; as well-paid mining sector jobs disappear, low, temporary wage work becomes the norm.[22]

George's testimony, reproduced at the beginning of this section, is common to most of the Canadian workers interviewed, for whom working for Inco was part of their local identity, their community ties, and even their family

---

20   Reuben Roth, Mercedes Steedman and Shelley Condratto, "The Casualization of Work and the Rise of Precariousness in Sudbury's Nickel Mining Industry", in *33rd International Labour Process Conference (ILPC)* (Athens, 2015), 7.

21   Ibid, 8.

22   Ibid, 7.

history. "Mother Inco" represents, as will be seen, in the words of many workers, a past built by their parents and grandparents. It is with sadness, therefore, that people talk about the failure of the merger between the two large mining companies in the city, since the workers preferred that the company should continue to be controlled by national capital. In their opinion, this would keep investments and profits in place, since being a small part of a TNC may weaken their capacity to put pressure on and intervene in management decisions.

> At that time, I was very disappointed because there was another North American company, a local company, that was wanting to merge with Inco: Falconbridge. And our hopes were that it was gonna happen. We could see that being good for the mining guys, for the people that work for these two companies and we could see that being good for the community ... Just because it's local, local dynamics, local people. It would be local management, it would be a local management strategy ... With Vale, we had a lot of concerns on the style that would come with a Brazilian-based company. We were concerned about that.[23]

> People call it 'mother Inco' ... There were still big mining companies in Sudbury at that time, Inco and Falconbridge. They tried to merge, to get together, which would have been the best thing for Sudbury obviously ... So you'd have a boom, right? Both companies have been around here for a hundred years. There are still tonnes of ore underground. The two companies together employ ... I don't know ... At one time there were 30,000 people that worked for Inco. They're still the two largest employers in Sudbury. So how could that not be good for Sudbury and Canada, obviously? Now you're seeing the profits go wherever ... It seems like they have to fight for capital money just to reinvest in Sudbury ... I didn't know anything about Vale really, but it was kind of said that Inco now had foreign ownership and operated in Brazil. You see the money just goes ... I don't know how to word it, maybe disappointment, I don't know. I really wanted that merger to take place, Inco and Falconbridge.
> LEONARD, Aguiar Interview

> Vale came in here and they tried to treat us the way that they treat their people down in Brazil: pay them nothing, treat them like shit, fire them at will ... It was a hostile takeover: 'This is the way it is. You don't like it,

---

23   Sean, miner, interviewed by Thiago Aguiar in Sudbury, Canada (November 2016).

leave.' And, I'm sorry, but in Canada you don't do that. That's not the way
we treat people. That's not the way anybody should be treated, you know?
You took over a company, take it over the way it is because it's working.
You didn't buy the company because it's failing. You bought it because
it was working and it was a well-oiled machine. We knew what we were
doing long before Vale was here. We've been mining since what? 1900s or
1850s? We know how to mine. We didn't need them to come in here and
tell us what to do or tell us how to do it or to shut our mouths in the meetings, you know? Or we make too much money, as per the [Brazilians]
that came here and said: 'Whose vehicles are these, the workers'? Are you
kidding?' Who the hell are they? We didn't want Vale here, we didn't ask
for them to come and they can leave at any point. The worst thing that
ever happened around here was Inco being sold.

GREGORY, Aguiar Interview

In 2006, Inco was bought by Vale for US$18.24 billion[24] and Falconbridge was
bought by Xstrata, now Glencore, for US$17 billion.[25] The former mining region
of Sudbury had become part of the globalized mining industry landscape. The
discomfort with the loss of "Mother Inco" would only increase after the new
management's first years, when the new contract began to be negotiated. Then,
in many moments, a feeling that was openly 'against Brazil' would arise. Many
workers, when talking about the issue – and, I imagine, especially because they
were in front of a Brazilian – stated that, with time, people started to differenti-
ate the country from the company. In any case, it is common, in the interviews,
for workers to refer to Vale as "Brazil":

Our management keeps saying that 'Brazil wants this, Brazil wants that.'
The worker here doesn't know what Brazil wants because Brazil doesn't
talk to us. There is no communication back and forth. All we know is that
everyday they're cutting benefits or cutting this, always losing money:
'We need more.' So, the workforce is demoralized ... We don't know Brazil
because we're not in touch. Just like in Brazil, regularly, the people would
know nothing of Sudbury. Unless when it comes up in the news or something like that. Your country is distant from ours. We're still the same people, we all think the same, we work the same, but we're a whole continent
away. So, yes, we did not know. I was hoping that we're gonna be part of a

---

24   Coelho, *Noventa por cento de ferro nas calçadas*, 241.
25   Peters, "Down in the Vale."

giant corporation. But it started right away that, basically: 'If you don't do what we tell you, you're only like 5% of our big organization, so you really don't mean anything to us.'

JOHN, Aguiar Interview

[There were anti-Brazil feelings], originally, yes, absolutely. It was Brazil, Brazil, Brazil ... Over time, I think part of this is the Brazilian thing. I also think that our corporate people are not connected to our people in Sudbury ... So, there's a population of workers that still think it's Brazil. I, myself, I think is partly a Brazilian thing, partly the corporate thing and partly our local management. Certain groups really don't have a connection to Sudbury.

SEAN, Aguiar Interview

This kind of discourse seems to be an unintended consequence of Vale's adoption, in its new global brand, of the green and yellow colors of the Brazilian flag, as a way to associate its image with that of the country. Among the objectives of such association, Judith Marshall's suggestion[26] – that the company used a supposed 'South-South' orientation of the country's foreign policy during Lula's government as a showcase to facilitate its entry into Mozambique to the detriment of Chinese competitors – seems to make sense.

Also on this issue, union advisor Susan recalled a case she learned about while organizing international solidarity activities for the Steelworkers during the strike in Vale Canada: an experienced Brazilian union member from Conlutas traveled to a fly-in fly-out unit of Vale in Voisey's Bay to participate in activities in support of the conflict, but "it seems he arrived there and found people with signs saying 'Brazilians, go home!' ... He got into a dialogue with them to explain that there are all kinds of Brazilians."[27] This case immediately came to my mind when, in one of the rooms of the USW Local 6500 union, I found a picture up on the wall of one of the 2009–2010 strike pickets, in which there was a group of workers standing in front of a company gate, under a sign, erected by them, with two arrows in opposite directions: to the left, Canada; to the right, Brazil. It must be remarked, also, that there are, in the union's several rooms, CUT and Brazilian social movement flags, mementos of the articulation

---

26   Judith Marshall, "Behind the Image of South-South Solidarity at Brazil's Vale", in *BRICS: an Anti-Capitalist Critique*, ed. Patrick Bond and Ana Garcia (Chicago: Haymarket Books, 2015), 163.

27   Aguiar Interview.

attempts with Vale's union movement in Brazil, which occurred during the strike period.

3   A Powerful Multinational Union with Deep Local Roots

Vale took control of Inco while the collective agreement signed earlier by the Canadian company and the USW Local 6500 union was in effect. The union is a local section of the powerful United Steelworkers (USW),[28] a binational US-Canadian union (with a presence in Caribbean countries as well), which claims to have 1.800 local unions representing hundreds of thousands of active and retired union members.[29] The USW is "the largest private sector union in North America, the union with the most global alliances, and the union with a tradition of militancy and innovation."[30] It is also considered the largest private sector union in the world.[31] For reasons such as these, the 2009–2010 strike is considered an "especially bitter" setback in the face of a powerful transnational.[32]

The USW is the main union of the US union federation AFL-CIO, which is made up of 56 national and international affiliated unions representing 12.5-million-member workers.[33] The Steelworkers also maintain a federated structure, since they represent workers in a wide range of economic sectors through affiliated local unions. According to Mary, a USW international leader[34] who worked in the Solidarity Center's São Paulo office years ago,

> really, in Brazilian language, the USW would be a confederation, almost a union centre. Because, to tell you the truth, we represent workers in several sectors: paper, rubber, petroleum, steel, aluminum, all metals, healthcare ... Puerto Rico, Virgin Islands, Barbuda. So it's not just mining.[35]

In Canada, the USW is affiliated with the Canadian Labour Congress (CLC), which plays the same role in Canada as the AFL-CIO does in the United States.

---

28   Created on May 22, 1942 as the United Steelworkers of America, according to information available in http://www.usw.org/union/history; accessed May 26, 2021.
29   Available in https://www.usw.org/union/one-member-one-vote; accessed May 26, 2021.
30   Peters, "Down in the Vale," 75.
31   Ibid, 76.
32   Ibid.
33   Information available in http://www.aflcio.org/About; accessed May 26, 2021.
34   Its headquarters is located in Pittsburgh, USA.
35   Mary, AFL-CIO advisor, interviewed by Thiago Aguiar (videocall, February 2016).

The CLC represents more than 3 million Canadian workers[36] out of approximately 20 million active workers in the country.[37]

As Mark Thompson and Albert Blum have shown,[38] there has historically been criticism in Canada of US-based international unionism, related to, among other reasons: the distribution of collected funds, which is unfair to local Canadian unions; the restrictions on the establishment of political and international ties, which are subject to the interests of US-based unions; and the fragmentation of the Canadian labor movement, due to the conflict carried out by many international unions active in the country. This criticism has led, over time, to breakaway movements and organizational changes within Canadian unions, who put pressure on international headquarters as their membership rates and relative political importance increased.

Four models of integrating Canadian unions into international ones have developed: 1) "assimilationist," whereby local Canadian and US unions are treated the same way, with no specifics for national issues; 2) "special status," whereby Canadian unions have different rights and functions than their US counterparts; 3) "self-governing," whereby Canadian unions exercise forms of financial and political autonomy; and 4) "sovereignty-association," whereby there are formal ties to the US headquarters, but the latter exercises no authority over the Canadian section.[39]

Throughout the 1980s, pressure began in the USW Canadian sections in favor of the self-governing model and for a Canadian district of the Steelworkers.[40] Today, the international USW is divided into thirteen districts – ten in the United States and three in Canada – linked to the international union, but constituting the immediate structure to which local unions report.[41] The Canadian unions that have moved to the models of self-governing or sovereignty-association have been more successful in retaining or expanding their membership base.

---

36   According to information available in https://canadianlabour.ca/who-we-are/; accessed May 26, 2021.

37   According to data from Statistics Canada available in https://www150.statcan.gc.ca/t1/tbl/en/cv.action?pid=1410001801; accessed May 26, 2021.

38   Mark Thompson and Albert Blum, "International Unionism in Canada: The Move to Local Control," *Industrial Relations* 22, no. 1 (Winter 1983): 71–85.

39   Thompson and Blum, 73–4.

40   Ibid, 76.

41   Information available in https://www.usw.org/districts; accessed May 26, 2021. The three Canadian districts are: District 3, with jurisdiction over local unions in the provinces of Alberta, British Columbia, Manitoba, Nunavut, Saskatchewan, the Northwest Territories, and Yukon; District 5, with jurisdiction over Quebec; and District 6, with jurisdiction over New Brunswick, Nova Scotia, Ontario, and Newfoundland and Labrador.

In turn, those that broke away entirely from the international unions became more weakened and isolated.[42] In addition, there would reportedly be a more "left wing" trend in Canadian unions, which would be more militant, oriented towards advocacy of public services and state presence in basic sectors of the economy, as well as of interunion mergers and the establishment of strike funds.[43]

Unionism in the United States and Canada have common roots, reinforced by the presence of binational unions.[44] However, over the course of the twentieth century, their trajectories began to separate, particularly in terms of union density. Both countries maintained similar unionization rates up until 1960, when they were just under 35%. Since then, the unionization rate has declined sharply in the United States, reaching 12.3% of workers in 2011 (with only 7.4% in the private sector), while the rate in Canada in the same year was 31.2%.[45] These changes can be explained by differences in the two countries' 'political incorporation' of the working class.

> In both countries, labor was politically incorporated as a result of struggles in the 1930s and 40s, in response to the crises of the Great Depression and World War II. As a result of these struggles, US labor was incorporated as an *interest group*, whereas Canadian labor was incorporated as a *class representative*. These different identities reflected different organizing logics that enabled or constrained labor's scope of action in each country. Canadian labor's role as a class representative fit into a *class idea* that broadened and legitimized its scope of action, while US labor's role

---

42   Thompson and Blum, "International Unionism in Canada."

43   Ibid, 83.

44   Barry Eidlin, "Class vs. Special Interest: Labor, Power, and Politics in the United States and Canada in the Twentieth Century," *Politics & Society* 43, no. 2 (2015): 181–211. For a reconstruction of the origins of US unionism and the model of business unionism which historically guided the union practice of the AFL-CIO and the Steelworkers, see Svétlana Askoldova, *Le trade-unionisme américain – formation d'une idéologie (fin du XIXème siècle)* (Moscow: Éditions du Progrès, 1981).

45   In dealing with LMEs, Peter Hall and David Soskice show that low unionization rates – an effect of the greater ability to hire and fire in these countries – are one of the main differences with CMEs. However, in exposing the characteristics of LMEs, the higher unionization in Canada compared to the United States is underlined. See Peter Hall and David Soskice, "An Introduction to Varieties of Capitalism," in *Varieties of Capitalism: The Institutional Foundations of Comparative Advantage* (Oxford, Oxford University Press, 2001), 1–68.

as an interest group fit into a *pluralist idea* that narrowed and delegiti-
mized its scope of action.[46]

As a result of such differences, labor in Canada placed greater importance on
independent mobilization to achieve broad demands, which offered better
conditions for unions to maintain their membership base, while labor's identity as an interest group in the United States linked its issues to a kind of particular demand to be defended by Democratic Party Representatives, eroding
workers' claims and union membership rates.[47]

These characteristics help frame the particularities of the Canadian labor
movement, even when it is part of binational, or multinational, US-based
unions. The international USW has representation of workers from all of Vale's
units in Canada. In Sudbury, representation of mine and production area
workers is handled by the union USW Local 6500. According to Michael, from
the local union's board:

> I think being part of an international union, a North American union,
> is important, more important than ever now because of globalization
> and because of Vale that came and bought Inco, you know? Before, we
> could stand on our own with Inco and we could do that within Canada
> and we would win. That's how we got our good collective agreements
> and everything to where we are today. But, with Vale coming over, it's
> not just a Canadian company we're dealing with now. Now we're dealing
> with a global conglomerate and we use our connections not only in North
> America but all over the world with our struggle against Vale. And Vale,
> you know? They know that we went on a strike for a year, it's hurt a lot
> of us, it wasn't easy, but they know we did it, they know we're tough and
> I think they realized that they may think twice about taking us on again.
>
> MICHAEL, Aguiar Interview

USW Local 6500 participates in the Sudbury and District Labour Council, an
umbrella body for all CLC-affiliated union organizations in the city. As Joseph,
leader of the Sudbury teachers' union and president of the Sudbury and District
Labour Council during the strike years, explained, CLC unions organize locally
into municipal councils and pledge not to compete with other unions affiliated
with the federation for union representation at a company, if that company

---

46   Eidlin, "Class vs. Special Interest", 183, emphasis added.
47   Ibid, 184.

is already represented by another organization. Michael explained how it is possible to gain representation at a company, according to the model known as the 'closed shop':[48]

> The way that our labor laws work in Ontario and most of Canada actually is that, if there's a workplace that doesn't have a union, you go to the workplace, you talk to the wokers at the workplace. We're not allowed in the workplace but we talk to the workers from that workplace and we organize them. We sign union cards and, when we get over 40%, in Ontario you can apply to the Ontario Labour Relations Board to have a vote to represent those workers. We normally wouldn't apply only with 40%, we like to have a lot higher. And one week to the day, seven days later, there's a vote that's held by the Ontario Labour Relations Board. They hold it and supervise it and it's in the workplace and all the workers in the workplace have a right [to vote]: 'Do you want to be represented by the union, yes or no?'. And if 50% plus one vote to be represented by the union, they're unionized. And from that point forward any new hired, anyone who starts automatically becomes part of the union.
>
> MICHAEL, Aguiar Interview

Once representation is gained, it doesn't need to be renewed, precisely because of the CLC's interunion agreement, whereby "unions can't raid each other. So we don't spend our resources fighting each other about controlling workplaces. We focus on places that are not unionized",[49] as Michael explained. In Sudbury, the Steelworkers gained representation at Inco in 1965, which is why the name of the local union is 6500. However, there had previously been a union representing those workers: the Mine Mill,[50] which lost representation, in Michael's words, because it "failed to maintain good relations" with the CLC. This is a somewhat more complex story, in fact, which intersects with the personal history of Leo Gerard, a Canadian and a miner in Sudbury, currently the international president of the Steelworkers in the United States, with deep ties to the town having been a former leader of USW Local 6500. His father had been

---

48   For a concrete description of the form of union activism in this model, considering the differences of historical period and sector studied, see Huw Beynon, *Working for Ford* (Harmondsworth: Penguin Books, 1984).

49   Aguiar Interview.

50   Currently Mine Mill Local 598, a member of the international union Unifor, which represents workers at the current Glencore facility in town. The union lost representation from Inco in 1965 but managed to keep representation from the former Falconbridge.

active in the local union since before USW membership.[51] For union advisor Susan, the determinant for Mine Mill's loss of Inco representation would have been its openly communist positions at the time:

> Sudbury is the heart of the Steelworkers, you may have heard that already, right? And the international president Leo Gerard comes from this mine in Sudbury. ... Interestingly enough, the father ... It's a fascinating story. A mining town with two big companies, historically Inco and Falconbridge. The Falconbridge workers were represented by the Mine Mill Smelter Workers, which was a union with a few people ... US-based, but a communist union, openly communist. However, their history in Sudbury is interesting, as a communist union, really a social union, a beauty of a union. They promoted camps in the summer for the miners' children, cultural activities. There was a time when the dance company from the city of Winnipeg ... was hired for a presentation, all done by the union. This was in the 1950s, in the middle of the Cold War, and it seems that this dance company was told that if they accepted the invitation of this communist union in Sudbury, they would never have the opportunity to perform in the United States again. ... At that time, the Steelworkers played an ugly role, trying to destroy the communist union. And Leo's father was a member of that generation. I don't really know the story, but it seems that Leo's father was from the other union and switched to the Steelworkers.
>
> SUSAN, Aguiar Interview

Hans Brasch, in turn, described the story somewhat differently, especially with regard to the union's relationship with communists, but he went in the same direction as Susan in showing the Steelworkers' role in getting Inco representation out of Mine Mill. Brasch worked at Inco for forty years: he was hired shortly after his arrival in Canada – before that he had worked as a waiter, a cleaner, and a lumberjack – seeking a better life than he found in his country

---

51 Which explains the view of many interviewees that the strike ended up becoming an almost personal conflict: "it was a clash of the titans: Roger Agnelli and Leo Gerard, and they were gonna prove who was the strongest", according to John's opinion (Aguiar Interview). In an article critical of the actions of USW Local 6500 in the strike, John Peters disagrees with this view. For him, one of the local union's mistakes was not to get closer to Leo Gerard and use his international president figure to put pressure on Vale, which may have occurred due to internal disputes in the board of directors during the period in which the strike took place. See Peters, "Down in the Vale."

after World War II. According to his account, in 1958 he participated in his first
strike at Inco, which lasted for 91 days, at which point the pressure on Mine
Mill would have increased.

> In 1958, you had this McCarthy, if you have ever heard of him, McCarthy
> from the United States ... Everybody was a communist ... And they blamed
> Mine Mill Local 598 communist, which I dispute even today. You might
> have some members there [who were] communists, I didn't know, but
> that's an individual situation ... Yeah, we had some communists there,
> but the union itself is not communist. But, anyhow, then in 1962 it came
> the United Steelworkers in ... And it came to a vote and the Steelworkers
> got in by 15 votes. Another thing I should mention: at that time, we had
> in Inco, I would say, about 18,000 people ... Because everything was done
> by hand, you didn't have so much machinery. When the Steelworkers
> came in ... You know, when you campaign to get the vote, you make lots
> of promises, even the United Steelworkers: 'We have more money, we are
> gonna show Inco!' ... In 1966, because the company didn't really know
> who represented, Mine Mill or Steelworkers, so they said: 'Listen, you
> gotta solve out this thing first, which union you belong. We will not nego-
> tiate with a union which might be going out.' It kept on negotiating ...
> But then it came a dispute underground and the guys started ... a wildcat
> strike because it was not authorized by the union, which were for 24 days
> at strike and then the union settled, the United Steelworker.
>
> HANS BRASCH, Aguiar Interview

One possible reason for the pressure on Mine Mill in Sudbury can be specu-
lated, inspired by the context of McCarthyism in the United States: in addition
to the historic presence of US capital at Inco, according to Brasch, the company
had been the main supplier of nickel during World War II and in the following
period would continue to be one of the main suppliers for the US war industry.[52] In any case, between 1965 and 1966, the USW consolidated its status as the
representative of Inco workers. In the following decades, the tradition of long
strikes and confrontations with the company continued, especially during
the negotiation of collective agreements, which, once expired, were immediately considered by the union a reason to picket and go on strike. Hans Brasch
described several long strikes which he participated in or documented after
his retirement:

---

52   Information also presented by Coelho, *Noventa por cento de ferro nas calçadas*, 233.

In 1969 there was another dispute with the company ... a strike here, 121 days, and then we find a settlement with the company and the union. Things modernized, mechanized [during that period, the use of dynamite was abolished in Sudbury by Inco] ... In 1975, we had another 10-day strike ... And then we have 1978–79, that was a big one, but you have to realize what happened at that time: the nickel price was very, very low ... [In 1982–83], we went on strike for 32 days, followed by a 275-day shutdown, which was very good: the union worked together with our members of Parliament, so that we got unemployment insurance ... In 1997, the 26-day strike, in 2003 we had another 89-day strike, and then we had the big one here from 2009 to 2010, 361-day strike. So, a total of 1,290 days in my lifetime here for 40 years.

HANS BRASCH, Aguiar Interview

As he spoke, the retired German miner looked up the dates and duration of Inco strikes in Sudbury in his book.[53] Out of the whole period covered by his research (1958 to 2010), the strike of 2009–2010, lasting 361 days, was by far the longest. After that, one can mention the long 261-day strike in 1978–1979, which is still remembered by many workers today, when, due to low nickel prices in the world market and the inability of the company to grant a higher wage increase, a 'nickel bonus' was negotiated with Inco, which was a bonus paid annually in accordance with the variation of nickel prices, as a way to supplement wages. Besides these, in 1982–1983 there was a large 32-day strike, followed by a mine shutdown carried out by the company's management which lasted another 275 days, as a way to avoid further losses due to the very low nickel prices in the period. At that time, the company laid off 159 workers and promoted dozens of early retirements. In the 1980s, the workforce at Inco was reduced to 10,000 men. A decade earlier, 18,000 miners worked at the company. The reduction was caused by the crisis in prices, but above all by changes in the production process, with the introduction of new machines.

When Vale took over operations at Inco in 2006, it began to deal with a group of workers strongly linked to the union, whose families had settled in the region for decades and worked in nickel mining. As was possible to notice in the interviews, for them, their job is seen almost as a craft inherited from previous generations. The union – whose presence in the town is still significant to

---

53   Hans Brasch, *Winds of Change: The Local 6500 USW Strike of 2009 to 2010* (Sudbury: Hans and Teresa Brasch, 2010), 130.

TABLE 1   Strikes and production shutdown at Inco/Vale (1958–2010)

1958	September 24 to December 23	91 days of strike
1966	July 14 to August 8	24 days of strike
1969	July 10 to November 15	121 days of strike
1975	July 10 to July 20	10 days of strike
1978–1979	September 16 to June 3	261 days of strike
1982–1983	June 1 to April 3	307 days – 32 days of strike and 275 days of production shutdown
1997	June 2 to June 27	26 days of strike
2003	June 1 to August 28	89 days on strike
2009–2010	July 13 to July 8	361 days of strike
Total – 1,290 days of strike and production shutdown		

SOURCE: BRASCH, *WINDS OF CHANGE*, 130

this day,[54] despite the aforementioned workforce decrease in the mines (USW Local 6500 currently has about 3,000 members) – has a history of organizing workers and of striking during tougher contract negotiations. Its stewards, the union representatives in the workplace, have a constant presence in day-to-day production, be it opining on occupational safety procedures or filing grievances. The latter are very important for the relationship between miners and supervisors. Historically, a three-stage grievance pattern was built at Inco, regulated in detail by the collective agreements.

Table 1 summarizes the strikes (and shutdowns) that occurred at Inco/Vale in Sudbury from 1958 to 2010. As a result, the workers' collective has obtained, over time, successive wage and benefit increases. According to information obtained from interviews with union members,[55] the average annual salary of Vale workers in Sudbury is 100,000 Canadian dollars, and can reach 150,000 in cases of workers who do a lot of overtime and whose productivity is higher. In the aforementioned report from *The Globe and Mail*,[56] it is stated that the city's average salary is higher than that of Toronto and Montreal, two large and wealthy Canadian urban centers.

---

54   Sudbury's main ballroom, for example, is located inside the headquarters of USW Local 6500, the rent for which is one of the union's sources of revenue.

55   Corroborating data also presented by Peters, "Down in the Vale."

56   McGugan, "The Great Canadian Mining Non-Disaster."

In Sudbury, therefore, there is a workers' collective and a union which are significantly different from the ones that Vale relates to in its Brazilian operations, in which workforce turnover, low wages and outsourcing are key characteristics, as well as the dispersion of unions, their distance from the workplace and the bureaucratization of their leadership. As shown in the previous chapters, these characteristics bring, as consequences, low union activism and restricted opposition to the initiatives of the company's management. These elements conform Vale's labor and union relations strategies, which the new Brazilian managers would take to Canada. The collective agreement signed by USW Local 6500 and Inco in 2006, shortly before the company's sale, was still in force. It would take three years for Canadian workers to understand the extent of the restructuring imposed by the new controllers and the concessions they required from their workers.

For Sérgio Rosa, then president of Vale's Board of Directors, the purchase of Inco was the main step taken towards establishing a "transnational company culture." On the one hand, he stated that, when establishing oneself in a new location, one must adapt to its conditions. However, when questioned about the restructuring promoted by Vale in Canada, Rosa answered that he considers it a pure and simple imposition of the economic logic under globalization, ahead of which there is nothing to do but regret it, from an individual point of view, and take advantage of the situation, as a business leader, to increase the profitability of investments:

> **Sérgio Rosa:** Vale was going international at that time, and still didn't have a clear internationalization policy. ... It still didn't have significant revenues abroad, nor had it created a culture of a consolidated transnational company. Inco was, in fact, the main step towards this direction. ... It was a desire to reduce costs. Obviously, you'll look for the company's internal parameters, but, deep down, it's a perception of how much you can negotiate the workforce at that moment. You can't impose a standard. You have to respect the local markets. ... You have to respect the local market, global legislation, local culture, local existing workforce or not. You can have some things that you generalize, but it's not everything. Vale was building that. The idea that Vale was going to become a transnational company would demand that it built an attitude in this sense, but this culture wasn't consolidated.

Thiago Aguiar: *Were labor and union relations at the former Inco taken*
into account in the acquisition?

Yes and no, man. Let's be very clear about this. I, as a
shareholder representative, have never denied what
I think about the labor world, about labor relations, etc.
etc. On the other hand, I couldn't put my ideological worl-
dview ahead of investment decisions. In fact, when I went
to Previ, I knew that. I can't do that and be the director
of an investment fund, because the guys who elected me
here want this to turn profitable. ... But labor relations,
unfortunately, aren't determined by a company and aren't
determined by a shareholder. We're within the context of
the local economy dynamics, the play of forces, etc. And,
unfortunately, the companies, when they can take some
advantage in this aspect, they take advantage in this aspect.
I say unfortunately because I think it's a systemically bad
vision. My conception of the world and my conception of
life is that the boss systematically taking advantage of the
workers is, for the system as a whole, for the world as a
whole, bad. But this is what happens: the boss is always
looking to take advantage. If he can reduce wages, he
does. If he can reduce benefits, he does. There was a cycle
in history when that was different. There were conquests
and continuous improvements, let's say so, right? The private pension system itself, both in the United States and
elsewhere, was obtained within a cycle of conquests, and
other benefits as well. And, unfortunately, starting in the
1980s and 1990s, the reverse cycle began, of globalization,
of migration of production to various places and, where it
could, of the precariousness of labor relations forced by
this flexibility that capital had.

But, from a management point of view, was this aspect dis-
cussed when buying Inco?

You have a concern and the Board's directive, in this case,
was even formally clear: we'll respect the best standards
of relationship with the union. We don't want conflict
with the union. We're going to respect the relationship
and try to keep labor relations at a level ... Obviously, this
is ... It's a very formal statement and it can be read and

implemented in practice in many ways, but it's what the
Board could do, right? The Board evaluated what it represented, the way the labor relations existed there, and
understood that it was something that we were going to
have to deal with. ... It's done, even legally, by the executive board, right? If you take the charter of a [publicly
traded] company, you have the Board ... The Board has a
... It seems like the Board can do anything. And actually
it can, it will ... I can fire the company's CEO if I don't
like him. So, I can say I want to hire a CEO who will do ...
But in practice, in practice, that's not how it works. You're
not going to fire the CEO of a company that's doing well
because you think he's a son of a bitch. If I were the sole
shareholder, I might. When it's a widely held company,
this is a possibility, but in practice, it doesn't work. So, as
I told you, I never had any doubt that we participated as
shareholders of the big companies, in a game of capital-
labor relationship, which was not a game we were going
to ... I could have small positive inflections, bring about
small positive orientations, but it wasn't going to be from
Previ's orientation that we were going to change the
capital-labor relationship game, neither here nor abroad,
right?

Aguiar Interview

André Teixeira, in turn, said that he took over the executive management
of labor relations right after the end of the strike in Canada, but that, having worked in the sector for some years, he followed the negotiations with
the Steelworkers after Inco's purchase and worked as a consultant in Canada
before the strike. According to Teixeira, there was a capital-labor relationship
at Inco that he did not like. The conflict between Vale and USW Local 6500 also
related to a different 'clash of cultures':

And I felt that I didn't really like the relationship at that time that I had in
there, capital-labor. I gave a few hints, but they were very much in charge
at that first moment. And we had more of an advisory role in that process.
The Steelworkers, at a certain moment, I know that they talked to some
people. Leo Gerard, who was the president, is still the president, if I'm
not mistaken, he even had conversations I think with Roger [Agnelli].

... You can't do business there without discussing a lot with the union before. The political issue there is very strong. ... And we didn't make any investments there for a long time. In the past years, no big investments were made there. And so, at first, ... there was a very strong culture clash between our culture and Canadian culture. And there was also prejudice against Brazilians, right? I heard that over there: 'Don't come to teach what you came to learn!' ... I believe that the capital/labor relationship has two columns: our relationship with the union and the supervisor's relationship with the employee. And we have to work on both. The conflict is born from the supervisor-employee relationship. And the relationship there was ... It had a history of many strikes, a history of strikes every year, a history of a lot of fuss. ... Inco is a century-old company and today, perhaps, we're breaking a record: ten years or almost ten years, going on ten years, that there hasn't been a strike there, after the last strike. Since the last strike up until now, we've never had such a long period without a strike at Inco.

ANDRÉ TEIXEIRA, Aguiar Interview

4   "It Can't Be Easy to Have Me as a Boss"

This was the statement of Roger Agnelli, then Vale's CEO, in an article in the *Financial Times* in March 2010,[57] which dealt with the long strike at the company's Canadian facilities. The conflict would last for another four months. The British economic publication pointed out the management changes introduced by the new Brazilian controllers, after the departure of many Canadian managers. A more participatory decision-making culture, adopted by Inco, was reportedly replaced by the centralization promoted by Vale, eager to increase worker productivity in its Canadian unit, who were too accommodated to the previous pattern. When addressing the strike in Sudbury, the article also questioned whether or not these events could be repeated in other parts of the world, with the increased presence of Brazilian companies setting up units abroad and buying competitors in other countries.[58]

---

57   Bernard Simon and Jonathan Wheatley, "Heading in Opposite Directions", *Financial Times*, March 11, 2010; available in https://www.ft.com/content/6de1ac42-2c69-11df-be45 -00144feabdc0; accessed May 26, 2021.

58   Gerdau and Marcopolo were also mentioned as similar examples.

Roger Agnelli still leaves bitter memories today among the Sudbury workers. Most of the interviewees mentioned how 'not easy' it really was to have him as a boss. Some, like Robin, expressed quite harsh positions about the Brazilian executive:

> I always thought the way he presented himself here in Vale that was almost like a Nazi, a German Nazi ... in the Second World War ... It almost feels like that when I watch military shows on television and then compare them to the way they run here. It almost reminds me the Nazi regime ... Because of the way they treat people, the way they segregate people. The way they run their business is either you comply or you're gone. And that's the way the Nazis ran their business and they're very similar. So, just a thought, you know?[59]

During the first three years of Vale's operations after the purchase of Inco, still under the previous contract, according to union members and workers interviewed, there were no major changes in the production process and in local administration. George classified the period as a "honeymoon":

> In the transition, there was ... what I call the honeymoon phase. So, from 2006 to 2009, it seemed like it was still the old ways, there were still a lot of management people that were local people. I call that the honeymoon phase. In 2009, I think that's when we saw the true colors of the company during the negotiations, in particular the negotiations. The classic example of that was hiring scabs. That was never done previously.
>
> GEORGE, Aguiar Interview

> They took the first three years, up to 2009, to plot their strategy on how they could take control because they felt the union was too strong ... The reason we made multimillions of dollars in great profits is because the union and the company worked together. At the end of the day, we could agree or disagree but it was forgotten the next day ... They just wanted to pulverize the union ... For me, their position was they wanted a long strike to break us. They didn't care about the employees, they didn't care about how much money they are gonna make.
>
> JOHN, Aguiar Interview

59   Robin, miner, interviewed by Thiago Aguiar in Sudbury, Canada (November 2016).

Other interviewees spoke of a 'study' period in which Vale was preparing a strategy to impose changes (involving pensions, bonus payments and grievance procedures) in the new contract negotiations: a meticulous plan, which involved: 1) obtaining permission from the union to stop the mines for just over a month, extending the expiring contract, to perform maintenance services; 2) hiring a law firm known for its anti-union activities; 3) hiring temporary workers (derogatorily called 'scabs') to put pressure on the strikers and maintain some of the mines' activities; 4) surveilling pickets and union activists, threatening them with dismissal and suing them as responsible for the damage caused by the strike; and 5) rejecting grievances and accumulating thousands of arbitration cases in order to erode the union politically (by the loss of ability to act in the workplace), as well as to put economic pressure (through the costs of arbitration proceedings) on it. These aspects of the plan organized by Vale to restructure its Canadian unit will be addressed below.

In 2009, when negotiations for a new collective agreement began, the union soon realized the direction of the changes. At that moment, as mentioned in Chapter 1, the effects of the global economic crisis were felt, which decreased the prices of minerals between 2008 and 2009, after years of robust expansion. I can point out a fundamental aspect for Vale to maintain a tough position and not show concern in negotiating the strike's termination:[60] resuming full operation of the mines with low nickel prices would not be as profitable as the eventual long term benefits brought by a successful imposition of the desired changes in the Canadian operations.[61] Bernard, one of the union's bargaining table members, who holds an important position in the USW Local 6500's management, does not fully agree with this assessment. For him, in addition to the price fluctuation caused by the shock of the 2008–2009 world crisis, there was a planned strategy to weaken the union and break the community ties

---

60   Following the argumentation of Peters, "Down in the Vale."

61   As stated in Chapter 1, during the same period, Vale fired 2,000 in-house workers and 12,000 outsourced workers in Brazil, claiming to make a necessary adjustment because of the economic crisis. See Laura Nazaré de Carvalho, "Análise da ação dos sindicatos dos trabalhadores da mineradora Vale S.A. na região Sudeste brasileira," *Textos & Debates*, no. 23 (January/July 2013): 93, note 2. At that point, Roger Agnelli clashed with the federal government's orientation to preserve jobs, an episode credited as responsible for his departure from the company's CEO position in 2011 and, in the aftermath, the appointment of Murilo Ferreira, who had previously commanded Vale's operations in Canada. See Marshall, "Behind the Image of South-South Solidarity at Brazil's Vale," 170–1. The crisis made Vale sell, between 2009 and 2010, US\$ 110 million in assets in Brazil and around the world to reduce the cash deficit caused by lower iron ore prices and lower orders in the international market. See Tádzio Peters Coelho, *Projeto Grande Carajás: trinta anos de desenvolvimento frustrado* (Rio de Janeiro: Ibase, 2014), 23.

which bind it to the miners. This would be, according to him, the most important reason for the hardening of negotiations:

> The economy was bad in 2009. However, it wasn't bad for Vale, it was good ... Vale was making millions and millions of dollars in iron ore. From the time they bought us in 2006 to 2009, alone in Sudbury, they made [more than] 3 billion dollars ... The company was doing good. All the company wanted to do was change. They wanted to change the culture here in Sudbury ... It was clear that they wanted to do that because we told the company that we were willing to do a *status quo*, not change anything in our contract. We understand times are tough and we would wait. But it didn't happen. And then the strike started ... They were trying to come and change the culture where our fathers, our grandfathers and our great-grandfathers fought for what we had. So we stood strong. Was it tough? It was very, very tough. Was it hard on families? It was very, very hard on families. Did it destroy our community? Yes, it did. But I blame all that on Vale because they wanted to bring scabs to do the work and we've never had that. We've had long strikes in the past. In 1979, we had a 9-month strike against Inco. I wasn't here at that time. But this was the longest strike. And this was a dirty strike where the company brought in their own security guards, where they had more security here than we had in the police, right? And that's Vale, that's the way they operate ... They would film us, they would follow us, they would sue us. We had lawsuits. I had personal lawsuits against me and my family: I think three different lawsuits ... After the year strike and after everything was resolved, all those lawsuits went away. But this was a matter of putting the stress and the strain on families and on people.[62]

For Artur Henrique, then president of CUT, who oversaw the strike in Canada, Vale in fact intended to diminish the union's importance in production, changing the local union "culture":

> Going to that strike showed me a few things. First, that you have a town that is basically made up of the mining business. ... Vale simply goes up there and buys it. Our struggle, or our dispute, was that we tried to make room for negotiation even before the strike. ... Vale would tell us: 'Look, this is a deal that will change the culture ..., because we can't allow

---

62   Bernard, union leader, interviewed by Thiago Aguiar in Sudbury, Canada (November 2016).

the miners themselves to take over production, with the power that the union has.' ... But at the same time, a very different relationship in Canada, because these were people who their grandfather had worked in the mine, their father had worked in the mine, and the guy was working in the mine. They expected their son to go work in the mine. The way the proposal was going, it was going to be a disaster from the point of view of ... with no concern for the local reality, with no willingness to listen to the people. So, our struggle with Vale started to be, here in Brazil, in addition to making room ... – we went to talk to Vale's CEO, Roger Agnelli ... – and, meanwhile, I thought that, given what we were discussing in terms of international solidarity, networks, workers in the chemical industry ..., it was necessary to get to know the thing up close. When the strike began, ... some things drew our attention because the workers' assembly was inside a hockey gym. And to participate in an assembly inside a gym full of workers, but also with women, family, children, shows what it was ... A surreal business, another kind of organization.

> ARTUR HENRIQUE, Aguiar Interview

In the negotiations, for the first time, the company was not represented by local managers and hired Hicks Morley, "the largest and most pro-employer human resources law firm in Canada,"[63] to represent it. According to the union members interviewed, the lawyers merely restated the proposals made from the beginning and would not agree to enter into any negotiations. Michael, who also participated in the negotiation team on behalf of the union, described the company's attitude during the strike:

> The very first red flag, the very first signal we got that there was going to be trouble was right away, you know? We heard rumors that they're maybe wanting to make big changes and there was going to be a strike, there were rumors about that. But when we got to the bargaining table their head spokesperson for the company was a lawyer. His name was Harvey Beresford. He was a very senior lawyer for a company called Hicks Morley, which in Canada is the biggest anti-union lawfirm ... Their job is to crush unions, you know? That's the whole reason that they're hired for: because they are trouble for unions. Hicks Morley had always been involved in bargaining in the backroom with Inco but they were never at the bargaining table face to face. They were there for advice. This time it

---

63   Peters, "Down in the Vale," 89.

was him [who was] in charge. He had the power all the way from Brazil
to negotiate these changes and that's the way it was gonna be ... There
were some local managers and people locally that were there too, but the
message from Brazil was: 'This is the way it's gonna be. Your bonuses are
too high, your pensions are too high compared to what Brazilian workers
have. We gotta bring you down.' They wanted to make sweeping changes
[in what] we had worked decades to get. I was there, I was at the bargaining and I remember they gave us our package and we responded to it.
And normally we look at it and give them a package and they look at ours
and change it. We go back and forth. We changed our package, gave it to
them, waited a little while. They came back [with the] exact same package as the first time and said: 'No, you don't understand. Here it is. This
is the new contract.' And we said: 'No, this is not how we bargain. We go
back and forth and come to an agreement. Not you dictating to us.' And
then in the third time they said: 'No, this is what it is ... Take it or leave it.
If you guys go on a strike, it's gonna be a very long strike'. And our members said: 'Then let's gonna have a long strike because we're not going
backwards that much the way that you think that we're gonna just give up
our stuff.' And that was the beginning of the 361 days. ... [Later,] We had
several attempts to negotiate. Everything moved from negociating here to
go into Toronto. We did a lot of negotiations, days and days ... a couple of
months in total. It was horrible. It was: 'No, this is how it's gonna be'. They
would move a little bit here, a little bit there, a little over here. They were
firing our people ... There were 300 guards they hired that came and lived
in hotels in town that were there with cameras and microfones ... They
were horrible. They wanted to break the union.

> MICHAEL, Aguiar Interview

André Teixeira, when talking about the strike in Canada in an interview, always
seemed to somehow remove the responsibility for the conflict from the company's Brazilian management. He stated that Canadian managers were in
charge of the negotiations during the strike, who received guidance from the
executive board in Brazil, but were responsible for conducting the process:

The negotiation was not by Brazilian managers, but the one in charge,
the one who defined the mandate, was Vale's executive board. It was
Brazilians who defined the mandate. Now, the handling was not Brazilian,
no. Never, in our model. For example, I have guided, I guide negotiations
in Mozambique: I guided the last one, this year even. Now, it's theirs to
conduct. And, when we define what we're going to do, they listen a lot.

It's very bad if you put a Mozambican at the table with a Brazilian, or a Canadian with a Brazilian. This never happened at a table ...

ANDRÉ TEIXEIRA, Aguiar Interview

The expiration date of the contract in effect was approaching: May 31, 2009. The impasse caused, even in the first rounds of negotiations, by the company's intransigence to obtain changes in pensions and bonuses, started to make workers apprehensive. Many interviewees said that they expected to go on strike if the negotiations were not concluded in time, but nobody imagined the conflict that was coming.[64] Perhaps this is why the union agreed to Vale's proposal to extend the contract from June 4 to July 12, 2009, so that negotiations could continue. During this period, the mines and the smelter's operations were paralyzed for maintenance services, also taking advantage of the market's setbacks with the economic crisis.[65]

> From the union perspective, it was bargaining in good faith. So, if there were still some openness and some conversation going on ... Because, historically, 6500 Local was known ... Work with no contract, we've never done that before. So, come May 31st [expiring date of the former contract], we don't have a contract, we're on picket lines on June 1st. But the bargaining committee thought in good faith ... to allow this shutdown and keep some people working and keep bargaining. Very controversial though because the union never did that before. Even some of our own members felt that that was wrong. And we've actually maintained and fixed the equipment for the replacement workers that we didn't know at that time were coming through the door ... There's no doubt they were preparing for the strike, probably much better than us.
>
> GEORGE, Aguiar Interview

The negotiation impasse was not resolved during the agreed contract extension period. On July 13, 2009, Sudbury workers went on strike, following the July 10 vote rejecting the contract proposal submitted by Vale. Out of the 3,062 then-members of USW Local 6500, 2,600 voted: 387 (14.88%) in favor of the contract

---

64   Vale's calculated preparation for the strike and the contrast with the union's troubles in anticipating and organizing for the conflict are highlighted by Peters, "Down in the Vale," 90 through a metaphor taken from one of his interviews in Sudbury. According to one union member, during the strike, "we went into a gunfight carrying a pencil and they had laser beams."

65   Brasch, *Winds of Change*, 38.

presented and 2,213 against (85.2%).[66] Following this, the Port Colborne and Voisey's Bay operations, represented by other USW local unions, also went on strike. Strikes are frequent in Canadian history and in Sudbury, but the one which took place at Vale's plant in the city, "3,300 workers were off the job for a year – approximately 845,000 lost workdays, making it the largest private sector strike in Canada in more than 30 years."[67] In Sudbury, the strike did not end until July 7, 2010, 361 days after it began. Days later, in Port Colborne, a new contract was signed. At Voisey's Bay, a smaller facility, the strike lasted another six months, bringing the total to eighteen months of stoppage.

As the workers interviewed recounted, staying on strike for so long brought many obstacles. The first one was the maintenance of the pickets themselves. The greatest tension was reportedly caused by the company's decision to hire a security team to watch over the strikers and to force the passage of inputs or of buses with temporary contract workers.

During the year on strike, Vale used temporary outsourced workers to maintain some of the production, and in particular to carry out maintenance and modifications in the mines. This is perhaps what irritated the interviewed workers the most. Many felt that the company wanted to demoralize them by showing that others were taking their place. The presence of the nearly 1,200 temporary outsourced workers hired by Vale during the strike was a major blow to the workers' resistance, as the company was able to maintain part of its activities, in particular completing pending maintenance services and modernizing the mines for the following period.[68] The company took advantage of the strike, at a time when nickel prices were low, to restructure its Canadian operations as it wished. All of the workers interviewed, without exception, mentioned the issue of hiring scabs with much resentment. "Scab," in the sense of scar or wound tissue, is the derogatory term which workers use to describe the temps.

Michael: Scabs we call them. People doing our work when we are on a picket line we call them scabs.

Thiago Aguiar: *What does this word mean?*
                     Oh, it's horrible. There's no lower life form on Earth than a scab. When somebody is on a picket line defending their working conditions, their family, their community, everything they work hard for, and someone takes advantage

---

66   Ibid, 40.
67   Peters, "Down in the Vale," 73–4.
68   Ibid.

of that and says: 'I'm gonna be a scab on you to go and do your work while you are there and I'm gonna do it.' That's the worst thing ... People call them replacement worker, temporary worker, contracted. No! They're scabs! They're stealing our jobs while we're on a picket line.

And did they cross the picket line?
Absolutely. With the security guards that they had, they would have a bus, a bus that had tinted windows so you couldn't see in. There would be a driver on the bus. They would pick the scabs up, they would go on the bus, there would be people with cameras on the bus. On the other side of the picket line there would be all kinds of security and they would try to go through our picket line to go in and to do our jobs. We know they didn't do much of our work. It was more to try to upset us and try to inflammate the situation and make us look like we're losing for our people to say: 'Holy Jeez, they're doing my job! I better just give up and go back to work before I have no job.' But it didn't work. There was violence here. It was a hard time in the city.
Aguiar Interview

If somebody crosses the picket line, they're called a scab worker, ok? And right away the company said: 'You can't use the word *scab* at work anymore.' So now they're trying to tell us what we can say, how we can act towards people who crossed the line and made top dollar while we starved. Do you know what? That's our right! They crossed the picket line, they should be able to take the shit that's coming from them because they went to do our jobs while we were starving. Who's Vale to tell us that we can't call them scabs?
GREGORY, Aguiar Interview

The hiring of temporary workers to replace the strikers was confirmed by André Teixeira. In his version, however, Vale carried out the hiring after episodes of threats to workers and managers had occurred. The company, according to the labor relations manager, chose to bring in workers from the province of Quebec, using the rivalry between Anglophones and Francophones in Canada. This type of expedience was "part of the game" in a strike, according to Teixeira, as well as the need to "operate" to face the workers' resistance on the picket lines:

André Teixeira: Look, they started threatening the working guys' families and all that. So, we hired what they call over there .... I forgot the name ...

Thiago Aguiar: *Scabs?*
That's the name they give them. ... They call them scabs, right? And it was the French. We got these people over in Quebec, and there's a huge feud between the English and the French. All of this caught on. Now, it's part of the game, right? I mean, some people, including [mentions the name of a manager], for example: he had to take his family away because he was the company's representative. ... He had to leave there with his family and take them to Toronto. There was a lot of suffering for everyone. It wasn't easy, no. Then, when the scabs came ... Not scabs: replacement workers, which they called scabs, that changed completely.

So, the company had to toughen up from that physical point of view as well, let's say ...
Yes, we needed, at a certain moment, to operate. If you look at it, it was a moment when they toughened up too: every action represents an equal and opposite reaction.
Aguiar Interview

Julian, a worker who was active during the strike, said that he suffered reprisals for his participation in the picketing: his supervisors handed over the lockers he used to a temporary worker during the strike. For him, it was offensive that another person had access to the space where personal belongings and pictures of family members were. Another locker, which he used to store items for lunch, was opened, and the stored utensils were discarded to make room for the temps.

It really bothered me that they had some guy, some worker in a bad position, a scab crossing a picket line ... And to not even have the decency to take my pictures down with my family. I just found it disrespectful to me and to that guy who was in a bad spot, right? And it shows the character of who they are. They don't care.[69]

Many workers also spoke of the pressure by security guards and watchmen on the picket lines, who would encourage confrontations to create pretexts for dismissals and persecution. Some union leaders also reported episodes of intimidation against the strikers' families. There were reports of company lawyers going to workers' homes to 'inform' their wives about the opening of lawsuits against activists and union members:

> They would say: 'Well, your husband was on a picket line and they stopped a truck today.' So somebody would go knock on a woman's door when her husband was on a picket line with ... papers and say: 'You are being sued for millions of dollars because your husband's actions stopped us from producing so we're suing you.' And the wife would be panic stricken: 'We're gonna lose our house! We are not gonna feed the kids! What's this all about?.' They'd never seen this before. Vale used the Hicks Morley law firm and they used more dirty tricks to intimidate our people. They followed people around with the guards in their car videotaping them. You'd be out for lunch with your family at the coffee shop and the guards would come and sit beside you to try to get something started. They used a lot of dirty tactics and they spent a lot of money doing it.
>
> MICHAEL, Aguiar Interview

During the strike, John was one of those responsible for organizing the pickets. He told how, at the time, he was sued for one million Canadian dollars for a conflict that occurred at a company gate:

> Nothing to do with me. When I stood up, there were security people who didn't even know who I was ... Many court cases resulted in different things, they were trying to demoralize the workers, right? But Sudbury has a very strong pride and we stand up for our rights. It's kind of hard to break a union in Canada. I don't know about Brazil if it's easy, but in Canada it's not.
>
> JOHN, Aguiar Interview

For André Teixeira, the strike ended in radicalization, in a dynamic where both the company and the union decided to make the other side lose more. In the

---

69   Julian, miner, interviewed by Thiago Aguiar in Sudbury, Canada (November 2016).

end, despite the troubles and the losses, the manager recognized that Vale managed to achieve results close to what he expected:

André Teixeira: And I followed up on it, I talked to people. At a very fast pace, things became radicalized, radicalized in a way that became difficult. And strikes, as you go towards radicalization, ... both sides become radicalized. And then what happens is this: one of them is really defeated ... Everyone loses, but who will lose the most? On that strike, everybody lost: they lost and Vale lost, too. Everybody lost. But you start losing more than I did in that process. And things went down the path of radicalization – radicalization that, for me, with my strike experience, what I saw at the time was totally out of control. ... It went ... towards a radicalization that I couldn't imagine, and no mediation would help. It was like this – the way I feel it - : either you give it up or we end it. In the end ..., after the strike, the results were much closer to what we wanted. ... Then, when we were about to complete one year, the union backed out. So, it was an example of radicalization that, I confess, scared me with how radical the journey was. The negotiation was not ours to conduct, it was actually the Canadians', but we acted as consultants.

Thiago Aguiar: *Given the radicalization that you have just reconstructed, in your opinion, did Vale also need to radicalize? What would it mean to radicalize in a conflict of this kind?*
What's radicalization in negotiations? It's that you have less flexibility to negotiate, to reduce your bargaining margin. The union would say: 'it's either this or this.' And Vale: 'it's either this or this.' That's radicalization. You reduce radicalization when you increase your range of items to negotiate.

So, Vale reduced flexibility to as little as possible?
I wouldn't say that Vale reduced it: Vale didn't expand it. The impasse arose from these two positions and neither of the parties expanded it.
Aguiar Interview

The interviewed workers and union members said that they did not plan to stay on strike for so long and that they were not prepared for this type of conflict. Even though the Steelworkers are a powerful union with many resources and an international strike fund, the support that the striking workers received from the union and the community was insufficient. According to Bernard, it was not possible, with the strike fund supported by the international union, to maintain the families' standard of living. At first, CA$200 per week were paid to the striking workers, an amount later increased to CA$300.

The organization of the strike fund by the union was also subject to criticism.[70] The low amounts made it difficult for the workers to stay on strike and put pressure on them to return to work. In addition, the union's decision to transfer the strike fund amounts to Vale – so that the company would deposit the money in the employees' accounts – made it difficult for the USW Local 6500's directors to have permanent contact with the workers. For Michael, the decision to transfer the funds to Vale did not have major consequences and was just an option of the union to facilitate the task of making the payments at a time when everyone was focused on negotiations and maintaining the picket lines.

Michael: We have a big strike fund. When people pay union dues it goes into our strike fund and when we go on strike they get a reimbursement of their union dues that goes back to them every week. So we had that but more importantly – because we had 3,500 workers – most people would only picket one day or two days a week, which would give them five or six days when they didn't have to picket. So, during that time, a lot of them got jobs. They got temporary jobs. Some of them left town and got jobs ... The reimbursement of the union dues was a help but it wasn't nearly the replacement of their lost wages. They could buy their groceries and pay maybe their hydro bill, but if they didn't have their own savings or if their wife wasn't working, a lot of people decided .... This seems like it may go on for two, three, four years, people didn't know. So a lot of them said: 'I'm not taking the chance. I'm gonna get a job while I can.' ... We could have survived for many, many, many years. The fund never bleeds out because ... we got over 800,000 members in North America continuing to work and their money goes into

70   Ibid.

that fund. So that's what it's about: it's about helping each other in times of need ... The international union holds the fund and every member in North America that belongs to the Steelworkers pays into it. It's very powerful ... And we spent lots on lawyers and bargaining. If we didn't have the resources of the Steelworkers union, we'd be in big, big trouble.

Thiago Aguiar: *I heard that the strike fund payments were made by Vale. Why did this happen?*

What happened there was we would transfer the money to Vale and Vale would ... Because everybody here gets paid by direct deposit so once a week, on pay day, you go online and your money is deposited in your account. And instead of us trying to write 3,500 checks every week and handing it and everybody coming to get it, Vale did the banking. We gave them the money ... and the company did the transaction to all the accounts and we continued to do it through that way.

Don't you think this could have empowered the company during the strike?

Well, it didn't empower the company. The company got to do it. It was easy for us because if people were working or if they weren't around, it was easy for them to get paid and it was done. But one of the downsides ... is that, if we spent two days a week writing checks and having everybody coming here to get checks, we would have a lot more communication with them, a lot more stuff. So, going forward, we will do the checks if and when it happens again: individual checks for everybody so we can have better communication. But at that time, for what we did, it worked well ... For our members it would be better to write the checks. As much work and how the hardship it is, it would be better to write the checks. ... Well, at the beginning of the strike, they said would do it [the transfers]. We made the arrangements and they agreed. They never took any money or didn't do it or delayed it or played any games. For a lot of the members they liked to get it that way because it was easy.

Aguiar Interview

Many workers had to look for temporary jobs in the region during the strike period; others simply decided to leave the company or move to another city with the strike's indefiniteness. Several people reported cases of divorce and family crises:

> You do what you can ... Credit cards, you manage your pre-save, knowing that there's a possibility [for strike] ... Because we worked for Inco for a long time, we know that there's a possibility, every contract, there's a possibility, there's gonna be a strike. So most people save at least enough money to last six months, three to six months ... Life circumstances could change that, but most people try to do that. If they could, they'd manage that way .... Other people, every credit card they had in their wallet was matched out by the end of the strike. A lot of people went to find other jobs. Some people just depended on donations, food banks. They had to do it, they managed. You gotta feed your kids ... [The strike fund] is not enough. It's controlled by our international [union] ... They haven't seen the need to increase that over the years. So it stayed down, it's still down ... So, everybody just managed. Some people did it, some didn't ... Marriages gone, houses gone, all the vehicles, anything they had, gone. There was a lot of that.
>
> SAM, Aguiar Interview

> The corporate strategy was to put us down as bad workers. They used the media, bloggers, all the time, to try to break people's minds and play games and all the stuff. A lot of people got hurt: there were a lot of suicides, there were 300 divorces, a lot of homes got lost. They hurt the workers. Then they come back and impose [what] I call a martial law, a strict code of ethics that got even worse, to the point where all they said now had to change because they're not getting production no more ... And now we're in a world where their production levels could double to what they are today, but they have to be willing to stop this dispersion of unions and stop trying to be in control. We know that Vale is the boss, but when you have a boss that you wanna work for, you produce more ... I'm lucky because my wife is a nurse so I had a certain income. I had [some savings] prior to the strike because I knew it was coming ... All the big nickel bonuses that they used to give us ... Our former president told us to put that money away, don't spend it because tough times were coming.
>
> JOHN, Aguiar Interview

The restructuring promoted by Vale brought about changes in sensitive aspects of labor relations in comparison with previous contracts. The concessions extracted by the company concerned three main issues, summarized below:

1)   End of the bonus paid according to the market variations of nickel, obtained in the long 1978–1979 strike as compensation for the low salary increase in that period. In recent years, with the ore's appreciation, this bonus meant high earnings for the miners. In some cases, according to union members, the bonus could exceed US$50,000 or US$60,000 per year.[71] Vale intended to reduce the bonus payment to a maximum of US$ 15,000 per year and link it to goals and productivity in line with its global bonus policy (especially with the profit sharing bonus model paid in Brazil), since, in the company's view, the bonus linked to nickel price variations would not stimulate workers to increase their productivity.[72] According to Bernard, the nickel bonus was replaced by the company's common bonus (known in Canada as the Annual Incentive Program – AIP): "It's something like the one in Brazil ... They see what they make in the whole year, what kind of profit and then after that every worker gets so much money."[73] The Ontario division, in the negotiations to end the strike, kept an additional bonus, the Earnings Based Compensation (EBC), based on the company's annual revenues. The changes in the bonus were a major blow to the workers, who were used to high earnings during previous years:

> We had a nickel bonus ... people were buying many cars ... So Vale, back when it was CVRD and the strike started, they came in and said: 'We aren't doing this anymore. We have a bonus system already and this is the one we're gonna use.' So, either just arrogance or not recognizing that we had a history and we bargained for this so, instead of raises, we have this nickel bonus. So, if you want to remove the bonus system, then we want wages.
>
> JULIAN, Aguiar Interview

2)   Change in the pension plan, ending defined benefit plans, by which workers keep their active salaries when they retire, and replacing them with private defined contribution plans, by which the pension depends strictly on the investment made by the worker over the years. The change is very similar to the one that Vale, after privatization, made in Brazil

---

71   Similar numbers can be found in Ibid, 88.

72   As stated by Roger Agnelli and the Vale directors interviewed in the aforementioned *Financial Times* article.

73   Aguiar Interview.

with the end of the Valia plan and the creation of the Vale Mais plan.[74] At
first, the company intended to impose this change for all Canadian workers, while the union said that this was a non-negotiable aspect. As the
months went by, company and union, at the end of the strike, agreed to
keep the defined benefit plan for the then active workers of the company,
while the new hires would be included in defined contribution plans.
Michael, perhaps in an effort to show that the concession made was not
so great, thus explained the changes in the pension plan:

Our members, before the strike, were on a DB pension, which is defined
benefit [plan] ... If the stock markets went down, Inco was responsible to
put in the extra money to top things up to make sure it was all guaranteed
... After the strike, the new hires, they are on a DC plan, defined contribution, where they're giving a percentage of their wages, they can put in
some of their own wages and the company matches that extra that they
put in. That money goes into a savings plan and when it's time for them to
retire they draw out of the savings plan whatever is there. If markets are
low, they might have to work longer. It's gonna be less of what a DB plan
workers are. So Vale didn't wanna have any responsabilty on the changes
... The new hires, which are now about 25% of our members, are in a new
pension plan, which is still a very good pension plan, compared to a lot
of places in Canada. It's still a very good one, but it's not this really, really,
really good one that the old workers had.

    MICHAEL, Aguiar Interview

With regard to the reduction of bonuses and changes in the pension plans for
Canadian workers, Sérgio Rosa and André Teixeira are explicit in stating that
the miners' compensation was high and needed to be revised. The defined
benefit plans, in turn, would not be in line with those offered in Brazil, besides
being unprofitable. The former president of Vale's Board of Directors and the
manager of labor relations also associated the changes which lowered the
workers' variable earnings and the new hires' pensions to the drop in nickel
prices after the 2008 crisis:

Some things were described to us as difficult to sustain within a positive labor relationship dynamic. The pension fund issue – contrary to
my conviction, where I see defined benefit plans as positive, but this is

---

74   As analyzed in Chapter 1.

a conviction which I couldn't even convince the Lula administration of, ... and the defined contribution became an international standard – any and every company in the world which had the opportunity to change its pension fund standard changed to defined contribution. If I took a stand like that within Vale ... , it would almost be an ideological battle which I would do. Secondly, the bonus policy, according to the description at the time, was a policy that didn't properly incentivize what the company wanted. It wasn't aligned with the ideas the company had of encouraging productivity, of rewarding labor productivity. It was an old-fashioned bonus policy that benefited people without matching the company's ability to encourage what it wanted for workers. It happens. Changes in pay policy in a company happen all the time. Obviously, crises are always very important factors, but it's not just because of a crisis. You have periods of growth, it encourages people to do certain things. You have different periods which will encourage other stuff, to reduce losses, development, anyway, you'll level. So, the vision they gave us was that the bonus policy was outdated, that it didn't correspond to the company's period and that it was no longer a correct instrument to deal with ... It was going to be replaced by incentive policies more adequate to the company's planning. That was the version we had.

SÉRGIO ROSA, Aguiar Interview

André Teixeira: There was a very strong history of strikes, and then that strike movement began. It started during a negotiation in which we were discussing ... We were negotiating in Brazil, and there was a private pension plan up there which was very unprofitable. It's the difference between defined contribution and defined benefit.

Thiago Aguiar: *Here in Brazil this was solved right after privatization?*
Right: 2001 or 2002. And the plan there was even proposed only to new employees at the time, but there was a lot of resistance in relation to that and we couldn't reach a consensus .... This was the main point. There was also the nickel price bonus that influenced it, which was their variable pay.

Did you also want to standardize by what is done in Brazil?
It was a period when the nickel price was high and a lot was being paid, that's to say, you had an employee there receiving 100,000 dollars a year, a mining employee.

Only with the bonus?
No, their total pay. That's what I've been told. I'm telling you what I heard. So, on these two points, an impasse was reached. I think – now, that's my opinion, get it? – [the Canadians thought:] 'These Brazilians are going to learn here!' .... Even though I was participating as a consultant, not leading the process, because at the time I wasn't even responsible for that at Vale.

In any case, the willingness to standardize the bonus and pension policy by the one in Brazil was a strategic decision for the company?
There was that. There was this decision because the pension plan up there is unprofitable. The amount of money you lose there with the pension plan is horrible. It's a lot. ... And also this happened: ... the price of nickel plummeted and the nickel stocks on the London Metal Exchange of nickel were sky-high, so ...

Vale could buy time to negotiate ...
We didn't lose sales, so to speak.
Aguiar Interview

3) Reduction of the number of workers by means of voluntary redundancy programmes, stimulated by incentives. The company intended to restructure production and increase the productivity of mines with fewer workers.[75] In addition, it modified the internal grievance system, restricting and centralizing the channels through which conflicts in production could be resolved. This was a direct attack on union action in the workplace. The grievance procedures exist to channel and deal with day-to-day issues and conflicts in production regarding safety, procedures, relationships with coworkers and supervisors, etc. The role of the stewards, the union representatives at the workplace, is very important in handling grievances.

---

75   In addition to layoffs promoted by Vale after the strike, many workers left the company and sought new jobs in other cities, as union members of USW Local 6500 recounted, because they could not stand the several months without wages. Vale's turnover data gathered by Carvalho, "Análise da ação dos sindicatos," captured this movement. The rate, which was 5% in 2008, jumped to 19.7% in 2009 and remained high, at 10.8%, in 2010.

Up until then there was a grievance system at the Inco mines based on three stages: first, at the local level, stewards and local supervisors sought to deal with the grievance; secondly, at the intermediate level, if the previous stage was not successful, a union representative and a mid-level member of management sought resolution; thirdly, the union and the company's top management dealt with the grievance. If no solution could be reached in the three previous steps, the case would go to arbitration, a process conducted by lawyers pre-established by the two parties in the contract. Arbitration is an expensive process, for which the support of lawyers is necessary.

Vale decided to reduce grievance procedures from three to two steps and referred all conflicts to arbitration, in order to reinforce its authority in the workplace and put pressure on the union with the high costs of this process. The reduction of internal grievance channels and the explosion of cases sent to arbitration were thus a "tactic to place political pressure on the union, in an attempt to both overwhelm, distract and drain the union's resources."[76]

This stance changed only on the eve of the 2015 to 2020 contract negotiation, when the company agreed to return to the three-step grievance system and to avoid referring grievances to arbitration. The return to the three-step grievance process in the 2015 agreement is always remembered by members of USW Local 6500 as a demonstration that they 'reversed' many concessions made in the 2010 post-strike agreement. Indeed, the return to the previous grievance procedure is a major victory for the union, as this was the most direct way in which Vale sought to weaken collective power by imposing a type of direct relationship with its workers, similar to that carried out by its managers in its Brazilian operations. As stated in Chapter 2, this is a central aspect of the company's labor and union relations strategy. The fact that USW Local 6500 was able to resume grievance procedures shows that the company needed to deal with the union's embeddedness by adapting its union relations strategy.

However, as will be seen below, the company sought other ways to extend its control over production, circumventing (or seeking to limit) the role of the union and stewards, particularly through changes in the safety policy and the alcohol and drug code. Moreover, 'reversal' is perhaps not the most accurate way to define the contract signed in 2015, since it did not bring any retreat by the company with regard to pensions and bonuses, the heart of the changes imposed by Vale in the restructuring promoted in 2009–2010.

---

76   Roth, Steedman and Condratto, "The Casualization of Work and the Rise of Precariousness," 12.

According to the union members interviewed, in addition to the workers' discontent with unresolved grievances, Vale's retreat was also economically motivated: the company started to consider that its arbitration costs were too high, as Michael argued:

> We had over 5,000 grievances going into arbitration. With arbitration, every day that we go to have a hearing without any lawyers involved, just the cost of the arbitrator for both sides is about 3,000 dollars a day ... They tried to weaken the union, make us ineffective, and tried to say: 'Look, guys, you don't need a union. You can do better without one.' ... The most anti-union thing that you can have. But what happened was, because of that, our workers were so mad at their situations not being addressed and not getting the answers ... they knew the company was doing it, not the union ... They had a lot of problems with unhappy workers so they went: 'Look, we better fix this, because if we don't fix this, it's gonna keep the relationship not going well.' So that's why we fixed it at this time.
>
> MICHAEL, Aguiar Interview

With nearly 5,000 grievances accumulating for arbitration, after the 2015 contract negotiation, the company reportedly agreed to speed up the resolution process. According to a member of the union's grievances committee, around 4,800 grievances accumulated since the strike period were resolved in just six months.

> There was a lot of bitterness from the company towards the union, towards the members. They were very heavy handed ... they disciplined. And it continued on. The bulliness they showed during the strike, they continued that going inside. For those members [fired during the strike] we took them all to arbitration and it cost thousands of dollars but we're a big union, we've got a big building that we rent out for weddings and stuff. So we're not a poor union, we can defend ourselves and our members. The company spent millions and millions on lawyers. And since the prices [of ore] have gone down now, it's more important for them to work with the union and get along with us because they don't have the extra money to spend on arbitration and lawyers and all of the problems. They want things to run smooth to make the profits they can. So let's hope it continues.
>
> MICHAEL, Aguiar Interview

5   **Defeat or Victory?**

There's the *Sudbury Star*[77] the day after the strike. At the end of the
strike, they wrote [in the headline], "A funeral." That's the feeling they
had. The strike changed .... I didn't follow it for many years later, but
at first it changed the way the supervisor acted. So, we had a win with
that strike. We didn't win, but one interesting thing about that strike was
that the responsibility – [like] I said, there are two columns, right? -, the
supervisor did very little in this relationship with the employees inside.
After that strike, the supervisor's relationship with the teams ... When
the strike was coming to an end, they held their own workshop there.
We participated, in terms of suggestions, ... to discuss what they had to
change after that. And the supervisor's relationship with the team was
one of the points, and it's something that we work on in Brazil. So, they
changed the relationship between the supervisor and the teams: this
was a gain we had. At the time, they even said: 'Look, in the long run
this will be good for us.' And we were also able to operate the plant, a
unit, with far fewer people, that's to say, it showed that there was also an
excess of people in there.

ANDRÉ TEIXEIRA, Aguiar Interview

I guess there was some mistrust against the local union because of the
length of time of the strike. A lot of people blame us too, right? It wasn't
easy, a lot of people needed to go back. But we fought for the good things,
we fought for the pensions, we fought for benefits, we fought for our
bonuses, we fought for our wages ... A lot of people say: 'Well, did you
guys lose the strike?' And I say: well, I won't say we lost the strike but did
we take concessions? Yeah, we did. At that time, how far do you keep
going? There were people that they just couldn't handle no more. It was
time to go back. So, what do we do? We go back and we fight again. That's
what we did. So, we continue that fight.

BERNARD, Aguiar interview

At the end of the day, there was stuff that after a year people voted to
accept not because they wanted the changes. They voted to get their jobs
back. They needed to go back to work. You know, a year is a long, long
time without a regular big pay check coming up. There were changes we

---

77   A local newspaper in Sudbury.

didn't like that we accepted but they weren't nearly what they wanted at the beginning of the strike ... We had some changes in pension for new hires, we had a change in the bonus plan. Eight people that got fired weren't all returned to work. They had to wait and go to arbitration ... some of them are back, some of them aren't.

MICHAEL, Aguiar Interview

After going on for months on end without Vale showing any willingness to back down from its central impositions, the workers' resistance was running out. On March 11, 2010, nine months after the beginning of the strike, a vote was held on a new version of the contract presented by the company. Once again, the rejection was categorical: of the 2,371 members of USW Local 6500 who voted, 2,105 (88.7%) did not accept the contract presented and only 266 (11.3%) voted in favor.[78] It was, however, a last attempt, a last breath. Many workers interviewed said that the March vote expressed outrage at a contract which was virtually the same as the one presented before the strike began.

However, the final three months exhausted the Sudbury miners' resources and capacity for prolonged resistance. On July 6, another vote approved the contract agreed to in negotiations between the union and Vale by 1,795 votes (75.5%) against 581 (24.5%) who rejected it, out of 2,376 USW Local 6500 members who voted in the Assembly.[79] Despite the decision to call off the strike, the significant number of rejection votes showed that there was still a lot of dissatisfaction with the signed contract. In the end, it was concluded that it was useless to continue. Perhaps corroborating Bernard's impression that there was some discontent with the union, Gregory stated:

> That collective bargaining agreement that they came up with the union, which, you know what? I'm not well impressed with our union there, but I also have to say that, with a company as big as Vale, it doesn't matter how good your union is, you don't have the power. You have no strength against a company like that. They can say and do whatever they want for as long as they want. It got to a point where the speech [the USW Local 6500 president during the strike] gave before the vote when everybody said yes [to the contract] was basically: 'This is the last you're gonna see. Take it or you're not gonna see anything for a long, long time.' Do you know what that did to all kinds of people, all young people who just

---

78   Brasch, *Winds of Change*, 91.
79   Ibid, 117.

bought houses, trucks, cars? Do you know what I mean? Right then they finally said yes and then we were fucked ... Then, what happens? We lose everything. So, right there, I see our union sold us out, which is despicable because at least, when it was Inco, our union had power. It was about equals, so they could actually bargain and we could gain.

GREGORY, Aguiar Interview

When evaluating the strike's results, the USW Local 6500 members usually, if not explicitly, at least indirectly, point to the ability to resist for a year to Vale's offensive as the greatest victory obtained by the strike. Demonstrating the ability to stay on strike despite the hardships, therefore, would be the workers' greatest victory. According to union leaders, the company will need to 'think twice' if it wants to face a strike again in Sudbury. That is why, for them, the 2015 contract negotiations occurred quite differently: the lawyers were out of the picture; the Brazilian managers were not in a prominent position in the Toronto or Sudbury head offices; the collective agreement was discussed and concluded by the local union and the Sudbury managers, without the direct participation of the international Steelworkers or of Vale's top management, as explained by Bernard, who was in a prominent position in these negotiations.

However, if, on the one hand, the conclusion of the 2015 agreement one month before the expiration of the previous contract would demonstrate the change of posture in the company's relationship with the union, one cannot disregard, on the other hand, that this occurred under the milestones imposed by Vale in the successful restructuring process carried out in its Canadian operations in 2009–2010. Considering the issue from this point of view, and from what the company sought to gain when negotiations began in 2009, it is clear that Vale won. The company got what it was looking for.

For Susan, the posture change in the 2015 negotiations is perhaps due precisely to the company's previous victory, so large that it would have been able to change the union's own posture:

A strike, for it to be effective, has to hurt the company and hurt the union, so each has a vested interest in resolving the strike. If one party isn't really affected by it, it can just go on forever. And I mean that was part of the dynamics of this strike ... These nickel properties in Canada, with low nickel prices, for Vale were just of no consequence. Another thing is that, historically, in these mining towns, management and workers all lived in the community. Everybody hurt when the strike was on. The families of workers on strike didn't shop at the grocery store anymore because they didn't have as much money ... They're all at the same church together, [their kids go to] the same schools together ... I was shocked to come across something in the *Sudbury Star*, which was a joint statement from Vale and the union to the community saying that bargaining would be beginning on such a date and that both sides were resolved to make a very efficient bargaining and the community needn't worry that there would be a repeat of something along those lines. I think it's pretty unusual for this kind of thing to ever happen: a union and the company to put out that kind of public statement before they sit down to bargain. So, some would say: 'That was the deal, the Steelworkers would stop challenging Vale on anything and Vale, in turn, would take through the next round of bargaining without big ripples.' ... It wasn't a strike that helped communication with different levels of the union. It wasn't a strike that the union came out of it stronger.

SUSAN, Aguiar Interview

It can be said that this assessment is shared, in his own way, by André Teixeira, for whom the strike was a 'learning experience' for both parties, the result of which were revealed in the 2015 negotiations, where a five-year contract was established, which has, among its clauses, the prohibition of strikes. At its end, in 2020, Teixeira celebrates that the longest strike-free period in the history of Inco/Vale will be completed:[80]

And the relationship with the union itself also matured from that. The union itself also, in a certain moment, changed the people who were

---

80   The information is not exactly accurate, since there were fourteen years without strikes at Inco, between 1983 and 1997, according to information from Brasch. In any case, the eleven-year strike-free interval between 2010 and 2021 was the second longest since 1958. In 2020, a one-year contract extension was negotiated during the COVID-19 pandemic, when Sudbury operations were maintained. In negotiations for a new five-year contract in June 2021, however, there was an impasse. Despite USW Local 6500's recommendation to vote in favor, 70% of member workers voted against the proposal offered by Vale, which included the withdrawal of health benefits and drug coverage for retirees and questioned the low readjustment and bonus values. A two-month strike began, ending in August 2021, when a new company proposal was accepted by the workers, despite criticism of the new concessions obtained by the company. See USW, "Steelworkers Reject Vale's Concessionary Offer, Call for Good-Faith in Negotiations as Strike Continues"; available in https://www.usw.ca/news/media-centre/releases/2021/steelworkers-reject-vales-conces sionary-offer-call-for-good-faith-negotiations-as-strike-continues; accessed December 4, 2021, and Martha Dillman, "Mine, Mill and Smelter Workers Vote 85% for Vale Contract, Ending 2-Month Strike," *CBC News*, August 4, 2021; available in https://www.cbc.ca/news /canada/sudbury/usw-vale-collective-agreement-1.6128851; accessed December 4, 2021.

leading it .... There was an exchange, from both sides there was an exchange. The people who were on one side left and the people who were on the other side left. If you take who was the leader of ... Local 6500, they changed the management of it there. So, I'd say that there was maturity on both sides. The strike helped both sides to mature and a five-year agreement was closed. We've now signed another five year agreement, which means that when we reach ten years, we've never had a ten-year period without a strike there. And, in the agreement, there is a strike prohibition. So, we'll have ten years, which we've never had in Sudbury's history of that operation. So, the agreement itself that was closed ... in 2015 was also for five years. And when you close a five-year deal, wow, it's very mature! In Brazil, you can only close a two-year one. The first big company that closed a two-year agreement without fixing the pay adjustment was Vale in Brazil. ... If you ask me, fifteen years from now, we'll say that the strike was good for both sides. I think that the strike allowed the company and the union to mature. The relationship changed, right? We had, afterwards, an HR manager who was from Sudbury, who lived there, ... was born next door, his father worked there, who had roots there, and he knew the people very well. So, that changed a lot over there. This is what I say: both sides changed their people, that is, both sides recognized that those people made mistakes.

ANDRÉ TEIXEIRA, Aguiar Interview

Reuben Roth, Mercedes Steedman and Shelley Condratto, in a case study on Inco/Vale in Sudbury,[81] showed a tendency to labor precariousness in the city's nickel industry. Traditionally, Canadian mining workers were considered part of the 'labor aristocracy' because of their high wages, benefits, and unionization, which guaranteed good contracts. Over the past few decades, gradually, the introduction of outsourcing began to erode collective bargaining capacity, reducing the USW Local 6500's membership base. By mapping outsourcing clauses in contracts between Inco/Vale and USW since 1969, the researchers concluded that the union opted to exchange workplace control for monetary gains and other benefits, gradually allowing the company to hire outsourced labor which is not covered by the contract signed between company and union, segmenting the company's workforce.

---

81   Roth, Steedman and Condratto, "The Casualization of Work and the Rise of Precariousness."

As of the 2000s, indeed, this process accelerated with corporate demands for labor flexibility. With the purchase of Inco in 2006, "Vale proceeded to implement centralized human resources systems and introduced an adversarial managerial approach that led to further erosion in its unionized workforce."[82] In addition, there was a loss of relative importance of the Sudbury operations, which went from representing 47% of Inco's revenues to just 4% of Vale's overall revenues. The 2009–2010 strike was not able to reverse the restructuring imposed by the company, and its results deepened the trend of the union's loss of workplace control, ensuring better conditions for Vale to gain flexibility in managing its mines in the face of volatile mineral commodity prices.

As seen in the previous chapters, workplace control and the weakening of the unions' collective power are key elements of Vale's labor relations and union strategy. The loss of bargaining power leads to the erosion of the ability of unionized workers to resist the power of transnational corporations. In this way, mining TNCs can deal with an apparent contradiction: the fact that you cannot move a mine by moving it to offshore operations. With restructuring, "using triangular employment relationships, [Vale] can in fact *offshore their responsibilities* while still remaining in Sudbury, and squeezing all available profits from their directly-employed employees, as well as those of their subcontractors."[83]

Several interviewees mentioned a 'bitter atmosphere' and veiled confrontation in the post-strike daily life. Bernard said that the pressure to diminish the union's importance continued after the new contract was signed:

> I can honestly say that when we came back from the strike in 2010, I think it was a lot more difficult than it was during the strike because they continued to really put worker against worker. They really made that 'division and conquer,' they really worked hard on that. They ignored the union, they ignored my position for a long time. I had to fight to have a conversation with them, to have meetings with them. And it's sad to say but there's a lot of it. When we came back, we worked so hard to try to get everybody

---

82   Ibid, 8.

83   Ibid, 20. Additionally, it can be said that this diagnosis is in line with the description of the characteristics of the LMEs presented in Hall and Soskice, "An Introduction to Varieties of Capitalism." Perhaps, it is possible to conclude that the restructuring promoted by Vale benefited from an institutional structure which concentrates responsibilities in the top corporate management and allows it greater ease in hiring and firing, making agile decisions in contexts of market fluctuation, as occurred in the sharp drop of nickel prices after the 2008–2009 crisis.

back together, build our union back because they weakened our union, right? Because a lot of people lost homes, lost their savings and lost a lot of things. We had people [who] comitted suicide, we had people that left the company and worked elsewhere and took their family, uprooted from here and went west. So there's a lot of different stories, a lot of personal stories that people went through some tough times. And that continued for a long time ... They would get disciplined because they said something to them or someone would get fired.

BERNARD, Aguiar Interview

The interviews also showed a major effort by the company to reduce work porosity and increase productivity. Supervisors have stepped up the drive for discipline. Attempts to reduce the stewards' intervention power should be seen against this background. Two changes illustrate the behavior adopted by managers and supervisors after the strike: 1) the introduction of a new safety policy in the mines,[84] aimed at avoiding production interruptions; and 2) the creation of an 'alcohol and drugs' policy, which, according to several interviewees, justified the widespread urine testing of workers. Through this policy, supervisors and managers could embarrass union activists or intractable workers in front of their colleagues.

Sean, who acted for years as a sort of risk inspector in the mines, described the changes in safety procedures as follows:

With Inco, it was a hazard-based management style where, if we had a hazard in a workplace that we knew about, we would fix it. And we went from a hazard-based with Inco to a risk-based model with Vale. And that essentially was a model that allowed us one way or another to get in and do the work even though the risk is there. [At] Inco, you get rid of the risk and then you go in ... Hazard-based approach was good and a lot better than the risk-based approach that Vale brought in ... Vale's safety model is behavior-based safety. The first thing they look at is the actions or the behavior or the thoughts of the worker. They forget about everything and look at the worker. We know that, when you look at one thing long

---

84   Which the union members associate with increased risks, since, according to their reports, in the two years since its introduction, there have been four serious accidents with three deaths at the Sudbury mines. USW Local 6500 found it difficult to conduct a joint investigation with the company, as was the custom at Inco, and decided to conduct its own investigation, whose report blames changes in procedures and mine failures for the events.

enough, you find a way to get what you want out of that situation. So, the company came back after the strike [saying]: 'I'm the boss and you're the worker.' And they were very clear that they were the boss. You wouldn't step out of the line, you wouldn't talk back ... Eventually, the company got what they wanted ... It's not worth it to push back on the company. So, the average worker would say: 'I'm coming into work and I'm gonna try not to get hurt and I'm gonna stay out of any type of conversation and I'm not gonna bring any issues to the forefront. I'll deal with it by myself. And I'll go home in the end of the fucking day with less bullshit.' That culture is alive today. It's slowly changing where people will bring things up ... So that's changing, but there's a real strong line between, we're gonna say, us and them, the workers and management ... That's not the culture of safety we want. We want people to be able to look for things that are gonna harm them or somebody else. You want that person to make a shot at fixing it and, if he can't, that person has to know that he can go to the supervisor and the supervisor has got his back ... Everything is all on the worker. It takes away the responsibility and the liability from the company because, if something weird happens, the company can say: 'Well, he was trained on that, he knew about it.' And the company says what? 'He chose to do that.' ... So, it's a way that the company can take one step back from many liabilities and, also at the same time, put the worker one step forward towards those liabilities.

SEAN, Aguiar Interview

For Sam, the alcohol and drug policy has been used to make activists a target, generating insecurity in the workers' collective – since a mistake in production can be a reason to suspect the use of some substance and generate an order to submit to a urine test – and bringing, as a consequence, exposure in front of colleagues:

A small incident, it doesn't have to be a big incident. Back in the old days, before all of this policy, as a welder, I made many repairs on equipment for little mistakes that guys made. Guys usually make mistakes when they are trying to make production. It's just a mistake ... Nobody gets hurt, a little bit of damage in the equipment, we fix the equipment, all good. Nothing was ever said ... In the real old days, they would smell his breath [referring to alcohol consumption] and say: 'You'd better go home.' The guy could have had a night out the night before, coming in the morning after having a night of drink the night before ... But the foreman had respect for the man, the man had respect for the foreman. The foreman would say: 'Listen, you smell a little bit heavy, you'd better go home.' Or: 'Go to sit somewhere, I'll come and get you in a couple of hours, let's see how you are doing.' Now, the guy can be absolutely sober or a nondrinker and he's gonna get piss tested if he bangs something off the wall ... The activists get targeted, right? Most of the activists are just regular guys. They maybe go out for a few beers, their social life may be known to some. But if he's an activist, let's say a miner, they would put him in a position ... If something happens, they would put him in a risky position and target him, so that they almost can assure something will happen so they can ... [claps] have reprisals. So, if he's aggressive, if he's a good steward, he's generally a little bit aggressive, right? He has to stand up for his guys, and the supervisors and managers get upset. They start, well, they formulate plans on how they're gonna either throw him down or get rid of him one way or another. It's all part of control, still part of control. When they've taken a guy who's too active, they try to control him.

SAM, Aguiar Interview

Gregory, a miner fired from Vale, expressed great resentment of the period spent at the company. A member of a family (grandfather, father and uncles) who worked at Inco for decades, he claimed to have confronted the supervisors in the post-strike period, which led to his dismissal. His account of the company's alcohol and drug policy is harsh, all the while showing the issue's multifaceted aspect. On the one hand, he acknowledged having dealt with addiction problems as a result of his underground work. At the same time, in his opinion, the company's drug policy was not aimed at recovering workers from chemical dependency – since drug and alcohol use underground would persist – but at pressuring and intimidating activists or workers critical of their supervisors, in a context of Vale seeking to strengthen their authority in the workplace.

The stress has become so much and so great that it affects [the workers] at home and it affects them at work to the point where I've seen guys shaking in a shower, not because they're cold. Because they're so stressed out they don't have a choice but to cope with their stresses the only way that they know how. And lots of people don't have a proper use to deal with stress. I myself learned that I did lots of things that were very bad for me. I used to do coke underground, you know? I used to do Oxicam underground. That's a pain pill, it's like a ... Anyway, it's very bad stuff. I used to smoke weed underground, but you know what? Smoking weed underground calmed me down, and I was just kind of able to brush them off and not take it home with me. The other stuff was not supposed to be done down there, you know? I could have hurt somebody, I could have hurt myself or I could have killed somebody. You never know, right? ... There's people who drink underground, there's people who smoke dope underground, there's still people who do other things underground but that's the only way that they know how to cope with it and to deal with having to come back to that place the next day.

... How it used to be before, when it was Inco? If your chief boss was in the cage with you, that's the elevator that goes down. If they were in the cage and they smelled booze on somebody then they would just send them home. Now, you get piss tested. So, you have to piss in a bottle in front of somebody to make sure that it's yours, you know? Cause everybody carries a bag of pee around with them ... obviously not! So, you have to do that in front of somebody, you get tested right there on the spot and, if there's any alcohol or drugs in your system, you're immediately fired. Like, no going to rehab or nothing: you're sent home without pay ... Whereas before, ok, there's something wrong with this guy: 'Hey, let's send him for help.' That doesn't happen anymore. The only way that it does is through the union and they have to fight tooth and nail to have that happen ... Even if you get into an argument with somebody [from the] staff ... If they just wanna push the issue because you're pushing back or you're asking questions: 'Ok, we're gonna piss test you, you are not being yourself.' That's all they have to say: 'You're not being yourself, we're gonna piss test you.' ... I've stood up in a meeting and said: 'That's fine. What you're doing with us, how about you going through all the staff? And we'll see how many on your side and on our side.' And then I got thrown out of the meeting and sent home for saying that.

... I'm even better now because I'm not the angry little shit that I was. I was angry at the world. I hated everything because I hated my job. I hated being treated like a number. Like I was saying about that meeting, [a staff member] came back to me the next day, the very next shift, he came down: 'Hi, Gregory 1542431!'[85] He recited my serial number that I didn't even know was my serial number. After that day, I recognized: ok, so they actually do think that we're just numbers. So anytime I introduced myself to a staff member, I would say: Hi, I'm 1542431! And they would take that as an insult.

GREGORY, Aguiar Interview

---

85   In addition to the name, Gregory's identification number has obviously been changed.

Testimonies such as these presented point to management's increased control of the workplace, through its calls for discipline, in a daily conflict over the suppression of the union's collective power in the workplace. At the same time, the imposition of restructuring, despite union opposition, showed a willingness by the company not only to align bonuses and pensions with those adopted in Brazil. In fact, the conflict showed how Vale does not accept the union having a relevant role in the intermediation between the company and the workforce, especially when it comes to controlling the work process. Its union relations strategy, as André Teixeira's statements reproduced in Chapter 2 show, seeks to subordinate the unions, making them play a role of indirect intermediation between company and workers, complementing the direct intermediation role performed by managers and supervisors.

As part of its 'social strategy,'[86] the company also strives to maintain relations with the community by funding education, cultural, and health facilities in Sudbury. Vale's influence in the city, however, seems to go beyond the production process inside the mines and its relationship to unions and to the community: interviewed union members reported the mining company's influence in the municipal election which took place right after the strike, when John Rodriguez, mayor from 2006 to 2010, was seeking reelection. Rodriguez is a member of the New Democratic Party, a social democratic party with ties to the USW that reportedly supported the striking workers:

> John Rodriguez was a supporter of the strikers. He spoke at the rallies about the importance of the workers ... My opinion and others' is that he was punished for that.
>
> JULIAN, Aguiar Interview

In the 2010 election, Rodriguez was defeated by Marianne Matichuk (who governed the city until 2014), a Liberal Party member who had had no previous experience of political activism or electoral performance. The mayor, before being elected, was ... a safety consultant for Vale.

> We had a mayor, for example, who had no previous business as a politician running against the mayor who was the mayor during the strike. She was a safety supervisor of Vale prior to running and she spent a ton of money on the election and she was elected.
>
> JULIAN, Aguiar Interview

---

86   See Bruno Milanez et al., "A estratégia corporativa da Vale S.A.: um modelo analítico para redes globais extrativas," *Versos – Textos para Discussão PoEMAS* 2, no. 2 (2018):1–43.

The case of the election of a mayor in Sudbury close to Vale is not, however, new when considering the company's 'institutional strategy.'[87] Some of its aspects have been presented throughout this book. We can mention: the economic dependence on mining activities, which submits local governments to corporate interests; the relationship to state institutions and public agents through lobbying and 'revolving door' mechanisms, by which managers or professionals linked to the company occupy seats on public boards and agencies; and the financing of electoral campaigns.

Regarding the last aspect, in the 2014 election,[88] companies belonging to the Vale group donated R$ 79.3 million to campaigns for the national and local executive and legislative branches. There were donations to the presidential candidacies of Dilma Rousseff (R$ 12 million) and Aécio Neves (R$ 3 million) and to the state governors of Minas Gerais and Espírito Santo elected on that occasion – respectively, Fernando Pimentel (R$ 3.1 million) and Paulo Hartung (R$ 300,000). Vale also financed the campaigns of legislators directly involved in committees of interest to the company, such as senators Antônio Anastasia (R$1 million) and Rose de Freitas (R$500,000), members of the Federal Senate's Temporary Committee for the National Policy on Dam Safety. In turn, out of the nineteen members of the commission established by the Chamber of Deputies to follow and monitor the consequences of the collapse of Samarco's Fundão dam in November 2015, ten had their campaigns funded by Vale.[89]

It can be concluded, therefore, that Vale's influence in the Sudbury municipal election, as pointed out by members of the USW Local 6500 union, is also part of the corporate strategy originally developed by the company in its operations in Brazil.

John Peters' assessment[90] of the strike's outcome is quite critical of the tactics used by the USW. For him, despite being perhaps the most powerful union in the world, with financial resources and international connections, there was little effort to gain support from the local community and little pressure put on Canadian politicians. International solidarity was reportedly protocol, despite the presence of some Brazilian union members during the acts in support of

---

87   Ibid, 20.
88   The last one before the 2015 electoral reform, which banned corporate campaign financing.
89   Tádzio Peters Coelho, Bruno Milanez and Raquel Giffoni Pinto, "A empresa, o Estado e as comunidades," in *Antes fosse mais leve a carga: reflexões sobre o desastre da Samarco/Vale/BHP Billiton*, ed. Marcio Zonta and Charles Trocate (Marabá: iGuana, 2016), 186–8.
90   Peters, "Down in the Vale."

the strike. As shown in the previous chapter, the fragility of Vale's unions in Brazil helps explain the meagre engagement of Vale's union movement in the international support to the strike. In the following section, this discussion will be resumed.

It may be useful to illustrate the assessment of the 2009–2010 strike in Canada through the account of Guilherme Zagallo, who advised USW Local 6500 during the strike. For Zagallo, who followed the conflict on site for a few weeks, the union was defeated by Vale and had to accept, after a year on the picket lines, the same impositions that the mining company had presented from the beginning.

> The comrades from Canada don't like it. For them, it was an important clash, in the union, it was an atypical movement of a Third World company, from a peripheral country, buying Inco. There's a bit of Canadian pride ... , there was a certain national identity. And they have an interpretation of the strike as resistance. It really was an important resistance, but I believe that, in this process in Canada, Vale was victorious. It managed to impose its agenda. So, the union makes victory speeches, but the concessions in the process were minimal. Almost one third of the workers ... They chose a very hard job, although Canadian miners are the best paid in the world, with average wages of about US$5,000 [per month]. It's a very hard job, a lot of young people don't want it, almost all of it are underground mines. So it ended up that a lot of people went to other jobs. The company managed, in a way, to impose a different level ... So much so that, in the subsequent collective agreement, there was no strike, there wasn't this more confrontational posture. The company had a billion-dollar loss. So, a one-year stoppage mustn't have cost less than a billion dollars in reduction of profitability, not in loss. There was also a cash loss in maintenance, hiring outsourced workers to do some minimal activities, especially in the industrial plants, with inventories, and so on. But you will hardly extract this reading from the comrades in Canada, this perception that it was a defeat for them. They read it as ... I think that it's part of the confrontation process: it's very difficult, after a year-long strike, to come out with the discourse that 'we were defeated.' But I think that, from a strategic point of view, Vale more or less managed to break the resistance there, the concessions that were made at the end of the process were minimal. Basically, the contract that was signed was very similar to the contract that was refused at the beginning, which generated the strike.
>
> GUILHERME ZAGALLO, Aguiar Interview

Although the union members do not say so openly, it is a 'bitter setback'[91] in which the union considered to be the most powerful in the world bowed to the dictates of a transnational from the Global South. The effects of the intense globalization of mining in the first decade of the twenty-first century were reaching the old Canadian mining town. An interesting dialogue with three workers from Vale in Sudbury illustrated the impasses and differences within the workers' collective regarding the course of the strike which became historical:

Leonard:	Although still a big enough group that said we should still [strike] ...
Sam:	Well, I know that some of the people that I talk to were gonna vote for [the contract] even though they disagreed with it. They just couldn't afford to go any longer.
Leonard:	Well, I don't think anybody would ever agree with it. It was a matter of choice. Can I hold on for another month ...
Sam:	I wanted another month at least.
George:	Yeah.
Leonard:	I was thinking like that myself but I said: it's not gonna be a month. It won't be a month, it'll be a lot longer than a month.
Sam:	But I don't know. You don't know that.
Leonard:	That was my thinking.
George:	Everyone had their own choice. Personally, myself I voted it down. I didn't want to accept it just on a matter of principle.
Sam:	I voted it down.
Leonard:	I voted for [Sam and George laugh]. But if you ask anybody, 80% or 90% are gonna say: I did! I turned that contract down! I didn't vote for that!
George:	[Laughing] That's Leonard!
Leonard:	I'm saying, I talked to many people in the workforce, I talked to many guys.
George:	And anyone had their own reasons: if you were more financially stable or if your wife was working, whatever. Personally, for myself it was for a matter of principle because the very issues that we went on strike for were exactly what we were being asked to sign for a year later.

91   Ibid, 101.

Leonard: It was identical, yeah.

George: Yeah. And then it was a no for me on a matter of principle.

Thiago Aguiar: *In your opinion, was the strike defeated?*

Sam: Yeah.

George: Yeah.

Leonard: Sorry, Thiago?

                  Was it a defeat?

Sam: Did the company defeat the union?

Leonard: Oh yeah ... Yeah ... If you look at what we got, yes. By
                  looking at it that way it's a defeat. The strike maybe ...
                  I think it ... How do you say that? The membership got
                  somewhat tired, right?

                  Aguiar Interview

The assessment presented by Brazilians involved in the conflict also pointed to a defeat of the strike, since Vale was able to impose, at the end of the process, the restructuring of the Canadian operations that it had planned. There are, however, differences of nuance: Artur Henrique, then president of the CUT who accompanied strike events in Sudbury, emphasized the USW's organizational capacity. For André Teixeira, there was learning and "maturity," which strengthened the capital-labor relationship. Sérgio Rosa, president of Vale's Board of Directors at the time of the strike, said that the conflict is part of an "unfortunately tough" capital-labor "game":

> Look, I don't think there were winners and losers. The process of the strike caused Vale's image, not only in Canada but also in other countries, to be strongly shaken. ... Of course, from the point of view of the change in management and of the pension fund, Vale was victorious. ... Vale ended up getting the result that it sought to achieve with the restructuring. ... And there it was demonstrated that the folks had organization.
>
> ARTUR HENRIQUE, Aguiar Interview

The exit from the strike, the end of the strike: I think both parties learned. Both parties changed their behavior. In this sense, it was a learning experience for both parties, and they came out with a five-year agreement. It was a nice way out, and even more, it showed maturity. I believe that the result: the relationship between capital and labor there became stronger after the strike, incredible as it may seem. It was a strike in which they felt defeated, but it meant ... And Vale also lost, Vale lost a lot there. If you look at the balance sheets, you can see how it lost. Vale lost in that strike. They lost too.

ANDRÉ TEIXEIRA, Aguiar Interview

Thiago Aguiar: *There is criticism from the unions on the company's impermeability in negotiating the Canada strike. What do you think about that?*

Sérgio Rosa: I think that, in practice, this is true, to the extent that no agreement was reached and the conflict was prolonged for a long time. It's obvious that when that happens, there's a struggle on both sides. Again, I'm not able – I wasn't able at the time and am not able today – to say that Vale was very tough, although this is implicit. Just as it's also implicit that the union was also very tough. And I'm not saying that one side or the other is wrong: it's a tough game of capital-labor. An unfortunately tough game, isn't it?

Aguiar Interview

Therefore, the case in question shows how – in the face of pressures to increase productivity to enhance value capture in a context of depressed commodity prices – mining TNCs restructure and reduce operating costs, increasing labor flexibility within the limits of legislation and weakening unions and their bargaining capacity. The result of the Vale strike in Canada exemplifies how, with globalization, the working class loses strength to confront a capitalist class who is transnationalized and has greater freedom of movement and global political articulation. Trapped within national borders and limited by language, political, cultural and economic barriers, the working class generally offers local and national responses to the impositions of the TCC, with less chance of success when dealing with global giants.[92]

Vale doubled down on the Canadian private sector's largest strike in thirty years, taking advantage of the stoppage to carry out maintenance and restructuring work at the mines, while waiting for more convenient nickel prices on the global market. The company was also able to do so because of the relatively lower importance of nickel exploration revenues in Canada in its overall global operations.

---

92   See William I. Robinson, *A Theory of Global Capitalism: Production, Class, and State in a Transnational World* (Baltimore, Johns Hopkins University Press, 2004).

TABLE 2   Changes in Inco/Vale Canada contracts compared to Vale Brazil

	Inco/Vale 2006–2009 contract pre-strike	Vale Canada 2010–2015 and 2015–2020 contracts post-strike	Vale Brazil
Bonus	Nickel bonus – varying according to the increase in nickel prices in the world market.	AIP – tied to the achievement of goals and profits reached by the company.	Profit sharing bonus – linked to the achievement of goals and profits reached by the company.
Pensions	Defined benefit plans	Defined benefit plans for legacy employees and defined contribution plans for those hired after 2010.	Vale Mais, defined contribution plan.
Role of unions in the workplace	Three-step grievance procedures, with stewards and union playing a role in handling complaints.	From 2010 to 2015, two-step grievance procedures; reduced role of stewards and union; referral of grievances to arbitration. From 2015 to 2020, return to three-step grievance procedure. From 2010, alcohol and drug code strengthens supervisors' role in production.	No union role in handling workplace grievances; difficult access of union leaders to production sites (Metabase Carajás); supervisors and managers with workplace control; managers present at union assemblies (STEFEM).

TABLE 2   Changes in Inco/Vale Canada contracts compared to Vale Brazil (*cont.*)

	Inco/Vale 2006–2009 contract pre-strike	Vale Canada 2010–2015 and 2015–2020 contracts post-strike	Vale Brazil
Safety policy	Safety policy based on stopping activities when there is exposure to danger (hazard-based style); union involved in occupational safety checks; joint accident investigations.	Behavior-based safety policy; union less involved in occupational safety checks; increasing number of accidents and no joint investigation with union; alcohol and drug code with urine testing by supervisors.	Company determines safety policy; little or no role for the union; eventual action by members of the *Comissão Interna de Prevenção de Acidentes* [Internal Commission for the Prevention of Accidents], or CIPA, complying with legal requirements.

SOURCES: INCO AND USW LOCAL 6500, COLLECTIVE AGREEMENT BETWEEN INCO LIMITED AND UNITED STEELWORKERS, LOCAL 6500, JUNE 1ST, 2006; VALE S.A. AND USW LOCAL 6500, COLLECTIVE AGREEMENT BETWEEN VALE CANADA LIMITED AND UNITED STEEL-WORKERS, LOCAL 6500, JULY, 8, 2010 – MAY, 31, 2015, ONTARIO OPERATIONS, 2010; VALE S.A. AND USW LOCAL 6500, COLLECTIVE AGREEMENT BETWEEN VALE CANADA LIMITED AND UNITED STEELWORKERS, LOCAL 6500, JUNE, 1, 2015 – MAY, 31, 2020, ONTARIO OPERA-TIONS, 2015; AND INTERVIEWS WITH LEADERS OF METABASE CARAJÁS, STEFEM, AND USW LOCAL 6500

As we will see in the next section, international trade union networks are an attempt to transcend the isolation of the working class in the face of global-ization by broadening the links of workers from TNCs in different countries. In Vale's case, however, as will be argued, there have been great difficulties in making such an articulation successful.

Before that, as a way of framing some elements of Vale's labor and union relations strategies presented thus far, Table 2 provides a summary of the changes in the contracts negotiated between Inco and Vale with USW Local 6500 (in 2006, 2010, and 2015) and of the information obtained through field observations and interviews conducted with union members and company workers in Brazil and Canada.

6   Vale's International Trade Union Network: A Frustrated Experience

The purchase of Inco in 2006, as we have seen, had a fundamental role in Vale's internationalization. In its corporate strategy, the acquisition was part of an ambitious plan: diversification of ore extraction; reduction of revenue dependence from iron ore extracted in Brazil; opening of new sources of financing, with a presence in a Global North country; and enhancement of value capture, with nickel prices appreciated in the world market, following the movement of the commodity boom.

The company's workers and unions in Canada, however, clashed with the company's union and labor relations strategies, which sought to restructure operations in that country, reducing operating costs and expanding its control over the workplace. Such a diagnosis is also present in a letter from the International Federation of Chemical, Energy, Mine and General Workers' Unions (ICEM)[93] to Vale's management, in which it demanded the reopening of negotiations with the USW during the long strike at the Canadian unit of Voisey's Bay:

> The picture of its relationship with unions in Brazil is very different from the one presented to us during our global campaign period. Vale workers in Brazil sign individual employment contracts and can be dismissed from their jobs at any time, without just cause and without union representation. There are no grievance systems in place and workers are routinely dismissed, even after several years of labor. There are a large number of work-related accidents, and there have been more than thirty deaths in the last three years.
>
> We are completely against this form of labor relations as practiced by Vale in Brazil and we are deeply concerned that Vale intends to export a

---

93   ICEM was the international trade union federation for chemical and other industries, which merged with IndustriALL in 2012.

model where workers' rights are not respected. If Vale is to succeed in its global expansion, it must change its practices and learn to respect workers and their unions around the globe.[94]

The strong strike of 2009–2010, therefore, can be understood as a workers' response to the globalization of mining in Sudbury,[95] even if unsuccessful in its attempt to prevent the changes promoted by the company in pay, pensions, and union relations. The conflict, moreover, allows us to reflect on a fundamental aspect of the relations between labor and globalization: the emergence of transnational cooperation initiatives among workers' organizations to react to the consequences of the expansion of TNC's activities.

With Vale's internationalization, and especially during the conflict in Canada, there were attempts to establish a greater exchange between the company's unions around the world. The Steelworkers, in particular, engaged in this effort, since, with the company's intransigence in the negotiations, it was necessary to expand the forms of pressure. Visits to Brazil and to Vale's unions, protests during shareholder meetings and in front of stock exchanges were held. As Bernard, leader of USW Local 6500, explained:

> This was already designed, they already had the playbook, Vale ... I'm sure this was designed a long time before this was started, a long time, because you could tell just [by] the way they played the cards all the way through, you know? They had this planned for a long time. I think they just want to destroy us. They just want to destroy this local union. And that's what it was all about: not just weaken us, but destroy us ... They just think about having control, showing that they got the power and suppressing their workers, like they do in Brazil, right? That's what they do ... I can't speak about everywhere. I can only speak for the times I did go to Brazil and had meetings and conversations in Brazil with workers at Vale ... It was all about control of the worker, making sure that they're the boss and you listen. So, there's a lot of 'divide and conquer.' I noticed that: they put worker against worker ... I think it was like a big war. It was a bigger war than a local war. It was an international union war and a Vale parent company war. Bringing people here was very good for solidarity and us going there for solidarity ... They didn't like that. I think that's one thing that

---

94 ICEM Letter to Vale's Labor Relations Office, September 10, 2010.
95 As was also pointed out by Roth, Steedman and Condratto, "The Casualization of Work and the Rise of Precariousness."

really hurt the company by us going to Brazil, or going to New York and running into Agnelli, or going to Africa, or England and Switzerland. We were everywhere meeting them. So I think that really helped. The unfortunate part is that the people from Brazil that came here, that were part of CUT from different areas, they were mistreated after. The people that came to support us, Vale in Brazil made them look bad, told the people that they were more interested in our Canadian strike than they are in their own people. So they really turned the workers against them. And that happened.

BERNARD, Aguiar Interview

Bernard's comments are very illustrative of the challenges for unions in their unequal relationship with transnationals with little reliance on isolated local operations, and thus a superior position of strength vis-à-vis the isolation of labor and its organizations bounded by national and regional boundaries. In addressing challenges to labor and society such as these, Peter Evans[96] pointed to what he saw as the 'failures' of neoliberal globalization – for example, its failure to offer sufficient protection to social and collective goods; its favoring of monopolies and their pursuit of rent-seeking and limiting innovation; its failure to gain consent for its domination; and its presentation of serious weaknesses in coordination and governance. He differentiates this from globalization, understood as the process of the reduction of geographical distances by the advances in transportation and communication, from neoliberalism, whose effects threaten social reproduction and even the accumulation of capital itself, given the accumulated contradictions.

Inspired by Polanyi's work, Evans calls attention to the possibilities of the emergence of counter-movements of society, protecting itself – eventually uniting actors with diverse interests – from the global expansion of neoliberalism. Such societal responses, in his analysis, cannot be anticipated, but the hypothesis of using the instruments offered by globalization in favor of counter-movements to neoliberalism (such as the struggle of workers, women, environmentalists, and in defense of human rights on a global scale) could make room for a 'movement of movements' in favor of a 'counter-hegemonic globalization,'

---

96   Peter Evans, "Is an Alternative Globalization Possible?," *Politics and Society* 36, no. 2 (2008): 271–305.

a globally organized project of transformation aimed at replacing the dominant (hegemonic) global regime with one that maximizes democratic political control and makes the equitable development of human capabilities and environmental stewardship its priorities.[97]

The proposition of a counter-hegemonic globalization does not entail that it is most likely trajectory for the replacement of the global order. Evans points to other possible paths, such as a change in the balance of national powers or even the emergence of 'regressive movements for social protection,' which claim authoritarian, nationalistic ways out, and in defense of internal and external repression.[98]

Labor, in turn, faced with the decline of its power at the national level and pressured by the mobility of capital, by the geographical displacement of productive activities and by the risk of unemployment, would have an opportunity with globalization: to develop a new transnationalism, building alliances and promoting campaigns which help create more durable institutions, transnational networks of labor that can offer a counter-hegemonic perspective to globalization.[99] This, for Evans, would be an alternative to the 'structural pessimism' of those who see neoliberal globalization as the twilight of labor organization.

For Michael Burawoy,[100] the studies on global labor which seek inspiration in Polanyi's work are marked by the same 'false optimism' of this 'thinker',[101] who could not have imagined the ideology of market fundamentalism taking over the world again because, among other reasons, he focused on the market and the counter-movement in opposition to it, reducing, moreover, the state to society. More than just a difference in the appropriation of Polanyi's work, Burawoy seeks to draw attention to the fact that the 'counter-hegemonic' movements to globalization, pointed out by Evans and other authors, may not be exactly *counter*-hegemonic. It is not clear "in what way they represent an alternative 'hegemony', nor what it is that they actually 'counter', nor that they effectively build transnational solidarity."[102] Thus, such movements could only be an adjustment to hegemonic neoliberal capitalism. Therefore, Burawoy

---

97   Ibid, 272.
98   Ibid, 281.
99   Ibid, 293.
100   Michael Burawoy, "From Polanyi to Pollyanna: The False Optimism of Global Labor Studies," *Global Labour Journal* 1, no. 2 (2010): 301–12.
101   Karl Polanyi, *Origins of our time: The great transformation* (London: V. Gollancz, 1945).
102   Burawoy, "From Polanyi to Pollyanna," 302.

asserts the need for research to focus more on the obstacles to contestation than on the embryos of a global counter-movement or counter-hegemonic globalization.[103] To avoid a kind of 'Pollyanna' optimism, Burawoy claims to have a stance of "uncompromising pessimism" in the face of labor's promise of global solidarity, since labor, considered globally, was on the defensive.[104]

Responding to such considerations, Evans, animated by his 'skeptical optimism,'[105] suggests that globalization – considered as a shortening of social and geographical space or in the form of contemporary neoliberal capitalism – stimulates the mobilization of labor solidarity at the transnational level, as well as the constitution of transnational labor movement networks and organizations.[106]

The reproduction of this theoretical debate, regarding the emergence of forms of labor transnationalism, is useful when dealing with a multifaceted case such as Vale's process of conversion into a TNC, as well as the labor and union relations in its GPN and the organized reactions of unions. A glance can be directed, on the one hand, to the possibilities of developing relations between Vale's unions worldwide, and on the other hand, to the failure of the embryonic international trade union network organized from 2007 onwards, boosted during the 2009–2010 strike in Canada.

After years of attempts to articulate the company's unions in Brazil, Vale's international trade union network was made official in 2007, with the signing of an agreement involving unions from Brazil, Canada and New Caledonia. Subsequently, the USW tried to bring union members from Mozambique closer to the initiative, which gained some momentum in international campaigns during the strike in Canada. Of the eight local and national Brazilian union organization representatives – whose presence was expected in Canada and whose names were included in the text of the agreement – there was a signature missing: precisely that of Tonhão, an important leader of Metabase Carajás, the largest Vale workers' union in Brazil,[107] who did not attend the founding meeting, showing, from the beginning, that the obstacle of Brazilian

---

103   Ibid, 307.

104   Michael Burawoy, "On Uncompromising Pessimism: Response to My Critics," *Global Labour Journal* 2, no. 1 (2011): 73–7.

105   Peter Evans, "National Labor Movements and Transnational Connections: Global Labor's Evolving Architecture under Neoliberalism," *Global Labour Journal* 5, no. 3 (September 2014): 258–82.

106   Peter Evans, "Is It Labor's Turn to Globalize? Twenty-First Century Opportunities and Strategic Responses," *Global Labour Journal* 1, no. 3 (Sep. 2010): 356.

107   According to the documents creating Vale's international network reproduced at Brasch, *Winds of Change*, 12–3.

union coordination would make the consolidation of Vale's international trade union network unfeasible.

If it is difficult to consider, following Burawoy,[108] the international union network *per se* as part of a counter-hegemonic initiative, we must recognize that the links between Vale's unions, as the interviews showed, created embarrassment for the company, which acted to hinder the network's consolidation. Vale's union strategy, empirically analyzed in the previous chapters, guided the measures taken by the company to stop the continuity of the development of common international campaigns and initiatives of its unions. André Teixeira made explicit his antipathy to international union federations and, as will be seen, to proposals that the company sign an international framework agreement.

> How did the Cold War influence the trade union in the world? ... When Russia saw communism and, especially after World War II, when several countries there became part of the Iron Curtain, they created the union centers, which weren't union centers at all. The United States at that time, capitalism at that time, Europe also, encouraged the emergence of international labor federations. The big federations appeared at that time and were a counterpart to the emergence of those centers. If you check, the international federations, for years and years and years, were utterly useless. If you look at it: what did the worker gain with the federations for so long? Not much. It was a structure that existed and that was encouraged by the Cold War.
>
> ANDRÉ TEIXEIRA, Aguiar Interview

As Bernard reported, during the strike in Canada, the USW organized a global solidarity campaign, involving press denunciations, protests in front of stock exchanges and during meetings of Vale shareholders, as well as trying to strengthen the links of the network created shortly before through visits to Brazilian unions and Vale's operations in the country. The interviewees said there had also been attempts at conversations with Vale's shareholder pension funds, such as Previ, and with members of the federal government.

In Chapter 2, it was possible to verify that Vale's union strategy aims at keeping the unions close to the company's management and making their joint action difficult. André Teixeira, when describing his conception of good relations between the company and the unions, said that he was against the negotiation of collective agreements' exposure through the press, making evident

---

108   Burawoy, "From Polanyi to Pollyanna," 301–2.

his opposition to public scrutiny of the company's actions. In addition, when talking about the strike in Canada, Teixeira mentioned what Vale had learned from the labor conflict involving Gerdau in the United States,[109] stating that he had sought information from this company to better deal with the Canadian strike and the type of action taken by the USW. The long reconstruction of the labor relations manager about the way the company dealt with the strike and the Steelworkers' campaign is useful to understand the troubles which Vale's international trade union network had to consolidate itself.

André Teixeira: Gerdau also had a problem with the Steelworkers in the United States. And we even started to talk to Gerdau at the time, when the problem began, before the strike itself, [about] the relationship between Brazilian management and Canadian and American companies, right? They went through similar situations. Now, at Gerdau, they tried at the time to get Lula to interfere in the process. There was a ... Lula was in Pittsburgh. ... There was a forum there ... in Pittsburgh or around it, which is where the USW headquarters is, I'm not sure, where they went after Lula to talk to him, right?

Thiago Aguiar: *What about in the Canada strike?*
They tried to get Lula to interfere: they came here and talked to Minister Dulci, ... they went after Paim, they went after a hearing here in Congress. They tried to get the government to interfere: to put pressure on the Lula administration at the time so that Lula would put pressure

---

109   Evans pointed to Gerdau's international trade union network as a successful example of "the new labor transnationalism." The network, created in 2003, played a key role in 2005, "when contract talks at a Gerdau-owned plant in Beaumont, Texas ended in a lockout after the Gerdau subsidiary Ameristeel demanded cutting vacations, overtime pay, and seniority rights as part of their 'last best offer.'" See Evans, "National Labor Movements and Transnational Connections," 264. The USW and the Gerdau international network organized a global campaign and pressured the company in Brazil, with support from Brazilian unions and the CUT, achieving in 2007 the end of the lockout and a change in demands and in the new contract's line of negotiation by the company. The mention, by Teixeira, of the search for learning from the Gerdau conflict seems to indicate Vale's concern that the organization of the international trade union network during the Canadian strike would create similar troubles for the company. For a detailed analysis of the Gerdau network see Chad William Gray, *Riding Bicycles When We Need Cars: The Development of Transnational Union Networks in Brazil*, PhD Dis. (Cornell University, 2015).

on Vale. They used that route a lot. They came here: they wanted to interfere in our negotiations, they wanted us to strike in Brazil in solidarity with them. I made a negotiation: ... I was in the Novo Mundo Hotel, in the meeting room, and they were upstairs and there was a union member there, at the time, with a computer, broadcasting live my negotiation to them. They had a representative here, whose name I forget, who was from the AFL-CIO as well. So they followed one of my negotiations and tried to interfere in one of my negotiations. Then the Brazilian unions went like: 'Wait a minute, calm down, this is our negotiation!' They went to Mozambique to ask for solidarity from the unions there, to encourage the strike there, and they said: 'Strange, when we needed you, you didn't come here. Now that you're in need, you've come.' They tried to hit us all over the world, right?

This is an interesting point: so, did an internationalization of the conflict occur?
It did. When I went to the ICEM, the [International Metalworkers' Federation] IMF[110] in Geneva, the [International Labour Organization] ILO ... And at the time they were discussing – now the unions have given up on this deal – International Framework Agreements. These were global agreements, which the companies made in order to guarantee the ILO's eight fundamental conventions and some other stuff. And I was under a lot of pressure at the time to sign this agreement. A lot of pressure.

And did Vale sign the agreement?
It didn't.

Why?
What's in it for me to sign this agreement? What do I get?

What do companies in general gain from this type of agreement?

---

110   International metalworkers trade union federation, which merged with IndustriALL in 2012.

Pressure. You get pressure: you sign, and then you get cornered. No company signed that out of its own free will. Have you ever seen any company come to the Public Prosecutor's Office: 'I came here to sign a Conduct Adjustment Agreement because I want to.' It doesn't happen, you know what I mean? So, the pressure that was made ... ... What was I concerned about with these international agreements? What's the international union movement's dream? To have global agreements defining wages. That was their dream, the one they had at the time. But those agreements never happened. The agreements' texts were ridiculous. Some companies: Petrobras signed it, Banco do Brasil signed it. If you take the text Petrobras signed and no text at all, it's all the same. Then I said: 'This is a picture on the wall, you know what I mean?' Several steel companies ... Automakers in Germany signed this agreement! The agreement foresees that you have a role in the production chain. ... They wanted a role in the production chain. I never received anything ... I'm part of the car industry's production chain, I'm part of the steel industry, and I've never received any pressure to follow that. Most, I would say 99% of these agreements, were a picture on the wall. So much so that they gave up. ... It's over. They're not doing these agreements anymore.

... So, we never signed, because I never saw what we would gain with that. And, at the time, Artur Henrique was the CUT's president. He put a lot of pressure on me to sign that. Then, one day, someone ... said: 'André, you're either going to sign this agreement here in Brazil or you're going to sign this agreement in Canada. You'd better sign it in Brazil.' I better not sign this agreement, okay? ... But what will I get? 'No, you have to commit to the eight fundamental conventions.' Of course! We have a GRI report: the first thing ... I declare I'm committed to the eight fundamental [ILO] conventions! I'm against child labor, I'm against slave labor! I'll make the commitment: I just don't want to sign an agreement with you. So we started to make this commitment in documents. ... Instead of using the agreement as marketing, I assume

it, of my own free will: we assume this commitment with
the international market.

*... But you were saying that somehow the unions tried to get
government support because of the government's relationship with the unions, in particular with the CUT ...*
But what I want to say is this: at no time did we identify
PT interference in our negotiations. ... We didn't identify that. I'm saying that they [USW] sought out Minister
Dulci. The minister greeted them. I had afterwards,
because of the Brazilian unions ... ... I even heard about
what they talked about and all that, but we didn't feel any
pressure from the government about this.
Aguiar Interview

One can conclude from André Teixeira's speech that the USW's international
campaign was successful in exposing the company. The USW's presence in a
negotiation with Brazilian unions seemed particularly uncomfortable, as did
the search for members of government. When questioned about this episode,
Artur Henrique, then president of the CUT, confirmed that the Vale strike in
Canada was the subject of debate in the government:

Oh, I think so. It may not have been, let's say, an official agenda that led
to ... But, for example, there was ... I don't remember if it was Gilberto
Carvalho or if it was still [Luiz] Dulci, but, for sure, Dulci, Gilberto
Carvalho and people who were close to the president had all the reports
and were going to make the complaint. ... Certainly, there must have been
some conversation, I don't know if it was with Roger himself, from Vale's
point of view, with someone from Vale, I have no information about that,
but it certainly became a debate, I have no doubt.
ARTUR HENRIQUE, Aguiar Interview

The union leader also confirmed the pressure put on Vale at the time for the
company to sign an international framework agreement. According to Artur
Henrique, there were initial attempts to discuss the agreement based on themes
such as health and safety, which would be easier to negotiate because they do
not influence profitability issues, but the conversations did not advance due to
lack of time, since, with the outbreak of the 2008 crisis, the situation became
more difficult.

But, at the same time, when we pushed to have meetings with international representatives to build the network, the obstacles were very big.
And I'd say that the obstacles were very big in the sense that they were very
afraid of establishing commitments that they couldn't control afterwards.
... Even business commitments, from the international point of view.

ARTUR HENRIQUE, Aguiar Interview

André Teixeira's testimonies showed, however, that perhaps there was even
less interest from the company than time. In any case, if the international
framework agreements (IFAs) were just a 'picture on the wall,' unimportant,
Vale's resistance to initiatives of this kind would not be so great. The IFAs

> are essentially aimed at ensuring respect for workers' rights by putting in
> place permanent mechanisms for information exchange and for control,
> which advocate the implementation of sound labor practices throughout
> an international company's operations. They are generally signed by com-
> pany management and at least one Global Union Federation (GUF) ....[111]

Initially driven by topics such as 'corporate social responsibility' and the quest
to enforce ILO clauses in global production chains, IFAs have become a useful
tool for ensuring international union mobilization and cohesion, stimulating
the emergence of international trade union networks.[112] Indeed, the lack of an
IFA, whose clauses could guide common trade union activities, contributed to
the obstacles in continuing the embryonic international trade union network
organized in 2007. André Teixeira associated the IFAs to the trade union networks as exogenous projects, stimulated by the international federations, with
remote chances of success in Brazil due to the union movement's characteristics in the country:

André Teixeira: The federations competed not with the agreement's con-
                  tent, but with the number of agreements. And they, as
                  they looked for their space, ... wanted to sign more and
                  more. Now they've given that up. They've done away
                  with that. Then, their concept is this: what I have to build

---

111   Marc-Antonin Hennebert, "Os acordos-marco internacionais e as alianças sindicais
      internacionais: instrumentos de uma necessária transnacionalização da militância sindi-
      cal," *Sociologias* 19, no. 45 (2017): 116.
112   Ibid.

are the trade union networks. ... Can you build the network? You can build the network. Now, you don't want my help to build the network, because what you want is the dominance of the European union over the Brazilian one. ... I'm not against the network, no, but don't ask me to help you to build a network.

Thiago Aguiar: *I imagine that the network leaders would be the Brazilian unions and not [the] European ones ...*
I doubt it! Now, why don't these networks work in Brazil? Why didn't these networks work in Vale? Because the people that came here didn't know about our union movement. ... Vale's union movement is split. Today you can't put Vale's union around the same table. ... So, they came here to organize the networks and found this problem. The union division in Brazil is what prevented the networks from growing here when they wanted them to grow. ... This is what happens in Vale and in many other companies.

So why don't networks work?
Because, in my opinion, the union can never distance itself from the workers. These networks aren't built by the unions. They're very much built by the centers. And the worker doesn't see any gain in that. He doesn't participate in it. ... So, these are beautiful models when they're outlined, but they're far from reality. 'Oh, no, but BASF, BASF's network works all over the world!' ... BASF itself pays for the BASF [network] meetings: it pays the ticket for the guys to go over there to Germany. ... To me this is just giving money to the union, money to the union members: they go there and they walk around. So, I haven't seen any trade union network where the money leaves the union and brings results. You may have two or three meetings, but it doesn't last. ... I'm not arguing if it's bad or if it's good. I'm just saying: the trade union network doesn't work without the company's support. ... The labor world started the International Framework Agreement, ended the International Agreement and then put on the trade union networks, which also didn't take off. ... Vale's trade union network has already been

created five or six times and never had a second meeting with the same people who created the network. We
never did anything against it either, because there's nothing to do against it. What will be their next step? I keep
thinking: what are they going to come up with?

Aguiar Interview

The increasing problem of "postulating the national interest as an interest of
the domestic bourgeoisie" makes the articulation of "class interests based on
a national discourse" less likely.[113] If this is not exactly news, there is, on the
other hand, a chance of a recovery of interest in labor issues in production
sites and on the factory floor, regaining strength and politicization precisely
because of the unexpected international articulation of workers based on their
common ties with a company.

The worker networks, or trade union networks, appeared in Brazil in the
early 2000s,[114] based on the organization of the same company's factories or
facilities spread throughout the national territory. The participation of the par-
ent country's unions and centers is usually decisive for the network's organization, in order for it to reach an international dimension. International trade
union networks, however, deal with a contradiction: while they are a 'cosmo-
politan' response to the crisis of traditional unionism, they face the obstacles
inherent to an action focused on a specific company or organization, even if
global.[115]

It is necessary, then, to question the capacity of networks to organize themselves as collective agents and not only as social agents captured by corporate
agendas in the context of globalization. By analyzing the features of successful

---

113   Leonardo Mello e Silva, "Inovações do sindicalismo brasileiro em tempos de globalização
e o trabalho sob tensão," in *As contradições do lulismo: a que ponto chegamos?*, ed. André
Singer and Isabel Loureiro (São Paulo: Boitempo, 2016), 96–7.

114   Leonardo Mello e Silva, "Redes sindicais em empresas multinacionais: contornos de um
sindicalismo cosmopolita? A experiência do ramo químico," in *Século XXI: transformações
e continuidades nas relações de trabalho*, ed. Maria Cristina Cacciamali, Rosana Ribeiro
and Júnior Macambira (Fortaleza: *Instituto de Desenvolvimento do Trabalho* [Labor
Development Institute], *Banco do Nordeste do Brasil* [Bank of Northeast Brazil], 2011). For
an analysis of the organization of trade union networks in various economic sectors in
Brazil, see Ricardo Framil Filho, *O internacionalismo operário entre o local e o global: as
redes sindicais de trabalhadores químicos e metalúrgicos no Brasil*, MA Thesis (University
of São Paulo, 2016), and Maurício Rombaldi, "Diferentes ritmos da internacionalização
sindical brasileira: uma análise dos setores metalúrgico e de telecomunicações," *Caderno
CRH* 29, no. 78 (2016): 535–51.

115   Silva, "Redes sindicais em empresas multinacionais."

trade union networks, we can locate some reasons for the failure of Vale's network:

> A trade union network is a horizontal organization which aims to articulate in the same space of information and action exchange the representatives of workers who perform tasks in the same transnational company in different locations. ... The relationship of the network to the union may be complementary or tense. In general, a network is always a workers' *trade union* network, as this avoids two possible risks: the first is the danger of co-optation of the network members by the company; the second ... is the employers' discretion.[116]

A study which analyzed the experiences of fifteen international union networks[117] pointed out four characteristics of successful networks: 1) the commitment of the network members to the continuity of actions, avoiding high turnover; 2) access to resources (claiming them from the TNC or through union funds); 3)[118] the existence of an action plan; and 4) the creation of a network coordination. In addition, it is fundamental that the GUFs offer support to the networks.

It is possible to affirm that none of these elements was found in the Vale network: 1) there was no commitment from all of the company's unions – on the contrary, there was opposition from Metabase Carajás and other unions[119] – which made any commitment from local organizations to the network impossible; 2) resources were scarce, dependent mainly on the USW and the AFL-CIO (as seen, there is intense opposition from Vale to fund the functioning of the networks); 3) the network sustained itself while there was a strike solidarity campaign in Canada, but had, due to the differences between the Brazilian

---

116 Leonardo Mello e Silva, Ricardo Framil Filho and Raphael Freston, "Redes sindicais em empresas transnacionais: enfrentando a globalização do ponto de vista dos trabalhadores," *Análise*, no. 5 (2015): 3.

117 Ibid.

118 This aspect has become even more sensitive after the changes promoted by the 2017 labor reform and the end of compulsory union dues. At least in the medium term, unions and centers will have fewer resources, which will probably be an additional obstacle for the maintenance of trade union network-building efforts in Brazil. An analysis of the labor reform can be found in José Dari Krein, Roberto Véras de Oliveira and Vitor Araújo Filgueiras, ed., *Reforma trabalhista no Brasil: promessas e realidade* (Campinas: Curt Nimuendajú, 2019).

119 As was also pointed out by Carvalho, "Análise da ação dos sindicatos," 107.

unions, no possibility of establishing long term plans; and 4) for the same reason, it was hardly possible to organize a stable coordination.

Moreover, we can highlight the troubles faced by the Brazilian union members who supported the organization of the Vale network. In Chapter 2, we mentioned Ronaldo's displacement from his position in the STEFEM leadership in retaliation against his support to the Canadian strike, as a union member, as well as a member of Vale's Board of Directors. Interviewed union members also reported pressure from the company on an active leader of Sindimina-RJ.[120] This union member left his organization as a result of the company's reprisals.

> I think the strike is done and then everyone kind of goes their way. I don't believe in that, I think that's wrong. I feel that we let down the people of Brazil ... that were there and supported us ... The bigger unions should have got together and continued ... I know they still have conversations ... But for me, personally, on the local level, I think it's important that we continue. I know it's a little different, how it works in Brazil, and that's why Ronaldo lost his position because the company made him look bad ... I felt so bad about what they did to them in Brazil.
>
> BERNARD, Aguiar Interview

> The unionized workers there [in Brazil] that helped us, the company then was telling the workers there: 'Why are you trying to help the Canadians when they make so much more money than you ... when you have your own problems here? ... You guys shouldn't be worrying about fighting for them. You should worry here.' So a lot of those leaders there lost their jobs in the union [in reference to the dismissal of a Sindimina-RJ union leader]
>
> MICHAEL, Aguiar Interview

> The main problem with Vale's [network] was lack of money, because the unions, with very rare exceptions, were [not] willing to pay for any expenses or tickets, all that, for their members, as in the case of Pará. In Rio de Janeiro, the leader of Vale's union was a front-line negotiator and a very tough guy. Vale did what they did until they removed him from the union's leadership. These unions live off the company. ... All of their union dues come from one company. The other companies [represented

---

120   A union which organizes port workers, engineers, and workers at Vale's central administration.

by them], all backyard companies. So, if the company wants to, it won't collect money from the members anymore – the company can just say: 'Oh, go collect the money at the factory door' -, it doesn't pass on the union dues and breaks [the union] up. It comes to the union president and says: 'Look, if you don't remove the guy from the board of directors, if you don't remove him from the negotiation table, you know the consequences.' ... Vale has an anti-union posture in Brazil. If Tonhão is still there in the union and you go to Pará, he'll say no. He won everything from Vale. ... And there was an opposition there, but they fought it with bullets. With bullets. I don't know how that union is doing.

    CARLOS ANDRADE, Aguiar Interview

And they also had ... I'm not going to say that there was financial help, but they paid a nice daily rate there, you know what I mean? You could see that the guys would leave here and come back full of laptops and start selling. There were very interesting rates to go there ... You pay for everything, and then you get paid a rate for coffee, a really good one! So, most of the Brazilian unions, the Brazilian union members, said: 'Look, they want to use me!' They really said to me: 'They want to use me!' And when they were on the hotel's top floor, on the second floor, and I was in the convention room, when they found out, they came to tell me: 'André, this happened. I'm ashamed of what happened.' But their reaction: in Brazil, in Indonesia ... They went to Indonesia too! They went to New Caledonia, to Mozambique ... In Mozambique, they were all disgusted. They went to Chile ...

    ANDRÉ TEIXEIRA, Aguiar Interview

According to Carlos Andrade, a CUT leader who coordinated the CUT-Múlti, a project to build trade union networks in multinational companies in Brazil,[121] there was interest on the part of Vale's workers' unions abroad, notably in Canada and Mozambique, to organize the Vale network. The obstacles, therefore, would be mainly in Vale's Brazilian union movement, for two main reasons: the company's pressure on union members to avoid approaching their counterparts in other countries; and the traditional articulation troubles of Vale's unions, stimulated by the company.

---

121   Which ran from 2000 to 2009 on the center's initiative, with support and funding from Dutch and German international trade union federations.

[In the attempts to set up the Vale network,] we met the railroad workers [STEFEM], who were younger and very cool people. A very good union, very militant people, who came from the construction of the railroad itself, knowing all the aspects of that railroad, struggles with Indians, squatters ... And they were lucky to have a lawyer [Guilherme Zagallo], who used to work for Vale and started to work for them. A very good guy, who was president of the Maranhão section of the OAB [Order of Attorneys of Brazil]. He was our lawyer for the network, who oriented the network in legal terms. He would go to the negotiation table along with the unions. ... He studied English, started studying Vale, the New York stock exchange. Suddenly, we would receive a report from him. ... So, based on these more militant unions we set up the Vale network: we made a manifesto, formed the network, with the support of the ICEM and the AFL-CIO, which represented these unions in Canada. ... It was a shame we couldn't organize this network in Vale. Because the Canadian people agreed. They had a historic strike there. By the way, Vale tricked us. ... They went behind our backs and sabotaged the meeting. Like this: we would call a meeting, then it would call Tonhão and say, for example: 'Tonhão, you know that health hazard we were discussing? The discussion will take place tomorrow, and there's a good chance of reaching an agreement. It will be tomorrow at 2 pm,' the same date we had invited him to the meeting in São Paulo. Then Tonhão called: 'Oh, I can't.' Tonhão, send someone else! He wouldn't, because Vale had put pressure on him to leave. ... The main problem in not being able to close a network agreement was this union divergence. You couldn't trust each other. There was a time when PSTU[122] got so pissed off that they said: 'Look, you can all go to hell! I can't stand these cowards anymore. I'm going to meet with our people from Peru – who had a Vale unit there – and I'm going to start the network .... If you don't want to build the network, I'll build the network our way.' PSTU never refused to participate in the network. It never refused, because here the idea is to have every force, every idea, because this will be a common struggle.

CARLOS ANDRADE, Aguiar Interview

In Chapters 1 and 2, it was possible to identify, in the Brazilian Vale workers' unions studied, tendencies towards conservation of union leaderships, bureaucratization, and distancing from the membership bases, either by the inertia

---

122   He refers to union members linked to the CSP-Conlutas trade union federation.

effects of the Brazilian union structure itself, or by the company's conscious pressure on the unions. As a consequence, relations of greater proximity and less conflict between Vale and the unions representing its workers have developed – even if against the orientation publicly expressed by the organizations. The interviews in São Luís (where there is a union which clearly opposes the company's attacks) and Parauapebas (where the local union often stands as a spokesperson for Vale's interests and profitability) showed how the company succeeds in fragmenting the unions and weakening their collective power.

A comparative case study of transnational union cooperation in three sectors[123] showed how the globalization of capital leads to increased intra- and inter-sectoral differentiation within countries, making transnational union partnerships a possibility, not an immanent necessity, as national and local union members struggle to maintain jobs, in a logic of competition between workers. Thus, 'parochial interests' can frustrate international cooperation. Hence, "transnational union relationships are pulled by the national industrial relations systems of the globalizing firm's home country",[124] and there are both push and pull factors for unions to engage in transnational cooperation initiatives. Among the push factors, in addition to various forms of competition between workers, is pressure from managers and companies on unions, pitting them against each other. In turn, the pull factors relate to the existence of previous transnational cooperation structures and a strong, unionized workforce.

If the role of the unions in the transnational company's home country is fundamental to the creation of instruments of international cooperation,[125] a decisive aspect of the failure of the attempt to organize Vale's international trade union network is evident: the weakness of the Brazilian unions and their division into groups were the main reasons for the discontinuity of the network's initiatives after the strike in Canada. While push factors are evidently present,[126] few (if any) pull factors for transnational action are found in the Brazilian Vale unions. USW Local 6500, on the other hand, had more elements – material (the economic resources of a huge multinational union), structural (the expertise of the AFL-CIO and Solidarity Center, for example), and of opportunity (the need to respond to Vale's impositions in the 2009

---

123   Mark Anner et al., "The Industrial Determinants of Transnational Solidarity: Global Interunion Politics in Three Sectors," *European Journal of Industrial Relations* 12, issue 1 (2006): 7–27.

124   Ibid, 14–5.

125   As was also pointed out by Silva, Framil Filho and Freston, "Redes sindicais em empresas transnacionais."

126   Identified by Anner et al., "The Industrial Determinants of Transnational Solidarity."

contract negotiation) – to encourage it to pursue network building. Once the strike ended and a five-year contract was signed with Vale, one could say that such an impulse also cooled down.

There is another fundamental aspect to understand the failure of the Vale network, and the reasons why international solidarity with the strike in Canada was limited to some isolated initiatives of Brazilian union leaders. It is the importance of pension funds, especially Previ, for Vale's control. Carlos Andrade and Guilherme Zagallo dealt with this issue:

> We tried several ways. We tried to talk to Previ, which had a guy appointed by the bank workers, because Previ had a stake in Vale do Rio Doce and didn't help us one inch. It didn't help us in Canada. It didn't help us to open a dialogue. It had a pro-employer position. Previ, with a representative from the bank workers' union, didn't want to know anything about it. Its position was more pro-employer than the boss's. It didn't even greet the foreign delegation who came to talk to them. It was very difficult.
>
> CARLOS ANDRADE, Aguiar Interview

> They tried to build a network in 2007. I met Carlos Andrade, at that time, in this activity of trying to build a workers' network ... , but it ended up not evolving and it didn't evolve, I think, especially due to the weakness of the Brazilian counterpart union movement. This deal of being a union movement that doesn't strike, a union movement more about negotiation and less about confrontation .... But that didn't advance much. It faced resistance, even internal resistance, here in Brazil. Why? Because of the fact that Vale has a *sui generis* position, being a company controlled by a pension fund very close to the workers' unions, Previ, and also a little bit by Caixa's pension fund, but a small part. Massively, if you add the government and Previ's shares, it's a majority in the Vale shareholders block, in the shareholders' agreement. ... It's a *sui generis* company from the point of view that the government and Previ had a majority in this agreement, in this shareholders block. And, in Previ's case, I think there was a certain conflict of interest. In what sense? It was Previ's main investment. There were times when Vale represented I think 30%, 32% of Previ's investments, of Previ's assets, at a time when Vale was growing, this stake was increasing. ... A certain conflict of interest happens. Vale's profitability in the golden years caused the generation of surpluses in Previ, it generated in certain moments a reduction of contribution values, an apportionment of the pension fund surplus, a certain extra value that's paid to the participants. So, even within the union movement, the CUT

union movement, which had, let's say ... Vale's unions are predominantly
CUT affiliates, although there are some unions from Força and Conlutas
.... But the fact is that there was a certain conflict of interest, let's say,
creating obstacles for this broader solidarity between the Brazilian union
movement, which had interests – my associate, who votes for me, who's
going to pay less pension or who's going to have an extra pension benefit
– versus what Vale does in Brazil and in the rest of the world. There was
a certain conflict of interest, which is a bit like this situation of modern
capitalism, which is the preponderant role of pension funds in global
investments. I consider this a typical case of conflict of interest: you end
up being divided between values of solidarity, of building a world with
more benefits, with wealth distribution versus your own interest. Some
union members, not from a personal point of view ... Some even from a
personal point of view, because they become managers, directors, permanent members on the Board of Directors. ... The pension fund leaders end
up, in time, incorporating capitalist practices and management vision.
It's a permanent conflict, that is, I let it happen to the Vale workers what
I don't want to happen to the bank workers of the union that I belong
to, of the unions' leadership. So, it's a very contradictory situation today
with the pension funds. It's not specifically a Vale problem, but in Vale we
could see very clearly that it's a factor like this: I support, I give solidarity,
but I do enough so that I don't seem ... I don't do as much as I can, but
I also don't say that I don't have any solidarity actions. When you have a
CUT president who is an electricity worker, with less links, at the time of
Artur Henrique, for example: he, as he had less links with the bank workers' union movement, with Previ, there was a more intense participation,
a more intense approach, for example, to the Canada strike. When you
have the succession and then comes Vagner Freitas, a bank worker, that's
to say, you have these workers' own interests, then there's a certain distancing ... of this solidarity that should distinguish the union movement.
    GUILHERME ZAGALLO, Aguiar Interview

Faced with criticisms such as these, Artur Henrique affirmed he understood
the role of pension funds and suggested that there was a lack of political formation and strategic discussion in the union movement so that sensitive issues
to the workers could be taken to the companies' boards of directors with pension fund participation. Sérgio Rosa, on the other hand, affirmed that there
were talks with the unions and that the – undesirable – alternative to the criticism received by Previ would be for the workers not to participate anymore in
the companies' management:

Thiago Aguiar:	*Many interviewed union members criticized Previ's behavior during the strike. For them, it actually defended Vale's profitability instead of making room for a negotiated end to the strike. Do you agree?*
Artur Henrique:	I find it very difficult to make such a statement. What I think, I mean, it's clear that the pension fund has as its priority and main goal to keep resources to guarantee the retirement of its participants, that you represent in the pension fund. That's obvious. So, that'll be my priority of action as a pension fund. Should this be done at any cost? That's the question. That's the point. ... You're not going to use the pension fund to be a socialist. We're talking about something else. What you can't want is: if you have to lay off half the employees to increase the profit to guarantee money, then are you going to lay off half the employees? That's when I say that this can't happen. So, when we call the pension funds' responsibility to a strategy that should have been built together to establish rules or, at the very least, boundaries, we're talking about something like this: firing one, five, ten employees, whatever, that has to go through the Board of Directors. The board member has the duty to talk, to articulate, to talk to the union. That was never the center of the board members' concern. ... I think that, there, we're talking about a need for formation, for a strategic discussion of the union movement, which we didn't do even in my time as president. I am not saying that CUT did it. I'm not talking about guilt. Aguiar Interview

Thiago Aguiar:	*Some CUT union members, who tried to mediate a solution to the strike in Canada, report a certain bad feeling about Previ ...*
Sérgio Rosa:	We talked about it. I imagine that feeling is this: they know that Previ had a relevant role inside and they thought that ... They didn't just want to talk. They wanted us to intervene to provoke flexibility, and we didn't have that capacity. It's a situation ... in which we could demand, try to sensitize, give generic directives, but I had no condition to go there and say: change this

right here in the agreement. This here makes a difference, please ... I don't have this capacity. First, that we
don't have the power to make decisions alone in the
Board and, second, that it's not natural for the Board to
make this kind of decision.

Do you consider this criticism unfair?
Not unfair or anything. I think it's normal. They're going
to criticize the company's management, they're going
to criticize their shareholders. ... I think they have every
right to criticize, as I think we have the right, when reading things, to interpret things: what were Previ's limits
as a shareholder of a company, how far it can go. Even
if it had a management that was 100% workers, with a
vision about the labor world, etc. etc., even so, within the
investor vision, it would have limits to make big changes
in the capital-labor relationship game. ... So, we hear
criticism, you know: so, no, workers shouldn't participate
in it. Workers should refuse to participate in this game.
Fine: then let the others, the company leaders manage
the resources that are ours, that are going to make our
benefits. What's the limit of that? Where's the limit in
which we participate or not in a capitalism that exists
and that has a class conflict within it? Where do I participate and where do I not participate? What's the limit
of me defending the interests of workers in Brazil to be
taking some measures that may be better than others
would take, even though I am not going to change ... So,
it's difficult. I'm going to have several answers for that ....
Aguiar Interview

The confluence of interests pointed out by Guilherme Zagallo – which allowed
Roger Agnelli to present himself around the world as someone close to the
Brazilian government and who led the country's union movement to promote
actions on the edge of keeping up appearances – had its origin in the defense of
Vale's profitability by the "financialized union bureaucracy,"[127] with origins in

---

127   Alvaro Bianchi and Ruy Braga, "The Lula Government and Financial Globalization," *Social
       Forces* 83, no. 4 (June 2005): 1745–62.

the CUT bank workers' union movement, which participated in Vale's adminis-tration through its presence in Previ.

The next chapter is dedicated to this question, well-defined in the dilemma expressed in the words of Sérgio Rosa, former bank worker and union member, former president of Previ and former president of Vale's Board of Directors: "What is the limit at which we participate or not in a capitalism that exists and that has a class conflict within it?" It will be the moment to assess, by way of conclusion, the 1997 and 2017 shareholders' agreements, and the recent changes in Vale's 'corporate governance.' Following this, the epilogue will offer the final reflections of this book.

CHAPTER 4

Conclusion: Global Capitalism, Pension Funds and Vale's 'New Corporate Governance'

The attempts to organize an international Vale union network and their failure, analyzed in the previous chapter, revealed, on the one hand, the open possibilities for the establishment of organizational links among the company's workers in several countries, and on the other, the setbacks for Vale's trade unionism in Brazil, nationally fragmented and the target of labor and union relations strategies which aim at controlling production and bringing unions and the company closer as a way to circumvent labor conflicts and guarantee flexibility to the company's operations. Due to the lack of national unity among Vale's Brazilian unions, the embryo of an international union network was sunk.

There is, however, an additional element to understand the relationship between the company and its unions, emphasized by Guilherme Zagallo when defining Vale as a '*sui generis* company,' due to the important participation of state-owned companies' pension funds in its capital stock. During Lula's and Dilma Rousseff's administrations, funds such as Previ – whose leaders are, in equal parts, appointed by the management of the Brazilian federal bank *Banco do Brasil* and elected by the bank workers' unions, mostly CUT affiliates – had strong ties with the PT-led federal government. Artur Henrique, former CUT president, described such closeness when talking about Vale:

> The case of Vale do Rio Doce, for example, is emblematic because Vale was a state-owned company and was then privatized. When it was privatized, it became commanded by the private sector, by private interests, but with a strong influence from the government, either because the pension funds had a strong influence on the company's shares at the stock exchange, or because part of the people appointed to the upper echelons of these companies were also appointed due to their influence on the government, be it the Lula or Dilma administrations or the pension funds themselves.
>
> ARTUR HENRIQUE, Aguiar Interview

The reduced solidarity of Brazilian trade unionism with the strike in Vale Canada and the obstacles created by the company to the development of the international union network can be seen, then, as an illustration of part of the union movement's contradictions, split between the defense of Vale's profitability – whose management was close to the government supported by CUT and on whose results the pension funds depend – and the struggle against workers' exploitation and in defense of solidarity typical of trade unionism.

It will be necessary, therefore, to analyze the relationship between Vale, in its period of intense internationalization in the first decades of the twenty-first century, and the Brazilian government, shedding light on aspects of the company's financial strategy, which, throughout its history, besides being financed externally, could count on important internal sources of financing, such as BNDES. The post-privatization shareholders' agreement in 1997 is central to the understanding of Vale's 'corporate governance,' in which pension funds and their shareholders, such as Bradesco and Mitsui, had a preponderant role. This discussion will be held as a way to frame the aspects of continuity and change in the new shareholders' agreement established in 2017, which, as will be seen, made the dispersion of Vale's capital stock possible.

In this chapter, as a manner of conclusion, I also intend to analyze the recent changes in Vale's 'corporate governance' aimed at consolidating its transformation into a transnational corporation. I hope to evaluate how internal financing and pension funds have contributed to the company's internationalization and, at the same time, have been linked to the dynamics of the Brazilian economy's integration inglobal capitalism, creating the conditions for Vale to become a company less limited to its Brazilian borders from the point of view of value capture, shareholder control and management, even though most of its revenues continue to be obtained from the export of iron ore mined in Brazil. Vale's transnationalization has affected not only its workers and unions, but also the multiple agents involved in its global production network. Therefore, these final remarks will promote an assessment of this process's consequences in the light of what was exposed in the previous chapters.

1   The Pension Funds and the Control of Vale after Privatization

In Chapter 1, through the statements of Sérgio Rosa, former president of Vale's Board of Directors, I described the process of the 'unwinding of shares' and the elaboration of the company's post-privatization corporate strategy, which enabled a leap in its internationalization. When the sale of Benjamin Steinbruch's stake in Vale was consummated, the pension funds of state-owned companies began having a majority share in Valepar, the holding company created in 1997, after privatization, to exercise control over CVRD.

The privatization of Vale established a dual ownership structure, in which common stock (with voting rights) and preferred stock (with priority in dividend distribution) were combined. Such "dual corporate ownership structures are a widespread component of Latin American capital markets"[1] and are intended to protect minority shareholders by offsetting the benefits of controlling shareholders, who possess voting rights. After privatization, foreign investors held the majority of preferred stock in Vale, while domestic capital held the majority of common stock, and thus controlled the company's Board of Directors and Executive Board. This dual structure was related to the growing search for external sources of capital in Vale's financial strategy, although under the leadership of domestic capital:

> In this sense, the dual shareholder structure of Vale has allowed, since privatization, for the operationalization of a financing strategy structurally supported on attracting external capital, even if led by domestic capital and strongly supported by the state. Considering the capital-intensive nature of mining, the oligopolization of the iron ore segment and the centralization of its consumer market, obtaining external resources to the corporation in increasing volume has assumed a central role in Vale's corporate strategy.[2]

The post-privatization shareholders' agreement was signed in 1997,[3] valid for twenty years, and provided that the parties could not sell, assign or transfer the ordinary shares involved in the agreement through which Valepar was created. In February 2017, as will be seen, the new shareholders' agreement was announced, by which Valepar was dissolved in Vale's capital. A device for converting preferred stock into common stock was then established, in order to change the dual ownership structure hitherto in place.

Figures 3 and 4 illustrate how Valepar, despite not having a majority of the company's total capital, exercised control over Vale by holding a majority of the company's common stock. In January 2017, one month before the

---

1 Rodrigo S. P. Santos, "A nova governança corporativa da Vale S.A.: um percurso político em direção à 'true corporation'," *Versos – Textos para Discussão PoEMAS* 1, no. 4 (2017): 3.

2 Ibid, 4.

3 This is "a specific type of contractually based institution internal to the firm ..., [which] defines and regulates the relations between its owners, as well as regulates the conditions under which the property rights of these agents are exercised," according to Rodrigo S. P. Santos, "A construção social de uma corporação transnacional: notas sobre a 'nova privatização' da Vale S.A," *Revista de Estudos e Pesquisas sobre as Américas* 13, no. 2 (2019): 242–3.

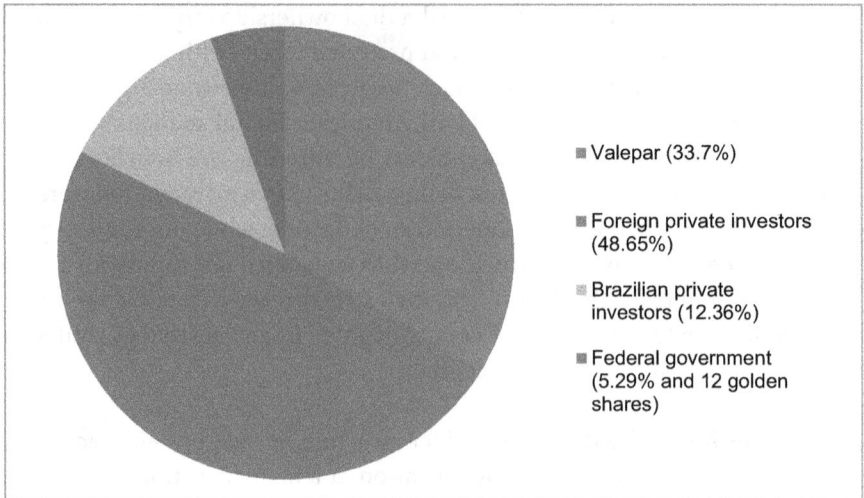

Valepar (33.7%)

Foreign private investors (48.65%)

Brazilian private investors (12.36%)

Federal government (5.29% and 12 golden shares)

FIGURE 3   Vale's shareholding composition (January 2017)
SOURCE: VALE S.A., *COMPOSIÇÃO ACIONÁRIA* (JANUARY 31, 2017); AVAILABLE
IN HTTP://WWW.VALE.COM/PT/INVESTORS/COMPANY/DOCUMENTS/ASS
ETS/201702_COMPOSI%C3%A7%C3%A3O_ACION%C3%A1RIA_JAN-17.PDF;
ACCESSED MAY 26, 2021

announcement of the new shareholders' agreement, as shown in Figure 3 (considering both common and preferred stock), 33.7% of Vale's total capital belonged to Valepar; 48.65% to foreign private investors; 12.36% to Brazilian private investors; and 5.29% to the federal government, which also holds 12 golden shares, by which the government has veto powers on changes in the company's name, headquarters location, and corporate purpose.[4]

Also in January 2017, as Figure 4 shows, Valepar, the controlling holding company, owned 53.88% of Vale's common stock; foreign investors owned 33.16%; Brazilian investors owned 6.48%; and the federal government also owned 6.48%.

Valepar's control, in turn, as shown in Figure 5, was divided between *Litel Participações S.A.*, with 49% of the shares; Bradespar S.A. (Bradesco's equity fund), with 21.21%; the Japanese group Mitsui, with 18.24%; BNDESPar (BNDES' equity fund), with 11.51%; and Eletron S.A., with 0.03%.[5] *Litel Participações S.A.*, therefore, held the largest share of Valepar, which in turn controlled Vale.

---

4   Vale S.A., *Formulário 20-F. Relatório Anual 2016*, 113; Available in http://www.vale.com/PT /investors/information-market/annual-reports/20f/20FDocs/Vale_20-F_FY2016_-_p.pdf; accessed May 26, 2021.
5   Vale S.A., *Formulário 20-F. Relatório Anual 2016*, 113.

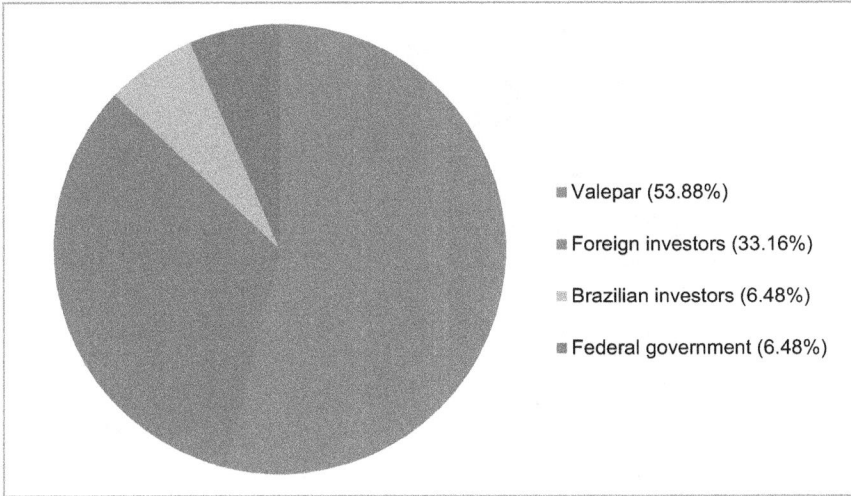

FIGURE 4   Distribution of Vale's common stock (January 2017)
SOURCE: VALE S.A., *COMPOSIÇÃO ACIONÁRIA* (JANUARY 31, 2017); AVAILABLE
IN HTTP://WWW.VALE.COM/PT/INVESTORS/COMPANY/DOCUMENTS/ASS
ETS/201702_COMPOSI%C3%A7%C3%A3O_ACION%C3%A1RIA_JAN-17.PDF;
ACCESSED MAY 26, 2021

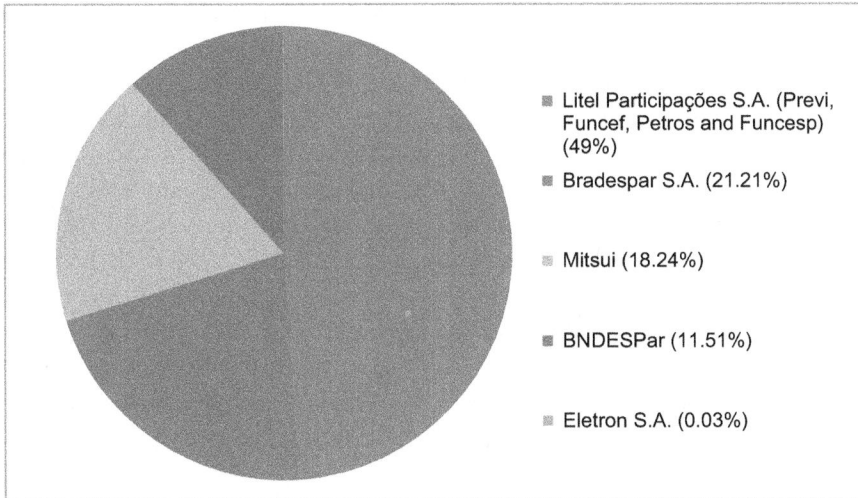

FIGURE 5   Distribution of Valepar's common stock (2016)
SOURCE: VALE S.A., *FORMULÁRIO 20-F. RELATÓRIO ANUAL 2016*

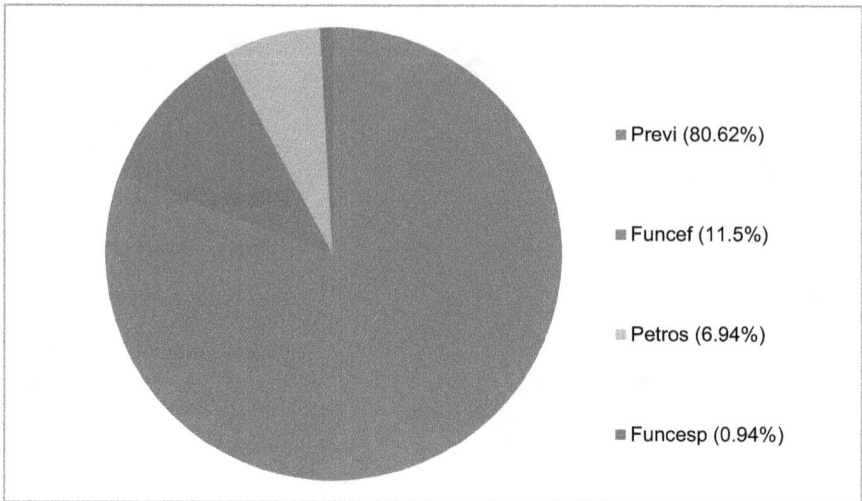

Pie chart legend:
- Previ (80.62%)
- Funcef (11.5%)
- Petros (6.94%)
- Funcesp (0.94%)

FIGURE 6   Litel shareholders (2017)
SOURCE: VALE S.A., *FORMULÁRIO 20-F. RELATÓRIO ANUAL 2017*

Also in 2017, as shown in Figure 6, Litel's control was divided among four pension funds: 80.62% owned by Previ, the fund for *Banco do Brasil* employees; 6.94% by Petros, for Petrobras employees; 11.5% by the *Fundação dos Economiários Federais* [Federal Economy Workers Foundation], or Funcef, for the employees of the *Caixa Econômica Federal* [Federal Savings Bank], a state-owned financial company; and 0.94% by the *Fundação de Empresas Elétricas de São Paulo* [São Paulo Electric Companies Foundation], or Funcesp, a fund originating from the *Companhia Energética de São Paulo* [São Paulo Energy Company], or CESP, along with other São Paulo electric companies.[6]

These data illustrate the important participation of pension funds, and of Previ in particular, in Vale's control and in the decisions taken in its Board of Directors after privatization. Vale shares are Previ's main investment, and therefore the profitability of the mining company remunerates the fund's investments and its benefit portfolios. In its organizational structure,[7] Previ's Deliberative Body, its highest body, is composed of six members – three of whom are appointed by *Banco do Brasil* and three elected by employees – with

6   Vale S.A., *Formulário 20-F. Relatório Anual 2017*, 115; Available in http://www.vale.com/PT
    /investors/information-market/annual-reports/20f/20FDocs/Vale_20F_2017_p.pdf; accessed
    May 26, 2021.
7   Available   in: https://www.previ.com.br/portal-previ/a-previ/estrutura-organizacional/;
    accessed May 26, 2021.

their respective alternates. Its audit committee is composed of four incumbent members – two appointed by *Banco do Brasil* and two elected by employees – with their respective alternates. Previ's Executive Board is composed of six members, appointed by the fund's Deliberative Body. The bank workers' unions from CUT's National Confederation of Financial Workers (Contraf-CUT[8]) have an important presence in Previ's Executive Board, committees and bodies.[9]

According to Roberto Grün,[10] in the 1990s, during the Collor and Fernando Henrique Cardoso administrations, the pension funds of state-owned companies were targeted in a process of delegitimization by government and market agents, who saw "arms of the corporatist scheme" in the funds. A dispute for the control of these entities began, involving their administrators – who came from the management of the state-owned companies which sponsored the funds -, bankers, especially from investment banks, and union members, who offered to represent participants who were workers. In the privatization process of state-owned companies, moreover, the funds

> were placed in the center ... , as 'capitalist partners' of the groups formed for the auctions, a situation which highlighted, on the one hand, their role in making viable the financial schemes necessary to give solvency to the bids and, on the other, their very limited power of intervention in the conduct of the companies of which they became co-owners.[11]

In this process, the pension fund leaders were driven by the idea that these entities should not be guided by the short term in their investments but should seek "a broader horizon – the long term related to the payment of pensions."[12] This would explain the twenty-year duration of the shareholders' agreement signed at Vale's privatization in 1997. Grün then proposes a hypothesis: with a PT electoral victory in 2002, pension funds would be "closer to the constellation of union political representation."[13]

In a dispute to extend their representation to the funds' participants, the unions sought greater participation in the decision-making bodies of the

---

8   Contraf-CUT brings together, mainly, bank workers unions from all over Brazil.
9   The slate supported by Contraf-CUT won the last members' representatives election at Previ, held in July 2020. Information available in https://contrafcut.com.br/noticias /chapa-1-obtem-quase-60-dos-votos-e-vence-eleicao-da-previ/; accessed May 26, 2021.
10   Roberto Grün, "Fundos de pensão no Brasil do final do século XX: guerra cultural, modelos de capitalismo e os destinos das classes médias," *Mana* 9, no. 2 (2003): 7–38.
11   Ibid, 9.
12   Ibid, 11.
13   Ibid, 26.

entities. During the Fernando Henrique Cardoso administration, PT leaders from the bank workers' union movement, such as Ricardo Berzoini and Luís Gushiken, played an important role in the discussions about the development of private pension funds in Brazil.[14] Sérgio Rosa had been close to both since the 1980s, when, then a Trotskyist militant, he joined *Banco do Brasil* and in 1985 was elected a director of the São Paulo Bank Workers' Union. Rosa was president of the National Confederation of Bank Workers, the precursor of Contraf-CUT; he was, for a short period, a city councillor in São Paulo (1995–1996) and was, in 2000, elected Equity Director at Previ. Considered "an exemplary case" of the "conversion of union leaders into financial managers,"[15] Rosa described the change in Previ's charter which allowed the election of participant representatives in the entity and his entry into the pension fund's leadership:

> Previ had a change in its charter in 1997, which democratized, in our view, Previ's management. So, a part of the board of directors is elected by the employees, and a part of Previ's Deliberative Body is also elected directly by the members. ... Six director seats were created: three were elected by the employees; three were appointed by the bank. In 2000 there was an election and I was elected Previ's Equity Director ..., which supervised the companies in which Previ had a more significant participation. ... The main motivation, which took place in 1997, was a very focused motivation ... Obviously people have political motivations, etc., but the main motivation was to defend the rights of Previ's members in that which is most fundamental, which were the plan's rules, the correct management of resources, so that there were no deviations. There was a very large volume of accusations regarding the use of Previ's resources. ... In 1997, then, they created a charter in which we could participate directly in the board of directors. ... These three seats gave the members the possibility to finally supervise, follow up, and feel more secure about managing PREVI's resources.
>
> SÉRGIO ROSA, Aguiar Interview

After Lula's election, Sérgio Rosa participated in the transition cabinet and was appointed to occupy the position of Previ's CEO in 2003 by his former

---

14   Ibid.
15   Alvaro Bianchi and Ruy Braga, "A financeirização da burocracia sindical no Brasil", *Correio da Cidadania* May 11, 2011; Available in http://www.correiocidadania.com.br/index .php?option=com_content&view=article&id=5816:submanchete120511&catid=25:polit ica&Itemid=47; accessed May 26, 2021.

colleagues Ricardo Berzoini, Luís Gushiken and Antônio Palocci, who had become Minister of Finance.[16]

One can point to the participation of the CUT union movement in Previ's leadership, as well as in those of other state-owned companies' pension funds, during the PT administrations as a "bridge which makes an organic alliance between sectors of the union bureaucracy and financial capital viable."[17] Seen this way, the 'financialization of the union bureaucracy' would be the corollary of the '*trasformismo*' process of the PT's union and party bureaucracy – based on the progressive increase of positions occupied by the PT in the state apparatus, with its parliamentarians, administrators and advisors – which found no hurdles within the party, given the pragmatism and theoretical uncertainty which have historically defined its leaders' practice.[18]

PT then assumed the 'passive revolution' as its program, "a gradual updating of the economic structure of capitalism through successive transitions commanded by the state, avoiding the active intervention of subordinate classes in the process."[19] In order to do so, "Brazilian trade unionism rose to the condition of a strategic actor regarding capitalist investment in the country"[20] and the PT-led federal government expanded and strengthened the financial market, instrumentalizing pension and salary funds. The financialization of salary and pension funds was also accompanied by the old class collaboration appeal for workers to defend the interest of their companies.

Such political orientation led to a symbiosis between the interests of pension fund administrators, coming from the union bureaucracy, and those of globalized financial capital, both searching for increased profits and valorization of the companies of which they were common partners. Certainly, this was Vale's case, since the federal government, through Banco do Brasil's management, appointed part of Previ's board members and leaders, while the CUT bank workers' trade unions supplied the directors representing employees. Therefore, a confluence of interests based on the promotion of Vale's investments and profits, as well as those of its national and foreign shareholders, was installed, leaving the interests of the company's workers and those of other actors affected by its activities on the back burner.

---

16   Consuelo Dieguez, "Sérgio Rosa e o mundo dos fundos," *Piauí*, no. 35, August 2009.

17   Alvaro Bianchi and Ruy Braga, "The Lula Government and Financial Globalization," *Social Forces* 83, no. 4 (June 2005): 1761.

18   Ibid.

19   Ibid, 1753.

20   Bianchi and Braga, "A financeirização da burocracia sindical no Brasil."

It is no coincidence that the orientation of the CUT bank workers' trade unions to occupy command positions in the pension funds was the target of criticism. Sérgio Rosa, when questioned about this, showed discomfort and justified this decision precisely because of the improvements in financial management achieved by Previ:

Thiago Aguiar:	*Were there any controversies within the bank workers' union movement about this orientation to participate in the funds' management?*
Sérgio Rosa:	There always is [laughs]. Absolutely nothing's ever not controversial [laughs].

I ask because, both in the literature and in the union movement, there are criticisms that claim that this choice somehow may have disarmed the union movement and generated some complicity of interest. How do you assess such criticism?

Well, that wasn't the focus of the interview. ... Like I said, everything's controversial. If you make an agreement, some people think that you shouldn't have made an agreement, you should have gone on strike. If you go on strike, some think that it shouldn't have ended on the seventh day. If you go all the way to the 20th, some people think that it shouldn't have ended on the 20th day, and that, more than the strike, you should overthrow the bankers and take over their banks. Well, that's one vision, isn't it? Previ, to this day, is the best example of a pension fund. It's the most successful from the financial management point of view. It has the best standard of benefits among all pension funds. Even though it's difficult to be too bold in the management of a fund dealing with third-party money and such, it has strict legislation regarding this. [Previ] was the one that innovated the most in terms of 'corporate governance,' of bringing the sustainable investment agenda to Brazil – it participated in the UN's international program called [Principles for Responsible Investment] PRI, the program for responsible investors. So Previ brought a management which had the participation of workers inside it, a lot of things that the system didn't have, a lot of guarantees that we managed to improve a lot for Previ's workers, a standard of results, of benefits ... So, our function, which is to protect the workers' interests, I think was much better performed with this function than just being outside, where you see only a few things, you can't know what's going on. See, you participate in the management of a company like Vale do Rio Doce! There are a lot of things that I participated in and supervised because I was there watching. And that, even though I was there, I couldn't tell others. You can't leave a Vale Board meeting and tell everyone: look, people want to do this, they want to do that. But you can intervene inside, if you're at the right time and in the right place. So, I think this decision was extremely important to protect the interests of Previ's members, and to improve governance standards. ... Up to 1998, Previ was frequently involved in scandals. At that time, it had two directors appointed by the bank's management. They had a lot of influence, it's said, at the time of José Serra, Ricardo Sérgio and other personages. And, in fact, afterwards, over time, we identified a lot of operations that Previ did that were very damaging to the fund ... Stakes in funds which were bad for Previ, acquisition of assets at low prices ... In short, this improved a lot after our participation in the fund started.

Aguiar Interview

Roberto Grün, moreover, stated that since the 1990s pension fund leaders "made a point of positioning themselves as financial market leaders, as capable as any of their counterparts from private banks."[21] In seeking legitimacy in the success of Previ's financial management and, as seen in Chapter 1, in the enormous growth of Vale's market value, Sérgio Rosa showed that the union leaders who took over the management of the pension funds did not differ from their predecessors in this respect.

In Chapter 3, the description of the strike in Canada and the failure of the attempts to build an international Vale union network revealed criticism of the company's, and especially Previ's, imperviousness in the negotiations. The

---

21   Grün, "Fundos de pensão no Brasil do final do século xx," 17.

obstacles created by Vale to the network's functioning – such as the pressures on union members who participated in it and the absence, in its organization, of unions close to the company, like Metabase Carajás – were pointed out by union members as a protection to the pension fund investments and to the company's good performance, whose managers used to display their proximity to the government. For Artur Henrique, the company's influence over the unions to make the international union network unviable was a possibility:

> I wouldn't say that it was visible, but Vale's influence in certain unions and in their forms of action was very big. ... I think it may have happened. I'm not going to assert it because I can't prove it, but it may have happened.
> ARTUR HENRIQUE, Aguiar Interview

The former CUT president also identified the estrangement between the pension funds' managers and the union movement's agenda: for Artur Henrique, pension funds' board members and directors, mainly appointed by the bank workers' trade unions, entered a roundabout that made them distance themselves from the entities to which they owed their positions:

> Not just because of Vale, but once I went to Rio de Janeiro for a meeting with the pension funds and it was a dinner, so it was out of the formal environment. And, at the dinner, there were representatives from several funds: Previ, Petros, Funcef. And I said: look, we're in a stage in which we need to make a leap, take a step. So, we need to create the conditions to make global framework agreements. We need to have social counterparts for BNDES investments. You can't take money from BNDES and go on financing companies that are just getting richer and richer, more millionaire, more profitable, only for them to find, in Brazil or abroad, a way to double or triple their profits with the dismissal of workers, with I don't know what else ... So, we went on ... There was a part of the people there, which were actually people linked to the financial sector, but not just that ... , some appointed by the financial sector, for the experience they had in the companies themselves, to be representatives of the pension funds in the companies' boards. And what we wanted to discuss was that, precisely on the board, where the strategic issues of the companies are discussed, is where we should have some room. Since I didn't have any room as CUT president, and I don't even think I should have – I even could, but why would they give me room as CUT president? But a guy who is a board member, appointed by a pension fund, who owns 10, 12, 15, 20, 22% of the company's shares ... Wait a minute! And some of these

board members said: 'No, look, Mr. Artur, if you need it, we can set up a meeting with Roger Agnelli.' I said: I'm sorry, but you don't understand what I came here to do. I don't need you to call Roger Agnelli. If Roger Agnelli won't answer the president of CUT – which is the fifth biggest union center in the world – and I need to ask you to articulate a meeting with Roger Agnelli, we are ... in trouble, we're fucked! Then, the guy got scared, looked at my face: 'But what do you mean by that?' I mean you're a board member! I mean that we have to discuss a strategy, and you're only there because you were appointed by someone from CUT! If you haven't realized that yet ... You're not there because of your beautiful blue eyes! You're there because you had a bank workers' union that was behind you when you went there. Because when the bank workers' union says you're not going anymore, you're not going anymore! Then they ... I think that was when it sunk in. I don't even criticize it, but I think it gets into a roundabout, into something so natural like: 'I was appointed! I have thirty years of experience.' Of course you do! Now, son, I'm sorry, but you're only there, first, because we're in government; second, because the company is bought with so many percent of shares; and, third, because the pension fund is financed by a union behind it! So, then it started to sink in.

ARTUR HENRIQUE, Aguiar Interview

The fund leaders, whose behavior was questioned by Artur Henrique, were not simply 'appointed' by the unions, but were in fact leaders and former leaders of union entities who maintained close ties with the top level of the federal government, which was ultimately the guarantor of these appointments. Sérgio Rosa, for example, in direct articulation with then Ministers Antônio Palocci and José Dirceu, had a fundamental role in changing the 'corporate governance' of the telecommunications company Brasil Telecom: a confrontation with the interests of banker Daniel Dantas which led the government and Previ to approach Citibank, whose international CEO was directly involved in conversations with the Ministers on the subject.[22]

The proximity between pension funds of state-owned companies and PT administrations can also be illustrated in a 2003 speech by former president Lula,[23] in which he emphatically defended that the funds should seek the highest possible financial return. On this same occasion, Lula said he had reviewed his position from the 1990s against pension fund participation in the

---

22   According to Dieguez, "Sérgio Rosa e o mundo dos fundos."
23   Reproduced by Bianchi and Braga, "The Lula Government and Financial Globalization," 1760–1.

privatization of state-owned companies, since these companies reportedly had experienced good results and had been successful with fund participation. Vale, as is well known, is the largest of the privatized state-owned companies with the participation of pension funds.

2   The Relationship with the Federal Government and the Role of BNDES in the Company's Financial Strategy

The debate about the relationship between pension fund leaders and PT-led governments is not new. By taking it up again, I intend to establish the links between this bond and Vale's labor and union relations strategies. The isolation of the company's unions and the problems of national and international coordination contribute to the existence of a regime of 'manipulated consensus.'[24] Field observations and interviews conducted in São Luís (in Maranhão) and Parauapebas (in Pará) identified the company's ability to prevent the emergence of contestation to corporate power.

As the strike in Canada and the failure of attempts to organize an international union network showed, the presence of state-owned pension funds – whose managers were former union leaders close to the government – in Vale's control contributed to the disarticulation of the company's unions and the weakening of collective power, as the union movement had little incentive to confront the company.[25] Another reason for the weakness of collective power, as analyzed in Chapter 2, was the incorporation of union leaders into Vale's Board of Directors, which reinforced the proximity of the unions with the company's management and contributed to the distancing between the entities and rank and file workers.

These characteristics are close to Ruy Braga's description of the 'Lulist mode of regulation,'[26] especially in its aspect concerning the active consent of the union movement's leadership. The changes occurred in the country after the crisis of the 'development model' promoted by the PT administrations,

---

24   As discussed in Chapter 2, based on research findings at Vale's operations in Itabira (in Minas Gerais) from Rodrigo S. P. Santos and Bruno Milanez, "Corporate Power and Economic Action: Considerations Based on Iron Ore Mining," in *'Civilizing' Resource Investments and Extractivism: Societal Negotiations and the Role of Law*, ed. Wolfram Laube and Aline R.B. Pereira (Zurich: LIT VERLAG, 2020), 255–277.

25   Especially CUT, of which most of Vale's unions are affiliates, including Metabase Carajás, whose leader adopts openly pro-employer positions, as presented in Chapter 2.

26   Ruy Braga, *The Politics of the Precariat: from Populism to Lulista Hegemony* (Leiden: Brill, 2018).

however, it did not seem to have changed the union movement's mood towards the company. Before dealing with the changes in Vale's corporate strategy after the 'commodities supercycle,' it is useful to deal with another aspect of the previous period, which is also related to the discussion about the role of the 'financialized union bureaucracy' at Vale. It is the confluence of the federal government and the company's interests in its internationalization process, and the importance of domestic capital, especially from the BNDES, in the financing of its investments, as in the S11D project, which greatly expanded Vale's iron ore extraction capacity.

Vale's interests in its internationalization process were close to those of the PT-led federal government's foreign policy. This proximity can be illustrated by two cases in which former president Lula personally engaged in the defense of Vale's interests in Africa.

In Mozambique, Lula introduced Roger Agnelli to the country's government on an official visit. Claiming to be an example of the 'South-South' orientation of his foreign policy, he reportedly advised the Mozambicans to grant an operating license for the Moatize coal mines to Vale instead of to the Chinese mining companies, which, he argued, would take their own workforce and not create jobs in the African country.[27] Contrary to his own statements when he presented Vale to the Mozambicans, years later, in 2012, already as a former president, Lula returned to the country accompanied by Murilo Ferreira, then CEO of Vale. Both met with the Mozambican Minister of Labor, Helena Taipo, "in lobbying ... to reduce the restrictions on foreign workers in Vale's Mozambique operations."[28] The mining company sought authorization to subcontract construction companies which would use Filipino labor, but was unsuccessful.

Sérgio Rosa, when asked about the eventual participation of the federal government in the Mozambique investments, answered ambiguously and stated that the business was aligned to the internationalization strategy formulated in 2000 after the 'unwinding' of shares with CSN.

> Look, here's what I think ... I can't say in detail how much. I confess, no bull, it's not ... Maybe, if I did know, I wouldn't say to you. Indeed, I don't

---

27   Judith Marshall, "Behind the Image of South-South Solidarity at Brazil's Vale," in *BRICS: an Anti-Capitalist Critique*, ed. Patrick Bond and Ana Garcia (Chicago: Haymarket Books, 2015), 165–6. For an analysis of Chinese mining companies' operations in Africa, see Ching Kwan Lee, "The Spectre of Global China," *New Left Review*, no. 89 (September–October 2014): 29–65.

28   Marshall, "Behind the Image of South-South Solidarity," 165.

know. I do know that, for example, evidently Lula is a person who, in my view, intelligently looked at Africa and made several diplomatic and commercial inroads into Africa, as all the other countries do. As all other countries do. China was present in Africa all the time. China saw Africa as an opportunity to expand, to grow, to take jobs, to take companies, anyway. Lula saw it too and went there. And he took business missions. Roger went there once or twice. ... It's all documented. As did Odebrecht people, as did OAS people ... He took people from Brazil on business missions. I mean, which country doesn't do it? So, first, to say that this is a ... Yes and no. Yes and no. It's a tradition, more or less, you can do it more or less. Certainly, Lula did it, and I think he did it properly. If there was a ... As far as I know, Roger, like Bradesco itself, although he never wanted to go against the government – no businessman wants to be frontally against the government, even more so against a government that had very popular characteristics – but he also doesn't do what the government wants just because the government asked him to. In my view, the Mozambique asset fitted very well with the investment strategy that Vale had outlined in 2000, that is, before Lula's administration. This growth strategy, with these parameters, had been given even before the Lula administration. It was executed during the Lula administration, let's say, but largely elaborated before. ... An asset that Vale knew how to develop very well. That's all it did here: develop mines, railroads and ports. Vale knew how to do that and there were these features over there. ... And of low political risk at the time.

SÉRGIO ROSA, Aguiar Interview

The lawyer Guilherme Zagallo, in turn, said that the proximity to the Brazilian government was used by Vale as a way to facilitate the opening of operations in Africa. Zagallo mentioned the hardships the company faced in Guinea:

Vale had a moment of very great expansion – today it's experiencing a moment of contraction, it has already sold assets in Peru, in fertilizers, in coal in Colombia, that has paralyzed, and it's trying to sell a potash asset in Argentina. At its peak, it was present in forty countries. Today it's present in a little more than half of them. So, it's experiencing a moment of contraction. Even with its initiative in Africa, in Mozambique, it has already sought partners, it no longer has the exclusivity of the process. Some of its initiatives in Africa didn't work out, with losses for the company as well. It advanced $500 million for an iron ore mine, a world-class mine in West Africa, two countries, Liberia and Guinea, a circumstance where the mine was one place and the port in another country, a railroad, but also corruption allegations. Apparently the corruption problems were with the previous owner, the way he had received the extraction rights. It was apparently able to absolve itself of further responsibility for that. But it took a big loss: it had advanced $500 million for this acquisition attempt, lost. Anyway, during this process, there was, yes, a very close relationship with the federal government, in this process of Vale's growth.

GUILHERME ZAGALLO, Aguiar Interview

Vale's entry into Guinea was through a partnership with Benjamin Steinmetz Group Resources (BSGR), owned by Israeli investor Benjamin Steinmetz, who obtained permission from the local government to extract iron ore in Simandou in 2008 for US$160 million.[29] Only a year and a half later, Steinmetz transferred his rights to Vale for US$2.5 billion, with the creation of the joint venture Vale BSGR Guinea (VBG). The feasibility of the operation depended on Vale building a railroad which would pass through neighboring Liberia. With the rise of a new government in Guinea, an investigation accused Steinmetz of obtaining the exploration rights by bribing the widow of former president Lansana Conté. The dispute over the Simandou mines involved major mining TNCs such as Vale and Rio Tinto. The conflict between Benjamin Steinmetz, Vale and the Guinean government led to arbitration and court disputes in several countries. The London Court of International Arbitration ordered Steinmetz to reimburse Vale $2.2 billion in 2019.[30]

Sergio Rosa said that the company withdrew from the partnership when the charges in Guinea against Steinmetz were formalized:

> There was a controversial case there in Simandou, a very controversial project. ... There was an international investigation about the hypothesis that the guy [Steinmetz] who bought it ... would have, through the wife of the Guinean president, corrupted that wife to gain the right to explore it. How did the idea come up inside Vale? That's a very important asset. I mean, as a mining asset, it's an asset of similar quality to Carajás, which has a very high concentration and volume of iron ore and the right to explore this mine all belonged to Rio Tinto. For a long time, it was all Rio Tinto. Suddenly, the government there in Guinea decided to withdraw

---

29   Consuelo Dieguez, "The billionaire behind the Vale", *Piauí*, no. 171, December 2020.
30   Details of the dispute, which involved other players such as Hungarian investor George Soros and several national governments, can be found in Dieguez, and in André Guilherme Delgado Vieira, *O mapa da mina* (Curitiba: Kotter Editorial, 2020).

half of that mine because Rio Tinto didn't invest in it either. ... Since Rio
Tinto didn't invest, it was using it only as a strategic reserve, that is, it
bought the mining rights, sat on it, and developed nothing. The guy over
there said: this is no good for the country. So, he took half of the concession and put it on the market and this Israeli guy bought it and offered it
to Vale because he didn't have the money to develop it either. He offered
it to Vale. Again: for a small amount, given the quality and volume of
reserves there. We had concerns about this, so we hired an international
investigation agency that did legal diligence on this aspect, to protect
Vale from participating in any process ... This company conducted an
international investigation and didn't reach any conclusions. The Board
decided to approve the purchase of this stake for a value, at the time, that
I don't remember, and that was it. Afterwards, the remaining investment
ended up not even being made. ... You had two problems there: the problem of the concession origin ... and the logistical issues. You bought the
mine in Guinea, but for it to be viable, you had to build a railroad to get it
out to a port in Liberia. So there was no plan that was ever put on paper
and negotiated. There were preliminary talks evaluating the risk and the
possibility of it working. The investment was made for an amount considered, at the time, reasonable enough to be buying a right for representing
a good future opportunity.

      SÉRGIO ROSA, Aguiar Interview

There is yet another element of Vale's troubled presence in Guinea: Lula,
already a former president, and Roger Agnelli, then the company's CEO, traveled to that country in 2011 to intercede with the Guinean government and
help Vale resolve the issues it found itself involved in due to the allegations
against its partner.[31]

    Another striking aspect of Vale's proximity to the PT-led administrations is the
volume of resources obtained through BNDES to finance the company's investments. Evidently, Vale was not the only company in the period to obtain resources
from the bank to finance investments and internationalization activities.[32]

---

31   According to news published by the Lula Institute, the former president was indeed in
    Guinea that year, invited by Vale, to inaugurate the cornerstone of the railroad which
    would allow the iron ore production flow from Simandou. Information available in
    http://www.institutolula.org/lula-participa-de-abertura-de-obra-da-vale-na-guine;
    accessed May 26, 2021. A description of Lula and Roger Agnelli's activities in Guinea at
    the time can be found in Vieira, *O mapa da mina*, 166–9.

32   An aspect emphasized by André Singer, *O lulismo em crise: um quebra-cabeça do período
    Dilma (2011–2016)* (São Paulo: Companhia das Letras, 2018), when dealing with the features

In fact, during Dilma Rousseff's first administration, there was a significant increase in BNDES financing for Vale. Only in direct loan operations, from 2011 to 2014, BNDES transferred R$ 14.150 billion to Vale.[33] Except for a large contribution (of over R$3.2 billion) for the modernization of the iron ore mines in Itabira (in Minas Gerais) in December 2012, and another (of about R$800 million) for the modernization of a copper mine in the Carajás complex, most of these funds went to the Carajás Iron Project S11D – "the largest mineral startup in human history, at 90 million tonnes per year"[34] – to implement the mine (a highly mechanized one, and planned to carry out the transportation of ore only by conveyor belts, without trucks); to expand and reform the Carajás Railroad; and to reform the port of Ponta da Madeira (in São Luís) to meet the increased production in Carajás.[35]

On just one day, May 19, 2014, for example, two billion-dollar loan agreements were signed between the mining company and the bank: one of them, for over R$2.5 billion, was for the "the construction of an iron ore mining and enhancement plant, with a 90-million ton capacity per year;"[36] the other, for over R$3.6 billion, for the expansion of the Carajás Railroad. The total investment in the S11D project was US$19.67 billion,[37] including the implementation of the mine, the expansion of the Carajás Railroad and the port, making it a "project of superlative dimensions that will represent the largest volume of private investment in Brazil in this decade."[38]

To make such large loans possible, in May 2012, the Central Bank of Brazil changed its norms to allow Vale to be included in a list of companies (which

---

of the 'developmentalist test' which was reportedly carried out during the Dilma Rousseff administration.

33   Information based on data from the consultation portal of BNDES's operations; Available in http://www.bndes.gov.br/wps/portal/site/home/transparencia/consulta-operacoes -bndes/; accessed May 26, 2021. Between 2006 and 2014, "the bank approved R$ 20.9 billion in resources for projects, being the corporation's largest financing agent in the period," according to Santos, "A construção social de uma corporação transnacional", 253.

34   Rodrigo S. P. Santos, "Desenvolvimento econômico e mudança social: a Vale e a mineração na Amazônia Oriental," *Caderno CRH* 29, no. 77 (May-August 2016): 303.

35   Vale S.A., *Projeto Ferro Carajás S11D: um novo impulso ao desenvolvimento sustentável do Brasil* (August 2013).

36   Information based on data from the consultation portal of BNDES's operations; Available in: http://www.bndes.gov.br/wps/portal/site/home/transparencia/consulta-operacoes -bndes/; accessed May 26, 2021.

37   Santos, "Desenvolvimento econômico e mudança social", 304.

38   Vale S.A., *Projeto Ferro Carajás S11D*.

already included Petrobras and Eletrobrás) to which BNDES could "lend more than 25% of its reference equity."[39] Years later, in June 2015, the Central Bank overturned this ruling,[40] as a sign of the reorientation of economic policy underway in the country.

Vale inaugurated the S11D Eliezer Batista complex on December 17, 2016.[41] As Guilherme Zagallo argued, in this context, investments in S11D, the world's largest iron ore mine, became strategic for the company. The ore extracted there has higher iron content and lower production costs, repositioning the company for international competition in the commodity post-boom period:

> Vale cruised a lot. A lot of the growth was pulled by China, by China's growth, which demands a lot of iron ore. Although it's in unfavorable conditions of distance – its Australian competitors are 8 or 9 days by ship from China, and Vale is 42 days from China -, ... it had a large quantity of good quality ore that allows for blending. China is also the largest producer of iron ore in the world, but it produces very poor quality ore, with very low iron ore content. This means that the cost of producing steel with only Chinese ore is very high: you burn more coal, you have more pollution, a lot more tailings, much more steel mill and blast furnace slag. You then have to blend it in this blast furnace, in this ladle, with a better quality ore, with a little bit of scrap, to have more competitive production costs. So, China pulls this growth up and pulls iron ore prices up. And Vale leveraged its production in this growth a lot. Today, it's around 340 million tonnes. When it concluded the S11D and other projects, there were plans to reach 450 million tonnes. The S11D alone is the biggest iron ore mine that has ever been opened in the world: one of the mines is 90 million tonnes, with new technology, which demands less truck use, lower production costs. Instead of taking the ore by truck, those gigantic trucks, to the processing plant, you take the plant. You dismantle it, with conveyor belts, so you do this transportation by belts. Not the whole plant. But you do it in modules and reduce the production cost. Vale's big

---

39   João Villaverde and Thiago Resende, "Vale entra para seleto grupo de empréstimos 'especiais' do BNDES," *Valor Econômico*, May 24, 2012; Available in https://valor.globo.com /brasil/noticia/2012/05/24/vale-entra-para-seleto-grupo-de-emprestimos-especiais-do -bndes.ghtml; accessed May 26, 2021.

40   Available in http://www.bcb.gov.br/pre/normativos/busca/downloadNormativo.asp?arqu ivo=/Lists/Normativos/Attachments/48516/Res_4430_v1_O.pdf; accessed May 26, 2021.

41   In honor of CVRD's former CEO.

wager, at this time when the [price of] ore is dropping, is to conclude the
S11D because ... the lower production costs will position Vale at a higher
level of competitiveness in relation to its competitors.

GUILHERME ZAGALLO, Aguiar Interview

As already analyzed in previous chapters, Vale's transformation into a TNC is
"conditioned to the privileged access to the world's largest iron ore reserve,
the Carajás Mineral Province."[42] With this in mind, it is possible to frame the
place of the S11D in the company's current corporate strategy. With the mineral
commodity price reduction in the post-boom period and the company's high
indebtedness, the company began to carry out divestments, seeking to reduce
its indebtedness from the level of US$ 25 billion at the end of 2016[43] to US$ 10
billion at the end of 2018.[44] It then decided to focus on its core business, i.e.
the extraction of iron ore, combining this orientation with "a product strategy
based on the diversification of revenue from existing assets,"[45] extracting more
value from its operations, such as base metals in Canada.

Ahead of such reorientation of product strategy, S11D came to occupy a fundamental place, since the gain of scale with the project and the higher iron
content of the ore extracted from it allow the company better conditions to
compete. Vale has also inaugurated a 'blending strategy,' "having launched
Brazilian Blend Fines (BRBF), a mixture of sinter feed ... with 70% of powder
from Carajás (in Pará) and 30% from the Iron Quadrangle,"[46] which has also
allowed the company to deal with the exhaustion of mines in the Southeast
and South systems (in Minas Gerais).

Vale's investments in the S11D Project, financed by BNDES, were therefore
fundamental to the company's repositioning ahead of the changes in mineral
prices after the 'commodity supercycle.' Vale's financial strategy is "fundamentally related to the available debt and ownership control options"[47] and relies

---

42   Santos, "Desenvolvimento econômico e mudança social," 302.
43   Francisco Góes and Renato Rostás, "Novo CEO terá desafio de reduzir dívida de US$ 25
      bilhões," *Valor Econômico*, March 28, 2017; Available in https://valor.globo.com/empre
      sas/noticia/2017/03/28/novo-ceo-tera-desafio-de-reduzir-divida-de-us-25-bilhoes.ghtml;
      accessed May 26, 2021.
44   Vale S.A., *Formulário 20-F: relatório anual 2017*; Available in http://www.vale.com/PT
      /investors/information-market/annual-reports/20f/20FDocs/Vale_20F_2017_p.pdf;
      accessed May 26, 2021.
45   Bruno Milanez et al., "A estratégia corporativa da Vale S.A.: um modelo analítico para
      redes globais extrativas," *Versos – Textos para Discussão PoEMAS* 2, no. 2 (2018): 11.
46   Ibid.
47   Ibid, 15.

on three main sources of funding in the company's financial strategy: 1) cash flow, dependent on ore price variation and, therefore, volatile; 2) loans and other forms of fundraising; and 3) the issuance of debentures and fixed income assets.[48] In recent years, as will be seen, Vale has sought to increase its financing from private agents, especially abroad.

> Nevertheless, the effective public loans ... continue to constitute its main mechanism to obtain external resources, followed by the issuance of bonds .... In these terms, BNDES is a strategic partner in Vale's access to credit, and it is relevant to observe the impact of the changes announced in the bank's financing policies, especially the substitution of the *Taxa de Juros de Longo Prazo* [Long-Term Interest Rate], or TJLP, for the *Taxa de Longo Prazo* [Long-Term Rate], or TLP, in its relationship with the company.[49]

The importance of BNDES in financing Vale's investments and the proximity between the company's board, pension funds and the federal government can be seen as an example of the international expansion of domestic capital, a consequence of the policy of creating 'champions' during the PT administrations, mentioned in this book's Introduction. Artur Henrique and Sérgio Rosa have commented on this hypothesis:

> We had the 2008 crisis, international, but also a recovery or the proposal of major interventions, of a policy, in Brazil, that strengthened the large Brazilian companies to operate abroad. You will remember ... BNDES's role in large companies, questionable at times, in some situations, even today. But it had the role of being a protagonist, an international actor with protagonism, but financing companies and the performance of companies outside, abroad.
>
> ARTUR HENRIQUE, Aguiar Interview

> There was a whole movement that was not only in Previ. It existed in the pension fund sector, in the economic sector ... It's not that we were, let's say, fond of one economic thesis or another, because it was not our role to manage the economy or to be the Minister of Development, or anything like that, but we could see these discussions going on, that is, Brazilian

---

48   Ibid.
49   Ibid, 17.

companies with some vocation, being able to grow and, instead of being companies whose natural trajectory would be to be acquired, instead of multinationals coming here to buy, to establish themselves here, we have a trajectory of the national company being able to grow and, eventually, to go abroad as well. That is, you can increase the presence of Brazilian companies in the world market, either defending the Brazilian market or going abroad. So, that happened, discussions of this kind, at Perdigão, you had a large presence [from Previ], at Embraer, which was a company where we also had a large presence, anyway, others in which we had a smaller participation, like Weg, we were a small shareholder in Weg, but we followed their discussion about doing it. Anyway, it was a movement that we followed and saw with positive eyes. It was good for us as shareholders, especially because Previ can only invest in the Brazilian market. Today, it can even invest a little abroad, but pension funds can only invest here. So, if the Brazilian market doesn't have a certain size, companies of a certain size, you will be limited to investing ... in whatever you have, right? ... It was a way to make the market more dynamic, to solidify it, make it stronger, and it was interesting for us.

SÉRGIO ROSA, Aguiar Interview

When asked if the internationalization of domestic capital was in any way stimulated or coordinated by the federal government, Sérgio Rosa affirmed that there were internal differences in the government in this respect and that, in reality, this process came from a 'will of the market,' made possible by the expansion of the capital market in Brazil and without the participation of the federal government.

Previ was not part of any coordination of this movement. I could see it, because I was a partner in BNDES in some situations, a debate about that, but this debate in BNDES also varied from the first BNDES management in the hand of [Carlos] Lessa ... [to] Luciano Coutinho. ... On the other hand, there was a great resistance to the so-called capital markets, which was ours ... I could only intervene, I could only invest, I was only interested in things within a capital market dynamic, which is the environment where I make my investments. So, having a healthy capital market, for me, regardless of any ideological discussion – knowing if the market is good, if the market is bad -, I was elected to do this: manage the investments. So, for me, thinking about 'corporate governance,' improving the standards of governance at Bovespa, improving the levels, level 1, level 2 ... For me, all of that was super important. In Lessa's case, for instance, I know he had a lot more problems in thinking that it was healthy. Anyway, I think that this question varied a bit within the government. What I think happened was an ambition of the entrepreneurs as a whole, of the investors ... It was a time when investment funds came here when there weren't any, when the Stock Exchange became something more [important]. ... So, there was a whole favorable environment to imagine that the Brazilian capital market, both in terms of bonds as well as stocks, had an opportunity to improve and this was going to bring a good thing for investors, it was going to attract capital for investment. Companies would be able to better finance themselves. In short, there was a broad movement around this moment and the companies with the ambition to grow, at the moment they saw this possibility: new managers, new shareholders, new economic environment, new capital markets. ... This will was in the market. ... The government didn't participate in these discussions. In this aspect, the government didn't participate. I can say that clearly.

SÉRGIO ROSA, Aguiar Interview

The former CEO of Previ and former president of Vale's Board of Directors presented the same arguments when dealing with BNDES's role. For Sérgio Rosa, the bank's loans were an opportunity to develop a movement which was underway in the market. In reality, for him, the expansion of Brazilian companies was stimulated by the presence of new investment funds and the development of capital markets, which would have been more important in financing Vale than the BNDES loans. Therefore, Rosa ruled out that there was any form of coordination, in the government or at BNDES, in favor of the internationalization process of Brazilian companies at the beginning of the 21st century.

Thiago Aguiar:	*But BNDES financed a good part of these investments ...*
Sérgio Rosa:	They were financed because Vale went there with the projects, showed them and convinced those guys that it was a good idea. In this respect, the merit goes to the BNDES technical teams, who saw and believed in the projects, ... but they weren't the original source of the idea. It wasn't there. It was the company. It wasn't BNDES that got there and said: 'Look, you have an opportunity. We can help you.' It wasn't.

Was there never any kind of debate, of coordination?
Look, we may like it, either from the Right in order to make a critique, or from the Left in order to positively

appropriate what happened, but the truth is that, in my perception, this happened much more as a movement from within the companies. Take Embraer, for crying out loud! Embraer's decision to invest in this [E]190 jet family is an engineering decision, a market vision within Embraer. It's something that happens inside. The guys in there saw the opportunity and thought they had to do it, because the [E]145 family was running out, it was completely exhausted. It was a huge sales success around the world, but the [E]145 was, after all, a small jet. They saw the market opportunity, they started to invest in the engineering of it, a cycle of, I don't know, almost ten years of product design .... There was no government. The decision to invest in the [KC]390 as a cargo plane, again, an internal discussion within the company, market vision. Obviously you have interactions with the government in this period. The guy goes and visits a Ministry, talks to a guy from the Air Force. Obviously, but you got interactions. To say that you have a center ... Unfortunately, in Brazil, you don't have a Chinese tradition of having a government with centers of thought. So, we don't have it. Here, we have something much more diluted, which some might like and others might not like, but it's much more diluted.

... I think this is good. Within the economic framework that we have, ... a Brazilian company that increases its participation in the global market is better than leaving it to others. It's a dispute. I am as sympathetic to the Australian worker, the English worker, as to any other, but, after all, within a world ... I'll encourage the Brazilian company to capture part of the market abroad. So, I think it was a good move. It was a positive moment: a moment in which Vale knew how to take advantage of the global economy dynamics, the movement of shareholders here, BNDES credit when it ... Now, most of Vale's credit was not from BNDES: it was from the capital markets. Vale had a very large capacity to finance itself in the capital markets, launch debentures, bonuses, etc.

Aguiar Interview

Sérgio Rosa's position is perhaps due to his caution in not associating himself, as Previ's former CEO, with some kind of investment coordination along with the PT-led administrations at a time when the BNDES and pension fund operations were the target of press attention and ongoing investigations.[50] In any case, his statement that the process of Brazilian companies' internationalization experienced in the 2000s was not driven by some form of government coordination, but in fact was led, above all, by the strengthening of the capital markets, deserves attention.

3   Pension Funds and the Transnationalization of Vale

One can speculate if the underestimation of governmental coordination is really what Sérgio Rosa thinks or just a way to dodge an uncomfortable question. The fact is that his analysis is close to Alvaro Bianchi and Ruy Braga's,[51] who relate the economic policy of the Lula administration to the expansion of the financial market, through the approximation of the union bureaucracy to the globalized financial accumulation regime, instrumentalizing pension and salary funds.[52]

From these considerations, it is possible to resume Chico de Oliveira's analysis in "The Duckbilled Platypus"[53] regarding the convergences in the party program between the PT and the PSDB, based on the "emergence of a new [social] class",[54]

> ... based on technicians and intellectuals doubling as bankers – the core of the PSDB; and workers become pension-fund managers – the core of the PT. What they have in common is control over access to public funds, and an insider's knowledge of the lay of the financial land. ... since classes are forged in class struggle, its dynamic lies in the appropriation of major portions of public funds. This is where its specificity lies: its lien is not

---

50   As mentioned earlier, the interview with Sérgio Rosa was conducted in January 2018 in Rio de Janeiro.

51   Bianchi and Braga, "The Lula Government and Financial Globalization," 1745–62.

52   Continuing a movement that had begun during the Collor and, above all, the Fernando Henrique Cardoso administrations.

53   Francisco de Oliveira, "The Duckbilled Platypus," New Left Review, no. 24 (November/ December 2003): 40–57.

54   Ibid, 53.

on private-sector profits, but on the place where part of those profits are made: public finances.[55]

The thesis of the emergence of a 'new social class' is recovered, at this point of the exposition, for the strength of Chico de Oliveira's insight, since in my view the 'financialization of the union bureaucracy'[56] is not sufficient to classify it as a 'new class.' Here I intend, therefore, to retain the diagnosis that PSDB's 'technicians and intellectuals doubling as bankers' on the one hand, and PT's 'pension-fund managers' on the other, have bridged the gap with the financial system based on the control of access to public funds and on a common ideology – the neoliberal restructuring of the state's function – formulated in elite schools such as the Pontifical Catholic University of Rio de Janeiro (PUC-Rio) and the Getulio Vargas Foundation (FGV).

Sérgio Rosa's statements, fifteen years after Lula's inauguration and the publication of Chico de Oliveira's essay, corroborate this diagnosis. Rosa stated that the capital market, which was expanding at the beginning of the twenty-first century, directed the internationalization of Brazilian companies as a way to increase their profits. In this process, capital from BNDES and from pension funds, along with new foreign and domestic funds (in addition to individual investors), were destined to the expansion of domestic operations and the opening of activities abroad of companies originally controlled by domestic capital, in addition to financing corporate mergers and acquisitions.

Now, this process is precisely what I sought to frame, in the book's Introduction, as the transnationalization of capital typical of globalization, an epochal change in capitalism. Seen from this angle, the strict symmetry between the PT and the PSDB's leading cores, formed in elite schools with a neoliberal ideological base, pointed out by Chico de Oliveira, is very similar to what William I. Robinson named the 'transnational elite',[57] the cadres at the service of the transnational capitalist class who work in the management of companies, in the state, in agencies and supranational bodies, in academia and in the press, to ensure the necessary conditions for global accumulation. It is certain that in this process, some high-paid members of this elite may become shareholders of TNCs and eventually join the ranks of the TCC.

In any case, at this point, it is less necessary to precisely delimit the boundaries between the transnational elite and the TCC – a task to which sociology

---

55   Ibid, 55–6.
56   Bianchi and Braga, "The Lula Government and Financial Globalization."
57   William I. Robinson, *A Theory of Global Capitalism: Production, Class, and State in a Transnational World* (Baltimore: Johns Hopkins University Press, 2004).

has much to contribute – than to point out the tendential character and the movement of integration to the global economy stressed by Robinson. For Sérgio Rosa, there was a movement of the "Brazilian company" in search of "greater participation in the global market", which may perhaps be only the appearance of a broader phenomenon, identified by Previ's former CEO as "the global economy dynamics."

Robinson addressed this apparent contradiction when dealing with the BRICS,[58] seen by many analysts as kinds of 'Southern challengers to global capitalism.' However, the governments of these countries, instead of promoting an agenda contrary to globalization, sought to expand it, integrating their economies into global capitalism and fighting for more space for the new members of the transnational capitalist class coming from these places. In this way, the struggle against agricultural subsidies promoted by the Brazilian government in international forums, for example, which appeared to be a confrontation with the protectionism of countries from the Global North in benefit of their own rural producers, in reality was very beneficial for the agribusiness TNCs which are active in the development of seeds, genetic modification, pesticides and fertilizers,[59] as well as for the companies and funds which operate in the purchase of crops and in speculation in futures markets around the world. Another example of the phenomenon in question is the important participation maintained by transnational investment funds in TNCs of Chinese origin, even in those controlled by state-owned capitals.[60]

From this perspective, the different 'varieties of capitalism' would therefore be different varieties of 'integration into global capitalism.' Robinson stresses the importance, within the BRICS, of state-owned companies and investment funds, such as sovereign wealth funds, which are being deeply integrated into transnational corporate circuits, in a "merger of interests between transnational capitalists from both statist and private sectors."[61] This does not mean

---

58   William I. Robinson, "The Transnational State and the BRICS: A Global Capitalism Perspective," *Third World Quarterly* 36, no. 1 (2015): 1–21.

59   The TNC resulting from Bayer and Monsanto's merger, announced in 2016, is a clear example of the kind of agents Robinson has in mind. In recent years, moreover, TNCs of animal protein processing based in Brazil have been consolidated, such as BRF, JBS, and Marfrig – the latter two, in particular, have acquired operations abroad, especially in the United States, and now get most of their revenues outside Brazil. The transnationalization of agriculture in Brazil and the TNCs which operate in it seem to be promising cases for the study of sociology.

60   In this regard, an analysis based on the theory of global capitalism can be found in Jerry Harris, "Who Leads Global Capitalism? The Unlikely Rise of China," *Race, Class and Corporate Power* 6, no. 1 (2018). DOI: 10.25148/CRCP.6.1.007548.

61   Robinson, "The Transnational State and the BRICS," 17.

that national differences and disputes cease to exist, but reinforces the importance of analyses which transcend the limits of the nation-state.

> To be sure, global capitalism remains characterised by wide and expanding inequalities whether measured *within* countries or *among* countries in North–South terms and grossly asymmetric power relations adhere to *inter-state* relations. ... But this cannot blind us to analysis that moves beyond a nation-state/inter-state framework. ... Breaking with nation-state-centric analysis does not mean abandoning analysis of national-level processes and phenomena or inter-state dynamics. It does mean that we view transnational capitalism as the world-historic context in which these play themselves out. It is not possible to understand anything about global society without studying a concrete region and its particular circumstances; a part of a totality, in its relation to that totality.[62]

The integration of state-owned (and parastatal) funds into transnational corporate circuits, then, may be a useful way to frame the relationship of state-owned pension funds and BNDES capital (through its equity arm) with transnational funds in Vale's ownership structure. If, during the effectiveness period of the post-privatization shareholders' agreement, domestic capital exercised control over the company, with the drop in mineral commodity prices and the Brazilian economic crisis which began in 2014, pension funds, as will be seen, lost profitability, and discussions began for a new shareholders' agreement which would allow for the release of the shares which were immobilized in Valepar in search of greater liquidity.

The political changes following the parliamentary coup which ousted Dilma Rousseff in 2016 and the rise of Michel Temer's administration facilitated the redefinition of the pension funds and the BNDES's role in the company.[63] Jair Bolsonaro's administration, in turn, has consolidated this reorientation with the ongoing sale of the BNDESPar share portfolio, and the expected liquidation of the state-owned development bank's equity arm in the aftermath.[64]

For reasons such as these, for Sérgio Rosa, the participation of pension funds in the control of large companies was part of a moment in the Brazilian

---

62 Ibid.

63 Santos, "A nova governança corporativa da Vale S.A.," 8.

64 Joana Cunha, "Brazilian Government Will Keep Only Petrobras and Two Federal Banks," *Folha de S.Paulo*, January 30 2019; Available in https://www1.folha.uol.com.br/internacio nal/en/business/2019/01/brazilian-government-will-keep-only-petrobras-and-two-fede ral-banks.shtml; accessed May 26, 2021.

economy and in the capital market, which is over. The funds, according to Previ's former CEO, will decrease their participation due to the growing need to pay pensions and even due to structural characteristics of the Brazilian labor market.

Sérgio Rosa: [Pension funds] Are going to be less and less [in the companies' control]. This debate is going to get old very quickly! First, it's that this was true in a specific period of history, either of the American economy or of Brazil for a very short time. And it's not going to be that way anymore. Pension funds are going to withdraw from the companies' capital and are going to stop ... So, this debate is going to get old, it's going to become history, it's not going to be important anymore.

Thiago Aguiar: *Why?*
Because in Brazil, except for us, who saw the stock market as an important opportunity to diversify investments, at a time when the capital market welcomed it and wanted pension funds to participate, today, pension funds, private pensions as such, are not expanding. On the contrary, it's contracting – either due to controversies within the union movement itself, from sectors that haven't embraced the idea of having a complementary pension as a worker's right ... At CUT, we were already debating: why does the CUT not embrace the discussion that the workers should demand for the improvement, where there already is a complementary pension plan, or the creation of ... CUT had no ... CUT has never ...

It has never defined a position?
That's never been very clearly defined. So ... And the economy today is going against that. I mean, today, the less benefits, the better. Labor precariousness is going in the opposite direction. I mean, what we have today is the storing of pension funds, which already existed, and there will be very little new things happening, right? So, the growth movement of pension funds has already happened. We're going to live off the management of those that are already there. And those that are there, as most

of them are already mature – mature, I mean, they're already in the cycle of benefit payment rather than accumulation -, the investments will accumulate in things that are much more liquid than stakes like these, like that of Vale's, where you can spend fifteen years participating in a company betting on growth. So, I mean, I bought Vale at a proportional value of [R$] 10 billion, and I ended up with [R$] 180 [billion]. So, it was worth an investment that took me twelve, thirteen years to see growing, but where would I get a profitability like that? Oh, I might miss three more of these bids. But that's okay: I got one of those right, and I pay for the whole ... That move's not going to happen anymore. The funds no longer have that time, they'll no longer have that perception. Whether from the Right or the Left, attitudes like ours, who went inside the companies to discuss ... The people on the Left think it's nonsense; the people on the Right don't even want to know about people with this kind of mentality discussing with them. So, this was a bubble: it happened at a certain moment and it'll become a historical debate. You're going to analyze what happened and it'll hardly serve as a lesson for what's to come.

Aguiar Interview

Sérgio Rosa, thus, questioned the future viability of pension funds, taking labor precariousness into account, as well as the lack of initiative from the union movement to stimulate the adhesion to existing funds and the creation of new ones. However, his statements regarding labor and union relations at Vale, presented in Chapters 2 and 3, illustrate how the defense of the companies' profitability by pension fund managers, who came from trade unions, leads to this very precariousness,[65] which is indicated as a risk for the future of pension funds themselves.

In the end, the implicit conclusion in Rosa's argument is that the very management of TNCs like Vale, who are successful in the neoliberal globalization 'game,' eventually led by pension funds like Previ, may end up undermining the future bases for the continued existence of these funds as they existed during

---

65   In a 'game,' as Rosa often says, between capital and labor, in which the unequal conditions of the latter in the face of corporate power are ignored or seen as part of a natural 'logic' to which there is no alternative but adherence.

the brief 'bubble.' The pension funds of state-owned companies, thus, fulfilled the role of stimulating Vale's capitalization and leading its internationalization (as part of the transnationalization process) to, in the end, leave the protagonist role, delivering it, gradually, as we will see, to transnational funds.

If, for Vale's private shareholders, the result of the company's privatization and internationalization was the exponential increase of its market value, when assessing the field observations and interviews carried out, one can say that the results of this process for the workers were the intensification of labor exploitation, the dispersion of unions and the weakening of collective power. In this sense, the case in question seems to be in line with the conclusions of Alvaro Bianchi and Ruy Braga:

> The financialization of the union bureaucracy is a process which fundamentally divides the working class and weakens the defense of its historical interests. As managers of pension funds, this group's main commitment is to the liquidity and profitability of their assets. ... Brazilian pension funds have acted as a strategic line in the process of mergers and acquisitions of the country's companies and, consequently, are financing the process of economic oligopolization with effects on the intensification of work rhythms, on the weakening of workers' bargaining power, and on the downsizing of administrative sectors. ... The curious thing is that, in the current period, the workers' savings, managed by union bureaucrats from the new trade unionism, are being used to finance the increase of labor exploitation and environmental degradation. [66]

What is in question, however, is less – as Rosa seems to believe – the risk to the existence of complementary pension mechanisms and pension funds, which is much to the taste of neoliberalism, and a lot more the reproduction of a certain circumstantial, concrete form of their regulation, in which characters like Sérgio Rosa were in the foreground. The bitterness which transpires in his speech and the constant hesitations and reticences in his discourse, somehow, accompanied the recognition of the period as a 'bubble,' underlining the circumstantial, not very sustainable, aspect of the Lulist mode of regulation. Once this phase is over, managers like Rosa, who come from the union movement, may no longer be necessary and welcomed 'by the Right,' as Previ's former CEO stated, despite his intransigent defense of productivity and company profits, which has always been criticized 'by the Left.'

---

66   Bianchi and Braga, "A financeirização da burocracia sindical no Brasil."

Seen in this way, Sérgio Rosa's answers about how he experienced the contradiction between his union origins and his work as a business manager seem to portray such an exhaustion:

Thiago Aguiar: *Have you at any point experienced this conflict between your convictions and your trajectory as a union member and the fact that you saw yourself making decisions as ...*

Sérgio Rosa: [Interrupting] I live it every day. As a car user, I live that conflict. I'm against climate change, I know that cars are the main instruments of climate change and I have my car, I drive a car. I live this conflict every day. Behaviors or demands in my personal life that are not completely in line with things I care about. Obviously. I've felt that conflict. I wish I could arrive inside a company and say: people, let's ... Several ... It's not just that I would like to arrive: many times I did, but I couldn't convince them, I couldn't ... Not even at *Banco do Brasil*, a state-owned company. I used to argue: 'Gee, now we have a democratic and popular government in Brazil. Why don't we change some labor relations inside *Banco do Brasil*? Why don't we democratize the companies' management?' We brought the examples we had learned in trade unionism. ... These contradictions are very present in our lives and I'm not going to say that I've never felt them ... No, on the contrary, I felt the contradictions many times a day. Between general ideas that we have, contradictions that we have, and such, and that can't be realized, that are in conflict with the specific function that you're exercising at that moment. Now, I totally accepted, when I ran for office, that it was a mission that I had to accomplish. I couldn't get there and ... You know? It was a function that I had to perform.

What is your final assessment of this relationship between pension funds and unions on the one hand, and between pension funds and company management on the other?
I don't believe that anything in society will ever exist without conflict. There will be conflict all the time. It's the nature of society that conflict exists. I think this relationship is less explored, less discussed, less talked about,

less understood than I think it could be. I think that Previ
showed, when we made an effort towards this direction,
that it had some capacity, given a very particular condition of the Brazilian economy, in which a fund like Previ
was quite big, big enough to influence – not to determine,
but to influence, to be heard, to be in the forums and to
speak. I don't think we were going to change the logic of
money, of capital, I don't believe it, but we were going
to make small pushes for ... for ... for ... for positioning.
Push for small things as a conscious investor. We would
be able to make small efforts that way if we were more
... So, when we were chosen, for example, to participate
in the UN's international program ... 'Oh, a great UN illu-
sion, a great nonsense.' True, we're not going to mess with
capitalism. We'll say that it has to be a little more socially
responsible ... But that's good: that manages to put a little
rule there. In this regard, of type, of respect to the international union movement. I mean, you have an international movement in which you take a little bit of the
Scandinavian funds, a Norwegian fund, bring a little of
the things that they were able to develop there and bring
it here and try to bring as an element of modernization
for our reality. I think that these are moves that you manage to make.

Aguiar Interview

4   Vale's 'New Corporate Governance' after the Commodity
Boom: Reorientation of Pension Funds and Increased Presence of
Transnational Investors

With the end of the 'commodity supercycle' and the mineral price drop, Vale
began a process of change in corporate strategy, which is analyzed throughout this book. In 2015, the mining company's losses, presented in Chapter 1,
affected the value of the pension funds' stake in the company. That year, Previ
reported, with regard to Vale, that

In 2015, Previ's stake in Vale/Litel depreciated by approximately R$8 bil-
lion compared to 2014. The main factor which influenced this result was
the sharp reduction in the price of iron ore, the company's main sales

product (the prices charged by Vale were reduced by around 40.8%), combined with the volatility of demand from China, the main purchasing market, which represents 34.9% of Vale's gross operating revenue. The devaluation of the Brazilian real against the dollar is positive for the company, but did not offset these factors.

Vale has reduced its production costs and expenses and increased its operational efficiency, in addition to its strategy of capital discipline and focus on its core businesses, with a program of divestments in non-core assets to strengthen its cash flow. It is important to highlight the annual production records verified in 2015 ....

In addition to the expectation that the price of iron ore will stabilize at higher levels, the S11D project, Vale's and the world's largest mining project, is scheduled to start operations in the second half of 2016. The S11D will help the company become even more competitive, due to its low production costs, as well as transport to the port and high quality iron ore.

Another factor which impacted the company in 2015 was the Samarco accident, which occurred on November 5th in the region of Mariana (in Minas Gerais). Vale, as a partner in Samarco (50% stake), has supported initiatives to mitigate the social and environmental impacts ....[67]

Among the changes promoted by Vale in the commodity post-boom period, one can mention the focus on its core business; divestments to reduce the company's indebtedness; operational cost cutting; the gradual increase in production at Carajás and S11D – with lower costs and higher iron content compared to the mines in the Iron Quadrangle; and the search for increasing the company's market value, after problems brought on by the ore price drop and the impact, mentioned in Previ's report, of the Fundão dam's collapse, operated by Samarco (which Vale controls in a joint venture with BHP Billiton) in 2015.[68]

As the end of Valepar's 1997 shareholders' agreement approached and in a context of economic crisis and political changes in Brazil, Valepar's controllers began discussions about changing Vale's 'corporate governance' with a view

---

67 Previ, *Relatório anual 2015*; Available in https://www.previ.com.br/quemsomos/relatorio2 015/files/PREVI_RA2015_20160415c.pdf; accessed December 4, 2021.

68 As will be seen below, Vale's dam failure in Brumadinho (in Minas Gerais) in January 2019 brought even greater impacts on production, on cash generation, and on the reputation of the company's management.

towards obtaining greater liquidity from their stakes and towards the company's financial recovery after the heavy loss recorded in 2015.

> [T]he members of the controlling group have reportedly opted for a pragmatic, short-term position oriented towards the financial recovery of the corporation and of its asset position. Under pressure from the expiration of the then current shareholders' agreement and the associated "political risk on the company's value"[69] of problematic economic and financial results in recent years, as well as from changes in the governance structures of the pension funds and in BNDES's command, this position has become major. Thus, "Previ, BNDESPar and Bradespar embraced the project,"[70] leading to a quick conclusion on the 'corporate governance' model.[71]

The removal of 'political influence' over Vale became one of the main justifications of the controlling shareholders for the changes in the company's 'corporate governance,' since the new shareholders' agreement provided for the incorporation of Valepar by Vale and for the two stock categories' merger into common stock with voting rights.[72] Up to 2020, when the deadline set by the new agreement expired, part of the shares of Valepar's former partners could not be traded. After that, shares of the pension funds, Bradespar, BNDESPar and Mitsui became freely tradable. Without a defined controlling shareholder and, above all, with the relative decrease in power of the former controlling shareholders vis-à-vis minority shareholders, the federal government's influence over Vale was reduced after the new shareholders' agreement. The "change in Vale's corporate governance regime"[73] has brought it closer to that of other mining TNCs.

However, the discourse on the end of 'political influence' in Vale, celebrated by rating agencies, consulting firms and economic journalists, is misleading, since 'corporate governance' was "reordered in an essentially political way – not restricted to a purely economic dimension" – and mobilized "a set of power devices" that established forms of "financial discipline" over the company's

---

69   Graziella Valenti, "Vale will only have an 'ownerless' management in 2021," *Valor Econômico*, February 21, 2017; Available in http://www.valor.com.br/empresas/4876120/vale-so-tera-gestao-sem-dono-em-2021; accessed May 26, 2021.

70   Ibid.

71   Santos, "A nova governança corporativa da Vale S.A.," 7.

72   Ibid.

73   Santos, "A construção social de uma corporação transnacional," 231.

management and even over its owners.[74] The unification of the ownership structure expanded the decision-making power of minority shareholders, including transnational investment funds, and opened space for the dispersion of company control.

'Corporate governance' is related to the institutional arrangements which define the forms of ownership and control of publicly traded companies, as well as the limits to agents' actions and to the distribution of results.[75] Roberto Grün, in turn, treats 'corporate governance' as a 'tool' related to financial domination:

> 'corporate governance' is the main 'tool' through which various sectors of society have become accustomed to and have accepted the assumptions of the financial worldview. Of course, calling 'corporate governance' a tool is uncomfortable. It is not an instrument with a limited scope and purpose, like a receivables fund or a bank certificate of deposit. Rather, it is a generic expression which designates the relationship between companies and all those who have a direct or indirect interest in their operation and its consequences. But to call it a 'tool,' I believe, is a necessary heuristic procedure to understand the recent profound transformations of the contemporary economic and political space, produced by the increased importance of financial assumptions, which we have been witnessing both in Brazil and in the international scene.[76]

In the new 2017 shareholders' agreement, in addition to the merger of the two stock categories, a relation was established for the exchange of the shares of Valepar, the defunct holding company incorporated into the mining company, for Vale's ordinary shares "with an increase of 10% over the original value,"[77] so that the former controlling group would obtain compensation for its stake in exchange for the disposal of decision-making power. This "alleged trade-off between political control and economic reward" should be analyzed in light of the reorientation of state action, of changes in the pension funds and in the BNDES's command after the 2016 parliamentary coup, and of "internal pressures from members, related to the cumulatively negative results" of previous years.[78]

---

74   Santos, "A nova governança corporativa da Vale S.A.," 2–3.
75   Ibid, 2, note 4.
76   Roberto Grün, *Decifra-me ou te devoro: o Brasil e a dominação financeira* (São Paulo: Alameda, 2015), 58–9.
77   Santos, "A construção social de uma corporação transnacional," 247.
78   Santos, "A nova governança corporativa da Vale S.A.," 8.

The conversion of preferred stock into common stock was presented by Vale as a way to join the Brazilian stock exchange B3's *Novo Mercado* [New Market], which demands:

> higher levels of transparency of economic and financial information and, mainly, special criteria of 'corporate governance.' ... With regard to the main criteria for listing on the *Novo Mercado*, three rules concerning governance structure and shareholders' rights seem to be central: the exclusivity of capital composition by common stock, the isonomy of sales prices among controlling and minority shares (tag along), and the maintenance of a minimum of 25% of shares outstanding (free float).[79]

Vale announced that it had completed, on December 22, 2017, the procedures for joining B3's *Novo Mercado*.[80] Following that, there was a significant increase in its share prices.[81] The incorporation of Valepar by Vale and the prospect that the company's shares would be in free float after 2020 were pointed out by economic commentators as the "completion of Vale's privatization."[82]

As shown in Figure 7, in effect, after the new shareholders' agreement, there was a dispersion of the company's shares and an increase in the presence of foreign investors in Vale's shareholding composition:

The changes in Vale's shareholding composition draw attention. First, I can highlight the BNDES's withdrawal from the company's capital,[83] concluded in February 2021, and the sale of the mining company's debentures held by the development bank.[84] The participation of Valepar's former controlling partners was reduced.

Figure 7 shows that 37.56% of Vale's common stock in April 2021 was owned by shareholders who each hold more than 5% of the company's total capital

---

79   Ibid, 6.

80   Vale S.A., *Formulário 20-F: relatório anual 2017.*

81   Indeed, for illustration only, Vale's ordinary shares at B3 were trading at around R$30 on February 20, 2017, the date the new shareholders' agreement was announced. On December 31, 2018, one month before the dam rupture in Brumadinho (in Minas Gerais), the shares were trading for about R$52. Information available in https://br.tradingview .com/symbols/BMFBOVESPA-VALE3/; accessed May 26, 2021.

82   Santos, "A nova governança corporativa da Vale S.A."

83   Francisco Góes and Maria Luíza Filgueiras. "BNDES sai da Vale e embolsa R$ 11,2 bi," *Valor Econômico*, February 24, 2021, C3.

84   Ana Paula Ragazzi, Talita Moreira and Maria Luíza Filgueiras, "Venda de debêntures da Vale soma R$ 11,5 bilhões," *Valor Econômico*, April 13, 2021; Available in https://valor.globo .com/financas/noticia/2021/04/13/venda-de-debentures-da-vale-soma-r-115-bilhoes .ghtml; accessed May 26, 2021.

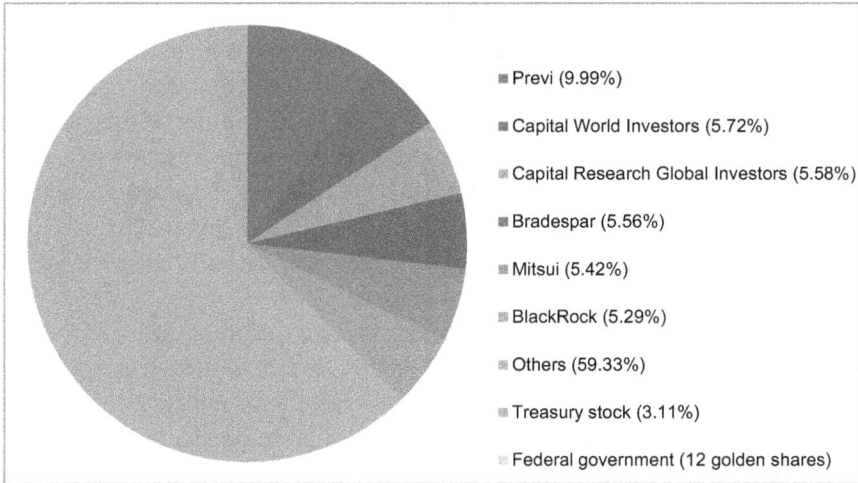

Legend:
- Previ (9.99%)
- Capital World Investors (5.72%)
- Capital Research Global Investors (5.58%)
- Bradespar (5.56%)
- Mitsui (5.42%)
- BlackRock (5.29%)
- Others (59.33%)
- Treasury stock (3.11%)
- Federal government (12 golden shares)

FIGURE 7   Vale's shareholding composition (April 2021)
SOURCE: VALE S.A., *COMPOSIÇÃO ACIONÁRIA* (APRIL 30, 2021); AVAILABLE IN
HTTP://WWW.VALE.COM/PT/INVESTORS/COMPANY/SHAREHOLDING-STRUCT
URE/DOCUMENTS/ABR_SHAREHOLDER%20STRUCTURE_P.PDF; ACCESSED
MAY 26, 2021. ACCORDING TO THIS DOCUMENT, THE DATA FOR CAPITAL
WORLD INVESTORS AND CAPITAL RESEARCH GLOBAL INVESTORS (BOTH
CAPITAL GROUP VEHICLES) ARE AS OF DECEMBER 31, 2020

stock. Another 59.33% of the stock belonged to shareholders with stakes lower than 5% of the total capital stock. Additionally, it should be noted that currently, at Vale, "65% of its capital is held by foreigners and 35% in the hands of national investors."[85]

Among the largest individual Vale shareholders (with their stakes in parentheses) are: Capital Group (17%[86]), Previ (11.36%[87]), Bradespar (5.56%), Mitsui (5.42%) and BlackRock (5.29%). Figure 7 shows, therefore, the important presence of transnational funds in controlling the mining company. After the changes introduced by the 2017 shareholders' agreement, the sale of BNDES's

---

85   Francisco Góes and Rafael Rosas, "Conselho da Vale será mais diversificado," *Valor Econômico*, May 4, 2021, B1.
86   US-based transnational fund which controls the investment divisions Capital World Investors and Capital Research Global Investors, mentioned in Figure 7. However, Góes and Rosas state that as of May 2021, Capital Group "participates in the mining company through three vehicles, holding, in total, about 17% of the company's capital stock".
87   Besides the 9.99% direct stake shown in Figure 7, Previ has another 1.37% indirect stake in Vale, totaling control of 11.36% of the company's total capital stock. According to Vale S.A., *Composição acionária*.

stake and the reduction of the Brazilian state-owned companies' pension funds' stake in Vale's capital, the largest shareholder of the mining company is Capital Group, "one of the world's largest investment management organizations, managing more than \$2.2 trillion."[88] BlackRock, in turn, is the world's largest investment manager, with \$8.7 trillion in assets under management.[89] The change in Vale's 'corporate governance' regime has thus favored institutional investors and transnational funds like the ones mentioned, which now have greater decision-making power in the company. These funds have equity stakes in Vale's competitors and in other TNCs.[90]

In addition, changes to Vale's bylaws established the presence of 20% independent members on the company's Board of Directors,[91] which expands the financial devices of corporate control and may create contradictions between a Board which is more oriented to shareholder remuneration and the Executive Board, which deals with decisions in the longer term.[92] In April 2017, Murilo Ferreira was replaced by Fábio Schvartsman as the company's CEO. The executive, who had worked at Klabin and at the Ultra group, followed the divestment process started by the previous management, led the 'corporate governance' reorganization process and the listing at B3's *Novo Mercado*, and started a policy of increasing dividend payment to shareholders.

Vale is heading, in this way, for greater denationalization and dispersion of its shareholder control, consolidating itself as a TNC. In recent years, the pension funds of state-owned companies have sought greater liquidity to pay their retirees. We can expect, then, the gradual reduction of their participation in the company.[93] Vale's new 'corporate governance' has consolidated the company's transnationalization, in progress since its 'preparation' for sale, through privatization, the leap in internationalization and the growth in market value at the beginning of the twenty-first century, as demonstrated throughout this

---

88   According to information available in https://www.capitalgroup.com/about-us.html; accessed May 26, 2021.

89   According to BlackRock data, *2020 Annual Report*, 26; Available in https://www.blackrock.com/corporate/literature/annual-report/blackrock-2020-annual-report.pdf; accessed June 4, 2021.

90   For example, in 2017, Capital Group owned 4% of Rio Tinto's shares and BlackRock owned 6.3% of that same company's common stock, as well as 10.1% of BHP Billiton's voting rights, according to data from Santos, "A nova governança corporativa da Vale S.A.", 3, notes 7 and 8.

91   Vale S.A., *Formulário 20-F: relatório anual 2017*.

92   According to Santos, "A nova governança corporativa da Vale S.A.," 13.

93   Previ, for example, since 2018, has sold R\$36 billion in equity stakes, including Vale shares, according to Juliana Schincariol, "Previ vende R\$ 36 bi em renda variável," *Valor Econômico*, May 12, 2021, C6.

book. In this process, domestic (state-owned and private) and transnational capital merged in the creation of a TNC headquartered in Brazil, but with global operations. It is necessary, therefore, to emphasize the aspects of *continuity* in the identified *changes*.

Thus, Vale "is possibly heading towards becoming a TNC with a shareholding composition similar to the mining's sector profile in general, and the iron ore's in particular."[94] The growing interest of Brazilian institutional investors and transnational funds in the company, in its financing needs and in the possibility, opened by the company's new bylaws, to increase its capital by issuing new shares, allows me to raise hypotheses about Vale's future, such as a possible breakup of the company or even the change of its headquarters.[95]

> If, in fact, corporate financialization also means the amplification of importance of the conditions of access to resources outside the corporation and, therefore, of the macro-political disciplining of capital markets, it does not seem unreasonable to raise the possibility of a future organizational dismemberment or even the change of Vale's headquarters. Thus, the corporation could directly access larger volumes and more diverse sources of capital. In the first situation, the organizational model that can serve as a guide to this possibility is related to the examples of the BHP Billiton and Rio Tinto groups, characterized by dual listing in Australia and the UK. In turn, the beacon of a potential change of headquarters could be the Anglo American group, which moved from South Africa to the United Kingdom.
>
> Certainly, changes of this magnitude would imply a radical transformation of state-market relationships at the corporate and domestic economic policy levels. However, smaller but cumulative changes have been supporting the strategic reorientation of the Brazilian state towards a profound reconfiguration of its roles in the economy ....[96]

It is possible to conclude, then, that the change in Vale's 'corporate governance' regime is related to the reconfiguration of the role played by the Brazilian state in the transnationalization of companies and in the economy ahead of the

---

94 Santos, "A nova governança corporativa da Vale S.A.," 14.

95 Vale is, for example, reportedly conducting "studies to separate its base metals operations [of which the most relevant are in Canada] with the possibility of launching shares of a new company on the Stock Exchange," according to Nicola Pamplona, "Vale volta a estudar IPO de divisão de metais básicos," *Folha de S.Paulo*, April 28, 2021, A24.

96 Santos, "A nova governança corporativa da Vale S.A.," 15.

shifting ground of global capitalism. André Teixeira and Guilherme Zagallo also analyze the effects of the dispersion of the company's shareholder control. When reflecting on the company's future, both manifested that the changes in its 'corporate governance' could mean less national linkage, from the point of view of its management and of its value capture. For Zagallo, Vale may be involved, in the future, in some merger or corporate acquisition operation.

> Vale's admission to the [B3's] *Novo Mercado* is just that. The best-managed companies are diffused. The more diffused your control is, the more professional it is. The Board of Directors, the company's management, are professionals. It's not because I'm friends with so-and-so, it's not the family, it's none of that, no: it's the professionalization of the company's management. I want results. This is how the world is! The world is moving towards being like that. Part of the valuation of Vale's stock is due to this change, that is, the state in Brazil, that interference, is no longer there. The more diffused control is, the presence of independent board members, this is part of a model that's all around the world, you know what I mean? And that's how it's going to be. ... But the existing tendency is this, in my opinion: an international dispersion of our capital ....
>
> ANDRÉ TEIXEIRA, Aguiar Interview

Thiago Aguiar:	*Do you believe that the new 'corporate governance' can allow for a takeover of Vale, in the medium or long term, by foreign capital?*
Guilherme Zagallo:	I think so, because, even though you have the limit per company – for example, there's a limit that no controlling company can have more than 25% – but I can't imagine what prevents, for example, ... the Chinese government from deciding, through different companies, to acquire 50% of Vale's share control. ... And that's possible. This design doesn't prevent this from happening in the medium or long term.
	Could mining transnationals competing with Vale have an interest in taking over its control?
	No, because of their volume, their size. I think they would need, if I'm not wrong, to go through a very high level of leverage, of financing, to be able to achieve it. I don't think it's probable at first. I think

it's more likely that it'll come from Chinese companies, in a geopolitical move by the Chinese government ... to control the market. With a large company, you regulate prices, you acquire control of a large company, individually the largest one, although not as close as the Australian ones. But from there, you regulate the price of that important input.

Which would lead to more accelerated extraction in Brazil ...
More accelerated. Definitively, we're heading towards a primarization or reprimarization, abdicating any control of the ore's flow as well as of its use. We would become a mineral province of China.

We are discussing a hypothesis here, but at this moment there is still no concrete indication in that direction ...
No, at this moment we don't see any shareholder movement. There are no signals. The signals that have come up are of small slices of shareholder control. I think that, if this were to happen, it would be with some of the large blocks being sold. So, I haven't noticed that yet. Also because I think it might not be necessary. Maybe it'll become necessary if iron ore returns to a growth rate that approaches or exceeds $100 a tonne. At the moment, in the current scenario, that might not be necessary.
Aguiar Interview

It can also be assumed that Vale, after reorienting its corporate strategy, would consider the acquisition of other iron ore mining companies to strengthen its market position. However, the focus in its core business – iron ore extraction – which favors the company over its competitors, may weaken its revenues in case of a new retraction period in iron ore prices, as experienced in the commodity post-boom period. In a context of shareholding dispersion, such a scenario could make Vale more vulnerable to acquisition or takeover bids. On the other hand, the instability of iron ore prices after the shock of the COVID-19 pandemic in 2020–2021, as we will see below, may make the occurrence of new shareholder movements in Vale possible, in the direction suggested by Guilherme Zagallo.

What is certain is that the consolidation of Vale's transformation into a TNC makes it less subordinate to national or local controls and more dependent on its ability to remunerate shareholders, bringing profound consequences for its workers and for the other agents involved in its global production network.

Epilogue

*Vale S.A., a Transnational Corporation on the Shifting Ground of
Globalization*

As the research on which this book was based was being completed, on January
25, 2019, dam I at Vale's Córrego do Feijão mine in Brumadinho (in Minas
Gerais) broke. In the following months, rescue operations identified 270 fatal
victims of the nearly 12 million cubic meters flood of mining tailings which
engulfed the region, took over the Paraopeba River and made its way to the São
Francisco River, affecting tens of thousands of families. Most of the dead and
missing were Vale's in-house or outsourced workers.

The rupture of the Brumadinho dam happened a little over three years after
the collapse of the Fundão dam, operated by Samarco (controlled by Vale and
BHP Billiton) in Mariana (also in Minas Gerais). As this work directed its focus
to Vale's transnationalization and to the company's labor relations and union
strategies, the dam failure was not the object of our analysis. It is clear, however, that there is no more brutal and concrete illustration of the effects of
globalized mining on workers, communities, and the environment than these
recent events in Minas Gerais.

At first, the terrible images of the tailings avalanche were not related to the
'shifting ground' which gives this book its title. The choice was actually due to
the instability which is characteristic of globalization and to the deterritori-
alization of capital, ahead of old national and local constraints for its circulation and appropriation. The title was also intended to refer to the instability
experienced by the working class and its unions in dealing with the strengthened transnational corporate power, as well as to the profound changes which
occurred during the four years of research.

Although we do not intend to analyze in detail the Brumadinho dam failure
and its effects[1] – especially the most important ones, related to the hundreds of
deaths and the thousands of people displaced and affected by environmental
degradation and by the disruption of the local economy – it is necessary to
highlight some of its consequences for Vale. The company stated that the event
had a "broad impact" on its "financial performance and operating results."
Among other consequences, in 2019, the company allocated $7.402 billion to

---

1   On this subject, see Bruno Milanez et al, "Minas não há mais: avaliação dos aspectos
    econômicos e institucionais do desastre da Vale na bacia do rio Paraopeba," *Versos – Textos
    para Discussão PoEMAS* 3, no. 1 (2019): 1–114.

expenses and provisions related to the mischaracterization of upstream dams and lost $235 million, "attributable to the write-off of the Córrego do Feijão mine and of other upstream dams."[2]

Several operations were suspended as a result of court decisions, revocation of licenses and on the company's initiative, affecting its production and revenues: the "suspension of operations at its most critical level totaled 92.8 million metric tonnes per year of production capacity, but part of these operations were resumed during 2019."[3] That year, on account of that loss, Vale's iron ore production was 302 million metric tonnes, down 21.5% from 2018.[4] Pellet production was 41.8 million metric tonnes, down 24.4% from 2018.[5] The mining company posted a loss of $1.683 billion in 2019, compared to a profit of $6.860 billion in 2018;[6] As already mentioned in Chapter 1, the reduction in iron ore production in 2019 and 2020 temporarily removed from Vale the position of this ore's largest global producer, held for years and assumed by Rio Tinto. However, in 2020, production began to recover, and the company made a net profit of $4.5 billion.[7]

The efforts of Fabio Schvartsman's management, described above, to reduce the company's debt, conduct divestments, and focus on core business – so that Vale could transform itself into a 'dividend machine' for its shareholders – suffered a temporary setback. Soon after the Brumadinho dam rupture, the mining company announced the suspension of dividend payments, resumed in September 2020, and, on March 1, 2019, received from the "Federal Public Prosecutor's Office, the Public Prosecutor's Office of the State of Minas Gerais, the Federal Police and the Civil Police of the State of Minas Gerais ... recommendations for the removal of certain executives and employees."[8] Schvartsman and three executive directors stepped down from their

---

2   Vale S.A., *Formulário 20-F: relatório anual 2019*, 7; Available in http://www.vale.com/PT/investors/information-market/annual-reports/20f/20FDocs/Vale%2020-F%202019_p.pdf; accessed May 26, 2021.

3   Ibid.

4   Vale S.A., *Relatório de sustentabilidade 2019*, 112; Available in http://www.vale.com/PT/investors/information-market/annual-reports/sustainability-reports/Sustentabilidade/Relatorio_sustentabilidade_vale_2019_alta_pt.pdf; accessed May 26, 2021.

5   Ibid.

6   Ibid, 113.

7   Vale S.A., *Relatório Integrado 2020*, 40; Available in http://www.vale.com/PT/investors/information-market/annual-reports/sustainability-reports/Sustentabilidade/Vale_Relato_Integrado_2020.pdf; accessed May 26, 2021.

8   According to a material fact disclosed by the company on March 2, 2019; Available in http://www.vale.com/brasil/PT/investors/information-market/press-releases/Paginas/Vale-informa-sobre-afastamento-temporario-de-executivos.aspx; accessed May 26, 2021.

positions.[9] Subsequently, Eduardo Bartolomeo, who had been the Director of Base Metals, took over as the company's CEO.[10]

While lawsuits were still in progress and the thousands of people affected awaited the resolution of reparation initiatives, an agreement was signed by the State of Minas Gerais, the State's Public Defender's Office, the Federal Public Prosecutor's Office and Vale, whereby the company will pay R$37.7 billion "to repair economic and environmental losses, and ensure compensation for moral, collective and social damages from the collapse of the Córrego do Feijão mine dam."[11]

Vale was still dealing with the corrosion of its reputation, the changes in the board of directors, and the operational, economic and judicial consequences of the Córrego do Feijão dam failure when the COVID-19 pandemic in 2020 and 2021 also affected its production, temporarily suspending the functioning of some of its operations. However, the pandemic shock, which initially disrupted global production networks and affected the supply of ores, was followed by the recovery of the Chinese economy and by stimulus packages in countries of the Global North, especially the United States, leading to an increase in demand and an unexpected rise in commodity prices, led by iron ore, which rose more than 150% in one year,[12] surpassing the US$200 per tonne mark, a record, in mid-May 2021. The rise in prices led to speculation about the possible beginning of a new commodity boom, which, in the end, did not occur.[13] The global economic instability and the drop in China's growth rates led prices back to the US$ 100 per tonne level by the end of 2021.

---

9   Available in http://www.vale.com/brasil/PT/investors/information-market/press-relea ses/Paginas/Vale-informa-sobre-afastamento-temporario-de-executivos.aspx; accessed May 26, 2021.

10   Initially an interim CEO, Bartolomeo was made effective in April 2019. In March 2021, he was reappointed by the Board of Directors for a three-year term.

11   Cibelle Bouças, Francisco Góes and Rafael Rosas, "Vale fecha acordo com MG e vai pagar R$ 37,7 bilhões," *Valor Econômico*, (February 5, 2021), B4. Criticism of the agreement's negotiation process and of its content, such as the allocation of part of the amounts paid by Vale to Minas Gerais government's mobility projects, can be found in Daniel Camargos, "Brumadinho: Vale quer reduzir em R$ 30 bi valor que pagará por reparação de danos," *Repórter Brasil* (November 19, 2020); Available in https://reporterbrasil.org.br/2020/11 /brumadinho-vale-quer-reduzir-em-r-30-bi-valor-que-pagara-por-reparacao-de-danos/; accessed May 26, 2021.

12   Neil Hume and Michael Pooler, "Vale chief rejects talk of iron ore supercycle," *Financial Times*, May 17, 2021; Available in https://www.ft.com/content/cb937f53-95fc-4558-a20e -63ac9fde80f2; accessed May 26, 2021.

13   Confirming the forecasts of Eduardo Bartolomeo, Vale's CEO, for whom the rise in prices would be temporary: "In the last supercycle we had urbanisation in China. It was a structural change. A shock in demand. ... We are not talking about a huge shock in demand

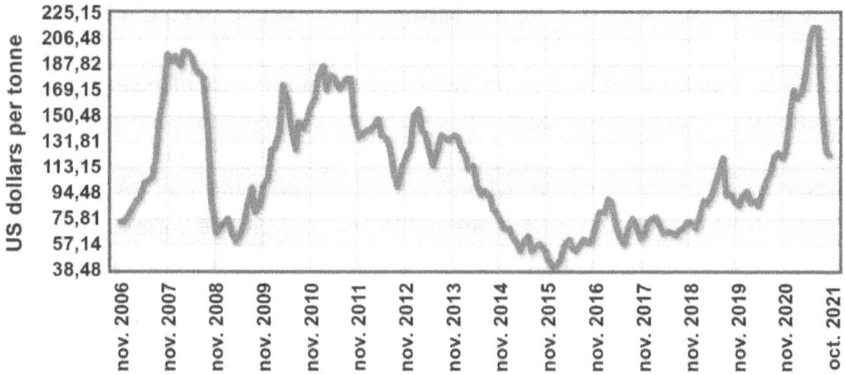

FIGURE 8   Monthly prices (in US dollars) for 62% grade iron ore (Nov. 2006–Oct. 2021),
            based on iron ore import prices per tonne in the port of Tianjin (China)
            SOURCE: INDEXMUNDI, WITH INFORMATION FROM THOMSON REUTERS
            DATASTREAM AND WORLD BANK. AVAILABLE IN HTTPS://WWW.INDEXMU
            NDI.COM/PT/PRE%C3%A7OS-DE-MERCADO/?MERCADORIA
            =MIN%C3%A9RIO-DE-FERRO&MESES=180; ACCESSED DECEMBER 6, 2021

Figure 8 shows the evolution of iron ore prices over a fifteen-year period, from November 2006 to October 2021. It shows the two previous price peaks described in Chapter 1, when the commodity boom and post-boom periods were analyzed: in April 2008, the iron ore price per tonne exceeded US$ 190, dropped sharply after the 2008–2009 crisis, and reached a new peak in January 2011, when prices approached US$ 190 again. Then, in the post-boom period, there was a consistent drop in prices, with some recovery moments. From April 2020, a steady increase can be seen, reaching previous price peaks again in mid-2021. However, as mentioned, in the second half of that year, there was a rapid and sharp drop in prices.

The maintenance of iron ore prices at this high level would be very beneficial to Vale after the conclusion of the S11D investments. In this scenario, with the changes in the 'corporate governance' regime described, institutional investors and transnational funds, with increasing presence in the company's capital, would have privileged conditions to expand value capture through the distribution of profits and dividends.

In May 2021, the first election for Vale's Board of Directors took place after the release of the former controlling group's shares, whose members hold

---

now. I would say it is marginal. It is not a shock.", in a statement reproduced by Hume and Pooler.

about 21% of the company's stock and acted together in the vote.[14] However, the shareholders' meeting was marked by intense dispute between the former controlling group and a group of minority shareholders, "backed by one of Vale's largest reference shareholders"[15] today: the transnational fund Capital Group. Four members linked to the former controlling group's shareholders and eight members considered 'independent' were elected, of which four names were put forward by the group of minority shareholders supported by Capital Group.[16] This consolidates the dispersion of the company's capital and a new internal balance of power in its Board of Directors, as analyzed in Chapter 4.

Throughout this book, I have sought to present the contours of Vale's trans-nationalization process and, in doing so, also to shed light on the ways in which the Brazilian economy has integrated into global capitalism in the first decades of the twenty-first century. The case in point offered a privileged look at this phenomenon, since, as mentioned before, Vale is a company which played a decisive role in industrial capitalism's structuring in Brazil in the twentieth century and even today "operates as an element of transfer and connection between international processes and domestic dynamics."[17] As closure, then, I present below a synthesis of the various dimensions of the mining company's corporate strategy, discussed in the previous chapters, and my final remarks.

Vale's labor and union relations strategy is decisive to ensure flexibility to the company's operations. In a commodity market with unstable prices, com-petition between powerful TNCs, and ore supply exceeding global demand, the company requires flexibility from its workers and unions in the face of varia-tions in revenues and profits, as seen in 2015 and 2016 – when, after experienc-ing a historic loss caused by the sharp drop in iron ore price, it imposed zero wage adjustment and profit-sharing bonus to its workers in Brazil. In other words, the tactics employed by the company in its relationship with workers and unions aim to contribute to the reduction of operating and labor costs, a way to expand value capture and to offer competitive prices in the global mineral market.

The control of production sites, before unions, social movements and other agents, is also a decisive aspect of corporate strategy. Supervisors are the prior-ity intermediaries in the relationship between the company and its workforce.

---

14   According to Góes and Rosas, "Conselho da Vale será mais diversificado."
15   Ibid.
16   Ibid. On Vale's Board of Directors, there is also a member elected by the company's work-
        ers: the seat was once again occupied by a STEFEM leader.
17   Milanez et al., "A estratégia corporativa da Vale S.A.," 2.

It is up to them, when necessary, to compete with the unions for the primacy of information. The unions also have a brokering role, whose goal is to stabilize and circumvent conflict. The mining company seeks to keep them close to its interests and strives to weaken the collective power of the entities through their fragmentation. This does not mean that Vale does not need unions. On the contrary, the strategy of union relations has the effect of perpetuating union leadership – be they more or less critical of the company – who become recognized and somehow trusted company agents. At the same time, opposition groups, particularly in strategic unions like Metabase Carajás, have little chance of success, as Vale acts to hinder their organization, according to the interviews and literature mobilized. The notion of "manipulated consensus"[18] seems to describe well the observations made in Parauapebas (in Pará) and São Luís (in Maranhão): the company is successful in its efforts to contain the exercise of collective power by unions and to prevent the public emergence of its workers' demands.

One episode confirms the important role assigned by Vale to its unions. In 2018, STEFEM approved in an assembly the establishment of a negotiation fee, in the amount of half a workday, to replace the union dues extinguished by the 2017 labor reform. Given its unprecedented nature and the possible obstacles to its application, the union and Vale established an unprecedented agreement in the Superior Labor Court, the first of its kind in Brazil, validating the measure. The reason seems evident: the unions need resources to continue existing. In their absence, opposing groups, whose behavior is unknown to the company, may become stronger and more competitive in relation to the union leadership established decades ago, with whom Vale has the habit of negotiating, discussing with, and, when necessary, imposing its determinations.

In Canada, Vale sought to restructure its operations, as described in Chapter 3, and clashed with the worker collective established there when searching, above all, for control over production and for the assertion of its corporate power before a powerful international union, which could bring problems to its corporate strategy's execution. The expiration of the collective agreement in 2009, in a period of sharp decline in nickel prices, allowed Vale to extend the impasse in negotiations for a year, weakening the union and the workers' collective power, who, in the end, gave in to most of the company's impositions in terms of pay, pensions, and relationships with supervisors and stewards in production.

---

18   Proposal to describe how Vale's corporate power operates in Itabira (MG) by Santos and
      Milanez, "Corporate Power and Economic Action."

It was also possible to identify that Vale seeks to avoid public scrutiny of its actions. Its institutional strategy aims at proximity to agents who influence its activities' regulation – not only in Brazil, since, as seen, a Vale supervisor was elected mayor of Sudbury in the election after the 2009–2010 Canadian strike. Mechanisms such as campaign financing and the 'revolving door' in regulatory bodies are described in the literature on the company.[19]

The ownership and financing structure changes, and the consolidation of Vale's transformation into a TNC, in turn, may have its 'disembeddedness' as a consequence, in what concerns, for example, value capture, primarily intended for its shareholders, who are spread around the planet, through the increasing distribution of profits and dividends – a possible 'disembeddedness,' also and therefore, of the national origins of the former Brazilian state-owned mining company. Obviously, this is not a one-way process, since the various agents involved in the company's global production network can mobilize to face the consequences of this process and the effects of mining.

This book also described the attempt to articulate Vale's unions around the world through an international union network, which, although it did not survive, proved to be an uncomfortable tool, at least temporarily, for the TNC's exercise of corporate power over its workers and unions. Here is an important lesson for the future: transnational labor organization, as pointed out by Peter Evans,[20] can be an alternative to the emergence of regressive social movements in the wake of the capitalist globalization crisis.

•••

The school of global capitalism has provided a key theoretical compass for framing issues which transcend national boundaries, such as those analyzed in this book. William I. Robinson also warned about the effects of the crisis of global capitalism, including the intensification of internal and external repression[21] – and its use as a source of accumulation –, and the emergence of even

---

19   See, for example, the analyses on the changes to the Mining Code, promoted in 2017 and 2018, by Bruno Milanez, "Governo Temer 'dialoga por decreto' para concluir mudanças no Código Mineral," (June 19, 2018); Available in http://emdefesadosterritorios.org/gove rno-temer-dialoga-por-decreto-para-concluir-mudancas-no-codigo-mineral/; accessed May 26, 2021; and by Bruno Milanez, Tádzio Peters Coelho and Luiz Jardim de Moraes Wanderley, "O projeto mineral no Governo Temer: menos Estado, mais mercado," *Versos – Textos para Discussão PoEMAS* 1, no. 2 (2017): 1–15.

20   Peter Evans, "Is It Labor's Turn to Globalize? Twenty-First Century Opportunities and Strategic Responses," *Global Labour Journal* 1, no. 3 (September 2010): 352–379.

21   William I. Robinson, *The Global Police State* (London: Pluto Press, 2020).

more restricted political forms, given the objective impossibility of the transnational capitalist class to organize new forms of hegemonic domination. In recent years, political movements and governments with neo-fascist features have gained strength, in addition to the intensification of financial speculation and militarized accumulation all over the world. Recent events in Brazil and the experience with the Jair Bolsonaro administration, certainly representative of that phenomenon, bring new challenges to the working class and to the popular masses.

Without wishing to develop such reflections at this point, it is also useful to point out the TCC's choices in such a crisis context. The overaccumulation of capital and the difficulty of valuing it led to the intensification of primitive accumulation forms and to the dispossession of common goods which are turned into commodities, in a process described by David Harvey as "accumulation by dispossession,"[22] to which natural resources, land and public services would be subjected. If accumulation by dispossession is one of the crises of global capitalism's faces, it makes even more sense to bet on transnational mobilization as a response to barbarity – manifested in the destruction of the lives and dreams of hundreds of workers and their families in Brumadinho or in the tragic and unprecedented scale of the millions of COVID-19 victims in the world. Regarding Brazil's place in neoliberal globalization, Chico de Oliveira came to a piercing conclusion almost two decades ago:

> Such is the platypus. It is no longer possible to remain underdeveloped, and take advantage of the openings allowed by the Second Industrial Revolution; and it is equally impossible to progress by digital-molecular accumulation – the internal requirements for such a rupture are wanting. What remains are 'primitive accumulations' of the sort fostered by privatization. But under the dominance of finance capital, these are now mere transfers of property; not, properly speaking, 'accumulation'. The platypus is condemned to thrust everything into the vortex of financialization. ... The capitalist platypus is a truncated accumulation and an unremittingly inegalitarian society.[23]

With the ethnographic inspiration of this research, based on Michael Burawoy's methodology of the 'extended case method,'[24] I intended to seek the social

---

22   David Harvey, *The New Imperialism* (Oxford: Oxford University Press, 2003).

23   Oliveira, "The Duckbilled Platypus," 57.

24   Michael Burawoy, *The Extended Case Method: four countries, four decades, four great transformations, and one theoretical tradition* (Berkeley: California University Press, 2009).

macro-forces in the micro-processes observed in the field. The dynamics of global capitalism, for this reason, have always been present as a backdrop to the object's analysis and to the transformations experienced during the investigation. The field trip to Sudbury and dealing with the long 2009–2010 strike in Vale's Canadian operations revealed the need to transcend analyses based only on national dynamics.

Such 'expansion' beyond the nation-state allows us to better frame local and global phenomena, the part and the whole: as in Drummond's poem which serves as this book's epigraph, a street begins in Itabira (or Carajás, São Luís, Sudbury ...) and leads anywhere on Earth. Once again, I contemplate the wonder and tragedy, the wealth and poverty of Brazil, just as I did when I stood on a viewpoint in front of the world's largest iron mine in the heart of the Amazon.

Bibliography

Aguiar, Thiago. *Maquiando o trabalho: opacidade e transparência numa empresa de cosméticos global*. São Paulo: Annablume, 2017.

Aguiar, Thiago. "Trabalhadoras lesionadas demitidas numa empresa global de capital nacional: trabalho, flexibilidade e gênero sob a 'nova condição operária'." *Revista da ABET* 15, no. 1, (January/June 2016): 138–156.

Andrade, Carlos Drummond de. *A rosa do povo*. São Paulo: Companhia das Letras, 2012.

Anner, Mark, Ian Greer, Marco Hauptmeier, Nathan Lillie and Nik Winchester. "The Industrial Determinants of Transnational Solidarity: Global Interunion Politics in Three Sectors." *European Journal of Industrial Relations* 12, issue 1 (2006): 7–27.

Antunes, Ricardo, ed. *Riqueza e miséria do trabalho no Brasil*. São Paulo: Boitempo, 2006.

Antunes, Ricardo, ed. *Riqueza e miséria do trabalho no Brasil II*. São Paulo: Boitempo, 2013.

Antunes, Ricardo, ed. *Riqueza e miséria do trabalho no Brasil III*. São Paulo: Boitempo, 2014.

Askoldova, Svétlana. *Le trade-unionisme américain – formation d'une idéologie (fin du XIXème siècle)*. Moscow: Éditions du Progrès, 1981.

Ban, Cornel. "Brazil's Liberal Developmentalism." *Review of International Political Economy* 20, no. 2 (2013): 298–331.

Beaud, Stéphane and Michel Pialoux. "Partir para o trabalho de campo em Sochaux com 'Bourdieu na cabeça'." *Cadernos CERU/Centro de Estudos Rurais e Urbanos* 24, no. 2, (December 2013): 31–51.

Beaud, Stéphane and Michel Pialoux. *Retour sur la condition ouvrière: enquête aux usines Peugeot de Sochaux-Montbéliard*. Paris: Fayard, 2010.

Beynon, Huw. *Working for Ford*. Harmondsworth: Penguin Books, 1984.

Beynon, Huw and Theo Nichols. *Patterns of Work in the Post-Fordist Era: Fordism and Post-Fordism*. Cheltenham: Edward Elgar Pub, 2006.

Bianchi, Álvaro and Braga, Ruy. "A financeirização da burocracia sindical no Brasil", *Correio da Cidadania*, May 11, 2011. http://www.correiocidadania.com.br/index .php?option=com_content&view=article&id=5816:submanchete120511&catid =25:politica&Itemid=47. Accessed May 26, 2021.

Bianchi, Álvaro and Braga, Ruy. "The Lula Government and Financial Globalization." *Social Forces* 83, no. 4, (June 2005): 1745–1762.

Blackrock. *2020 Annual Report*. https://www.blackrock.com/corporate/literature/ann ual-report/blackrock-2020-annual-report.pdf. Accessed June 4, 2021.

Boito Jr., Armando. *O sindicalismo de Estado no Brasil*. São Paulo: Hucitec/Editora da Unicamp, 1991.

Boito Jr., Armando. "Governos Lula: a nova burguesia nacional no poder." In: *Política e classes sociais no Brasil dos anos 2000*, edited by Armando Boito Jr. and Andréia Galvão, 67–104. São Paulo: Alameda, 2012.

Bond, Patrick and Ana Garcia, eds. *BRICS: an Anti-Capitalist Critique*. Chicago: Haymarket Books, 2015.

Bouças, Cibelle, Francisco Góes and Rafael Rosas. "Vale fecha acordo com MG e vai pagar R$ 37,7 bilhões." *Valor Econômico*, February 5, 2021, B4.

Braga, Ruy. "Terra em transe: o fim do lulismo e o retorno da luta de classes." In *As contradições do lulismo: a que ponto chegamos?*, edited by André Singer and Isabel Loureiro, 55–92. São Paulo: Boitempo, 2016.

Braga, Ruy. *The politics of the precariat: from populism to Lulista hegemony* Leiden: Brill, 2018.

Brasch, Hans. *Winds of Change: The Local 6500 USW Strike of 2009 to 2010*. Sudbury, Hans and Teresa Brasch, 2010.

Bresser-Pereira, Luiz Carlos. "Do antigo ao novo desenvolvimentismo na América Latina." In *Desenvolvimento econômico e crise*, edited by Luiz Carlos Prado, 27–66. Rio de Janeiro: Contraponto, 2012.

Bresser-Pereira, Luiz Carlos. "O governo Dilma frente ao 'tripé macroeconômico' e à direita liberal e dependente." *Novos Estudos*, no. 95 (March 2013): 5–14.

Burawoy, Michael. "From Polanyi to Pollyanna: The False Optimism of Global Labor Studies." *Global Labour Journal* 1, no. 2 (2010): 301–12.

Burawoy, Michael. *Manufacturing Consent: Changes in the Labor Process Under Monopoly Capitalism*. Chicago: The University of Chicago Press, 1979.

Burawoy, Michael. "*Manufacturing Consent* revisited" *La Nouvelle Revue du Travail*, no. 1 (2012). https://doi.org/10.4000/nrt.143.

Burawoy, Michael. "On Uncompromising Pessimism: Response to My Critics." *Global Labour Journal* 2, no. 1 (2011): 73–7.

Burawoy, Michael. *The Extended Case Method: four countries, four decades, four great transformations, and one theoretical tradition*. Berkeley: California University Press, 2009.

Burawoy, Michael, Alice Burton, Ann Arnett Ferguson and Kathryn J. Fox. *Ethnography Unbound*. Berkeley: University of California Press, 1991.

Burawoy, Michael, Joseph A. Blum, Sheba George, Zsuzsa Gille and Millie Thayer. *Global Ethnography*. Berkeley: University of California Press, 2000.

Camargos, Daniel. "Brumadinho: Vale quer reduzir em R$ 30 bi valor que pagará por reparação de danos." *Repórter Brasil*, November 19, 2020. https://reporterbrasil.org .br/2020/11/brumadinho-vale-quer-reduzir-em-r-30-bi-valor-que-pagara-por-re paracao-de-danos/. Accessed May 26, 2021.

Cardoso, Fernando Henrique and Enzo Faletto. *Dependency and Development in Latin America*, translated by Marjory Urquidi. Berkeley: University of California Press, 1979.

Carroll, William. "Global, Transnational, Regional, National: The Need for Nuance in Theorizing Global Capitalism." *Critical Sociology* 38, no. 3 (2012): 365–371.

Carroll, William. *The Making of a Transnational Capitalist Class*. London: Zed Books, 2010.

Carvalho, Laura Nazaré de. "Análise da ação dos sindicatos dos trabalhadores da mineradora Vale S.A. na região Sudeste brasileira." *Textos & Debates* 23 (January/July 2013): 91–114.

Castel, Robert. *Les métamorphoses de la question sociale: une chronique du salariat*. Paris: Galliard, 2016.

Chesnais, François. *La mondialisation du capital*. Paris: Syros, 1998.

Coelho, Tádzio Peters. "Minério-dependência e alternativas em economias locais." *Versos – Textos para Discussão PoEMAS* 1, no. 3 (2017): 1–8.

Coelho, Tádzio Peters. *Noventa por cento de ferro nas calçadas: mineração e (sub)desenvolvimentos em municípios minerados pela Vale S.A.* Doctoral dissertation. Rio de Janeiro State University, 2016.

Coelho, Tádzio Peters. *Projeto Grande Carajás: trinta anos de desenvolvimento frustrado*. Rio de Janeiro: Ibase, 2014.

Coelho, Tádzio Peters, Bruno Milanez and Raquel Giffoni Pinto. "A empresa, o Estado e as comunidades." In *Antes fosse mais leve a carga: reflexões sobre o desastre da Samarco/Vale/BHP Billiton*, edited by Marcio Zonta and Charles Trocate, 183–227. Marabá: iGuana, 2016.

Coutrot, Thomas. *L'entreprise néo-libérale, nouvelle utopie capitaliste?* Paris: La Découverte, 1998.

Cunha, Joana. "Governo quer ficar só com Petrobras, Caixa e Banco do Brasil, afirma secretário." *Folha de S.Paulo*, January 29, 2019. https://www1.folha.uol.com.br/merc ado/2019/01/bndespar-vai-se-desfazer-de-suas-acoes-e-ser-fechado-nos-proximos -quatro-anos-diz-salim-mattar.shtml. Accessed May 26, 2021.

De la Garza, Enrique. "Epistemología de las teorías sobre modelos de producción." In *Los retos teóricos de los estudios del trabajo hacia el siglo XXI*, edited by Enrique de la Garza, 71–85. Buenos Aires: CLACSO (Consejo Latinoamericano de las Ciencias Sociales), 1999.

Dicken, Peter. *Global Shift*. London and New York: The Guilford Press, 2015.

Dieguez, Consuelo. "Sérgio Rosa e o mundo dos fundos." *Piauí*, no. 35, August 2009.

Dieguez, Consuelo. "The billionaire behind the Vale." *Piauí*, no. 171, December 2020. https://piaui.folha.uol.com.br/materia/the-billionaire-behind-the-vale/. Accessed June 27, 2022.

Dillman, Martha. "Mine, Mill and Smelter Workers Vote 85% for Vale Contract, Ending 2–Month Strike." *CBC News*, August 4, 2021. https://www.cbc.ca/news/canada/sudb ury/usw-vale-collective-agreement-1.6128851. Accessed February 4, 2021.

Dubar, Claude. "La sociologie du travail face à la qualification et à la compétence." *Sociologie du travail* 38. no. 2 (April-June 1996): 179–193.

Durand, Jean Pierre. "A refundação do trabalho no fluxo tensionado." *Tempo Social* 1, no. 15 (April 2003): 139–158.

Eidlin, Barry. "Class vs. Special Interest: Labor, Power, and Politics in the United States and Canada in the Twentieth Century." *Politics & Society* 43, no. 2 (2015): 181–211.

Evans, Peter. "Counter-Hegemonic Globalization: Transnational Social Movements in the Contemporary Global Political Economy." In *The Handbook of Political Sociology*, edited by Thomas Janoski, Robert R. Alford, Alexander Hicks and Mildred Schwartz, 655–70. New York, Cambridge University Press, 2005.

Evans, Peter. "Is an Alternative Globalization Possible?" *Politics and Society* 36, no. 2 (2008): 271–305.

Evans, Peter. "Is It Labor's Turn to Globalize? Twenty-First Century Opportunities and Strategic Responses." *Global Labour Journal* 1, no. 3 (September 2010): 352–79.

Evans, Peter. "National Labor Movements and Transnational Connections: Global Labor's Evolving Architecture Under Neoliberalism." *Global Labour Journal* 5, no. 3 (September 2014): 258–82.

Evans, Peter. "Predatory, Developmental and Other Apparatuses: a Comparative Political Economy Perspective on the Third World State." *Sociological Forum* 4, no. 4 (December 1989): 561–89.

Framil Filho, Ricardo. *O internacionalismo operário entre o local e o global: as redes sindicais de trabalhadores químicos e metalúrgicos no Brasil.* MA Thesis (University of São Paulo, 2016).

Gereffi, Gary, John Humphrey and Timothy Sturgeon. "The Governance of Global Value Chains." *Review of International Political Economy* 12, no. 1 (2005): 78–104.

Gereffi, Gary and Miguel Korzeniewicz, ed. *Commodity Chains and Global Capitalism.* Westport: Praeger, 1994.

Godeiro, Nazareno, ed. *Vale do Rio Doce. Nem tudo que reluz é ouro. Da privatização à luta pela reestatização.* São Paulo: Sundermann, 2007.

Góes, Francisco and Maria Luíza Filgueiras. "BNDES sai da Vale e embolsa R$ 11,2 bi." *Valor Econômico*, February 24, 2021, C3.

Góes, Francisco and Rafael Rosas. "Conselho da Vale será mais diversificado." *Valor Econômico*, May 4, 2021, B1.

Góes, Francisco and Renato Rostás. "Novo CEO terá desafio de reduzir dívida de US$ 25 bilhões." *Valor Econômico*, March 28 2017. https://valor.globo.com/empresas/noti cia/2017/03/28/novo-ceo-tera-desafio-de-reduzir-divida-de-us-25-bilhoes.ghtml. Accessed May 26, 2021.

Gordon, Todd and Jeffery Webber. *Blood of Extraction – Canadian Imperialism in Latin America.* Halifax and Winnipeg: Fernwood Publishing, 2016.

Gray, Chad William. *Riding Bicycles When We Need Cars: The Development of Transnational Union Networks in Brazil.* PhD Diss. Cornell University, 2015.

Grün, Roberto. *Decifra-me ou te devoro: o Brasil e a dominação financeira.* São Paulo: Alameda, 2015.

Grün, Roberto. "Fundos de pensão no Brasil do final do século XX: guerra cultural, modelos de capitalismo e os destinos das classes médias." *Mana* 9, no. 2 (2003): 7–38.

Hall, Peter A. and David Soskice. "An Introduction to Varieties of Capitalism." In *Varieties of Capitalism: The Institutional Foundations of Comparative Advantage,* Peter A. Hall and David Soskice, 1–68. Oxford: Oxford University Press, 2001.

Harris, Jerry. "Who Leads Global Capitalism? The Unlikely Rise of China." *Race, Class and Corporate Power* 6, no. 1, article 8, (2018). DOI: 10.25148/CRCP.6.1.007548.

Hartmann, Michael. "Internationalisation et spécificités nationales des élites économiques." *Actes de la Recherche en Sciences Sociales* 190, no. 5 (2011): 10–23.

Harvey, David. *The Condition of Postmodernity: an Enquiry into the Origins of Cultural Change.* Cambridge: Blackwell, 2015.

Harvey, David. *The New Imperialism* Oxford: Oxford University Press, 2003.

Henderson, Jeffrey, Peter Dicken, Martin Hess, Neil Coe and Henry Wai-Chung Yeung. "Global Production Networks and the Analysis of Economic Development," *Review of International Political Economy* 8, no. 3 (2002): 436–464.

Hennebert, Marc-Antonin. "Os acordos-marco internacionais e as alianças sindicais internacionais: instrumentos de uma necessária transnacionalização da militância sindical." *Sociologias* 19, no. 45 (2017): 116–43.

Hirata, Helena. *Sobre o modelo japonês: automatização, novas formas de organização e de relações de trabalho.* São Paulo: Edusp, 1993.

Hirst, Paul and Grahame Thompson. *Globalization in Question: the International Economy and the Possibilities of Governance.* Cambridge: Polity Press, 1997.

Hume, Neil and Michael Pooler. "Vale chief rejects talk of iron ore supercycle," *Financial Times,* May 17, 2021; https://www.ft.com/content/cb937f53-95fc-4558-a20e-63ac9 fde80f2; Accessed May 26, 2021.

Inco and USW Local 6500. *Collective Agreement between Inco Limited and United Steelworkers, Local 6500.* June 1, 2006.

Knowles, Caroline. *Flip-flop: a Journey through Globalisation's Backroads.* London: Pluto Press, 2014.

Krein, José D., Roberto Véras de Oliveira, and Vitor Filgueiras, eds. *Reforma trabalhista no Brasil: promessas e realidade.* Campinas: Curt Nimuendajú, 2019.

Lee, Ching Kwan. "The Spectre of Global China." *New Left Review,* no. 89, (September/ October 2014): 29–65.

Lima, Raphael Jonathas da Costa. "CSN e Volta Redonda: uma relação histórica de dependência e controle." *Política & Sociedade* 12, no. 25 (2013): 41–64.

Lira Neto. *Getúlio (1930–1945): do governo provisório à ditadura do Estado Novo.* São Paulo: Companhia das Letras, 2013.

Lukes, Steven. "Power." In *The Blackwell dictionary of twentieth-century social thought*, edited by William Outhwaite and Tom Bottomore, 516–7. Oxford: Blackwell, 1996.

Lukes, Steven. *Power: A Radical View*. Basingstoke: Palgrave Macmillan, 2005.

Madrid, Sebastián. "Elites in Their Real Lives: A Chilean Comment on Robinson." *Critical Sociology* 38, no. 3 (2012): 389–393.

Marshall, Judith. "Behind the Image of South-South Solidarity at Brazil's Vale." In *BRICS: an Anti-Capitalist Critique*, edited by Patrick Bond and Ana Garcia, 162–85. Chicago: Haymarket Books, 2015.

Marshall, Judith. "Tailings Dam Spills at Mount Polley and Mariana: Chronicles of Disasters Foretold." *CMP; CCPA–BC Office; PoEMAS; Wilderness Committee*, 2018. https://www.policyalternatives.ca/sites/default/files/uploads/publications/BC%20 Office/2018/08/CCPA-BC_TailingsDamSpills.pdf. Accessed January 12, 2019.

Marshall, Judith. "The Worst Company in the World." *Jacobin*, no. 19 (Fall 2015): 53–59.

McGugan, Ian. "The Great Canadian Mining Non-Disaster." *The Globe and Mail*, November 5, 2016. https://www.theglobeandmail.com/report-on-business/indus try-news/energy-and-resources/sudbury-mining-foreign-acquisition/article32675 450/. Accessed May 26, 2021.

Mello e Silva, Leonardo. "Inovações do sindicalismo brasileiro em tempos de global- ização e o trabalho sob tensão." In *As contradições do lulismo: a que ponto chega- mos?*, edited by André Singer and Isabel Loureiro, 93–122. São Paulo: Boitempo, 2016.

Mello e Silva, Leonardo. "Redes sindicais em empresas multinacionais: contornos de um sindicalismo cosmopolita? A experiência do ramo químico." In *Século XXI: transformações e continuidades nas relações de trabalho*, edited by Maria Cristina Cacciamali, Rosana Ribeiro and Júnior Macambira. Fortaleza: Instituto de Desenvolvimento do Trabalho, Banco do Nordeste do Brasil, 2011.

Mello e Silva, Leonardo. "Trabalho e regresso: entre desregulação e re-regulação." In *Hegemonia às avessas: economia, política e cultura na era da servidão finan- ceira*, edited by Francisco Oliveira, Ruy Braga and Cibele Rizek, 61–91. São Paulo: Boitempo, 2010.

Mello e Silva, Leonardo, ed. *Exercícios de sociologia do trabalho*. Belo Horizonte: Fino Traço, 2016.

Mello e Silva, Leonardo, Ricardo Framil Filho and Raphael Freston. "Redes sindicais em empresas transnacionais: enfrentando a globalização do ponto de vista dos tra- balhadores." *Análise*, no. 5 (2015): 1–28.

Micussi, Pedro. *Empresário industrial e governos do PT: o caso do IEDI (2003 – 2016)*. MA Thesis (University of São Paulo, 2021).

Milanez, Bruno. "Governo Temer dialoga por decreto para concluir mudanças no Código Mineral." June 19, 2018. http://emdefesadosterritorios.org/governo-temer -dialoga-por-decreto-para-concluir-mudancas-no-codigo-mineral/. Accessed May 26, 2021.

Milanez, Bruno and Rodrigo S. P. Santos. "Topsy-Turvy Neo-Developmentalism: An Analysis of the Current Brazilian Model of Development." *Revista de Estudios Sociales*, no. 53 (July/September 2015): 12–28.

Milanez, Bruno, Rodrigo S. P. Santos, Lucas Magno, Luiz J. M. Wanderley, Maíra S. Mansur, Raquel Giffoni Pinto, Ricardo J. A. F. Gonçalves and Tádzio P. Coelho. "A estratégia corporativa da Vale S.A.: um modelo analítico para redes globais extrativas." *Versos – Textos para Discussão PoEMAS* 2, no. 2 (2018): 1–43.

Milanez, Bruno, Rodrigo S. P. Santos, Lucas Magno, Luiz J. M. Wanderley, Maíra S. Mansur, Raquel Giffoni Pinto, Ricardo J. A. F. Gonçalves and Tádzio P. Coelho. "Minas não há mais: avaliação dos aspectos econômicos e institucionais do desastre da Vale na bacia do rio Paraopeba." *Versos – Textos para Discussão PoEMAS* 3, no. 1, 2019, 1–114.

Milanez, Bruno, Tádzio Peters Coelho and Luiz Jardim de Moraes Wanderley. "O projeto mineral no Governo Temer: menos Estado, mais mercado." *Versos – Textos para Discussão PoEMAS* 1, no. 2 (2017): 1–15.

Minayo, Maria Cecília de Souza. *De ferro e flexíveis: marcas do Estado empresário e da privatização na subjetividade operária*. Rio de Janeiro: Garamond, 2004.

Moody, Roger. *Rocks and Hard Places: the Globalization of Mining*. London: Zed Books, 2007.

Munck, Ronaldo. *Globalization and Labour: The New "Great Transformation."* London: Zed Books, 2002.

Munck, Ronaldo. "Labour Dilemmas and Labour Futures." In *Labour Worldwide in the Era of Globalization: Alternative Union Models in the New World Order*, edited by Ronaldo Munck and Peter Waterman, 3–23. London: Macmillan Press, 1999.

Nogueira, Marta. "Vale perde posto de maior produtora global de minério de ferro para Rio Tinto." *UOL*, February 11, 2020. https://economia.uol.com.br/noticias/reut ers/2020/02/11/vale-perde-posto-de-maior-produtora-global-de-minerio-de-ferro -para-rio-tinto.htm. Accessed May 26, 2021.

Oliveira, Francisco de. "The Duckbilled Platypus." *New Left Review*, no. 24 (November /December 2003): 40–57.

Oliveira, Francisco de, Ruy Braga and Cibele Rizek, eds. *Hegemonia às avessas: economia, política e cultura na era da servidão financeira*. São Paulo: Boitempo, 2010.

Pamplona, Nicola. "Vale volta a estudar IPO de divisão de metais básicos." *Folha de S.Paulo*, April 28, 2021, A24.

Peters, John. "Down in the Vale: Corporate Globalization, Unions on the Defensive, and the USW Local 6500 Strike in Sudbury, 2009–2010." *Labour/Le Travail* 66 (Fall 2010): 73–105.

Pochmann, Marcio. *Nova classe média? O trabalho na base da pirâmide social brasileira*. São Paulo: Boitempo, 2012.

Polanyi, Karl. *Origins of our time: the great transformation*. London: V. Gollancz, 1945.

Previ. *Relatório anual 2015.* https://www.previ.com.br/quemsomos/relatorio2015/files /PREVI_RA2015_20160415c.pdf. Accessed December 4, 2021.

PWC. *Mine 2020: Resilient and Resourceful,* 2020. https://www.pwc.com/gx/en/energy -utilities-mining/publications/pdf/pwc-mine-2020.pdf. Accessed May 26 2021.

Ragazzi, Ana Paula, Talita Moreira and Maria Luíza Filgueiras. "Venda de debêntures da Vale soma R$ 11,5 bilhões." *Valor Econômico,* April 13, 2021. https://valor.globo .com/financas/noticia/2021/04/13/venda-de-debentures-da-vale-soma-r-115-bilh oes.ghtml. Accessed May 26, 2021.

Robinson, William I. *A Theory of Global Capitalism: Production, Class, and State in a Transnational World.* Baltimore: Johns Hopkins University Press, 2004.

Robinson, William I. "Debate on the New Global Capitalism: Transnational Capitalist Class, Transnational State Apparatuses and Global Crises." *International Critical Thought* 7, no. 2 (2017): 171–89.

Robinson, William I. *Global Capitalism and the Crisis of Humanity.* New York: Cambridge University Press, 2014.

Robinson, William I. *The Global Police State.* London, Pluto Press, 2020.

Robinson, William I. "The Transnational State and the BRICS: A Global Capitalism Perspective." *Third World Quartely* 36, no. 1 (2015): 1–21.

Robinson, William I. "Transnational Processes, Development Studies and Changing Social Hierarchies in the World System: A Central American Case Study." *Third World Quarterly* 22, no. 4 (2001): 529–63.

Robinson, William I. "Trumpism, 21st-Century Fascism, and the Dictatorship of the Transnational Capitalist Class." January 20, 2018. http://www.socialjusticejournal .org/trumpism-21st-century-fascism-and-the-dictatorship-of-the-transnational -capitalist-class/. Accessed May 27, 2022.

Rombaldi, Maurício. "Diferentes ritmos da internacionalização sindical brasileira: uma análise dos setores metalúrgico e de telecomunicações." *Caderno CRH* 29, no. 78 (2016): 535–551.

Roth, Reuben, Mercedes Steedman and Shelley Condratto. "The Casualization of Work and the Rise of Precariousness in Sudbury's Nickel Mining Industry." In *33th International Labour Process Conference (ILPC).* Athens: 2015.

Rueschemeyer, Dietrich and Peter Evans. "The State and Economic Transformation: Toward an Analysis of the Conditions Underlying Effective Intervention." In *Bringing the State Back In,* edited by Peter Evans, Dietrich Rueschemeyer and Theda Skocpol, 44–77. Cambridge: Cambridge University Press, 1985.

Saad Filho, Alfredo and Lecio Morais. *Brazil: Neoliberalism Versus Democracy.* London: Pluto Press, 2018.

Sampaio Jr., Plínio de Arruda. *Crônica de uma crise anunciada: crítica à economia política de Lula e Dilma.* São Paulo: SG-Amarante Editorial, 2017.

Sampaio Jr., Plínio de Arruda. "Desenvolvimentismo e neodesenvolvimentismo: tragédia e farsa." *Serviço Social e Sociedade*, no. 112 (October/December 2012): 672–688.

Santos, Rodrigo S. P. "A construção social de uma corporação transnacional: notas sobre a 'nova privatização' da Vale S.A." *Revista de Estudos e Pesquisas sobre as Américas* 13, no. 2 (2019): 230–270.

Santos, Rodrigo S. P. "A nova governança corporativa da Vale S.A.: um percurso político em direção à '*true corporation*'." *Versos – Textos para Discussão PoEMAS* 1, no. 4 (2017): 1–20.

Santos, Rodrigo S. P. "Desenvolvimento econômico e mudança social: a Vale e a mineração na Amazônia Oriental." *Caderno CRH* 29, no. 77 (May/August 2016): 295–312.

Santos, Rodrigo S. P. and Bruno Milanez. "Corporate Power and Economic Action: considerations based on iron ore mining." In *'Civilizing' Resource Investments and Extractivism: Societal Negotiations and the Role of Law*, edited by Wolfram Laube and Aline R.B. Pereira, 255–77. Zurich: LIT VERLAG, 2020.

Santos, Rodrigo S. P. and Bruno Milanez. "Redes globais de produção (RGPs) e conflito socioambiental: a Vale S.A. e o Complexo Minerário de Itabira." In *Anais do VII SINGA*. Goiânia: PPGEO; LABOTER; IESA, UFG, 2015a, 2093–2108.

Santos, Rodrigo S. P. and Bruno Milanez. "The Global Production Network for Iron Ore: Materiality, Corporate Strategies, and Social Contestation in Brazil." *The Extractive Industries and Society* 2 (2015): 756–765.

Santos, Rodrigo S. P. and José Ricardo Ramalho. "Estratégias corporativas e de relações de trabalho no Brasil: uma análise preliminar de 4 grupos multinacionais." In *Anais do XIV Encontro Nacional da ABET*, 2015.

Schincariol, Juliana. "Previ vende R$ 36 bi em renda variável." *Valor Econômico*, May 12, 2021, C6.

Schneider, Ben Ross. "Hierarchical Market Economies and Varieties of Capitalism in Latin America." *Journal of Latin American Studies* 41, no. 3 (August 2009): 553–75.

Schrank, Andrew. "Conquering, Comprador, or Competitive: The National Bourgeoisie in the Developing World." In: *New Directions in the Sociology of Global Development (Research in Rural Sociology and Development, Vol. 11)*, edited by F.H. Buttel and P. McMichael, 91–120. Bingley: Emerald Group Publishing Ltd., 2005.

Simon, Bernard and Jonathan Wheatley. "Heading in Opposite Directions." *Financial Times*, March 11, 2010. https://www.ft.com/content/6de1ac42-2c69-11df-be45-00144 feabdc0. Accessed May 26, 2021.

Singer, André. "A (falta de) base política para o ensaio desenvolvimentista." In *As contradições do lulismo: a que ponto chegamos?* edited by André Singer and Isabel Loureiro, 21–54. São Paulo: Boitempo, 2016.

Singer, André. *O lulismo em crise: um quebra-cabeça do período Dilma (2011–2016)*. São Paulo: Companhia das Letras, 2018.

Singer, André. *Os sentidos do lulismo: reforma gradual e pacto conservador.* São Paulo: Companhia das Letras, 2012.

Singer, André and Isabel Loureiro, eds. *As contradições do lulismo: a que ponto chegamos?* São Paulo: Boitempo, 2016.

Sklair, Leslie. *Globalization: Capitalism and Its Alternatives.* New York: Oxford University Press, 2002.

Souza, Jessé. *Os batalhadores brasileiros: nova classe média ou nova classe trabalhadora.* Belo Horizonte: Editora UFMG, 2010.

Swift, Jamie. *The Big Nickel: Inco at Home and Abroad.* Kitchener: Between the Lines, 1977.

Thompson, Mark and Albert Blum. "International Unionism in Canada: The Move to Local Control." *Industrial Relations* 22, no. 1 (Winter 1983): 71–85.

USW. "Steelworkers Reject Vale's Concessionary Offer, Call for Good-Faith in Negotiations as Strike Continues", 2021. https://www.usw.ca/news/media-centre /releases/2021/steelworkers-reject-vales-concessionary-offer-call-for-good-faith -negotiations-as-strike-continues. Accessed December 4, 2021.

Vale S.A. *Composição acionária,* January 31, 2017. http://www.vale.com/PT/invest ors/company/Documents/assets/201702_Composi%C3%A7%C3%A3o_ac ion%C3%A1ria_Jan-17.pdf. Accessed May 26, 2021.

Vale S.A. *Composição acionária,* April 30, 2021. http://www.vale.com/PT/investors /company/shareholding-structure/Documents/Abr_Shareholder%20Structure _p.pdf. Accessed May 26, 2021.

Vale S.A. *Demonstrações contábeis Vale S.A. 4th quarter of 2015.* February 25, 2016. http://www.vale.com/PT/investors/information-market/financial-statements/Fina ncialStatementsDocs/itr_IFRS_BRL_4T15p.pdf. Accessed January 20, 2019.

Vale S.A. *Formulário 20-F: relatório anual 2015.* http://www.vale.com/PT/investors /information-market/annual-reports/20f/20FDocs/Vale%2020-F%202015_p.pdf. Accessed May 26, 2021.

Vale S.A. *Formulário 20-F: relatório anual 2016.* http://www.vale.com/PT/investors /information-market/annual-reports/20f/20FDocs/Vale_20-F_FY2016_-_p.pdf. Accessed: May 26, 2021.

Vale S.A. *Formulário 20-F: relatório anual 2017.* http://www.vale.com/PT/investors/info rmation-market/annual-reports/20f/20FDocs/Vale_20F_2017_p.pdf. Accessed May 26, 2021.

Vale S.A. *Formulário 20-F: relatório anual 2019.* http://www.vale.com/PT/investors /information-market/annual-reports/20f/20FDocs/Vale%2020-F%202019_p.pdf. Accessed May 26, 2021.

Vale S.A. *Formulário 20-F: relatório anual 2020.* http://www.vale.com/PT/investors /information-market/annual-reports/20f/20FDocs/Vale%2020-F%20FY2020%20 -%20Final%20Version_pt.pdf. Accessed May 26, 2021.

Vale S.A. *Projeto Ferro Carajás S11D: um novo impulso ao desenvolvimento sustentável do Brasil.* August 2013.

Vale S.A. *Relatório de sustentabilidade 2015.* http://www.vale.com/PT/investors/info rmation-market/annual-reports/sustainability-reports/Sustentabilidade/relatorio -de-sustentabilidade-2015.pdf. Accessed May 26, 2021.

Vale S.A. *Relatório de sustentabilidade 2016.* http://www.vale.com/PT/investors/info rmation-market/annual-reports/sustainability-reports/Sustentabilidade/relatorio -de-sustentabilidade-2016.pdf. Accessed May 26, 2021.

Vale S.A. *Relatório de sustentabilidade 2017.* http://www.vale.com/PT/aboutvale/relato rio-de-sustentabilidade-2017/Documents/v_VALE_RelatorioSustentabilidade_201 7_v.pdf. Accessed May 26, 2021.

Vale S.A. *Relatório de sustentabilidade 2019.* http://www.vale.com/PT/investors /information-market/annual-reports/sustainability-reports/Sustentabilidade /Relatorio_sustentabilidade_vale_2019_alta_pt.pdf. Accessed May 26, 2021.

Vale S.A. *Relatório Integrado 2020.* http://www.vale.com/PT/investors/information -market/annual-reports/sustainability-reports/Sustentabilidade/Vale_Relato_Int egrado_2020.pdf. Accessed May 26, 2021.

Vale S.A. and USW Local 6500. *Collective Agreement between Vale Canada Limited and United Steelworkers, Local 6500.* July 8, 2010 – May 31, 2015, Ontario Operations, 2010.

Vale S.A. and USW Local 6500. *Collective Agreement between Vale Canada Limited and United Steelworkers, Local 6500,* June 1, 2015 – May 31, 2020, Ontario Operations, 2015.

Valenti, Graziella. "Vale só terá gestão "sem dono" em 2021." *Valor Econômico,* February 21, 2017. http://www.valor.com.br/empresas/4876120/vale-so-tera-gestao-sem-dono -em-2021. Accessed May 26, 2021.

Veltmeyer, Henry, James Petras and Steve Vieux. *Neoliberalism and class conflict in Latin America: a Comparative Perspective on the Political Economy of Structural Adjustment.* New York: St. Martin's Press, 1979.

Vieira, André Guilherme Delgado. *O mapa da mina.* Curitiba: Kotter Editorial, 2020.

Villaverde, João and Thiago Resende. "Vale entra para seleto grupo de empréstimos "especiais" do BNDES." *Valor Econômico,* May 24, 2012. https://valor.globo.com/bra sil/noticia/2012/05/24/vale-entra-para-seleto-grupo-de-emprestimos-especiais-do -bndes.ghtml. Accessed May 26, 2021.

Wagner, Anne-Catherine. "La bourgeoisie face à la mondialisation." *Mouvements,* no. 26 (2003): 33–39.

Wallerstein, Immanuel. "Dependence in an Interdependent World: the Limited Possibilities of Transformation within the Capitalist World Economy." *African Studies Review* 17, no. 1 (April 1974): 1–26.

Wanderley, Luiz Jardim de Moraes. "Do boom ao pós-boom das commodities: o comportamento do setor mineral no Brasil." *Versos – Textos para Discussão PoEMAS* 1, n. 1 (2017): 1–7.

Williamson, John. "What Washington Means by Policy Reform." In *Latin American Adjustment: How Much Has Happened*, edited by John Williamson, 7–20. Washington, D.C.: Pearson Institute for International Economics, 1990.

Wisnik, José Miguel. *Maquinação do Mundo: Drummond e a mineração*. São Paulo: Companhia das Letras, 2018.

Zaluth Bastos, Pedro Paulo. "A economia política do novo-desenvolvimentismo e do social-desenvolvimentismo." *Economia e Sociedade* 21 (December 2012): 779–810.

Zonta, Marcio and Charles Trocate, eds. *Antes fosse mais leve a carga: reflexões sobre o desastre da Samarco/Vale/BHP Billiton*. Marabá: iGuana, 2016.

Index